I0804684

The End of the Beginning

A People and a Land

VOLUME 1

The End of the Beginning

Joshua and Judges

Johanna W. H. van Wijk-Bos

William B. Eerdmans Publishing Company
Grand Rapids, Michigan

Wm. B. Eerdmans Publishing Co.
4035 Park East Court SE, Grand Rapids, Michigan 49546
www.eerdmans.com

© 2019 Johanna W. H. van Wijk-Bos
All rights reserved
Published 2019
Printed in the United States of America

25 24 23 22 21 20 19 1 2 3 4 5 6 7

ISBN 978-0-8028-6838-1

Library of Congress Cataloging-in-Publication Data

A catalog record for this book is available from the Library of Congress.

For my students

Louisville Presbyterian Theological Seminary

1977–2017

Now this is not the end. It is not even the beginning of the end. But it is, perhaps, the end of the beginning.

—Winston Churchill, "The End of the Beginning"

Contents

Preface

The Former Prophets of the Hebrew Bible are a part of the great arc of biblical narrative that begins with the creation of the world and ends with the Babylonian exile. The framework of entry and exile encloses the four books of Joshua, Judges, Samuel, and Kings, texts that include some of the most familiar and some of the least known material in the Bible. In Christian circles, where there is a certain amount of acquaintance with the Bible, the outlines of the David and Goliath story will be remembered, as well as the story of Solomon and the two prostitutes. Few, however, will recall the tricky Gibeonites or the prophet killed by a lion on his way home after dining at the house of one of his colleagues. The names of the prophets Elijah and Isaiah we recognize, but Deborah and Huldah are unlikely to have importance in the collective memory even of those who attend church or synagogue.

One purpose of this writing is to offer a close reading of the Hebrew text in translation to reacquaint us with the path taken by the people called Israel as they cross the Jordan into the land of the promise, live there—first under loosely organized tribal leadership but eventually embracing a form of monarchy—and finally lose the land and go into exile. In studying these books, we traverse more than six hundred years of history, much of it periods of great turbulence for the people of the Bible as well as the surrounding nations. The land the Israelites believed to be granted to them as a gift from God is a reality into which they cross, where they learn to live together, become divided from one another, and which they eventually lose. This land is not only the place where they live but it betokens for them the presence of God, a utopian ideal concentrated in the city of God, Jerusalem/Zion, and most of all in the temple. In the end, ironically, it is not land or city or temple, even less kingship, that guarantees for this people their ongoing identity, orientation, and self-definition. Rather, the words spoken, written, and read—deposited in documents—became the lodestar for the community out of which Rabbinic Judaism and Christianity were born.

Some of the stories we find here may move us; some may appall; all will speak to the imagination if we let them. The histories were written for education, edification, and also entertainment. This is the way the people went; this is the way God went with them as they saw it and described it. It is a remarkable collection describing an ancient people in an ancient world—far removed from ours, that at the same time invokes contemporary situations and questions. In considering these accounts, we also look in a mirror. We engage in our own quandaries regarding our communities and the God of our faith. The people who wrote the narratives, the ones who collected and edited them, believed that God was involved in their story—in the way they went, with all its ups and downs. By getting closer to their story, we may find a guiding hand in our own lives as individuals and communities. There is no boilerplate here, no script to copy, but in it and through our reading, we too may encounter the presence of the Holy One and derive a moral compass for our lives.

As always, I have written as a scholar of the Bible with deep commitments to feminism and issues of gender and to analysis of patriarchal structures and ideologies. Women's voices and the roles they play in the various accounts have received special attention. I also write as a child of World War II who absorbed in mind and heart the sights and sounds of atrocious violence and inhumanity that infested communities and individuals when entire groups were defined as outsiders, deprived of the basic claim to have a share in the human race. My awareness as a writer and interpreter of Scripture is attentive to the historical Christian dishonoring and victimization of the Jewish people, and it has been my aim to be respectful toward a part of Scripture that describes a history of which Jews are the direct descendants. The history we find here may not be history as it would be written today in the modern world. It is nevertheless history in the sense of a people writing about its past. The name in the Jewish community for what Christians call the Old Testament is "Tanakh," or "Miqra." Because Christian communities are unfamiliar with these terms, I have for the most part chosen "Hebrew Bible" to refer to the first part of Christian Scripture. The sacred Name of God, called the Tetragrammaton for its four consonants, is often presented as "LORD" in translations but is here rendered "Adonai," which is how it is read in Reform Jewish congregations.[1]

All translations of biblical texts are my own, based on the accepted Hebrew text of the Bible. For biblical quotations, set on the page as inserts, I use short, so-called colo-metric lines, giving the appearance of poetry.[2] Setting the biblical text on the page in short lines was advocated by Martin Buber and Franz Rosenzweig in their translation of the Hebrew Bible into German.[3] Their method was adopted and explained in the United States by Everett Fox in his translation of the Torah and the Former Prophets.[4] More recently, Susan Niditch has advocated the method and discussed it in her commentary on Judges.[5] The short lines emphasize the structure of a

1. For an extensive discussion of responsible Christian references to the sacred Name, see Johanna W. H. van Wijk-Bos, "Writing on the Water: The Ineffable Name of God," in *Jews, Christians, and the Theology of the Hebrew Scriptures*, ed. Alice Ogden Bellis and Joel S. Kaminsky (Atlanta: Society of Biblical Literature, 2000), 45–59.

2. Hebrew poetry distinguishes itself from prose mainly by a sequence of clauses in which the second one corresponds to the first, a phenomenon usually called *parallelism*. However, the dividing line between prose and poetry in the Bible is to my understanding often not sharp. For insight into issues of poetry and prose, see Robert Alter, *The Art of Biblical Poetry* (New York: Basic Books, 1985); Robert Alter, *The Book of Psalms* (New York: Norton, 2007), xx–xxviii; and James L. Kugel, *The Idea of Biblical Poetry: Parallelism and Its History* (New Haven: Yale University Press, 1981).

3. Martin Buber and Franz Rosenzweig, *Scripture and Translation*, trans. Lawrence Rosenwald with Everett Fox (Bloomington, IN: Bloomington University Press, 1994); trans. of *Die Schrift und ihre Verdeutschung* (Berlin: Schocken, 1936).

4. Everett Fox, *The Five Books of Moses* (New York: Schocken, 1995); Everett Fox, *The Early Prophets: Joshua, Judges, Samuel and Kings: A New Translation with Introductions, Commentary, and Notes* (New York: Schocken, 2014).

5. Susan Niditch *Judges*, OTL (Louisville: Westminster John Knox, 2008),

unit, reveal the parts that create the whole and emphasize key words that serve the interpretation of a passage. Translators who follow in Buber's footsteps also focus more on being as faithful as possible to the word order and word choice of the Hebrew original and less on the accessibility of the translation in the receiving language. The purpose of my translations and of this book is to draw the reader/listener "into the world of the Hebrew Bible." To paraphrase the German scholar Franz Rosenzweig, we "need to hear its alien tone in all its alienness . . . its cast of mind, its heartbeat." For Rosenzweig, the translator becomes "a mouthpiece for the alien voice that transmits it across the chasm of space and time."[6]

In the books of the Former Prophets, this alien world unfolds itself before us in all its variety, its different sights and sounds, its foreign nature and texture, and especially its multiple voices. The multivoiced character of the text is on full display in these books of the Bible. The voice that calls for complete eradication of the indigenous population of Canaan is heard together with the voice that commands hospitality and extends grace to the stranger. The voice that endorses a spontaneous, charismatic form of leadership sounds alongside the one that argues for hereditary kingship. We find here the voice that understands the absence of a king to be the cause of chaos and failure as well as the voice that holds kingship accountable for the dissolution of the bonds of kinship and the loss of the land. The same individuals appear as heroes and as villains. Modern and Western desires for uniformity and order may get in the way of a text that sets the reader on a course that opens up in different directions. A second purpose of this book is to present exactly, as an essential part of the complex history of their community, the multiplicity of voices which the collectors of this material let stand. In listening to the different voices, we will prefer some to others; we may turn our

---

19–26. See Phyllis Trible, *God and the Rhetoric of Sexuality* (Philadelphia: Fortress, 1978); Phyllis Trible, *Rhetorical Criticism: Context, Method and the Book of Jonah* (Philadelphia: Fortress, 1994); J. P. Fokkelman, *King David*, vol. 1 of *Narrative Art and Poetry in the Books of Samuel* (Assen: Van Gorcum, 1981), 1–20.

6. Franz Rosenzweig, "On the Scriptures and Their Language," in *Franz Rosenzweig: His Life and Thought*, ed. Nahum L. Glatzer, 2nd ed. (New York: Schocken, 1961), 253.

backs on texts that sing a melody we are no longer able to join. Our task is in the end not to agree or disagree but to enter into the text with our questions and, in our very questioning, tentatively find a way forward, drawing closer to the presence of the Most Holy.

The writing and shaping of this book took place in the absence of my primary conversation partner of more than forty years, my beloved husband, A. David Bos, of blessed memory. Our son, Martin, is a daily example of one who had the courage to traverse his own boundaries, stepping forward into an unknown land to embrace a new way of being, showing us what it takes to cross a river and daily confront the giants on the other side.

Other important conversation partners were present. They patiently listened to my enthusiastic ramblings and responded with interest and insight. I acknowledge with gratitude my colleague and friend Heather Thiessen, who was always ready to address issues vital to writing on the Bible; my former student Manasses Fonteles, whose knowledge of Scripture never failed to enrich our exchanges; and my assistant Christiaan Faul, who combed through the manuscript to check on the accuracy of biblical citations and who eased my transition from full-time professor to full-time writer in so many ways. My special thanks go to my friend Aaron Guldenschuh Gatten, whose presence supported me through the grievous loss of my beloved only sister, who made my garden a place not only of beauty but also of rest and tranquility, and who was always ready to exchange thoughts about the latest Scriptural adventure. My friends at Saturday morning Torah study not only gave me a place for weekly intense concentration on Scripture but made this stranger in the house of Israel feel welcome and loved. Rabbi David Ariel Joel of Temple Adath Israel Brith Sholom in Louisville, Kentucky, has a special place in this list. I am deeply indebted to his outstanding teaching and his meticulous, unfailing attention to the biblical text and the rabbis and sages who comment on it. I am profoundly appreciative of his patience and readiness to respond to my inquiries.

I am grateful to Louisville Presbyterian Theological Seminary, its board of trustees, and its faculty for allowing me to articulate the first outlines of this book and begin my work during a sabbatical leave. To my first editor at Eerdmans, Allen Myers, and my present editor, Andrew Knapp, go my thanks for their patience with this "slow professor" and for their meticulous oversight of the project. The copyeditor, Samuel Kelly, also has my gratitude for his judicious work cleaning up this book. I dedicate the book to my students at Louisville Seminary, who provided the stimulus and the sounding board for all my writing during my forty years of teaching.

The texts under consideration in this book do not have a happy ending; the adventure that begins in great expectation and hope with the crossing of the Jordan River ends in loss and exile. Yet out of ruin and destruction, a new way was found toward life as a community that discerned guidance and divine presence in the words it preserved and guarded. The Teaching enjoined upon Joshua at the beginning of the Former Prophets, authorized by the prophet Huldah in a document at the end, endured in time.

> *When Torah entered the world, freedom entered it.*
> *The whole Torah exists only to establish peace.*
> . . .
> *Let us learn in order to teach.*
> *Let us learn in order to do!*[7]

7. *Mishkan T'filah: A Reform Siddur* (New York: Central Conference of American Rabbis, 5767/2007), 257.

Introduction

Visions of the Past

We need a story to see in the dark.[1]

The Hebrew Bible depicts history as a series of ruptures in which various identities are cut and recut, formed, broken, and reformed, rather than as a continuous process in which a stable entity called Israel develops.[2]

Joshua and Judges belong to the division of the Tanakh called the Prophets. Together with Samuel and Kings, they constitute a subsection entitled the Former Prophets, also known as the "Historical Books."[3] Both designations, prophecy and history, may raise questions for contemporary readers. In what sense exactly is this material prophetic? We understand the prophets of ancient Israel to be those who, before the Babylonian exile, called the community and its leaders to their task of exemplifying in their common life the interest of God in the outcast, the poor, the orphan, widow, and

1. Peter Schaffer, *Equus* (New York: Samuel French, 1973) as cited in John Westerhoff III, *A Pilgrim People. Learning through the Church Year* (Minneapolis: Seabury, 1984), 3–4.

2. Regina Schwartz, "The Histories of David: Biblical Scholarship and Biblical Stories," in *"Not in Heaven": Coherence and Complexity in Biblical Narrative,* ed. Jason P. Rosenblatt and Joseph C. Sitterson Jr. (Bloomington: Indiana University Press, 1991), 198.

3. In the Hebrew Bible, Ruth is not included in this section and is instead placed in the third major division, called the Writings, where it may be found between Proverbs and the Song of Songs.

stranger. They were those who constantly warned the people of future disaster if they did not change their unjust conduct, presenting them with the option for a reversal of course, a decision that would open up a future for them as God's covenant people in the land.[4] Joshua through Kings presents itself as story rather than a speech, as description rather than oration. Joshua and Judges contain the stories of Israel's past that recount the entry of the ancient Israelites into the land of the promise and its initial uncertain existence in the land amid much hostility and disorganization. Yet the function of the material is at least in part intended to be instruction. There are, after all, lessons to be learned from the past, lessons that are especially evident through the voice of the editors who wove the texts into the one tapestry we have before us. These texts may thus be understood as prophetic in the sense that they provide a vision of the ancient Israelite past, the land, its inhabitants, and its leaders in order to chart a path for the future.

The term "historical" fits the four books insofar as they describe the history of the Israelites from the time they entered the land of Canaan until they gradually lost it, first to one and then to another foreign power. All the same, this is not history writing as we know it today. Sequences are not always linear; they may be interrupted by long lists or seemingly incongruous material. Some events are portrayed in fine detail while others receive only a few summary lines. Episodes may be repeated, some more than once, at times providing contradictory information. It is not as if there is no history in these books, not as if history is unimportant for understanding them, not as if all of it is fabricated. But the historical facts, exactly how it all happened, are described in a different way than we might expect. The narratives arose in a world that prized the category of mythos rather than logos, meaning that ancient Israel shared the

4. "The true prophet did not announce an immutable decree. They spoke into the power of decision that resided in the moment, and in such a way that the message of disaster touches this power. . . . The power and ability are given to every human being to take this choice. . . . It is to the personal decision of humanity that the prophetic announcement of disaster calls" (Martin Buber, *The Prophetic Faith* [New York: Harper, 1956], 104).

manner of its history writing with that of the world around it, especially when it came to describing conquest and military campaigns.[5] Myth-making, in respect to its importance for identity formation, has of course not entirely disappeared from the world and may come to the fore today especially in times of great trauma, but it is not the primary category we associate with historiography. Taking the differences between the ancient world and the modern era into account, we may ascribe the category of historiography to the Historical Books of the Bible.[6]

There is no doubt that the Babylonian exile and its aftermath constituted traumatic events for biblical Israel, not only in the experience of the extreme violence of war and the loss of a homeland but also in terms of raising doubts about the relationship of the people to their God and even about the nature of God.[7] Although most of the material in Joshua through Kings did not originate in the period after the Babylonian exile, we date its final collection and editing to that period.

Why do traumatized people look to their past for uplift and instruction? In my elementary school when I was very young, we often sang a song called "Every Man of Holland's Clan."[8] The song

5. For a thorough comparison of the descriptions of the campaigns in Joshua 9–12 with ancient Assyrian, Hittite, and Egyptian conquest accounts, see K. Lawson Younger, *Ancient Conquest Accounts: A Study in Ancient Near Eastern and Biblical History Writing* (Sheffield: Sheffield Academic Press, 1990).

6. See the extensive arguments of Rachelle Gilmour in her book *Representing the Past: A Literary Analysis of Narrative Historiography in the Book of Samuel*, VTSup 143 (Leiden: Brill, 2011). For another defense of this material as an example of ancient history writing, see Baruch Halpern, "The State of Israelite History," in *Reconsidering Israel and Judah: Recent Studies on the Deuteronomistic History*, ed. Gary N. Knoppers and J. Gordon McConville (Winona Lake, IN: Eisenbrauns, 2000), 540–65.

7. It is not coincidental that Isaiah 40–55, chapters we assign to the postexilic period shortly before the edict of the Persian king Cyrus in 538 BCE, focuses more than any other biblical material on the nature of Adonai, the God of Israel, and specifically on God's power to liberate the people of God's love.

8. Also titled, tellingly, "A Netherlandish Song," emphasizing the "typical" Dutch nature of the lyrics.

details the glorious past of the Dutch people, who originated from one "ancestral tribe," fought off the enemy with "fists of steel," eventually experienced "glorious liberation," and could live once again freely in the land of their "inheritance," to which they had a just right.[9] My early school years took place in the Netherlands on the heels of World War II—for Holland, a time that entailed five years of defeat, deprivation, fear, and loss of life under German occupation.[10] Famine, deportations, and destruction due to bombardments had been regular experiences. Loss of Jewish life was especially severe, with a higher percentage of Holland's Jewish population murdered than any other occupied country in Western Europe. One of the few battles fought and lost in Holland, following the German invasion on May 10, 1940, took place only a few miles from my home, and memories of those days were alive and well, recounted in stories told at family gatherings during the years of my childhood. Although, without doubt, bravery manifested itself during the war years, both in the early days and afterwards there had been little evidence of "fists of steel" and "nimble hands."

The songs in our collection dated for the most part to the nineteenth and early twentieth centuries, when Holland, together

9. The song goes:
Every man of Holland's clan
Knows his strong ancestral lineage,
Seeks life on his little acre
As his free inheritance!
His own boss, no servitude,
Right and just!
Fists of steel and nimble hands,
People of the Netherlands!

Author's translation of J. G. Nijk and Melody H. J. den Hertog, "Alle Man Van Neerlands Stam," in *Kun je nog zingen zing dan mee,* ed. Veldkamp and de Boer (Utrecht: Wolters-Noordhof, 1972). Our songbook, *If You Can Sing, Sing Along!* was composed by two idealistic Dutch schoolteachers at the beginning of the twentieth century. They believed that singing would endow children, especially those from a rural or illiterate background, with culture and taste.

10. While the Dutch army initially resisted the German invasion, it was forced to surrender after five days of engagement.

with other Northwestern European cultures, turned to patriotic and nationalistic sentiments as civic virtues considered to be an important teaching tool for young schoolchildren. Our songbook, *If You Can Sing, Sing Along!*, was extremely popular, not only in the schools but among the population at large, printed throughout the twentieth century in at least forty-one editions. The songs were not composed from the perspective of the losses of World War II, but they were used with fresh purpose in the period following that experience. In the aftermath of the war, our people tried to reestablish themselves and find their identity anew, seeking responses to unanswerable questions of suffering and brutality. In this context, references to historic triumphs in story and song provided escape from the brutal realities of the most recent past, brought comfort in the face of a more recently experienced sense of shame over defeat, and above all solidified our identity as a free people who had a right to live freely in our land with our own language and traditions. The songs were part and parcel of an anxious search for a claim to national identity through casting a spotlight on historic victories.[11] The focus of "Every Man" is the long-lasting war with Spain in the sixteenth and seventeenth centuries, a time when Holland established itself as the first democratic republic in the Western world. It was the golden age of Dutch power, when, according to the second stanza of the song, "the fatherland was in deep danger," and "*we* fought eighty long years" to preserve what the song writer identifies as "*our* heritage."[12]

The language of "Every Man," shared by many songs of this nature, has biblical overtones. Land is an "inheritance" rather than a mere possession, for which "men" who belong to an "ancestral tribe" fought "justly." The purpose of teaching such lyrics to young children was of course not to incite them to war but to instill in them pride in their homeland, culture, and families and a sense of belonging in the land of their ancestors. Values such as liberty and resistance to

11. In addition to songs, there were many children's books and collections of stories set in the heroic Dutch past.

12. The Eighty Years' War, also called the Dutch War of Independence, officially lasted from 1568 until 1648.

tyranny were also a strong part of the lessons of the past. The recall of the Dutch War of Independence was not so farfetched, because it invoked a period of despotism and threats against freedom when our ancestors had indeed successfully thrown off the yoke of the oppressor. Those were days when "lovely liberation" had finally arrived, as another line in the song records, pointing obliquely to a divine hand ready to rescue the land and its people from the chains of servitude.[13]

The books that constitute the Torah are in great part driven by a passionate belief in the divine promise of a land for the people to dwell in, a land they are still to enter at the end of Deuteronomy. The next four books of the Bible contain the stories and songs of their adventures during the times of entering, conquering, and possessing that land. Like all peoples, the ancient Israelites had their stories; like all peoples, they had songs that endured in recorded memory. These songs and stories, told at festive gatherings and family and religious celebrations, were perhaps written down at some point in the early period of ancient Israel's existence. Within the framework of the larger historical collection, Joshua and Judges tell stories of their great past, their mighty battles and their flawed but larger-than-life superheroes. These are the stories that later combiners and editors collected and arranged into their final form for a new context, a context in which the community that produced the narratives was once again at home, but not in the way it had once envisioned.

13. In this respect, it is worthwhile to bring to mind the famous lines of the poem by H. M. van Randwijk, engraved on the wall of the park named after him in the center of Amsterdam. The lines proclaim that a nation's "light dies" when it "yields to tyranny." Van Randwijk begins the stanza, "Together we face judgment/ to choose between good and evil," making clear that "yielding to tyranny" involves a choice. I am not here equating modern nationalism with allegiances belonging to the ancient world. Rather, my interest lies in the common urge of all communities to use the recall of the past in story and song for the purpose of forging renewed bonds of common culture and identity.

Far from Home

Israel is always on the move from land to landlessness, from landless to land, from life to death, from death to life.[14]

With roots in much earlier times, Joshua and Judges were not finalized as collections among the Historical Books until after the Babylonian exile—in the early period of the restoration of Judah perhaps, a time when the people were sadly diminished and suffering under the yoke of the Persian overlord. This was a time when they were living in the land of the promise under Persian sufferance: not a land but a province; not a possession but an overtaxed piece of property.

Nehemiah 9:36–37

36 Look, *we*:
today slaves,
and the land you gave to our ancestors
to eat its harvest and its bounty—
look, *we*:
slaves upon it;
37 its plentiful bounty for the rulers,
whom you gave to us for our failings.
Our bodies they govern, and our cattle at their pleasure;
and in great distress [are] *we*.

Thus ends the communal prayer in Nehemiah following the public reading of the Torah. The lines echo with the first-person plural pronoun (Hebrew *anahnu*) at the opening and in the center, preceded by the attention-drawing word "look" (*hinneh*). They end with the pronoun repeated again, as reflected in the literal translation provided here, so that the prayer culminates with this emphatic reference. In between the pronouns, the references to the land present a striking antithesis: Instead of the land God "gave" to "our" ancestors,

14. Walter Brueggemann, *The Land: Place as Gift, Promise, and Challenge in Biblical Faith* (Philadelphia: Fortress, 1977), 14.

God has "given" to "us" foreign rulers who own the land and all it produces, the livestock, and "our" persons. Twice the lines repeat the word "servants/slaves" (*avadim*). This community in Judah of the fifth and fourth centuries BCE—a small province in the large Persian Empire, insignificant and impoverished—constitutes the "we" of Ezra's prayer.[15] Beside the fact that their current home does not really belong to them, the people carry in their memory the even more distressing experience of exile, a dislocation that has marked their communal identity forever.

During the summer and fall of 2015 and the spring of 2016, hundreds of thousands of refugees streamed from their different countries into Western Europe. They arrived in Greece from war-torn lands, from Syria, Afghanistan, and Iraq, but also from Kosovo, Eritrea and other places where they could no longer lead sustainable lives.[16] In the United States, the newspapers daily portrayed details of families and individuals entering Greece, a land ill-equipped to deal with the flood of human misery attaining its shores. The papers almost daily analyzed European incapacity to deal in an orderly fashion with the problem presented by the overwhelming hordes of human beings seeking shelter while the US government quibbled about admitting a paltry number of refugees (100,000) by 2017. Various US communities were already gathering in fear of the impending "invasion." Photographs depicted human beings desperate for a safe haven in some country of their preference, anywhere except their homelands, which could no longer afford them a home: fathers holding young children, mothers helping their children and other relatives off unsafe rafts and overcrowded boats, all of them on the run from home toward a new place, a new land where they might

15. Ezra's prayer in Nehemiah 9 is essentially penitential, providing a review of both God's goodness and the people's unworthiness and moving to a plea to Adonai to not minimize the trouble that has befallen God's people. This general plea is followed by the description cited here.

16. On February 4, 2016, *The New York Times* reported that the total of refugees fleeing to Europe was likely around one million and that in the first month of the year 2016, more than 67,000 migrants had arrived in Europe. Of this number, 19,781 were minors. The countries of origin of the asylum seekers in Europe in 2015 numbered 148.

find safety.[17] It is difficult to fathom the extreme sense of dislocation most of these folk have experienced and that awaits them still in the future. In our Western culture, it is commonly understood that moving from one house to another, even in the same town, can be one of the more stressful experiences of a lifetime. Surely, the flood of migrants who out of fear and desperation are driven from their homelands, seeking frantically for a new home, constitutes a traumatized group of people.

It is not too farfetched to view the people of Judah exiled from their homeland by the Babylonian conqueror in the first decades of the sixth century BCE through the lens of desperation that colors the profile of those who have lost their homelands in the second decade of the twenty-first century CE. In his book *Holy Resilience: The Bible's Traumatic Origins*, David Carr defines trauma as "the haunting experience of a disaster so explosive in its impact that it cannot be directly encountered and influences an individual/group's behavior and memory in different ways."[18] Carr is especially interested in the indirect impact of the traumas experienced by ancient Israel and how this impact shaped Holy Scripture.[19] I agree that the modern concept of trauma is a helpful starting point to read and analyze the stories and songs in the biblical texts under our purview. From the vantage point of past dislocation during the destruction

17. Recent years have witnessed the stimulation of antagonism toward and fear of a perceived "invasion" of the United States at its southern border by "hordes" of immigrants, especially from Central America. Compared to the millions seeking refuge in Europe in 2015 and 2016, these groups constitute a trickle, but the outrage whipped up by the American president and his administration found echoes in Europe and shows the deep well of anxiety in host countries that is easily tapped.

18. David M. Carr, *Holy Resilience: The Bible's Traumatic Origins* (New Haven: Yale University Press, 2014), 7.

19. Carr, *Holy Resilience*, 7–9. Carr's review extends to Christianity and the New Testament, while I will stay on the ground of the Hebrew Bible, specifically that of the Former Prophets, or the Historical Books. While my perspectives on ancient Israel's religion and texts differ in many respects from those of Carr, I underline here the significance of the starting point of communal trauma as giving final shape to these texts.

of Jerusalem in the early decades of the sixth century BCE, of the subsequent exile, and of eventual return to a devastated homeland, together with the situation of current servitude, the editors of the Historical Books reviewed their past and tried to reestablish their identity and find responses to unanswerable questions. In this review, they too gloried in "the fists of steel" of the days of old, in their "just right" to the inheritance God had promised them, especially in the accounts of the people's early existence in the land as we find it in Joshua and Judges.[20]

The material before us contains tales of the most off-putting violence and savagery one encounters in any part of the Bible. It is difficult to come to terms with its presence in what many consider sacred literature. But the stories were not written to incite war—a farfetched notion for those attempting to restore their community in the small Persian province of Judah in the fifth century before the Common Era. The stories and songs of the four Historical Books of the Bible contain the myths of the glorious exploits of the people and their heroes when they were a young nation, when they assailed the land as David took on Goliath, with little chance of survival—let alone conquest—with only their faith in a divine promise and their wiles to outwit the enemy. Initially with hardly a chance to survive, the loosely organized groups that came from the other side of the Jordan with Joshua managed to find at least certain footholds in the land; besieged by hostility within and without, they clamored for more central leadership and finally became more organized. They were a people rarely at peace in the more than six hundred years of their existence. It was a violent age, and violence raged both inside and outside of their borders for most of the period covered by the Historical Books. The mayhem of war and its associated acts of violence are not glossed over in the stories, but neither are they

20. The transgenerational aspect of traumatic experiences is a well-established phenomenon. See, for example, Natan P. F. Kellermann, "Transmission of Holocaust Trauma: An Integrative Review," *Psychiatry: Interpersonal and Biological Processes* 64 (2001): 256–67; and "The Long-Term Psychological Effects and Treatment of Holocaust Trauma," *Journal of Loss and Trauma* 6 (2001): 197–218.

denounced in principle; perhaps they were too much a part of the landscape for the storytellers and singers to achieve any distance for judgment. Then, too, the telling of the story itself will have functioned as part of the post-traumatic healing process.

Judgment, however, is not absent. The voice of the editors can be heard in these texts, sometimes subdued or in the background, sometimes loud and clear, but present always to denounce the people and their leaders for their lack of faith, their betrayal of their God, their disloyalty and disobedience.[21] The stories and songs were at hand; the editors had only to set them in the proper frame to achieve their didactic purpose.[22] While initially the purpose of the material may have been to entertain and glorify, as a collection it served not only to establish the identity of the community in Judah after the exile but it also served as a warning: a warning to the remnant of returned exiles that past disobedience had caused disarray and suffering, raising an alert for the postexilic community that they stood to lose even the little they had left were they to repeat past disloyalty. A part of the retelling, after all, retains the memory of an exile that resulted in permanent dislocation, when the Assyrians overran the Northern Kingdom in 722.[23] Possession of the land had

21. "The voice of the theologian regards Israel's history as dependent upon its relationship to Adonai. Faithfulness brings success, military, economic, and political, whereas unfaithfulness and covenant breaking bring defeat and oppression" (Susan Niditch, *Judges,* OTL [Louisville: Westminster John Knox, 2008], 11).

22. I take for granted that much of the material before us in Joshua, Judges, Samuel, and Kings goes back to a time long before the editorial process was undertaken, some of it close to the actual periods of which it tells. For each book under discussion, a review of a possible process of composition and compilation will be provided.

23. I am at this point not taking up the issue of the veracity of the material in the Historical Books. I will consider truth claims and historical context for each book separately. In the main, I will hold to a fairly conservative reading of the texts as to their historical value while considering all of it under the category of mythos, as argued by Karen Armstrong and elaborately discussed in my own work. See Karen Armstrong, *The Battle for God* (New York: Knopf, 2000), xiii; and Johanna W. H. van Wijk-Bos, *Making Wise the Simple: The Torah in Christian Faith and Practice* (Grand Rapids: Eerdmans, 2005), 62–65.

been central to the self-understanding of the biblical community. What were they to do in view of the fact they ended as they began, squatters in territory belonging to others?

The Land

On balance, Israel's identity is tied less to possessing the land than to desiring to possess the land. They are not the "people of the land," but the "people of (frustrated) desire for land."[24]

We must take into account the radical differences in the physical environment and the social configurations of biblical antiquity.[25]

Between memory and dream there is no here and now. . . . There is no place for the land as it is.[26]

DEUTERONOMY 8:7–8

7 For Adonai your God
is bringing you into a good land;
a land with streams of water,
fountains and deeps,
springing from valley and hill.

I consider the sharp division between writing about the past as history, as it existed in Israel, and the category of myth argued, for example, by Yairah Amit (*History and Ideology: An Introduction to Historiography in the Hebrew Bible* [Sheffield: Sheffield Academic Press, 1999], 16) a mistaken one. Likewise the category of history as fiction or literary art does not address the issue of which mode of speaking of the past addressed essential truths in the most adequate way.

24. Regina Schwartz, *The Curse of Cain: The Violent Legacy of Monotheism* (Chicago: University of Chicago Press, 1997), 55.

25. Carol Meyers, *Discovering Eve: Ancient Israelite Women in Context* (Oxford: Oxford University Press, 1988), 8.

26. Ari Shavit, *My Promised Land: The Triumph and Tragedy of Israel* (New York: Spiegel & Grau, 2013), 25.

8 A land of wheat and barley,
of vine, fig, pomegranate,
a land of olive oil and honey.

It is probably a universal tendency to consider one's land beautiful. So the Dutch laud their country as a lush, fertile, realm of beauty with broad, slow-moving rivers and lowlands issuing in endless horizons.[27] In reality, the Netherlands is a rain-soaked, low-lying, exceedingly small piece of real estate, crammed full of people—the fertility of its soil due to its being situated in a river delta where the most important river, the Rhine, which in Germany indeed flows wide and deep, rapidly narrows, hastening on to the sea. Yet even today, the vista of wide rivers moving sluggishly through a vast tranquil landscape conjured by one of our famous poets evokes for me powerful images of the country of my birth. It may be worth noting that the idealized perspective depicts exactly what in reality is lacking: endless horizons and vast proportions rather than the narrow strip of land that constitutes Holland.

In a similar manner, the description of the land in Deuteronomy 8 quoted above emphasizes the abundance of water; streams, fountains, and subterranean water sources abound there. A country with an uncertain water supply elaborates on all the water that will make the ground produce what is needed for sustenance and tasty delights: wheat and barley, essential for nourishment, but also delicious fruits and other produce that enhances consumption. The Hebrew word "good," *tov*, can also be translated as "beautiful" and may be joined by the term "expansive," "wide." The land God promised to the ancestors may be identified as a "land flowing with milk and honey."[28] A small narrow country with much of its terrain inhospitable for crop production and an uncertain climate is thus envisioned in images that contrast with its reality.

Possession of the land of Canaan as a gift from Adonai takes up a central place in the Torah.[29] Beginning with Abram, to whom

27. From the well-known Dutch poem by Hendrik Marsman (1899–1940), "Thinking of Holland" ("Denkend aan Holland").

28. See Exod 3:8, 17; 13:5; 33:3; Deut 6:3; 11:9; 26:9, 15; 27:3.

29. Occasionally, the land is identified as belonging to the Canaanites

God promised the land as a gift to his multitudinous offspring (Gen 13:14–17), continuing with God's promise to deliver the descendants of the ancestors from servitude in Egypt and to make them "go up . . . to a land wide and good, a land flowing with milk and honey" (Exod 3:8, 17), through the long sojourn in the wilderness until the Israelites tread the verge of Jordan, the promise of the land beckons: a vision of their future. They almost get there, but not quite. For all of the Torah, the people are, for the most part, landless.[30] When they do get to Canaan, according to the testimony of the books under review here, they also discover the nature of the land: in reality, a "poor, drought-plagued land, leaving its inhabitants to struggle not only against invaders from without but against famine from within."[31] Above all, they find out what it means that there are already people in the land and what the tribes must do to establish themselves there. The promise had not stopped at superlative description, after all, but included the announcement that this land was the place of many peoples already inhabiting it. Land possession turned out to be a perilous gift, not only in the acquiring but also in the holding on.

Even a cursory view of the land of the promise reveals above all its diminutive size.[32] Small as compared to the large aggressive domains in its immediate surroundings, with relatively few portions that could be described as fertile or even arable, there was little in it to attract a flourishing population such as the verses following the text cited above go on to describe:

(Exod 3:8; 13:11; Deut 1:7; Josh 13:4), at times accompanied by a list of other peoples (Gen 15:19–21; Exod 3:17; 13:5; Num 13:29; Deut 7:1; Neh 9:8).

30. The exceptions were the tribes of Reuben, Gad and the half-tribe of Manasseh, who conquered regions east of the Jordan as recorded in Numbers and Deuteronomy (Num 34:14–15 and Deut 3:1–22).

31. Schwartz, *The Curse of Cain*, 45: "Palestine was a tiny strip of land battled over in various times by Syrians, Assyrians, Philistians, Egyptians, Babylonians, Persians and Romans, to name only the more familiar contestants."

32. The designation "from Dan to Beersheba," found to indicate "all Israel" in Judg 20:1; 1 Sam 3:20; and 2 Sam 3:10, for example, measures about 155 miles, with the distance from the Jordan to the Mediterranean an average 45 miles.

Deuteronomy 8:9–10

9 A land where you will not eat bread in poverty,
where you will lack nothing;
a land where the stones are iron,
and from whose hills you will quarry copper.
10 You will eat and be satisfied
and bless Adonai your God
on the good land he has given you.

Not blessed with the certainty of water supply from great rivers, with steady rainfall, or with vast stretches of fertile plains, the land of the promise was instead beset by difficult terrain to conquer, as well as the threat of droughts and consequent famine, of which the repeated mention in the narratives is not coincidental.[33] While subsistence farming characteristic of the socioeconomic period was possible and could be made successful through ingenious exploitation of land and available resources, droughts or locust invasions were regular catastrophes resulting in widespread devastation.[34] For all its insignificant size, Canaan was at the same time practically the only thoroughfare available for communication and trade between the great empires northeast and southwest of biblical Israel and thus a vital path for contacts in peaceful times as well as periods of hostility. Bounded to the east and south by desert, two main routes led through Canaan, making it a type of land-bridge between Eurasia and Africa.[35] Its size did not allow for isolation, and especially its western regions along the coast and the eastern sector in the Transjordan were witness to a great variety of travelers traversing the country for diverse purposes, including warfare, but also to exchange goods and culture. In addition, the original inhabitants of

33. For example, Gen 12:10; 26:1; 41:30; Ruth 1:1; 2 Sam 21:1; 24:13; 1 Kgs 8:37; 2 Kgs 6:25.

34. For a detailed description of agricultural methods and application in different regions of the country, see B. S. J. Isserlin, *The Israelites* (Minneapolis: Fortress, 2001), 149–59.

35. See, for example, Isserlin, *The Israelites*, 21.

the land of Canaan were not exterminated as demanded by the stern voice of the theologian-editor.[36] The text of the Historical Books testifies to the presence of other ethnic groups throughout the period of ancient Israel's existence in Canaan. The population of the early settlers of ancient Israel was apparently far from homogeneous and did not consist solely of those who traced their ancestry to the patriarchs and matriarchs who first migrated there from Mesopotamia.

The land had boundaries, but its borders fluctuated, and borders were in any case more permeable in ancient times than they are for modern nation-states. Canaan's natural boundaries consisted of desert to the east and the south, with the sea to the west and mountains in the north. The Jordan River formed another natural border, but from the time of their first settlements, Israelite communities established themselves east of the Jordan. It was there, especially, that commingling with outsiders was inevitable, as Israelite clans lived cheek by jowl with those of Moab, Ammon, and Edom to name just a few of the closest neighbors. West of the Jordan, the group we know from the Bible as the Philistines, part of the so-called "Sea Peoples" who immigrated into Canaan at approximately the same time as Israelite kinship groups, inhabited the maritime plain on the west coast for centuries. While the Israelite-Philistine relationship was hardly cordial, consisting of many encounters on the battlefield, some exchange of culture must have been inevitable by lives conducted in such close proximity. Witness the relative ease with which Samson moves back and forth between the two communities (Judg 13–16).[37]

The land was certainly an important and powerful entity, especially according to the religious utopian perspective, reflecting in its most idealized version a mirror of the Garden of Eden. In the garden, too, there had been rivers and subterranean water to provide moisture and fruit trees and vegetables of all kind. The creation as it came into being by God's word is repeatedly defined as "good/beautiful,"[38]

36. See, for example, Josh 13:2–13; 16:10; 17:12; Judg 1:1; 3:3; 4:11; 2 Sam 5:6.

37. In a later day, David would find a place among them with relative ease (1 Sam 27–30).

38. See Gen 1 *passim*.

an identification used also for the land. Conversely, as biblical scholar Regina Schwartz has argued, the "paradisal garden is an idealized, and lost, land of Israel," the exile of the first human creatures from the garden a foreshadowing of the exile of Israel.[39] Possession of this idealized entity proved elusive and in the end did not in itself guarantee the existence of the community that gave birth to the faith of Judaism and Christianity. Identity formation through land possession is both a blessing and a curse. It can give rise to gratitude and a life that reflects such gratitude in the just treatment of the unfortunate "other," but it can also occasion acts of appalling violence and justification for such violence.[40] The text with the narratives of common origin and survival, of the unbreakable bond created between Adonai and the community, containing instruction regarding its conduct in the social as well as the religious sphere—that text turned out to provide the guarantee of the survival of the people rather than possession of the land.

In conclusion, land is probably for all peoples at all times as much vision as concrete entity, and it certainly was that for ancient Israel.[41] It was, moreover, both as vision and concrete reality, un-

39. Schwartz, *The Curse of Cain*, 50.

40. As Schwartz points out (*The Curse of Cain*, x), the so-called conquest of Canaan was mostly a fantasy, but it was a fantasy that came to life in monstrous ways in cultures that adopted biblical views and biblical justifications for genocidal treatments of indigenous peoples. "Conquering the Canaanites was a fantasy of an exiled people; it could only carry force when it was adopted by groups who held the reins of power in Christendom." For the biblical underpinnings of, for example, North-American self-understanding in the United States, see also Christopher Buck, *God and Apple Pie: Religious Myths and Visions of America* (Kingston, NY: Educator's International, 2015); and Richard T. Hughes, *Myths America Lives By* (Chicago: University of Illinois Press, 2003).

41. For a modern description of the land as vision, see Ari Shavit's description of his great-grandfather Herbert Bentwich, one of the early British Zionists, and his blindness to the presence of the Arab population in the land when he first entered it in 1897 (*My Promised Land*, 13). "My great-grandfather," Shavit observes, "does not see because he is motivated by the need not to see." Shavit renders accurately both the idealism and the danger of "the seeing that does not see."

derstood to be God-granted. It was God who promised the land to them. God brought them there out of the "house of bondage," Egypt, and to God they owed the gift of this land and its produce (Deut 26:1–11). The flip side of that conviction was, however, the notion that what God gave, God could also take away. In return for God's gift, the people owed to God their loyalty, walking in God's ways and hearkening to God's instruction. Mishaps and disasters that overcame the land—drought and famine, invasion and eventual exile—were thus interpreted by the editorial voices in this literature to be a direct result of the people's refusal to be loyal to their God alone and to let commingling with indigenous peoples taint their perspective and worship.

The People

Blest be the ties that bind.[42]

When Israel depends upon kinship to chart its identity, that identity is far from clear.[43]

The people identified in the Bible as the "children of Israel" (*beney Yisra'el*) lived in kin-groups—small households that together formed clans that derived their unity from a common ancestor. Together, the clans constituted the tribe. Although the social and political organization of tribes is not clear, the tribal designation served the function of identity formation and was a dominant signifier for person recognition. Narratives often begin by introducing a person, usually a man, identified by region, name, ancestry, and tribal association in no particular discernible order.[44] House and clan, together with

42. John Fawcett, "Blest Be the Ties that Bind," hymn, 1782.

43. Schwartz, *The Curse of Cain*, 78.

44. The order of identifiers varies, with sometimes the tribe and sometimes the region coming first. See, for example, Ruth 1:1; 1 Sam 1:1; 16:1. Men who come on the stage only identified by name and perhaps place frequently play a negative role. See, for example, the story of the Levite in Judg 19:1–30 and the mention of Nabal in 1 Sam 25:3. The Levite never receives a name,

tribe and region, were the primary units for self-understanding and identity formation in biblical Israel rather than the larger notions of "people" as nation or the land in which it lived.[45] "Whose" you were and "where" you hailed from constituted the important pieces of information about a person and disclosed what needed to be known, not only about ancestry but likely also about class and economic status.[46] When the wealthy landowner Boaz in the book of Ruth asks his overseer to identify the unknown young woman who is gleaning on his fields, his question "*whose* is that young woman?" (*lemi hanna'arah hazzot,* Ruth 2:5) characterizes what Boaz considers essential information about Ruth. Patronymic and region of origin in most cases also identified tribal association. Much of the significance of these identifiers may be lost to outsiders, and also

---

while Nabal's tribal association can be understood negatively. It is noteworthy that few women are introduced with ancestral identifiers, and we may assume that the lack of such identifications signals the greater importance attached to her family association through her husband. A woman is ordinarily introduced as someone's wife. The prophet Huldah in 2 Kgs 22:14 receives family identification with references to the names of her husband and his father and grandfather, but the residential reference is to her person: "she resided in." Similarly, Yael in Judg 4:17 appears on the stage as "the wife of Heber the Kenite," though alternatively this may be read as "a woman of the Kenite tribe." At times, women who play an important role may be identified only by their region, as the shaman of Endor in 1 Sam 28:6–25 and the "wise" women of 2 Sam 14 and 20:16–23. Presumably listing a woman by her name, let alone a patronymic, heightens her prominence in an account. On the other hand, a woman who plays a significant role but remains unnamed may lend an air of mystery.

45. The overriding importance of local and kinship context, rather than that of nation, was doubtless one of the factors that contributed to the fracturing of the kingdom into two competing monarchies at the end of the tenth century following the reign of king Solomon.

46.Cf. Ruth 2:5. The question "whose is that young woman?" for Boaz includes the essential information about Ruth. In the Dutch village where I grew up in the 1940s and '50s, the important question was always about the identity of one's parents and perhaps the ones before them. Next came the issue of the precise location in the area one hailed from, as villages could be spread out and include distinct sectors housing people of a certain class and income.

to today's readers of the Bible, but they were clearly essential to the biblical writers.

With primary allegiance belonging to house, clan, and tribe, a question arises as to how much there existed a sense of national unity among the children of Israel as they entered the land and established an existence there. Evidently, the tribes were expected to support one another in periods of crisis and in engagements on the battlefield, but from the outset of their entrance into Canaan, it is also clear that fragile connections of kinship among tribes quickly moved into tension and even potential fracture—a harbinger of the reality that the monarchy with one king and one administration governing one people would last for only two administrations of the Davidic house, splintering into the permanent division of two kingdoms after the reign of Solomon (1 Kgs 12:1–19).[47]

The size of the average household was low on account of the short life spans of ordinary people and the high mortality rates of infants and children. Isserlin estimates the household to have consisted of no more than eight and perhaps as few as four people.[48] Households under the governance of the male head may have consisted of family members and servants or slaves, but only the fairly well-to-do were able to afford more than one wife or more than one indentured servant or slave.[49] As the notion of land is permeable and unstable, so it is with kinship. While some voices in the biblical

47. While Josh 1:12–15 provides an example of intertribal loyalty, illustrations of tension and conflict are abundant. For examples of friction in the early stages of Israel's existence in Canaan, see Josh 22:1–34; Judg 5:16–18; and Judg 18–21.

48. Isserlin, *The Israelites*, 101. The household (*bet av*) can appropriately be called "nuclear."

49. Slavery, though ubiquitous in the ancient world, including ancient Israel, was not of the type that was later practiced in the Roman Empire, nor was it like the chattel slavery of the United States. Even the richest households would have included perhaps three or four slaves. Isserlin writes that "there is no indication . . . that large gangs of them were toiling in deplorable conditions to cultivate big estates, as in the later Roman world" (*The Israelites*, 101). See also Daniel C. Snell, *Life in the Ancient Near East: 3100–332 BCE* (New Haven: Yale University Press, 1997), 36, 54–55.

text strongly oppose intermarriage with those not belonging to the ancestral line, many texts include close bonds with outsiders and do not fit into the endogamous pattern. On the one hand, father Abraham is concerned enough about marriage outside of his lineage to send his servant to find a woman for Isaac from the family clan (Gen 24:3); on the other we read about Judah taking a Canaanite woman for a wife (Gen 38:2). Joseph, the savior of his family and by extension his people, marries an Egyptian woman from a priestly family (Gen 41:50), while Moses marries a woman of Midianite, and also priestly, descent (Exod 2:16–22), to name just a few examples. All of this is recorded without comment from the writers or editors. Further down the historical path, the Canaanite Rahab finds a place among Israel (Josh 2; 6). There is little evidence of emphasis on endogamy in Judges, and Samson marries into a people hostile to the Israelite tribes (Judg 14). The many regulations pertaining to the stranger in the Torah also reflect the reality of a society that was far from homogeneous and the proximate presence of many who traced their familial descent to those from outside the Israelite ancestral lineage.[50]

In defining households as patriarchal, under the leadership of the most important male, we keep in mind that this arrangement has undergone considerable change in history. With biblical scholar Carol Meyers, I understand the "dynamics of gender hierarchy" to be context specific. Without presenting an idealized picture of the status of women in biblical times, I aim for a more nuanced view of relations between female and male than is sometimes assumed by modern interpreters, and I especially take into account the acute need for reproduction and the anxieties surrounding this need as well as the essential contributions made by women in the self-sustaining agricultural environment that constituted the biblical world.[51] In her extensive examination of biblical women, Tikva

50. Schwartz, *The Curse of Cain*, 78: "The process of defining who is an Israelite and who is not takes on subtle distinctions. How foreign is foreign? How close is close enough? How far is too far to qualify as an Israelite?"

51. Meyers, *Discovering Eve*, 26–29. In her analysis, Meyers remarks that "patriarchy may always be present, but it is not always the same" (30). Meyers

Frymer-Kensky points out that the Bible does not depict women as the "other" and does not "justify or explain" their subordination.[52] In other words, the position of women in ancient Israelite society was not supported by ideological underpinnings in the biblical text. This does not make of the biblical world a "feminist paradise" or imply that women were not at a disadvantage, but at least "the Bible does not add insult to this disadvantage, does not claim that women need to be controlled or need to be directed because they are passive, or any of the other justifications for male domination that have been prevalent in Western culture."[53] In addition, the binary gender code that has strongly dominated Western culture and biblical interpretation most likely did not function in the same way if it functioned at all in biblical times.[54]

Life was conducted mostly in an agricultural setting and in very small settlements and towns. Population size overall in the periods

---

revisits the issue of using the term patriarchy for ancient Israelite society in her book *Rediscovering Eve: Ancient Israelite Women in Context* (Oxford: Oxford University Press, 2013). See especially chapter 10, "Gender and Society: Reconstructing Relationships, Rethinking Systems" (180–202). While I am in overall agreement with Meyers that the "patriarchal label" as we use it today does not do justice to the complexity of ancient cultures, specifically ancient Israel, it still appears to fit best in terms of women's overall political and economic power (male administrations of the country land being owned for the most part by men), and female sexuality (controlled by men). See Meyers, *Rediscovering Eve*, 199.

52. Tikva Frymer-Kensky, *Reading the Women of the Bible: A New Interpretation of Their Stories* (New York: Schocken, 2002), xv. See also Frymer-Kensky, *In the Wake of the Goddesses: Women, Culture and the Biblical Transformation of Pagan Myth* (New York: Macmillan, 1992), 187–202.

53. Frymer-Kensky, *Reading the Women of the Bible*, xvi.

54. All gendered readings, as well as those with intentional queer interpretive frameworks, need to take this difference in context into account. The failure to question the biblical text on its particular gender ideology seems to me a problem in, for example, Deryn Guest's reading of Yael in her otherwise stimulating essay "From Gender Reversal to Genderfuck: Reading Jael Through a Lesbian Lens," in *Bible Trouble: Queer Reading at the Boundaries of Biblical Scholarship*, ed. Teresa J. Hornsby and Ken Stone (Atlanta: Society of Biblical Literature, 2011), 9–44.

reflected in the Historical Books of the Bible is difficult to imagine in today's context of the postindustrial societies of the Western World. Those of us at home in the United States may not have the mental capacity to conceive of a total land population between one and two hundred thousand or of towns considerably smaller than New York City's Central Park with a number of inhabitants that currently would barely fill some of the sanctuaries of Manhattan, not to speak of present-day megachurches or sports and entertainment arenas.[55] Jerusalem, a city that has occupied much of the religious imagination of three of the world's major religions, in the biblical period of varied acreage and number of inhabitants, grew by current estimates from perhaps a dozen to 150 acres in the monarchic era, while its residents never exceeded twenty thousand.[56] Such estimates, with measurements provided of necessity in acreage rather than miles, are made in comparison to the existence of fair-sized cities, even by today's standards, elsewhere in the ancient world. Not only was the land small, the towns were tiny, unimportant, and easily overrun and gobbled up in the larger region of aggressive empires. The powerful hold of land and city on the imagination is all the more astonishing, then and now.

Size matters. It matters for our understanding of the text because it is an essential feature of the historical context. The small scope of settlements and towns meant that most everyone knew everyone—certainly those who lived in the same town, but also perhaps in a wider area. In a country of which a good deal is not arable because of the conditions of the soil and other topographical features, human communities were not far apart. Rahab is most likely acquainted with the spies from the Israelite armies who visit her; Yael knows the conquered general Sisera is coming her way

55. For size and population comparisons, see Michael Patrick O'Connor, "The Biblical Notion of the City," in *Construction of Space II: The Biblical City and Other Imagined Spaces,* ed. Jon Berquist and Claudia V. Camp (London: T&T Clark, 2008), 29–30. O'Connor identifies Palestinian cities as "pint-sized" in the Middle and Late Bronze Ages. O'Connor argues that the translation "city" for the Hebrew *ir* is a mistranslation creating an impression that is altogether false for contemporary readers of the Bible.

56. Isserlin, *The Israelites,* 114.

and goes out to meet him, sure of recognizing him; the townsfolk of Gibeah know who the outsider is in their midst and that he has a guest.[57] Unknown groups of people who by profession move about, perhaps soldiers or servants, are founts of information in many stories because they reflect a historical context of small groups living in close proximity. Such communities throughout history, especially if they were small and close-knit, had their larger-than-life figures, who are central to a good story.

Heroes

The Bible was . . . intended to teach Israelites about the relation between their God and his people with whom he entered into a covenant.[58]

Remembrance of olden times always includes heroic deeds of some kind, extraordinary bravery, smarts, trickery, often including violence. When Isserlin writes that the Bible "was put together for a religious purpose," he may be correct in terms of the final editing and collecting process, but many of the narratives, especially in Judges, breathe the air of ancient storytelling not so far removed from the events, when kinfolk gathered to recount their family history in order to solidify their sense of community, especially in view of the experience of traumatic violence.

Because so much of biblical Israel's history includes the violence of war, community trauma was never far away. I have elsewhere written the account of my father's heroic-comic part in the roundup of able-bodied males in occupied Holland during World War II to be transported for work in German factories.[59] In the aftermath of the war, the need to come to terms with our identity as a community and as families was high. Not all our stories had

57. For examples of the easy flow of information in a small country, see Josh 2:9–12; Judg 4:17.

58. Isserlin, *The Israelites*, 11.

59. Johanna W. H. van Wijk-Bos, *Making Wise the Simple: The Torah in Christian Faith and Practice* (Grand Rapids: Eerdmans, 2005), 64–66.

a good ending, and some were tragic, such as the one in which a four-year-old Jewish girl from my village was betrayed, put on transport, and murdered in the gas chambers of the Auschwitz-Birkenau extermination camp.[60]

So were the remembered accounts of the Israelites sometimes comic, sometimes tragic, and sometimes both. Left-handed Ehud tricks fat Eglon by stabbing him with his dagger, hidden under his cloak on the "wrong" side of his body, most likely while Eglon, the "fatted calf," was relieving himself, sitting on his "throne" (Judg 3:15–25).[61] Non-Israelite Yael "mothers" defeated Canaanite general Sisera and kills him with her woman's tool, the tent peg (Judg 4:17–21). Both Ehud and Yael function as unexpected heroes: a left-handed man and an outsider woman get the best of the powerful opponent.

Other tales, starting on a seemingly mundane level of family discord, descend into descriptions of horrifying violence and eventual intertribal bloodshed and mayhem (Judg 19:1–30). The deeds of the heroes may undergo embellishment and exaggeration, but often they take their place on the stage warts and all. Even righteous Joshua is tricked by the wily Gibeonites (Josh 9:3–16); Barak will fight only if Deborah goes with him (Judg 4:8); Jefta foolishly makes a vow that condemns his only child to death (Judg 11:30–40); Samson marries not only outside clan or tribe

60. Johanna W. H. van Wijk-Bos, *Reformed and Feminist: A Challenge to the Church* (Louisville: Westminster John Knox, 1991), 13. The story of Ellie Frank and her family came to public consciousness long after the war with the discovery of her uncle's collection of family films, currently housed in the Jewish Historical Museum in Amsterdam. In 2008, Dutch television aired an episode about this Frank family in the series *Different Times* entitled "The Other Frank Family." My own account in *Reformed and Feminist* erroneously assigns the role of the traitor of little Ellie to the family servant who housed her. In reality, the mayor of our town was the culprit. Today, the elementary school I attended, in bitter irony then called the Mayor Kamp School, has been renamed, and a statue of Ellie erected on its playground. Ellie's first full name was Esther.

61. One of the many humorous inferences is Eglon's name, likely a diminutive version of the word for bull. The text records him as a fat man (Judg 3:17).

but cohabits with Philistine women, as well as with at least one prostitute, and stands out among violent protagonists in a warrior culture for his gratuitous ferocity involving animals as well as humans (Judg 14–16). We look in vain for words of condemnation of what appears to us to be unjust or immoral behavior. The narrators and writers let the tale tell its own truth, leaving judgment up to the listener.

Every culture has its heroes, the majority of them male. In Holland, we celebrated famous leaders, the "father" of our country William I of Orange, and especially the great seafarers, captains and explorers of the sixteenth and seventeenth centuries, important for their role in the expansion of the Dutch colonial empire toward the East. Few among the celebrated leaders of our past were women.[62] Comparatively speaking, the Historical Books of the Bible contain a significant number of accounts in which women play an important role, even that of savior. Especially in Judges, women appear in all their complexity and in different roles: victims and survivors, instruments in the hands of powerful men, warriors and deliverers. Rahab, Deborah, Yael, Delilah, and others take their place in the annals and make up a vital part of the act of biblical remembering.[63]

62. During the period of the Dutch revolution, when the Dutch republic (1581–1795) was established after renouncing allegiance to the Hapsburg royal house, one woman is remembered for her historic role in the siege of Haarlem: Kenau Hasselaer. Reportedly, she participated actively in the defense of the city, though the historical veracity of her role has come under scrutiny. In my youth, for a woman to be called a "Kenau" was far from positive and rather indicated an angry threatening woman, a "battle-ax."

63. As Frymer-Kensky explains it (*Reading the Women of the Bible*, xvii), the biblical portrayal of women does not "add prejudice to powerlessness," and in fact the "Bible's view of women became central to Israel's thinking [about itself], for it provided a paradigm for understanding powerlessness and subordination without recourse to prejudicial ideas. . . . Israel was subject to the power and authority of others on an international level just as women were subordinate within Israelite society, and the Bible's own image of women enabled its thinkers to accept this powerlessness without translating it into a sense of inferiority or worthlessness."

The Art of Remembrance

Collective memory readily acknowledges its invented character.[64]

We are wrong about what it means to be wrong.[65]

Remembering in the Bible usually connects directly to action rather than merely to the recall of a forgotten fact. When God "remembers" the covenant with the ancestors in the opening chapters of Exodus, this leads straight to the act of freeing the people from their oppressed conditions in Egypt through the agency of Moses (Exod 2:24).[66] "God's remembering is . . . an efficacious and creative event."[67] For its part, the covenant community is required to *remember* the deliverance God provided for them in the past. Following the liberation from bondage in Egypt, the stipulations for the Feast of Unleavened Bread in Exodus 13 begin with the words "remember this day" (Exod 13:3). In other words, as the crucial events of the liberation from Egypt unfold, the community is charged ahead of time with remembrance and passing the story on to the next generations, because in speaking of the past, the story takes on renewed authority.[68] In the same vein, the future community is called to remember the miraculous crossing of the Jordan at the time of Joshua (Josh 4:6–7, 21–24). For biblical Israel, the act of remembrance was an essential part of creating its identity. The ubiquitous presence of genealogical lists testifies to the importance of remembering past generations, an act through which their lives continue to have significance.

In her book *Being Wrong: Adventures in the Margin of Error*, Kathryn Schulz discusses the unreliability of memories, especially

64. Schwartz, *The Curse of Cain*, 144.

65. Kathryn Schulz, *Being Wrong: Adventures in the Margin of Error* (New York: HarperCollins, 2010), 5.

66. Cf. Exod 6:5; Lev 26:42; Pss 106:45; 111:5.

67. O. Michel, "μιμνῄσκομαι," *TDNT* 4:675. See also H. Eising, "זָכַר," *TDOT* 4:64–82.

68. P. A. H. de Boer, *Gedenken und Gedächtnis in der Welt des Alten Testaments*, Franz-Delitzsch Vorlesungen (Stuttgart: Kohlhammer, 1960), 37.

those associated with traumatic events. Many people are convinced they remember exactly their whereabouts and actions at the time of huge national disasters. Such memories have mostly proven to be erroneous.[69] "Our memories," she states, "are riddled with errors." What interests Schulz especially is how attached we are to our wrong remembrances and how we cling to them with profound conviction. Schulz calls this "the feeling of knowing." I have already mentioned the fate of the four-year-old Jewish girl in my village, betrayed and murdered during the years of occupation by Nazi Germany. I was only two years old at the time and thus have no personal memory of Ellie Frank and her disappearance; I know only what we were told in our household and in the family circle after the war. In writing about it more than four decades later, I had important details wrong, such as, for example, the identity of the betrayer.[70] In the end, this did not make a difference to the point I was making: the vulnerability of certain groups among a generally vulnerable population during the war years. Jews were not only illegal—people without rights—but they were free game and marked for certain death unless others were willing to risk their own lives in order to protect them. What we were told was that the former housekeeper of the Jewish family betrayed the little girl she had promised to shelter. Closer to the truth is that the authorities, including the mayor and the village constable, aware of the presence of little Ellie with the housekeeper, went to the house and forcibly took the child to send her to her death, although at the time they may have had no way of knowing what would happen to her.[71] Multiple versions of this story or combinations of them do not alter the fact of the murder of an

69. Schulz (*Being Wrong*, 72–73) cites research showing that only 7 percent of people remember with total accuracy the details of their activities and whereabouts during events such as the explosion of the space shuttle Challenger or the attacks of September 11, 2001, for example.

70. See above, p. 25n60; van Wijk-Bos, *Reformed and Feminist*, 13.

71. Only the very few in the occupied territories at the time had suspicions, let alone knowledge, of the reality of extermination camps. It should also be kept in mind that hiding Jews was judged to be a criminal act by the occupying authorities and that savage reprisals in case of discovery were commonplace.

unprotected four-year-old girl—surely one of the most defenseless among those lacking defense.[72]

Memories vary; ancient Israel's memories varied. Stories and events can be told in duplicate or triplicate. The different versions do not alter the essential truth of the story; in fact, they enrich it.[73] The conquest of the land under Joshua is at times portrayed as total and final, with the land at rest from war (Josh 11:23), and at other times a long list of the land and peoples still to be conquered belies that very claim (Josh 13:1). The story of prophet/judge/warrior Deborah and the Kenite tent-dwelling woman Yael is told in two versions, in narrative and song, each lending its perspectives and emphases to the events remembered (Judg 4; 5). The different versions add important detail and create a richer and more complex canvas of remembered experience. The collectors and editors of the text were no doubt aware of discrepancies and duplicates and were not concerned with the factual veracity of the details or "the feeling of knowing" but rather attempted to convey complicated truths in narrative form. They needed to make sense not only of the past but of the past as it impinged on the present. Land was conquered and occupied, annihilation of peoples inhabiting Canaan was demanded, but from the beginning boundaries were not clearly drawn and the existence of indigenous peoples continued, as mentioned throughout the book of Joshua, becoming a dominant theme in Judges. Deliverance from distress was achieved by unlikely people, and not only by those from inside the tribal circle (Deborah and Yael). Kingship was desired, and

72. Interesting questions arise from the identities of the betrayer in the different stories. Is a housekeeper an easier target for condemnation than a mayor? Was a rumor started right away that the housekeeper must have had something to do with it? Did she go and report Ellie's presence to the authorities, trusting that they would do "the right thing"? The mayor was held in high esteem until his death, as evident from the fact that the village elementary school was named after him. See above, p. 25n60.

73. My husband and I regularly invited the partners of couples who were guests at our dinner table to take turns in telling the story of how they first met. It was striking how the stories of the same couple differed from each partner's perspective, including my husband's and mine. In addition, our stories were not static and changed over time.

it came, but it had a shaky beginning, and its attainment happened in stages, with both encouragement and resistance from the Deity. Kingship, from its initial convoluted beginning to its ignominious end, had positive results but did not finally save the land for the people. Ancient stories, whether existing in multiple versions or in a single one, speak to the people's ups and downs throughout their history with their flawed leaders and to their perception of how the sphere of holiness and the divine impinged on their existence, which in the end was not dependent on possession of the land. What they were left with was not land but their memories as reflected in text.

If memories vary, they are also political. There was probably a political element at work in the erroneous remembering of the primary agent in the betrayal of little Ellie Frank in my village. More convenient and plausible, perhaps, to put blame on the housekeeper than on a respected authority in our small town! The even less convenient truth is that, in some way, the entire community was accountable for Ellie's murder, even in the face of the high risk. Solid communal support might have saved her life.[74] An element of evasion of communal responsibility thus crept into the preserved memory regarding the identity of the betrayer.

Political interests were surely not alien to the preservation of the communal memories of biblical Israel. It is then all the more remarkable that a number of competitive accounts remained intact and are present in the canon in an unresolved fashion. The collection of ancient Israel's memories into text arose by scholarly consensus in response to national devastation and crisis: Assyrian and Babylonian conquests followed by the threat of Hellenistic assimilation prompted the editing and collecting efforts that produced

74. Such communal and individual support did exist, as is evident from the history of Le Chambon-sur-Lignon, a village in the French Cévennes where villagers saved hundreds of lives by collaborating in efforts of support for Jewish refugees. Pierre Sauvage, a child born in the town during that period, memorialized that history in his film *Weapons of the Spirit.* See also my account of the New York taxi driver who survived the war in occupied Holland as a child in a town not far from my own because of the unflagging protection afforded by the town and individual members of the Dutch Underground (van Wijk-Bos, *Reformed and Feminist,* 15).

the Torah, the Prophets (including the Historical Books), and the Writings, which presently make up the canon of the Tanakh. The editing process of Joshua, Judges, Samuel, and Kings, however, did not create the collection ex nihilo. There had been text for a long time before the fifth century BCE.[75]

With others, I believe the composition of song and story in textual form to go far back into Israel's history. Writing was already very old by the time ancient Israel appeared on the scene, and extant documents from ancient Mesopotamia and Syria, for example, predate the existence of ancient Israel. It would be incongruous to assume that literacy and text composition arose only at a late date in biblical history or that it was confined to a very small group of professionals. Archaeological discoveries have shown that literacy may have been more widespread than previously supposed.[76] Ordinary folk—tradespeople, including women—had at least rudimen-

75. Regina Schwartz has argued that to "define a group is to delimit its story." In this way, "a fixed narrative" was created from "what had been a fluid, evolving set of memories" (Schwartz, *The Curse of Cain*, 145). Yet, text can also preserve fluid memories, as is evident from different versions of narratives left intact in the collection.

76. See Isserlin, *The Israelites*, 219–24. In this context, the recent find of military correspondence dated to ca. 600 BCE as reported in *The New York Times* is worth noting (Israel Kershner, "New Evidence on When Bible Was Written: Ancient Shopping Lists," *The New York Times*, April 12, 2016). The text written in ink on clay was analyzed to contain orders regarding wine, flour, and oil—in Kershner's words, "mundane ancient shopping lists"—and appears to have been written by army personnel rather than professional scribes. While the claim of the title may go too far, an argument for more widespread literacy than is sometimes assumed in at least Judah before the Babylonian exile is carefully made in an article by archeologists engaged in the discovery (Shira Faigenbaum-Golovin et al., "Algorithm Handwriting Analysis of Judah's Military Correspondence Sheds Light on Composition of Biblical Texts," *Proceedings of the National Academy of Sciences of the United States of America* 113 [2016]: 4664–69). In this review, the authors state that during this period shortly before the destruction of Jerusalem in the early part of the sixth century BCE, "the entire army apparatus from high ranking officials to humble quarter-masters of small desert outposts far from the center was literate, in the sense of ability to communicate in writing."

tary knowledge of reading and writing. I am not convinced that schooling and writing was limited to a scribal class or to one particular gender, and I assume female authorship not only possible but probable for certain biblical texts.[77] Be that as it may, if preserving memories in text is a political act and, as Schwartz puts it, the result of "protracted struggles for authority between competing communities," it is remarkable that one political vision does not dominate the Historical Books and that a proliferation of memories was preserved and passed on.[78]

The Long Arm of the Past

Nationalism has stubbornly held fast to this legitimation by transcendence. Nations are the will of God. National borders are the will of God. National expansions and colonization are the will of God. National military confrontations are the will of God. Every nation is the one nation under God.[79]

Political aspects of remembrance surface not only in who tells the story and how it is told but also in how it is interpreted. If the material in the Historical Books of the Bible was not intended to incite the survivors of the Babylonian conquest and exile to war and genocide, the text as adopted and interpreted in Christian culture and through colonial aspirations indeed served as the underpinning of immoral political action and as justification for social and political violence resulting in the conquest of indigenous peoples and institutionalized slavery in the colonies of Western Europe.[80]

77. Female authorship can be argued for the narrative of Tamar and Judah in Gen 38, for example, and for Judg 4 and 5. Among biblical books, both Ruth and Qohelet can be traced to female authorship.

78. Schwartz, *The Curse of Cain*, 149, 153–58. Schwartz argues cogently for such interpreting and reinterpreting within the Bible and also by biblical critics and historians.

79. Schwartz, *The Curse of Cain*, 11.

80. "The biblical narratives, for better and for worse . . . have wielded so much influence, even more than the classics, with the result that the Bible

While other ancient peoples may have had as much of a sense of divine-given right to their land, and while documents from their cultures are extant, only one people's writings survived to wield authority for centuries past the date of their creation with an impact on ever widening circles of peoples beyond the boundaries of the community and its direct descendants through the spread of Christianity.[81] Text is vulnerable to manipulation. So it happened that in subsequent interpretation of Holy Writ, the multiple levels of truth in the biblical stories were eradicated and the variety of perspectives was reduced to one that validated one people's superiority over another and legitimated its claim to conquer another people's land and even eradicate its existence. The extension of the biblical notion of chosen-ness to European peoples, already promulgated by William Tyndale in England in the sixteenth century, found new expression in the powerful vision of the United States of America as the New Israel, its land the promised land in which the Canaanites (i.e., the native peoples) could be rightfully displaced and conquered.[82]

Thus, America's Puritans applied Israel's past to their present, and while noble ideas of building a new community as a "shining city set upon a hill"[83] contained much that inspired exemplary com-

could be deployed against whatever 'Canaanites' people wanted to loathe, conquer, or exile" (Schwartz, *The Curse of Cain*, x).

81. Thus Schwartz (*The Curse of Cain*, 43): "It was through the accidents of religious history that the perishable book of a small persecuted people came to speak far more authoritatively about land to future generations. Its message has not perished. That book records the wish of a people in exile to be landed, of a homeless people to have a home, and it depicts their aspirations as synonymous with the very will of God. Monotheism has left a troubling legacy of the belief in land entitlement, one that continues to ghost territorial disputes."

82. "By the time Henry VIII died and Edward VI took the throne (1547), the notion that England was in some sense a chosen people, standing in covenant relation with God, had become a working assumption for many English people" (Hughes, *Myths America Lives By*, 28).

83. From John Winthrop's famous sermon onboard the *Arbella*, "A Modell of Christian Charity," in *God's New Israel: Religious Interpretations of American Destiny*, ed. Conrad Cherry, rev. ed. (Chapel Hill, NC: University of North Carolina Press, 1998), 40.

munal living it "contained also the seeds of expansion by conquest."[84] American exceptionalism of the seventeenth century eventually found a new formulation in the concept of manifest destiny, "the doctrine that Euro-Americans had a God-given right to conquer and colonize North Americans, and eventually to civilize and imperialize Hawaii, Cuba, Puerto Rico, Guam and the Philippines."[85]

I have elsewhere proposed the importance of a biblical ethic foundational to Israel's Torah that runs like a consistent requirement through the entire Bible: the mandate to exhibit ongoing concern for the "stranger" (i.e., the other as s/he faces the insider group, with the needs of one who does not belong). In the context of this ethic, the prohibition of oppression and the mandate to love constitute the outer markers, "determinative as continuous ethical requirements" for religious communities that "view themselves as inheritors of the promises and the directives contained in the Torah."[86] While we can readily agree to consider the material in the Historical Books of the Bible as illustrative of a people struggling to find its identity through considering its past, this characteristic also faces us with a conundrum. How does material that contains episodes of extreme violence, violence originating with and sanctioned by the Deity, speak an instructive word to religious communities that confess this text as

84. Buck, *God and Apple Pie*, 57. Also see Hughes, *Myths America Lives By*.

85. Buck, *God and Apple Pie*, 60. The term "manifest destiny" was coined by John L. O'Sullivan (1813–1895), founder and editor of the *United States Magazine and Democratic Review*, who wrote that there were hostile forces "limiting our greatness and checking the fulfillment of our manifest destiny to overspread the continent allotted by Providence for the free development of our yearly multiplying millions" ("Annexation," *The United States Magazine and Democratic Review* 17 [1845]: 5). There were notably dissenting voices to this vision. Sara Stanley wrote in 1856 that the American ideal of liberty was for her and her people "a phantom, shadowy and indistinct, a disembodied form, impalpable to our sense or touch" ("What, to the Toiling Millions There, Is This Boasted Liberty?" in *Lift Every Voice: African-American Oratory, 1787–1900*, ed. Philip S. Foner and Robert James Branham [Tuscaloosa, AL: University of Alabama Press, 1998], 284–87, 286). Frederick Douglass said, "I have no love for America as such, I have no patriotism, I have no country" ("Speech on American Anti-Slavery Society," 246–68 in *Lift Every Voice*, 248).

86. Van Wijk-Bos, *Making Wise the Simple*, 196–97.

Holy Scripture today? Even if the type of wholesale destruction commanded in Deuteronomy and executed in Joshua never happened or could not have happened, religious people who inherit these texts must take their distance and turn their backs on inclinations to use them as justification for their own violent tendencies.[87] The abuse of these texts for violent ends was not intended then and should not be its purpose now. For the moment, we let the conundrum stand of what the text may have to offer in response to pressing questions for today's religious communities, for there is no easy answer. Only by picking our way carefully through the narrative, with patience, curiosity and a willingness to befriend and listen, may we find surprises along the way.[88] The Bible was not intended as a blueprint and certainly does not provide a blueprint in the texts before us.

For all that, the biblical writers did not construct history in the way we understand historiography, because their mindset was not a logical positivist one. Christian interpretation of biblical texts, including the material under review here, has persistently sought to reconstruct the story of "what really happened." Questions about the facts of the "conquest" of Canaan, the identity of the conquerors, or whether there even were outsiders who did any conquering have occupied the attention of scholars of the modern era and produced a maze of theory and counter-theory. Similarly, the identity and agenda of the compilers and editors of the texts have unleashed a torrent of investigation and suppositions, making it difficult to chart a path through the competing theories of historical event and literary composition. Even if the biblical writers did not compose historical accounts as we understand them today, the historical context matters: both the one in which they constructed the material and the one about which they told. Understanding the context of Nazi occupation during World War II matters if we are to understand the

87. "We must turn our backs on it, as we turn our backs on an outdated piece of an ancient past that was never played out, should not have been played out, and will not be played out by us" (van Wijk-Bos, *Making Wise the Simple*, 261).

88. See Ellen Davis, "Losing a Friend: The Loss of the Old Testament to the Church," in *Jews, Christians and the Theology of the Hebrew Scriptures*, ed. Alice Ogden Bellis and Joel S. Kaminsky (Atlanta: Scholars, 2000), 83–94.

complexities of victim and victimizer, of betrayer and betrayed—for example, in the case of Ellie Frank. We will pay attention in what follows to what arises from the stories about possible historical events even when the reading engages us primarily on a literary level. *When* the tale is said to have taken place counts, as well as *how* it is told.

A defeated people composed collections of stories and songs about the past—the ancient days of victory, the gradual development of the scattered communities into a people with a central administration, its breakup and eventual demise—in order to regain a sense of who they were and who they could yet become. Their identity in past and present was closely wrapped up with their perspective on the way God had gone with them, from wilderness into the land and from their existence in the land to their being cast out and returned to live there not as owners but as servants of a foreign overlord. A people that saw itself as existing in a close relationship with its God also revisited its past in terms of this bond, trying to come to terms with ways to live anew within this covenant relationship guided by text. They longed to forge a path forward into an uncertain future and hoped God would begin again with them, even in view of past failures. The Historical Books of the Bible issue one chorus of voices in response to that uncertainty. Christians enter the stories of Israel's past in a certain sense as outsiders, laying claim to a bond with the same God, and as such they expect more from the text than lessons of the past intended for a different people. These are not our stories, but we too hope for insight and for a guiding word in our own uncertain future. With those of Nineveh in the Book of Jonah, trying to avert disaster, we too may say "who knows," *mi yodea'* (Jonah 3:9). In spite of our failures, God may yet be merciful to us, and we may begin again to live more closely in accordance with God's vision for creation.

JOSHUA

Entering the Land

Introduction

Content

Deuteronomy must be followed by something like Joshua if the history of Israel with God is to continue.[1]

Joshua easily divides into two main sections, chapters 1–12 and 13–21. Three concluding chapters, 22–24, contain distinct units with shared thematic links. The first part, Joshua 1–12, recounts the details of the entry into the land with a focus on specific events in detailed narrative style, such as the encounter of the spies with Rahab (ch. 2), the campaigns on Jericho and Ai (chs. 5–8), and the ruse of the Gibeonites (ch. 9). The final chapters of this part squish together a large number of conquests, first in the south (ch. 10) and then the north (11:1–15) to finish with an overview of vanquished territories and defeated kings (11:16–12:24). Chapter 11 ends with the following summary:

JOSHUA 11:23

So Joshua took the entire country
as Adonai had spoken to Moses.
Joshua gave it as an inheritance to Israel
in their tribal divisions.
And the land had rest from war.

1. J. Gordon McConville and Stephen N. Williams, *Joshua*, Two Horizons Old Testament Commentary (Grand Rapids: Eerdmans, 2010), 1.

The second part, Joshua 13–21, consists of specific land allotments to the tribes interspersed with narrative segments. This section opens with Adonai pointing out to Joshua his advanced age and the fact that there is still a lot of land not conquered, so there is a great deal of work ahead:

JOSHUA 13:1

Joshua was old, advanced in years,
and Adonai said to him:
You are old, advanced in years,
and the land that remains,
there is still a very great deal to possess.

In the recital that follows, God lists a raft of lands and peoples, concluding, "I myself will dispossess them for the Israelites" (13:6c). The allotment of the land thus anticipates *future* conquest rather than following *completed* occupancy. There were already hints of the need for more conquering and occupying to be done in the directly preceding account in chapter 12, but the specific listing of peoples and territories that remain to be taken in the first six verses of chapter 13 is surprising in view of the statement at the end of chapter 11. Provided the tribes will in the long run possess the entire land of Canaan, each tribe is promised an allotment. Possession is assured by direct divine action in the future.

At different stages in the dizzying recital of regions and towns assigned to each tribe that ensues, narrative interruptions enliven the proceedings. First, Caleb, one of the survivors of the wilderness wanderings, requests an inheritance, presenting his case in an eloquent description of past and current issues relevant to his situation (14:6–15). Caleb conquers his territory, and in a sequel his daughter Achsa comes to the fore by demanding more than just a field; she also needs a water supply. What good is land, after all, if there is no water to make it arable (15:16–19)? We also meet the five daughters of Zelofhad, who appeal to Joshua to make good on a divine promise relayed in the wilderness by Moses regarding their inherited share of the land (Num 27:1–11; Josh 17:3–6).

The final chapters include an entertaining and at the same time troubling account of altar building by the Transjordanian tribes and the conflict that follows (22:1–24). This story, with its description of potential intertribal conflict, even warfare, forms a bridge between the section of territorial listings and the final material, consisting of a farewell speech with warnings by Joshua and an assembly that includes a covenant making ceremony at Shechem (ch. 24). A theme of anxiety about the sometimes tentative cohesion of the community permeates each section of these final episodes. The book concludes with notations on the death and burial of Joshua and priest El'azar, and the interment of Joseph's bones (See Gen 50:25; Exod 13:19).

Historical Setting of Events

Something extraordinary happens in Joshua. Reports of failures to acquire cities and lands challenge the triumphal descriptions of conquests.[2]

Curiosity about historical issues does not disappear even in the face of acknowledgment that biblical texts do not record history in a way that conforms to contemporary notions of historiography. Central questions concern the nature of the entry into the land and the identity of those who settled in Canaan and east of the Jordan. How exactly did the "children of Israel" get into the land and who were they?

Responses to these related questions do not necessarily become clear by closely following the accounts in the book of Joshua, which present contradictory statements side by side: on the one hand a completed occupation with no more war in present or future (Josh 11:23), on the other a task that is not yet done, for "there is still a very great deal of land to possess" (Josh 13:1). Nor are these the only references in which the point of total violent takeover under Joshua's leadership finds a counterpoint in the mention of remaining territories and peoples that exist in Israel "to this day." The perspective of

2. L. Daniel Hawk, *Joshua,* Berit Olam (Collegeville, MN: Liturgical Press, 2000), xiii.

completed conquest at the end of chapter 11 runs up against other texts with promises of the completion of this task (see, for example, 13:6b; 17:18; 23:5). In addition, there are continuous references to indigenous populations that remain with Israel "to this day," beginning with the story of Rahab in chapter 2, which is concluded in the story of Jericho's fall (Josh 6:25), continuing with the ruse of the Gibeonites in chapter 9, the list of remaining peoples in chapter 13, and the mention of the Jebusites in 15:63 and the Canaanites in 16:10 and 17:12–13. One may also deduce the presence of groups other than the invaders from chapter 24. The fabric of one united country that "had rest from war" is everywhere rent by mention of families and indigenous peoples that remain in the land.[3]

An idealized or utopian view of the land as a gift from Adonai existed side by side with a, doubtless more realistic, reflection of the way events actually unfolded, and thus different perspectives are present in Joshua in terms of the extent of land and the number of existing peoples conquered by the invading Israelites. Apparently, the collectors and editors were satisfied to let the contradictions

3. It is incorrect to claim, as Anthony R. Ceresko does (*Introduction to the Old Testament: A Liberation Perspective* [Maryknoll, NY: Orbis, 1992], 90), that the book of Joshua recounts a total takeover in which "the whole land is brought under Israelite control and most of the Canaanite population either driven out or exterminated." Ceresko is not the only scholar to paint the Joshua account in contradiction to both archaeological discoveries and to the book of Judges. See, for example, Israel Finkelstein and Neil Asher Silberman, *The Bible Unearthed: Archaeology's New Vision of Ancient Israel and the Origin of Its Sacred Texts* (New York: Touchstone, 2001): "The Book of Joshua tells the story of a lightning military campaign during which the powerful kings of Canaan were defeated in battle and the Israelite tribes inherited their land" (70). One can hardly call the few campaigns described in Joshua "lightning." It takes five chapters to get to Jericho, just across the Jordan, and once the Israelites are there, the details of the fall of Jericho are most unlike a campaign. The battle against Ai initially meets with defeat, and the eventual conquest is the only episode in Joshua one could qualify as a battle scene. This is not to mention the multiple references to the presence of "peoples that remained in the land." Only a superficial reading of Joshua could give the impression of the idealized view of completed conquest as the only perspective present in the text.

stand, since conflicting points of view on the reality of the past do not necessarily undermine essential truth that needs to be told (see pp. 28–29). Living together as a community with its own religion and ritual among and together with peoples of different persuasions and practices was most likely always a part of the landscape and certainly arose as a new challenge in the period of the exile. While boundaries around land and groups—what belongs to whom, who is outside and who is inside—dominate in Joshua, the permeable nature of these issues does not remain hidden.

In reference to the possible invasion of Canaan, the question of *how* is closely tied to the question of *who.* Weaving a path through the thicket of theories that bear on this question is no easy task, but it is possible to discern three main perspectives. One view hews closely to the idealized version present in Joshua 11:23 and in the following chapter, which features a list of all the defeated kings, as well as in 23:1.[4] A second theory claims a gradual settling of Canaan by different "groups entering Canaan at different times"—the so-called "peaceful infiltration" model.[5] Third, there is the "revolution model," which proposes an internal upheaval in Canaan, a process of "social revolution" at the end of the thirteenth century BCE.[6] The

4. This view was advocated in an earlier era by William F. Albright, *From the Stone Age to Christianity: Monotheism and the Historical Process* (New York: Doubleday, 1957). Contemporary authors Iain Provan, V. Phillips Long, and Tremper Longman III emphasize the importance of adhering closely to statements proclaiming a total takeover by Joshua in their work *A Biblical History of Israel* (Louisville: Westminster John Knox, 2003), although they make distinctions between the concepts of capture and destruction and acknowledge the presence of text that points to "the Israelite tribes' occasional . . . failures to dislodge their foes" (156). In regard to 11:23, they observe: "The chief historical point is that the war of *subjugation* has been successful . . . and the *occupation* can now commence" (155).

5. This theory is represented by the German scholars Albrecht Alt, *Essays on Old Testament History and Religion* (New York: Doubleday, 1967); and Martin Noth, *The History of Israel* (New York: Harper & Row, 1960).

6. For an early representative of this perspective, see George E. Mendenhall, "The Hebrew Conquest of Palestine," *BA* 25 (1962): 66–87. Later, a similar point of view was argued by Norman K. Gottwald, *The Tribes of [YHWH]: A Sociology of the Religion of Liberated Israel* (Maryknoll, NY: Orbis, 1979).

three models do not cohere with the biblical text of Joshua, which in many places contradicts a total takeover while at the same time testifying to great violence. If none of the hypotheses are entirely satisfactory and none have support in biblical traditions, the truth may be more complex than simplified models allow. In the words of biblical scholar Benedikt Isserlin: "The origins of Israel may in fact have been far more complex, involving not only conquest by a limited group with a novel religion, but also some peaceful infiltration, as well as the adhesion of dispossessed elements."[7]

Recently, German scholar Rainer Albertz has argued for a modified version of the revolution model which allows for an exodus group to have entered the land of Canaan in the late thirteenth century BCE, to be joined there by indigenous movements of marginalized groups in revolt against the hierarchical and oppressive social and economic systems that prevailed in the city-states of Canaan at the time.[8] This model has much to be said for it. With Albertz and others, I assume that a kinship group, tracing its antecedents to a common ancestor-family, after hardship and oppression in Egypt, having undergone a transformational experience in the trek through the wilderness on the way to Canaan, arrived at the Jordan River in the late thirteenth century BCE and took violent possession of parts of the country as recounted in Joshua. At the time of the invasion, the indigenous people of the land were at a stage of social change, and the invaders were occasionally joined by other disaffected groups seeking to establish themselves. At other times they had to be content to live side by side with indigenous populations which they were unable to conquer. The stories of Rahab and Gibeon are thus illustrative of a tradition in which the conquest was remembered as "a process during which many inhabitants of the land survived, became aligned with Israel, and ultimately joined it."[9] I agree with Albertz

7. B. S. J. Isserlin, *The Israelites* (Minneapolis: Fortress, 2001), 59.

8. Rainer Albertz, *A History of Israelite Religion in the Old Testament Period*, trans. John Bowden, vol. 1, *From the Beginnings to the End of the Monarchy* (Louisville: Westminster John Knox, 1996); trans. of *Religionsgeschichte Israels in alttestamentlicher Zeit* (Göttingen: Vandenhoeck & Ruprecht, 1992).

9. Tikva Frymer-Kensky, *Reading the Women of the Bible* (New York: Schocken, 2002), 43.

that the exodus group exhibited some form of democracy, as testified to in the books of Joshua and Judges, and that there was "minimal social stratification."[10] Albertz holds that the sociopolitical system of the invaders was against domination and knew little established political leadership, apart from that which arose in times of crisis.[11] Such a view appears to cohere best with the text we have before us.

The book of Joshua contains a genre of ancient literature called conquest accounts. Such reports, often in poetic form, are extant from other peoples in the ancient Near East, and they exhibit common features with some of the Joshua material. In his extensive analysis of Assyrian, Hittite, and Egyptian conquest literature, K. Lawson Younger cites many parallels between the genre and Joshua 9–12. Other ancient conquest accounts share, for example, the convention of citing support from a deity who fought on behalf of his people and employed natural phenomena of a miraculous nature. There is the commonality of figurative and hyperbolic language, especially evident in the descriptions of total destruction and absence of survivors. In certain reports, there are parallels to the ruse used by the Gibeonites (Josh 9) to avoid total annihilation. Kings fleeing and taking refuge in a cave is also a common motif (Josh 10:17–27). As Younger points out, "The Hebrew conquest account of Canaan in Joshua 9–12 is, by and large, typical of any ancient Near Eastern [conquest] account."[12] In all the material he reviews, Younger finds a "common transmission code" with "an intermingling of the texts' figurative and ideological aspects." Such features do not "negate the fact that a war took place, that someone won or that the army performed certain specific actions." As we would most likely not call into question the fact that Tiglath-Pileser actually went on military

10. Albertz, *History*, 72–75.

11. "The tribal alliance of Israel derives from a political option which is opposed to domination, and which by deliberately standing apart from the monarchical Canaanite city-states allows the institutionalization of political power only to the degree that is absolutely necessary for safeguarding the survival of families and clans" (Albertz, *History*, 75).

12. K. Lawson Younger Jr., *Ancient Conquest Accounts: A Study in Ancient Near Eastern and Biblical History Writing*, JSOTSup 98 (Sheffield: Sheffield Academic Press, 1990), 265.

campaigns in the twelfth and eleventh century BCE as narrated in his annals, we may accord to the Joshua records a similar kind of trust while at the same time being aware that the book reflects a common ancient mode of record keeping that makes abundant use of hyperbole and figurative language.

The *Herem*

The God of Joshua not only sanctions war, he orders it. He not only orders war, he leads it. He not only commands total extermination, he abhors mercy. . . . The whole business . . . is nauseatingly repulsive.[13]

Violent conflict in the text of Joshua takes the form of both aggression and defense. Defensive warfare follows, however, upon aggressive assaults perpetrated by the Israelite invaders, and one can thus hardly speak of a defensive war on the part of the Israelites. All the Historical Books breathe the air of war, and in reality, Israel in the six hundred years of its existence before the Babylonian exile rarely experienced an extended period of calm and absence from the turmoil of armed conflict (see p. 10). Of particular concern and interest in Joshua is the practice of the so-called "ban" (*herem*). The verbal root of the word means "to consecrate" or "to devote" and denotes something or someone that belongs to the Deity (Lev 27:28–29). In the context of Israel's wars of conquest, it means that what is so devoted is to be entirely destroyed.

While the practice may indeed feel "nauseatingly repulsive," it is important to understand the nature of the ban in Joshua and in other parts of the Historical Books. In the context of war that involves the *herem* as we encounter it in Joshua, the defeated community is viewed as a sacrifice to the Deity, as Susan Niditch cogently argues in her book *War in the Hebrew Bible.* In that framework, the practice exhibits a certain respect for the other party without demonization or the further victimization that often accompanies armed conflict, such as rape or enslavement during and after mil-

13. McConville and Williams, *Joshua*, 109–110.

itary engagements.[14] To leave no survivors, as was commonly reported in other ancient conquest accounts also, may not have been the worst fate to inflict. The victims are consecrated or dedicated in the way sacrifice is consecrated. If the conquering party violates the *herem* by taking for itself what does not belong to it, the people become equally "consecrated," as is clear from the story of Achan (Josh 7), in the aftermath of which God declares that the Israelites "have become *herem*" (7:12).

The term *herem* occurs as a historical reference especially in the Historical Books of the Bible and may also be invoked because of injustice or an evil that needs divine punishment demanded by God's justice. Both the ban as sacrifice and the ban demanding God's justice make killing in war acceptable, the one by reducing guilt that might accompany killing, the other through a desire to eradicate evil. It is perhaps not entirely clear whether in Joshua the *herem* (i.e., the annihilation of all life and property) is invoked as an issue of justice or is the dedication of the conquered territory, livestock and people as a sacrifice. Usually, where injustice or evil demands the *herem,* mention is made of past or future deeds that require it. Deuteronomy 7:2–4 contains the instruction to completely destroy the peoples already living in the land the Israelites will enter because otherwise they would become intermingled with Israel through marriage, which would lead the Israelites to commit idolatry.[15] This

14. Susan Niditch, *War in the Hebrew Bible: A Study in the Ethics of Violence* (Oxford: Oxford University Press, 1993). See also the insightful discussion of Richard Nelson on the issue of *herem* as essentially something that is the possession of Israel's God in *Joshua: A Commentary* (Louisville: Westminster John Knox, 1997), 19–20.

15. Deut 7:2–4:

2 And Adonai your God will deliver them up to you,
and you will slay them; you must utterly destroy them [with a 2× repetition of the root *haram*].
Do not make a covenant with them and do not have pity on them.
3 Do not intermarry with them; your daughters do not give to their sons
and its daughters do not take for your sons.
4 For that will cause your sons to turn aside from me,
and they will serve other gods.

point is hammered home in all of chapter 7 and picked up again in Deuteronomy 9.

DEUTERONOMY 9:5

It is not because of your righteousness
or the integrity of your heart
that you are entering to take possession of their land,
but because of the wickedness of these nations
that Adonai your God is dispossessing them . . .

Neither the wickedness of the nations in the land the Israelites invade nor the danger of idolatry is featured as a reason to annihilate the peoples of Canaan in the conquest accounts of Joshua. Only in the concluding chapters does the issue of idolatry come to the fore as threatening the cohesion and the very existence of the tribes in the land. In this connection, it is worth noting that the final material is also clearly in the hortatory style of Deuteronomy, in which idolatry is the major reason for the threat to the people's continued existence in the land. Until this point, the wickedness of the inhabitants of Canaan, or the danger of intermarriage with them—the first step on the road to idolatry—has not been mentioned as a motivation for the invading Israelites to conquer the land.

Historical Setting of the Text

History writing is artistically constructed and does not necessarily follow a strict chronological format of presentation.[16]

Joshua as we find it today in the biblical canon was not composed at the end of the thirteenth century. The text reflects a long process of collecting and editing old material, as already mentioned, perhaps being finally completed by editors in the period of the restoration of Judah following the return from exile (see pp. 7–8). Theological con-

16. Younger, *Ancient Conquest Accounts*, 35.

cerns in the form of demands to follow God's instruction and trust in the divine promise of the gift of the land bind the narratives and lists together into a whole. Where these concerns are notably present, we hear the voice of the editors, the postexilic theologian(s) who wove the tapestry of Joshua into one whole.[17] This voice is prominent in certain parts of Joshua and takes a backseat in others.

There is throughout an emphasis on the obligation of individuals and the community to adhere to instruction or teaching (*torah*), at times referred to as written down: the "scroll of the Teaching" (so Josh 1:8; 8:34) or the "scroll of the Teaching of Moses" (implied in 1:8 and 8:34; explicit in 8:31 and 23:6), in the final chapter called the "scroll of the Teaching of God" (Josh 24:26). The text opens with emphatic references to the Teaching of Moses (1:7, 8), takes it up on the important occasion of the liturgical celebration after the defeat of Ai (8:31, 32, 34), and returns to it in the penultimate chapter (23:6). All the references culminate in the mention of "the scroll of the Teaching of God" in 24:26. I take these references to a written document to derive from the text-centered postexilic community in Judah, as reflected in, for example, Nehemiah 8:1–8, without excluding the possibility that a core of written instructions was available at an earlier date. The tradition of Joshua's leadership—not only as the principal planner of military campaigns but also as the one in charge of providing social and religious guidelines and policies—is thus dated to the very roots of Israel's presence in the land.

While there are many different ways of presenting the text of Joshua, which may on the surface appear unorganized and messy, I have chosen to approach the book as unified whole, and to facilitate our review I have organized the material using an adaptation of the

17. These editors are most often identified as the Deuteronomists or Deuteronomistic Theologians in scholarly analysis, with the editing process going through a number of stages. They are called Deuteronomists insofar as they reflect concerns and style prominent in Deuteronomy. While the stylistic and thematic concerns of Deuteronomy are evident in certain sections of Joshua, in other places there is greater emphasis on Priestly interest. It is possible that editors mainly from the Deuteronomistic and Priestly schools were both active in combing the material in Joshua through Kings.

scale designed by Jan Fokkelman.[18] In my design, the book consists of three Cycles: Joshua 1–12 ("Crossing and Conquest"), Joshua 13–21 ("Occupation"), and Joshua 22–24 ("Conflict and Unification"). These three are then divided into smaller units: Acts, Scenes, and Sequences.[19] The Crossing and Conquest Cycle (1–12) is marked by direct speech from God to Joshua, which is lacking in only three chapters. In the second and third Cycles of the book (13–24), direct divine address is generally absent, occurring only in chapters 13 and 20. Apart from those occasions, Joshua is the protagonist in these chapters, without prompting from Adonai, the God of Israel. In addition, groups of people occasionally move into the center of the action, or individuals other than Joshua take center stage.

Generally, the first Cycle presents the Deity issuing instructions to Joshua upon which Joshua takes action rather than presenting a dialogue between the two. The lack of interchange contrasts with the characteristic liveliness that marks the exchanges between God and Moses in the Torah, especially in sections of Exodus and Numbers, and creates a sense of distance between the human and divine realm. In a few places, this sense of separate spheres is interrupted, as, for example, in the encounter of Joshua with the commander of the divine host on the eve of the capture of Jericho (5:13–15) and on the occasion of Achan's violation of the ban on Ai (7:6–15). Both of these incidents are exceptions to the rule. The lack of dynamic verbal intercourse between the Deity and the main human character lends

18. This scale is an adaptation of J. P. Fokkelman's twelve-step scale found in *The Crossing Fates*, vol. 2 of *Narrative Art and Poetry in the Books of Samuel* (Assen: Van Gorcum, 1986), 1–21. Fokkelman's analysis is noteworthy because he constructs it as a ladder, beginning from the ground with sounds, words, and phrases and building up to the entire book. My use of it is an adaptation in that I also take into consideration reflection on possible historical contexts of textual origins and final composition, as well as interpretive horizons—the levels that Fokkelman calls "subsequent horizons" (7). For a close literary analysis of Joshua, see also Piet van Midden, "Jozua," in *De Bijbel Literair: Opbouw en gedachtegang van de Bijbelse Geschriften en hun onderlinge relaties*, ed. Jan Fokkelman and Wim Weren (Zoetermeer: Meinema; Kapellen: Pelckmans, 2003), 133–44, esp. 134.

19. Fokkelman, *Narrative Art*, vol. 2, 5.

an air of flatness to the portrayal of Joshua, who shows few flaws, whose failings when he does fall short are not highlighted, and who never receives divine punishment.[20] God speaks and Joshua acts, executing God's instructions as he is told to do from the beginning in almost perfect obedience. There is certainly nothing here like the defiant Moses who turns down God's call to lead the people out of Egypt (Exod 3:1–4:17), or the Moses who is indignant on behalf of a rebellious people in the wilderness (see Exod 32:7–20; 33:12–23; Num 11:1–25; 12:10–15; 14:13–25, for example).

In the second half of the book, Joshua stands in sharper relief as he is active in both allotting and receiving land, and even more so in the final chapters, where his interaction with the community is that of a lawgiver and policy maker. On the other hand, the latter part of Joshua mentions his advanced age at least twice (2× each in 13:1 and 23:1–2), a statement that is made of Moses only to point out his continued vigor in old age (Deut 34:7), creating at least a subtext of frailty for Joshua that undermines the strength of his character as protagonist.[21]

20. Sarah Lebhar Hall, on the other hand, views Joshua as a "full-fledged character, one whose authority is established largely in relation to that of his predecessor but whose leadership exhibits several distinctive features" (*Conquering Character: The Characterization of Joshua in Joshua 1–11* [London: T&T Clark, 2010], 9). In her extensive review of the first eleven chapters of Joshua, Lebhar Hall highlights many interesting features of the text and argues her case for Joshua's distinctiveness throughout. However, it is perhaps not so much uniqueness as vivacity that is lacking, possibly because Joshua shows few flaws. When he comes up short, the errors are not highlighted, and they never receive divine punishment.

21. In the Historical Books, references to old age with an implied negative connotation are made in regard to Eli in 1 Sam 2:22; 3:2; 4:15, 18; to Samuel in 1 Sam 8:1; and later to King David in 1 Kgs 1. Certainly the comment on Moses's vigor appears to be unique.

Cycle I: Crossing and Conquest (Joshua 1–12)

Act I: Capture of the First City (Joshua 1–6)

If a people and its land share an inseparable bond, how can an immigrant people claim an attachment?[1]

The first Act of the Cycle consists of episodes leading up to and including the conquest of Jericho. Two chapters, 1–2, prepare directly for the crossing of the Jordan River and following conquest, as well as for the entire book. Joshua is commissioned and commissions the people in turn, and two spies on a reconnaissance mission are protected by a Canaanite prostitute, an act that is central to the success of the invading army but also to protecting her own life and that of her family. Moreover, her presence at the start and at the end of the first act (6:22–23, 25) reflects the lived experience of early Israel as one of coexistence with many of its immediate neighbors. The crossing of the Jordan is related in fine detail in chapters 3 and 4, ending in the construction of two memorials. Chapter 5 describes the important marking of the separation between wilderness existence and conquering the land with ceremonies of circumcision and Pesach. Finally, the city of Jericho is captured, beginning with an initial appearance of a heavenly messenger followed by a ceremonial procession around the town for seven days, at the end of which the city falls without resistance.

1. L. Daniel Hawk, "Indigenous Helpers and Invader Homelands," in *Joshua and Judges*, ed. Athalya Brenner and Gale A. Yee (Minneapolis: Fortress, 2013), 109–22, 113.

Act I, Scene 1: Commission and Reconnaissance (Joshua 1–2)

Complete obedience and complete conquest.[2]

Canaan, like Rahab, is portrayed as an open space.[3]

Although chapter 1 can be understood as a unit by itself, considering it together with chapter 2 makes for a more interesting and thematically complex beginning to the book. Both chapters are placed at a point in time before the crossing of the Jordan (and as such the two belong together), while at the same time they are linked through matching as well as divergent concerns. Joshua 1 represents the commissioning of Joshua in a direct speech from God, and in his turn, Joshua commissions the leaders of the community. The chapter is thoroughly theological, with strong links to Deuteronomy and references to other texts of the Torah. God makes pronouncements, and male characters are in positions of leadership, with Joshua in first place. In chapter 2, God is not actively present and the initially male characters make way for a female non-Israelite who lives on the margins of her community.

In chapter 1, the stage is crowded with people: Joshua is present throughout, receiving instruction and encouragement from God and passing it on to official representatives of the people. Those of the tribes already in possession of land east of the Jordan get special mention and instructions. The chapter ends with the people pledging obedience to Joshua and adding their voice to the divine assurance of support. Almost the entire chapter consists of speech, exhibits the slow tempo that defines such a text, and leaves the people positioned in one place. Chapter 2 opens with Joshua and two unnamed male spies before immediately introducing a named Ca-

2. Sarah Lebhar Hall, *Conquering Character: The Characterization of Joshua in Joshua 1–11* (London: T&T Clark, 2010), 15.

3. Nāsili Vaka'uta, "Border Crossing/Body Whoring: Rereading Rahab of Jericho with Native Women," in *Bible, Borders, Belonging(s): Engaging Readers from Oceania*, ed. Jione Havea, David J. Neville, and Elaine M. Wainwright (Atlanta: Society of Biblical Literature, 2004), 152.

naanite female with an untraditional profession. Joshua speaks only one line in the chapter, four words in Hebrew (2:1), and disappears from the scene until the end of the episode. The woman, Rahab, is in the center of the action in virtually the entire chapter, is assigned a major role in the survival of the spies, and is thereby in control of at least the opening moves of the conquest. She also receives the largest amount of speech. There is a good deal of narration and movement: of the spies to the house of Rahab, of the Canaanite pursuers sent by the chieftain of Jericho, and of Rahab herself, ending with the spies returning to home base. Speech is rendered as conversation rather than monologue as in the first chapter, and in addition is for the most part not stereotypical but betrays lively interchange and delineates character. Speech in the first chapter takes place to a great extent in the open, while in chapter 2 the crucial action and speech happen in the enclosed spaces of city and house.

Finally, the tone of the two chapters is strongly contrastive. Joshua 1 testifies to the hortatory style one encounters in Deuteronomy, hammering home certain phrases and themes, while Joshua 2 engages from the start in double entendre and word play.

These two chapters together are, on the other hand, linked by the concern of "crossing," a major theme in the opening scenes of Joshua. The first words of God to Joshua contain the command to "cross the Jordan." The first people to do so, although the verb is absent in the opening lines of chapter 2, are the spies who must cross the Jordan twice in order to fulfill their task. The people as a whole stay east of the Jordan in both chapters. The spies cross more than the boundary of a river by bedding down in the house of a prostitute, and Rahab herself crosses the limits of loyalty to her own people by her alliance with the spies and through them with the invaders. She is moreover, as a prostitute, a person who professionally and habitually crosses the borders of propriety and acceptable behavior and owns an unstable identity to begin with—her marginal existence exemplified by her dwelling inside the wall of the city. Her only obvious power in the story consists of possessing information regarding the whereabouts of Joshua's emissaries. She is able to negotiate this power to her own advantage as well as that of her Israelite visitors.

We can break down chapter 1 into two sequences of approximately the same length, both consisting almost entirely of speech: verses 1–10 and 11–18. Only verses 1 and 12 and the first words of verse 16 comprise descriptive narration. In the first half, the opening lines set the time period as one directly following the death of a major character, Moses, a standard opening that serves as a transition point, closing off previous episodes and setting the stage for new events. Moses is identified as "the servant of Adonai" with Joshua positioned as "the assistant of Moses." Only at the end of the book will Joshua be promoted to the title "servant of Adonai" (24:29). Without further detail as to time or place, the text launches into the speech of God to Joshua, a speech that continues until the halfway point of the chapter. The speech consists of the formal commissioning of Joshua, with an elaboration of earlier commissions reported in Numbers and Deuteronomy (Num 27:18–23; Deut 31:14, 23). It is made up of commands and promises. The commands relate to action but above all to the appropriate mindset; the promises concern the gift of the land and the assurance of God's presence.

Now that Moses has departed this life, it is time for action. Hence God's first command is to "arise" and "cross." Joshua and the people are located on the side of a river they need to cross before they can take possession of the land. It will take a good deal of text before this crossing is accomplished, but its importance is indicated by these two verbs of action. The place where they (i.e. Joshua and "all this people") are is where they will leave behind wilderness existence under the guidance of Moses and the place from where they will begin their existence in the land under the guidance of Joshua. It is a land that God is "giving" to them. The fact of the gift is repeated in the opening part of the speech (2–3) and is emphasized in Joshua's instructions to the people that follow (11, 13, 15; 3×). The extent of the gift of land is specified in verse 4 but in such a way that its boundaries are unclear, only generally indicated as running from south to north and east to west, with the southern and western borders marked by the geographical endpoints of desert and sea. Daniel Hawk, in his commentary, suggests that this imprecise delineation "injects a sense of uncertainty into the very important matter of defining the boundaries of the land."[4] A purposeful ambiguity is possible, or it may be that the unrealistic limits in north and east—as far as the great river Euphrates no less!—point to the ideal of land possession, hearkening back to other delineations and the description of the land as "wide and good" (Gen 15:18; see p. 61). The promise of the land is followed by a promise of presence. Just as God had once promised ongoing presence to Moses at the outset of his mission to free the slaves from Egyptian bondage (Exod 3:12, 14; 4:12), God promises presence to Joshua at the conclusion of this mission: "As I was with Moses, I will be with you. I will not desert or abandon you" (5). This promise forms the capstone to all that precedes it.

The second part of the first sequence (1:6–9) is in the form of a command but concerns disposition rather than action. The "strength" and "courage" mentioned relate to the mindset required of Joshua rather than to the amassing of a proper army. The gift of the land is, after all, conditioned on sticking closely to the instruction Joshua has received (7), for that way lies success. It looks as if the obstacle to Joshua's success is not the difficulty of meeting a hostile indigenous population or the weakness of his own crowd but a potential lack of resolve and caving in to fear. Twice the admonition sounds to "be strong and courageous" (6, 7), to be repeated a final time in the form of a rhetorical question (9). This mindset will express itself in acting on the "Teaching" (*torah*) of Moses, God's servant (7). It is a written text which needs to be pondered and repeated so that proper action will follow what is "written" (8).

The divine speech concludes with an admonition not to be afraid, ending with a renewed promise of presence (9). Strength, courage, persistence in attention to Moses's instruction, and lack of fear, qualities that need to characterize Joshua's disposition, are enclosed in a divine dedication to presence (5, 9). The encouragement not to fear will be repeated three times in the conquest episodes (8:1; 10:8; 11:6), most likely indicating that there was a great deal to be afraid of rather than pointing to a flaw in Joshua's character. The

4. L. Daniel Hawk, *Joshua*, Berit Olam (Collegeville, MN: Liturgical Press, 2000), 8.

other caution, not to veer from the instruction of Moses, is a crucial component of the task ahead for Joshua and, at the same time, a warning to the community in which the final version of Joshua was composed. Their identity lay not in numbers, which had never characterized them, nor in extraordinary equipment or strength in battle. Those were certainly not resources they could trust after the Babylonian exile and return to the land. What identifies them is the text, the "scroll of the Teaching [*torah*]" referred to in Joshua 1:8, to which they must turn for guidance. Acting on it would be their way to any prosperity and success, which at the time of the Judean restoration consisted of surviving as a unique, cohesive community.[5]

The voice of the Deuteronomistic Theologian(s) is strong in this speech, providing many links with Deuteronomy. Joshua is connected securely to Moses, who is mentioned four times in the first three verses and twice more in what follows.[6] There are literal repetitions between Deuteronomy 31:1–8 and Joshua 1:6, 7, and 9. There is a strong emphasis on the land as gift—a gift contingent on the observance of the instruction given by Moses. The adjective "all" resounds throughout in the lines "all this people" (2), "all places" (3), "all the land of" (4), "all the days of" (5), "all the Teaching" (7), and "all that is written" (8).

The second sequence consists of three parts. First, Joshua addresses the "commanders of the people" to get the people ready for the river crossing that is ahead (1:10–11); the second part, sitting in the center of this sequence, contains a detailed instruction to the tribes that already inhabit the Transjordan (12–15); finally, the chapter closes with a response from those who receive Joshua's instructions (16–18), so that verses 16–18 correspond to verses 10–11. The short report in 10–11 begins with an order to the commanders to "cross" through the camp and to "command" the people to get

5. In Jewish liturgical tradition, Joshua 1:1–18 is the haftarah for Simchat Torah.

6. "Joshua is in a long line of Israelite leaders in the former prophets whose leadership is evaluated against the backdrop of the law of Moses" (Lebhar Hall, *Conquering Character*, 13).

ready because they are about to enter "the land that Adonai your God is giving you to possess."

Joshua's words are not a literal repetition of the divine speech but omit some elements while they add others. A new aspect is that the trip will happen in three days and that they are to prepare provisions. Instead of readying their weapons, they are to make sure to have enough nourishment—certainly an interesting touch for an army that is about to invade hostile territory. Perhaps this is the first hint that Jericho will be taken in an unusual fashion. Nothing is said here about armed encounter. Neither does Joshua encourage the commanders as God had encouraged him. Instead, he emphasizes the fact that there will be "entrance" and "possession" because the land is a "gift" from God. Joshua thus picks up the emphasis on the land as gift, a notion that will recur even more strongly in the speech that follows. Here he points out only that the gift will be in order to "possess" (*lerishtah* from the root *yarash*). The first section of the chapter uses the root *nahal* (v. 6), a verb with subtle differences from *yarash*. The former indicates a perpetual rightful inheritance, while Joshua speaks to the commanders about an acquisition through conquest.[7]

The next part contains instructions to the tribes already settled in the region east of the Jordan, Reuben and Gad together with half the tribe of Manasseh. Joshua reminds them that Moses had given this land to them but that they will not take "possession" of it until they have joined their kin, who still await the gift God has in store for them, in the military campaigns on the other side of the Jordan.

Joshua 1:12–15

12 To the Reubenites, Gadites and half the tribe of Manasseh,
Joshua said:
13 Remember the word that Moses,

7. Thus Norbert Lohfink ("ירש," *TDOT* 6:371): "By right of conquest one people or nation succeeds another in ruling over a territory. This right of conquest is undergirded by divine providence and action, which can be expressed in a play on words using the Hif of yarash (Deut 9:1; 11:23; 18:14; Judg 11:23 ff.)."

the servant of Adonai, commanded you:
Adonai your God is giving you rest
and will give you this land.
14 Your women, children and cattle will remain
in the land that Moses gave you, across the Jordan;
and you will cross in fifties before your kin,
all battle heroes, to help them
15 until Adonai will give rest to your kin as to you,
and they will take possession, even they,
of the land that Adonai is giving to them.
And you will return to the land of your possession
and take possession of it,
which Moses, the servant of Adonai,
gave to you across the Jordan, in the east.

The unit is tightly constructed around the theme of "giving," and with this emphasis not only summarizes the main subject of the first chapter but sets in motion the substance of the entire book. God, by the word of Moses, had already provided "rest" (i.e., land) for a part of the tribes (13), a gift that in the next breath issues forth from Moses (14). This motif is picked up in the second half of the speech in the point that for most of the tribes, their "rest," the land as the gift that God "is giving to them," still lies in the future. At that point, the root *yarash*, "to take possession," moves to prominent place, occurring side by side with the "gift" motif, each repeated three times in the span of one verse (15).

Reuben, Gad and half Manasseh have already received their land, but they may claim it as their abiding place, their rest and possession, only *after* they have come to the aid of their kin who also need the divine gift of rest. In the center of the speech stands the instruction to line up war-fashion, literally "in fifties," joining their kinfolk who are ready for "battle." The importance of family relationship comes to the fore here with the word "kin" (lit. "brothers"), used twice, to make clear that all members of this kinship need the same gift: "rest to your kin as to you." This is an elegant example of the need for cohesion among the tribes and not the last time that Reuben, Gad, and Manasseh will receive special attention in the book.

The last three verses reflect the response of the troops to Joshua in words that echo the instructions he received from God in the opening section (5–9). They promise complete observance of Joshua's instructions to the point that they threaten with death those who fail to do so, strongly underlining Joshua's authority.[8] The phrase in verse 18 used to describe rebellion against Joshua is elsewhere used only in reference to God. Moses is the benchmark in terms of their own listening and in terms of God's presence, and they end with the same encouragement given to Joshua by God: "Only be strong and courageous" (7, 18).

JOSHUA 2:1

Joshua, the son of Nun, sent from Shittim
two men as spies in secret, saying:
Go, look at the land and Jericho.
And they went and came to the house of a whore,[9]
whose name was Rahab,
and they slept there.

The first chapter has created the expectation that Joshua and the people will follow through on God's command to begin crossing into hostile territory, and in some ways this is what happens, but not in other ways. In chapter 2, we are looking at an opening narrative sequence in three parts with lots of movement (1–7), setting the scene

8. The beginning of v. 18 literally speaks of "every man who rebels against your mouth," rendered by most translations as "everyone who rebels against your orders" or something in that vein. The specific expression used here in Hebrew is a Deuteronomic phrase, occurring also in Deut 1:26, 43; 9:23; and 1 Sam 12:14, for example. As Lebhar Hall points out, Josh 1:18 is the "only place in the Hebrew Bible where the phrase is used of rebellion against a human leader"; elsewhere the reference is always to God's authority. Thus "as far as the Israelites are concerned Joshua speaks for the Lord" (*Conquering Character*, 17).

9. The verb I translate "came" in Hebrew is *bo'*, a word also used in the Bible for sexual intercourse. For more on the sexual nuances of this passage, see p. 62 below.

for the longer middle sequence in which action stops and speech takes over (8–21). A brief narrative sequence (22–24) concludes the episode in short lines filled with activity that cover a substantial time period, and at the end, everyone is back where they started.

Whereas chapter 1 places the action in terms of time, after the death of Moses, the second chapter opens with a location, Shittim, a place with specific associations. In Shittim, the Israelites committed "whoredom" with Moabite women and practiced idolatry, actions with gruesome consequences according to the story in Numbers (Num 25:1–9).[10] Joshua's commission to the spies is straightforward: "Go, look at the land and Jericho." In the next breath, the two spies have entered the house of a whore, where they sleep. For the careful listener, the place of "whoredom" thus leads straight to a whore. Perhaps the spies intended to set out from Rahab's place to do further reconnaissance; the story does not say, for their presence is discovered almost immediately. Two spies are sent out on a mission like the spies charged by Moses to reconnoiter the land, but unlike on that occasion, Joshua's charge lacks specificity (cf. Num 13:1–16). Also, Joshua sends the spies "in secret," unlike the group in Numbers, and there are only two of them. Instead of battle heroes lined up for war crossing the Jordan for all to see, two men on foot cross over in secret and without delay seek shelter in the house of a whore who is known by name, so that at the opening and ending of the introduction two named people, Joshua and Rahab, surround an anonymous party setting out in secret. The spies must have crossed the Jordan somehow, although any reference to "crossing" is absent. Joshua says "go" and they "went." Remarkably, the woman is identified not only by her profession but by name, Rahab, meaning *broad* or *wide*, the same root that indicates one of the crucial aspects of the land when it is said to be "wide" and good (see p. 56). So far in Joshua, only God and Joshua have appeared by name. They are now joined by a whore who remains in a prominent place in the story. Hebrew has two main words for prostitute, and Rahab is here called a *zonah*,

10. It is worth noting that in Num 25:1, the root *zanah* occurs, from which the Hebrew word "whore" (*zonah*) in Josh 2:1 derives.

a woman who sells sexual intercourse, rather than a *qedeshah*, a prostitute connected to the sanctuary.[11]

The spies' commission is to look at the land and the city, but they remain in one house in the city for almost the entire story. The narrative gets them to the house of Rahab as quickly as possible with strict economy of language that also manages to be suggestive. Shittim invokes "whoredom," followed by a reference to a "whore"; the verbs "to come/enter," used six times in the first four verses, and "to sleep" can both be used to refer to sexual intercourse (Gen 19:32–35; 30:16; 38:2; 39:12–14; 2 Sam 13:11; etc.), while Rahab's name means "wide" or "broad." The spies, literally "the men on foot," are indeed looking and entering, but perhaps not in a way Joshua had in mind, and these "footmen" cross more than one border.

The storyteller takes no time to moralize, for the movement goes on, with the first verse stating all that needs to be said at this point, including the mention of Jericho as a significant first place of conquest. Joshua and Rahab enclose the setup, deliverance and promise of a good land connoted by their names. Shittim and Jericho define two places, one from which the people must depart (licentious and idolatrous behavior) and another toward which they move: occupation of the land with all it implies, violence mixed with deeds of faithfulness, victory and inability to conquer. Notes of ambiguity and inconsistency in what lies ahead are already present.

11. On the difference between the two roles and on the role of the prostitute who plies her trade for a fee, see Phyllis A. Bird, "Prostitution in the Social World and Religious Rhetoric of Ancient Israel," in *Prostitutes and Courtesans in the Ancient World*, ed. Christopher A. Faraone and Laura K. McClure (Madison: University of Wisconsin Press, 2006), 40–58; "The Harlot as Heroine: Narrative Art and Social Presupposition in Three Old Testament Texts," in *Women in the Hebrew Bible*, ed. Alice Bach (London: Routledge, 1999), 99–119; and *Missing Persons and Mistaken Identities: Women and Gender in Ancient Israel* (Minneapolis: Fortress, 1997), 209–216. Also see Talia Goldman, "Prostitution in Classical and Jewish Antiquity," Hashta UMD: Jewish Voices on a Secular Campus, https://sites.google.com/site/hastaumd/contents-1/prost. On Rahab in particular, see Leila Leah Bronner, *From Eve to Esther: Rabbinic Reconstructs of Biblical Women* (Louisville: Westminster John Knox, 1994), 144–51.

In the second part of this initial sequence, the ruler of the city has got wind of the presence of Israelites at Rahab's place and orders her to give them up, for he is informed about the purpose for which they have "entered" Rahab's house. Verses 2 and 3 repeat the root "to come/enter" four times, with a telling escalation in verse 3:

JOSHUA 2:3

So the king of Jericho sent word to Rahab:
Bring out the men who came to you,
who came to your house,
for to search out all the land they have come.

The third line appears redundant, for the message is clear enough without it, but the phrase underlines the fact that the entering of Rahab and her house is a pretext for entering the land. It is the Canaanite land that is vulnerable to penetration rather than Rahab.[12] The king goes unnamed, and his role in the story is only perfunctory; he is acting as a proper administrator on behalf of his city should. Rahab's place is one where men come and go, and so it is not entirely surprising that word of the Israelites has reached the authorities.

In the next part of this first sequence (4–7), there is a great deal of action, dealt with by the narrator by tacking back and forth between past (4a and 6) and present (4b and 5) and anticipating the future (7). Rahab's action of hiding the spies is thus interrupted by her speech to the Jericho pursuers, and the detail of her activity of hiding the men is followed by the detail of the pursuit which is still to happen.[13] The first lines raise the tension of what will happen. The

12. Vaka'uta maintains that Rahab should be read as a "naming game by the Deuteronomist with intention to portray the land of Canaan as an open and dangerous place" ("Border Crossing/Body Whoring," 150). Tikva Frymer-Kensky wants to hold to both a positive and negative interpretation of her name: "Her name is emblematic of the permeable boundaries of Israel. She is the wide-open woman who is the wide-open door to Canaan, or maybe (in the negative view) the wide-open door to apostasy" (*Reading the Women of the Bible* [New York: Schocken, 2002], 44).

13. The verb usually translated "she hid *them*" literally reads "she hid *him*"

initial announcement of her hiding them could have been followed by the entry of the pursuers in the house and their looking for them. Instead, she disrupts any such potential activity by her announcement that the men were indeed in her house, but they have already gone, and if the posse goes after them right away they may still get them! Providing the specific time the spies left her house, when "the gate was about to close at dark" (5), alerts the reader to the detail that the gate may already be closed or is about to close, a factor that is confirmed in verse 7, which resolves the tension by noting that it closed behind the pursuers so that they are now outside, while the spies are hidden inside the city, guaranteeing them at least a short span of safety. In addition, verse 7 highlights that the pursuit goes in the direction of the Jordan, no doubt because they deduce that the Israelites are fleeing back to their encampment, and that the pursuers go "to the fords," revealing there are places in the river where it may be crossed fairly easily, knowledge the spies must have used to get to Jericho.

It is worth noting that, as of verse 3, the story drops Rahab's name to refer to her once as "the woman" (4) and subsequently simply with the personal pronoun "she," either explicitly, as in verses 6 and 8, or through the Hebrew verb form, which includes the gender of the subject and thus highlights the agency of the female. Verses 4 and 5 establish that this woman is not just anyone and not a fool. In order to hide the spies so quickly, she must have had her own network of people who tell her things and perhaps already had word of the king's intentions, or else she had hidden them foreseeing that pursuit might occur. In the face of the chieftain's envoys, she displays great sangfroid, speaking of "men" who "came" from who knows where and "left" for a destination equally obscure just before gate's closing. What began in the opening verse as "two men" has turned into a vague unspecified number. Who knows how many there were

---

and is used elsewhere in the Torah and historical books only in Exod 2:2, 3, of the mother of Moses. Tikva Frymer-Kensky points out the presence of the singular object pronoun as well as the relatively rare usage of this verb, especially with a feminine subject, and its connection to the saving act of Moses's mother (*Reading the Women of the Bible*, 36).

and where they are now? Rahab verifies that they indeed were in her house and does not deny that they may have been Israelites. She follows the truth with a lie and counsels the pursuers that they can still catch them if they go fast. It's all between "the woman" and "the men": on the one hand there are the Israelite spies, who, as the reader knows, are more or less safely hidden away, and on the other hand there are the Jericho police, on a wild goose chase at the end of the sequence with the city behind them and inaccessible. Logically, the exit from the city would now no longer be available to the spies either, but relevant information in that regard is held back until a later moment in the narrative.

Verses 9–21 consist of two speeches between Rahab and the spies with a proportional reversal: In the exchange of verses 9–14, Rahab contributes the largest amount of speech, while in verses 16–21, the spies take up the greater space. Yet even the second exchange is set in the framework of Rahab's words: "she said" (16, 21). In both parts, the action is almost at a standstill. Action occurs in the bridge between the speeches and in the concluding verses, which complement one another: "She lowered them" (15) and "she sent them off" (21). The hinge between the two parts is verse 15, which reveals the location of Rahab's dwelling. Her opening speech to the men under the flax is powerful and aims to persuade, with everything leading up to her plea in verse 12. Until then, she testifies to the things she "knows." She begins in the first person singular and moves quickly to the plural.

Joshua 2:9

She said to the men:
I know that Adonai has given the land to you
and that terror of you has fallen on us
and that the whole populace of the land quakes before you.

Quickly, she presents the entire matter as between you (plural) and us. "You" Israelites are the beneficiaries of the land and "we" Canaanites have fallen apart already. By mentioning the gift of the land as a done deal, Rahab also picks up the main theme of chapter 1 with its emphasis on the gift of the land. Rahab's word choice is of particular interest: "Terror" and "quaking" in fear have already taken place—verbs that outside of Joshua occur also in Exodus 15, the Song of Moses at the miraculous crossing of the Sea of Reeds—and in this way anticipate the events of chapter 3.[14] The news of the crossing following the exodus from Egypt spread far, so that even the inhabitants of Philistia, Edom, Moab, and Canaan experienced the same terror and quaking: "Then fell on them terror and dread" (Exod 15:16). Thus, Rahab follows her announcement with a reference to that occurrence and to the defeat of the Amorite kings across the Jordan, using the term "to devote to destruction" (*haram*) for the first time in the book (see p. 46). To bring home her point, she again mentions the defeated spirit of her people: "Our heart failed, and no spirit arose in any man before you" (11). Generally, the heart fails in the face of great odds, often in battle. References to hearts failing or melting occur also in regard to the people in the wilderness (Deut 1:28; 20:8) and again in Joshua of the heart of the Israelites after their initial defeat at the hands of Ai (Josh 7:5). She finishes her testimony with a confession about "Adonai, your God," who is not only the God of the Israelites but of all that exists, of "in heaven above and on earth below," a phrase reminiscent of Deuteronomy 4:39 (cf. 1 Kgs 8:23). In the words of Daniel Hawk, "The confession dresses Rahab in Israelite garb. She knows the songs Israel sings, can recount Israel's history, and acclaims Israel's God.[15]

The conclusion and objective of her speech come at the end: She wants a guarantee that her faithful deed in saving the spies will be reciprocated. "As I have dealt faithfully with you, you will also deal faithfully" (12). Logically, the recipient of the Israelites' reward

14. The word "terror" (*'emah*) occurs also in Genesis 15 of the fear that befalls Abraham on the occasion of the covenant God concludes with him, a covenant that consists of the promise of the land. See Gen 15:12–18. Outside of these passages, the word occurs twice more in the Torah, of the fear of Adonai that will make peoples flee before Israel (Exod 23:27) and of the terror God will send upon Israel because of its waywardness (Deut 32:25). The term connotes ominous fear connected with the presence of the divine. See also Job 9:34; 13:21; Ps 88:16[15].

15. Hawk, *Joshua*, 45.

for her action should be Rahab herself, but instead she expands the recipients to her entire family: "the house of my father." Just to make sure that they get it right, she spells it out as father, mother, brothers, sisters and "all that is theirs"—not a small group but as large as she can make it. What she wants is for all of them "to live" and to save their lives "from death." The last word of her speech, "death," thus forms the logical counterweight to her opening statement about God's gift of the land to the Israelites. What is life to them will be death to her and hers. She asks them to swear and give her a truthful or trustworthy sign.[16] So the men promise faithful act for faithful act: her life saved if she does not tattle and God indeed gives them the land (v. 14). It sounds almost mean-spirited for them to put a condition on their terms, since Rahab has surely proven her loyalty to them and their cause already. But apparently, their words suit Rahab's purpose, for she sends them on their way.[17]

The hinge verse returns to action and at the same time communicates crucial information.

JOSHUA 2:15

And she lowered them with a rope through the window,
for her house was on the outside of the wall
and in the wall she lived.

Clearly, letting them down into the town would have been counterproductive, so the narrator explains the location of her house on the outside of the city wall, repeating a word for "wall" three times; the text literally states that she lived in "the wall of the wall."[18] It is

16. Note that the word I have translated "faithfulness" is the Hebrew word *hesed*, a word with connotations of love, loyalty, and dedication that is also used to describe qualities of God. *Hesed* and *emet*, the word for "truth" or "trustworthiness," are often found together. As Bird notes, it will be "hesed for hesed" ("The Harlot as Heroine," 107).

17. Literally, the men say "our life instead of yours to die," picking up on the root of Rahab's last word, "death." In Hebrew, Rahab ends with *mawet*, death, and the men respond by pledging on their own *mawet*.

18. The text in Hebrew uses two words for wall in the second line, so

useful to know this, but more than usefulness is at stake here, and more becomes clear of the entire story. While it is possible that the position of her house is one with easy access to potential clients, this reality does not diminish the symbolic value of the location. Rahab is not an insider in her own community; she lives literally on its margin and may not feel any loyalty to the townspeople or their leaders. That prostitution was practiced in the ancient world is well-known. While Israel may not have had outright legal prohibition of the practice and may have viewed it as a necessary evil, the extension into its use as a metaphor for idolatry, along with other negative connotations of both the noun and verb in narrative and prophetic biblical texts, makes clear that both person and profession did not have a sign of approval and were marginalized in their societies. The house in the wall is thus illustrative of Rahab's position in her community. It turns out, of course, to also be extremely convenient for the spies, as she is able to lower them to an area outside the closed city gate.

The second speech sequence (16–21) begins with Rahab counseling the men as to the direction they should go: to the hills rather than the Jordan (i.e., west rather than east) so they may not be detected after all. She gives precise instructions: First, go where nature will provide some protection; then wait for three days and go back where you came from. Then it is the turn of the spies to demand conditions, opening and closing their address with the phrase "we shall be free of the oath you made us swear" (lit. "free from the swearing you made us swear"), picking up the phrase "we shall be free" in the course of their speech so that it occurs three times in four verses. Her life, together with that of her family, depends on three further requirements: Rahab has to mark her house; her entire family needs to be with her inside; and she must keep mum, a condition they had already stated when they first made their promise (14, 20).[19] We note that keeping silent

that the Hebrew literally reads "her house was in the wall of the wall/and in the wall she lived." With others I have taken this to mean that she lived in a house built into the outside of the city wall. Such houses were still present in the walls of the Old City of Jerusalem until they were demolished in the 1920s during the British Mandate.

19. The red cord, as others have observed, is reminiscent of the blood of the lamb on the doorposts when the Israelites left Egypt. Then, too, the sign

must have meant she could not tell her family about the state of affairs either and would have to convince them by other means to be with her in the house at the time of the attack. The house in the "wall of the wall" will exchange its marginal position for the center of survival. Rahab has the last word, pledging her intention to follow through on their conditions. Between Rahab and the spies, the tale is concluded with her final command that they be "on their way," giving her a last word and also a last position of some authority in that they do not leave until she "sent them off." The red cord is already on the window.

The last three verses bring everything to a satisfactory conclusion in a final narrative sequence in which the action once more speeds up. After the spies wait for three days in the hills, the pursuers return to Jericho without finding anyone (22). Once the posse from Jericho has gone back, the spies too can "return," and only then the narrator states that "they crossed" (23), thus making them the first ones to obey the divine command of the first chapter to "arise and cross this Jordan" (1:2). They tell Joshua "all that had befallen them," an account that must have included references to Rahab, as we find out later when Jericho falls to the Israelites (6:25–27). With their last words, the two spies echo the observation made earlier by Rahab that God has "given the land" and that "the populace quakes" in fear of the Israelites (24).

In Review: Point and Counterpoint

The indigenous helper is the pivot upon which the land turns away from the indigenous nations and toward the immigrant people.[20]

Two chapters set the stage for what is to follow. First is the encouragement and admonition to the leader of the conquest campaign

on the house saved the lives of those inside (Exod 12:7, 13). In addition, the red cord recalls the cord on the heel of Zerach, the twin brother of Peres, born to Tamar by her father-in-law Judah in Genesis 38—another story filled with sexual innuendo and even impropriety (Gen 38:28–30).

20. Hawk, *Indigenous Helpers and Invader Homelands*, 121.

and from him to his captains and back again as they get ready to cross "this Jordan" (1:2, 11). Tribes are lining up in battle array; obedience is pledged to the leader. In three days "the gift of the land" will begin. Within those three days, however, unanticipated action takes place, undertaken in secret, and negotiations are completed inside Canaan by a mission of two in alliance with a Canaanite woman of ill repute, with mutual loyalty (*hesed*) pledged between the two parties. The importance of the word *hesed*, just at this place, put in the mouth of a Canaanite prostitute, can hardly be overemphasized.[21] The term used in the Bible for both God's covenant loyalty and the reciprocal loyalty of people toward God and each other occurs only here in Joshua and originates from outside the covenant community with a member of a group logically hostile to the invaders and targeted for annihilation. How much it weighed in the balance will play itself out in the end when Rahab's life, together with all that is hers, will be spared at the destruction of Jericho.

The two spies cross the Jordan at a fordable place on their way to a location convenient for a number of possible reasons. We know Rahab lived not too far from a shallow part of the river where "the fords" were, for this is where the Jericho pursuers go, since they naturally assume it to be the place where the spies had initially crossed and would eventually return. At this point in the narrative of Joshua, then, it is possible for the Israelite armies to cross the river and annihilate the inhabitants of the land. But rather than this logical sequel to chapter one, the first thing that happens is a crossing by two men in secret to stay with a Canaanite woman of low status, whose entire family will survive the catastrophe about to befall her city.

Chapter 1 represents the commissioning of Joshua as the leader of the expedition by God and by his troops on the other side of the Jordan. Chapter 2 presents the messy and intimate interaction of people when they undertake a mission, land in a tight spot, and find help. In the first chapter, everything takes place in open spaces, within the encampment of the Israelite invaders east of the Jordan; in the second chapter, the important exchanges take place in a

21. Johanna W. H. van Wijk-Bos, *Making Wise the Simple: The Torah in Christian Faith and Practice* (Grand Rapids: Eerdmans, 2005), 255–56.

house, west of the Jordan. God's presence is not mentioned in the second episode, and Joshua does not extend encouragement to his spies, who are simply told to "go and look at the land and Jericho," an order they never fulfill, for they stay at Rahab's and subsequently hide in the hills. All they have is Rahab's words that her people have already mentally caved in to the power of the God who is on the side of the Israelites, and this word they bring back to Joshua. In chapter 1, expected promises of presence and encouragement flow from God to Joshua, from Joshua to his troops, and back again. In chapter 2, help arrives from an unexpected quarter, from a member of a group targeted for annihilation, and the only reference to God comes from this quarter.

But then, perhaps the help from this particular Canaanite was not entirely unexpected. The opening verse of chapter 2 states laconically that the spies went to the house of a whore by the name of Rahab, without comment from the narrator.[22] It leaves the question open as to why they went just there. While her house may have been the first place they came to, this is not necessarily the case, because the section of the wall in which Rahab's house was built may not have faced the Jordan. After she lets them down, she sends them to the hill country, a logical instruction from a location facing west. Or the reason they went to her house may be that the spies, who were, as we will find out, "young" men (6:23), decided they needed some R and R, and Rahab's house was recognizable as a brothel. They may have thought such a place helpful for gathering information.

All this may be true, but heading straight for this particular house, belonging to a woman mentioned by name, at least opens up the possibility that the narrator assumes previous acquaintance between the parties.[23] The Israelites were gearing up for battle.

22. As Bird argues, "There is no evidence that prostitution was ever outlawed in ancient Israel or that the prostitute was ever punished simply for her activity as a prostitute." Thus, "the prostitute in ancient Israel should be seen as the 'other woman,' tolerated but stigmatized, desired but ostracized" ("Prostitution in Ancient Israel," 42, 47).

23. Here I disagree with Bird, who observes that the story has given "no reason to believe that there was any previous relationship between the two parties" ("The Harlot as Heroine," 107).

Where there are armies, there are prostitutes, and there may have been traffic going both ways. As we have noted, nothing was very far apart in the country the Israelites are about to enter. The distance between Jericho and Shittim would have been manageable, and there is a place where the river can be crossed not too far away (see v. 7). The chieftain of Jericho appears to have had the necessary information to flush the spies out, and the implication in the story of Joshua 2 may be that he was both acquainted with the activities of the troops across the Jordan and prepared for the eventuality of some reconnaissance. He may have had spies of his own on the lookout for this eventuality. Rahab knew these particular customers also, and their arrival at her house came as no surprise. The implication is that her actions were prepared well in advance of this particular episode.

Finally, these two chapters set the tone for what is to come in the rest of the book: entry into the land accompanied by violence and all the horrors of war, and at the same time the need for human cooperation and coexistence to mutual benefit. Jericho is already signaled as the first city of importance to capture. A sequel to chapter 2 will certainly follow. Jericho will be under the *herem*, mentioned for the first time by Rahab, and she will play a role in the first violation of the same. Willy-nilly, the invaders will settle in the land of the promise with uncertain boundaries and fluctuating relations with indigenous populations and neighboring peoples. A less than perfectly tailored fabric in regard to the exact geographical territory violently conquered and possessed by the invaders, a less than homogenous community of insiders entirely closed-off to the outside, is what we meet first of all in the text of Joshua.[24]

24. In a challenging essay, Erin Runions presents Rahab as "a queer figure in the way that she troubles sexual- and ethnic-identity divides." She also argues that the story with its humor uses Rahab to cause "discomfort that both solicits interpretation and conscripts interpreters to laugh" ("From Disgust to Humor," in *Bible Trouble: Queer Reading at the Boundaries of Biblical Scholarship*, ed. Teresa J. Hornsby and Ken Stone [Atlanta: Society of Biblical Literature, 2011], 47, 70).

Act I, Scene 2: Crossing and Standing (Joshua 3–4)

As the Red Sea crossing brings the Israelites safely out of Egypt, so the Jordan crossing ushers them into Canaan.[25]

Draped in the numinous.[26]

After the first chapters, the stage is set: Joshua is commissioned, the people have been instructed and have pledged their loyalty, the spies have brought news of Canaanite weakness, and the river can be crossed with facility. Surely, a swift crossing and attack on Jericho will be next. Instead, what follows is a lengthy account of a miraculous march through the river with the Ark of the Covenant in the center of the action, followed by the erection of memorials to commemorate the occasion. The Ark, which appears out of nowhere and is present prominently only in the first part of Joshua, *stands* in the river, with the priests carrying it *standing* on dry ground, while the waters around it *stand* in a heap. Constant repetitions and anticipatory references slow down the tempo of the story and render it almost as motionless as the waters of the Jordan that stand on either side of the people moving through the river. The multiple designations of the Ark allude throughout to the powerful presence of God, to the extent that in 4:13, the Ark and the Deity have become one, and forty thousand warriors cross "in front of Adonai."[27] The

25. Lebhar Hall, *Conquering Character*, 57.

26. J. Gordon McConville and Stephen N. Williams, *Joshua*, Two Horizons Old Testament Commentary (Grand Rapids: Eerdmans, 2010), 168.

27. There are 17 references to the Ark in these chapters. In the initial verses, it is called "the Ark of the Covenant of Adonai your God," but it is also called by the shorter form "the Ark of the Covenant of Adonai" (3:17; 4:7, 18), and by "the Ark of the Covenant" (3:6[2×], 8, 14; 4:9), "the Ark of the Covenant of the lord of all the earth" (3:11), "the Ark of Adonai, the lord of all the earth" (3:13), "the Ark of Adonai, your God" (4:5), "the Ark of Adonai" (4:10, 18), simply "the Ark" (3:15 2×; 4:10), and once "the Ark of the Testimony" (4:16). The last designation is elsewhere found regularly in Exodus but occurs only here in Joshua. Scholars surmise that there may have been an independent Ark narrative that is reflected in the Historical Books, which

power of God acknowledged by Rahab in 2:9–11 manifests itself in these episodes in its full miraculous aspect. It is this manifestation of God's presence that is to be remembered for generations to come.

Joshua 4:6–7

6 So that this will be a sign in your midst:
When your children in the future ask:
What do these stones mean to you?
7 You shall say to them:
The waters of the Jordan were cut off
in front of the Ark of the Covenant of Adonai;
when it was crossing the Jordan,
the waters of the Jordan were cut off.
So these stones will be for an enduring memorial to the
Israelites.

While there will be no lack of "asking" in the Historical Books, Joshua 3 is the only place where an event leads to the goal of remembrance by future generations, thus providing another link, already established in chapter 2:9–11, between entry narrative and the liberation from slavery in Egypt (Exod 13:8, 14). The most obvious connection to those events is the stopping of the water so the people can cross on dry ground, as the people had once crossed the Sea of Reeds, although in this case there is no pursuing army and the Israelites are invaders rather than escapees. The chapters exhibit attention to priestly and ceremonial matters, constituting what may be called a "liturgical narrative."[28] In this first act, the emphasis on priestly engagement and representation will last through its final chapter, reporting the taking of Jericho. The entire account of the crossing appears to be a display of God's awesome power all accomplished "in order that you may be in awe of Adonai your God always"

surfaces in chapter clusters where the Ark has a prominent role but then more or less disappears from view. See also 1 Sam 4–6; 2 Sam 6.

28. Robert Polzin, *Moses and the Deuteronomist: A Literary Study of the Deuteronomic History*, vol. 1 (New York: Seabury, 1980), 92.

(4:24). In chapter 3, the crossing of the Jordan is accomplished, while the fourth chapter concentrates on the creation of two memorials of twelve stones. The memorials underline the ending of the people's wanderings and the beginning of their entry into the land of the promise.

Everything in the first sequence, 3:1–13, is preparatory, with a final action sequence, 14–17, bringing the passage through the river to a satisfactory conclusion. An introductory unit (1–4) is followed by three speeches: from Joshua to people and priests (5–6), from God to Joshua (7–8), and from Joshua to all the people (9–13).

The introductory unit sets Joshua and the people in motion from Shittim to the Jordan in expectation of the crossing and presents instructions not from the Deity but from the Israelite commanders anticipating events before the Ark has yet been carried forth. There is movement and awaited movement, beginning with Joshua "arising early in the morning" (3:1) (one verb in Hebrew), indicating haste and urgency—belatedly responding to the first divine instruction Joshua received to "arise and cross" (1:2)—and in contrast to the slow-motion account that follows. While the verb "to cross" is central to the narrative, it is balanced in chapter 3 by the verb "to stand." The contrast between lack of motion and crossing is underlined already in the opening verse, in which an army on the move "rested . . . before crossing" (3:1). A rest of three days commences, the third time that this ceremonially significant number appears in the opening chapters (see 1:11; 2:22).

Each unit in this sequence serves the purpose of getting the people closer to the Jordan to witness the miracle that will occur. The first ones to commence "crossing" are the commanders, but in their case it constitutes still a preliminary movement, a passing through the camp to make an announcement. They order the people to stay at a distance from the Ark when they "see it" being carried by the priests.[29] Coming too close to the numinous can be dangerous.

29. Joshua 3:3 reads "the priests, the Levites" (*hakkohanim haleviyyim*), sometimes rendered in the translation as "Levitical priests." This verse and Joshua 8:33 are the only two places in which the Levites are mentioned in the first cycle. Some variants add the copula "and" in 3:3, which provides the

The reason for keeping the Ark in sight is so the people may "know the way" they must go (3:4). This is interesting advice, implying that the most natural place to cross the Jordan is *not* where they should head. Access needs to meet a difficulty in order for a miracle to happen. A miracle is not necessary at a place where the river can be easily forded. The orders of the commanders anticipate what is to follow, since there is as yet no Ark in sight, while at the same time they introduce the overriding importance of the presence of the Ark.

In the next unit (3:5–6), Joshua first commands consecration to the people because of the "wonders" they will experience the next day. While the consecration recalls the Sinai experience (Exod 19:10, 14, 22), the word for "wonders" mostly occurs in poetry and appears in its verbal root also in Exodus 15, the song celebrating the parting of the waters at the Sea of Reeds, thus linking the event that is about to unfold to that experience (Exod 15:11; cf. Exod 3:20). The plural noun can be found also in Exodus 34:10, as well as in Nehemiah 9:17, Ezra's prayer, as he rehearses the rebellious past of the people during the exodus from Egypt when they were "unmindful of the wonders" God performed for them. Motion resumes as the priests follow Joshua's instruction to take up the Ark and carry it to the front so it will be in the lead. The second "crossing" is the passing of the Ark in front of the people.

A further instruction directly from God to Joshua looks ahead to the priests moving with the Ark to the water's edge, where they are to stand in the river (3:7–8). While God's words consist only of one encouraging phrase and a brief instruction, Joshua, in his following speech to the Israelites, expands on them (9–13). As Mo-

reading "the priest and the Levites." The history of the Levites and their place in the tribal community is complicated. In the blessings of Jacob to his sons in Genesis 49, Levi and Simeon are cursed together because of their violent treatment of the Shechemites (Gen 34:25–29). According to Numbers, the Levites became those who tended to the the Ark (Num 8:13–26), a commission connected to their role in the rebellion of Korah (Num 16:1–10). The expression *hakkohanim haleviyyim* is Deuteronomic and may have entered the text at this point under the influence of Deuteronomistic theology. The Levites and their land allotment will come into sharper focus in the second cycle, Joshua 13–21.

ses did in the past, he speaks here on behalf of God, a feature that flows directly from the assurance of presence made to him in verse 7: "As I was with Moses, so I shall be with you." Joshua is now able to promise the entire people God's presence (3:10), and he assures them they will receive a sign of this presence. A promise of divine presence, resuming God's first address to Joshua (1:5), thus echoes in the two speeches: from God to Joshua personally, then from Joshua to the people (3:7, 10). Joshua refers to the Deity as "the God of life," a unique expression, perhaps used to emphasize the contrast between the Israelites and the nations they are to conquer, for whom Israelite presence will not mean life.[30]

Heretofore in the Sequence, the Ark has been called "the Ark of the Covenant," underlining its representation of the bond between God and people. Joshua names the Ark twice, once identifying it as "the Ark of the Covenant of the lord of all the earth" (3:11) and the second time giving it the title "the Ark of Adonai, the lord of all the earth" (3:13). These designations hearken back to the testimony of Rahab, who confessed the God of the Israelites to be the "God of heaven and earth."

Joshua's final announcement comes as a surprise; it was not explicated in the divine speech.

Joshua 3:13

Now when the heels of the feet of the priests
carrying the Ark of Adonai,
the lord of all the earth,
will touch the waters of the Jordan,
the waters of the Jordan flowing down will be cut off
and will stand as one heap.

Nothing has happened so far except the movement of commanders and priests with the Ark and announcements of what is to come.

30. The list of six nations that will be driven out occurs elsewhere (Exod 3:8, 17; 13:5; 23:23; 34:11; Deut 20:17), though here the Girgashites are added, as in Deut 7:1 (see also Josh 24:11).

The description of the waters standing in one "heap" forges another link with the Sea of Reeds crossing (Exod 15:8), the only other place where this word occurs in the Hebrew text besides Psalms 33:7 and 78:13. Everything points to a future moment, and nothing more so than verse 12, the selection of twelve men, each representing a tribe, whose role does not take place until the next chapter although the order appears to be one to execute momentarily, anticipating an action central to the next episode (4:2–3).

The second sequence (3:14–16) presents the resolution of all that has been anticipated, with both people and priests on the move "to cross the Jordan" (14). The miracle of the waters standing in one heap receives a good amount of attention, still giving the impression of everything happening in slow motion, especially since the initial verses contain dependent clauses: "When the people set out. . . with the priests carrying . . . when the carriers came . . . and the feet dipped . . . with the Jordan overflowing. . . . Then stood the waters." The verb for the "standing" of the water is held back to the end of the unit, placed at the beginning of the phrase in contrast to everyone and everything else that is in motion, including the tumultuous waters which "came down" and now "stand." While the word "heap" is used for the collection of water in Exodus 15:8, the verb for "standing" in the Joshua account differs. The verb *amad* repeats twice: in verse 16 for the waters, in verse 17 for the priests with the Ark. This evocation of the stillness of water and priests creates an opening for the possibility of the people's crossing. The waters stand, the priests stand, so the people can move.

Joshua 3:16–17

16 Then stood the waters that came down from above;
they rose in one heap from as far as Adam, the city near
Zaretan,
while those that go down to the Sea of Aravah,
the Sea of Salt, were wholly cut off.
And the people crossed near Jericho.
17 And they stood, the priests carrying the Ark of the Covenant of
Adonai,

on dry ground in the middle of the Jordan,
and all Israel crossed on dry ground
until all the people finished crossing the Jordan.

The waters stood and the priests stood, while "the people crossed," "all Israel crossed," "all the people finished crossing." The threefold mention of the fulfillment of the first goal of the expedition puts the capstone on the miracle of "getting into" the land, the counterpart to that of the "getting out" of the land of oppression.[31]

Chapter 4 has its focus less on the event of the crossing than on ritual with a goal of establishing a memory for the generations to come, repeated twice (4:6–7; 4:21–24). The first nine verses are a coherent unit, followed by a sequence with emphasis on the role of Joshua as the successor to Moses (4:10–14), which resumes describing the finished safe passage through the river of all the people and takes up again explicit mention of the tribes who already possess land on the other side. The final sequence (4:15–24) concludes the crossing with the priests bringing the Ark to dry land and the water of the river returning to its normal flow; it continues with movement to another location, with action regarding the memorial stones, and with a resumption of instructions to future generations.

In 4:1–9, once again, movement is first announced and then delayed. Initial instructions from God to Joshua are followed by Joshua speaking to the people regarding what needs to take place immediately while, in addition, the eventual goal of the action they are about to undertake is spelled out. The first verses resume the action of 3:17, repeating the satisfactory conclusion of crossing the Jordan. In fact, this line will again be reiterated in verse 11, stressing the importance of completing this stage of the process. The first three verses make clear the directive in the previous episode in chapter 3 for a representative selection of twelve men (3:12): They will need to bring twelve stones out of the river and put them down in their camp. The purpose of the stones will become clear later. As often happens in these chapters, Joshua's speech (4:4–7) adds elements that were not

31. Note also the emphasis on "crossing" in Exod 15:16: "Until it crossed, your people, Adonai,/ until it crossed, the people you acquired."

a part of the instructions he received from the Deity. He begins by making the selection of the twelve and instructing them to "cross" facing the Ark "to the middle of the Jordan" and pick up stones, evidently large enough to be lifted on the shoulder (5). That is where the projected action stops to proceed with the explanation of the meaning of the stones. The reference to future generations and their remembrance is unusual in the Historical Books and reinforces the links to the exodus experience when, on the verge of leaving Egypt, the first Pesach is instituted with a similar directive (Exod 13:8, 14; cf. Deut 6:20). Later in chapter 4, there will be a time indicator (19) making clear that Pesach is once again around the corner. We will revisit the remembrance instructions below.

As in chapter 3, action follows speech, with twelve men removing twelve stones from the middle of the Jordan, which they take back to the camp to put down (4:8). Not anticipated is the action of Joshua, who takes stones into the Jordan to put them up there (9). Evidently there need to be two memorials: one in the Jordan and one on dry land; one to mark the boundary where the people crossed and one to mark the dry land, denoting accomplished action and hoped-for future. "Joshua fulfilled every command of Adonai—and then some."[32] Once the act of erecting the river memorial is accomplished, we expect the conclusion that takes place in 4:15–18, a sequence that follows seamlessly on verse 9. The narrator nevertheless has something more to say of importance and fits it in right here.

The next five verses (10–14) summarize and also look forward, treating the action of the priests and the Ark exiting the river as if it had already taken place, while in the timeline of the story this event is still to happen. In verse 10, the priests are still standing in the river while the people "quickly" cross—the only time that haste marks the event of crossing the river. Next, the crossing of the people as well as that of the priests with the Ark is viewed as if it was already in the past. The Ark is for the second time the subject of a verb: "The Ark of Adonai crossed with the priests" rather than the priests crossing while they

32. Polzin, *Moses and the Deuteronomist*, 109. Polzin considers the stones Joshua sets up in the river as a "testament to the necessity of change and mobility in the understanding, interpretation, and application of God's word."

carry the Ark (11). One of three times that the Ark is subject of the verb "to cross" in the two chapters (see 3:11; 4:7), it is placed at this point in close proximity to the battle formations "crossing before Adonai" (4:13), underlining the close identification of the Ark with God's presence. As in chapter 1, the tribes with land allotment east of the Jordan come to the fore, openly exhibiting their loyalty to the rest of the Israelites. Tribal unity, especially with those across the Jordan boundary, remains an issue in Joshua, coming to a head in the final chapters of the book.

The entire sequence of 4:10–14 serves to tighten the link between Moses and Joshua, each mentioned three times, with Moses absent from the lines only in verses 11 and 13. Everything happens as Moses commanded it on God's orders; the authority of God thus flows directly through Moses to Joshua, connecting the narrative to episodes occurring in Exodus, Numbers, and Deuteronomy (see Exod 33:11; Num 27:12; 32:18; Deut 1:38; 3:21, 28; 31:3, 23). Logically, the sequence ends with an affirmative statement about Joshua's authority, which is now comparable to that of Moses, while the people show him the same respect. The gist of the depiction of Joshua as well as of Moses thus presents an idealized picture both of leaders and of people, omitting references to Moses's disputes with God and his anger with the people and to the people's quarrels with, disrespect of, and rebellion against Moses during their wanderings in the desert (e.g., Exod 3:1–4:17; 16:1–3; 17:1–4; 32:1–6, 19–20; Num 11:10–14; 14:1–4; 20:9–13).

The conclusion of the crossing episode takes place in 4:15–18, picking up the thread from verse 9.

Joshua 4:15–17

15 Then Adonai spoke to Joshua as follows:
16 Command the priests carrying the Ark of the Testimonies
and let them come up from the Jordan.
17 Then Joshua commanded the priests as follows:
Come up from the Jordan!

The Ark is named in connection with the testimonies, or institutions, only here in Joshua and elsewhere only in Exodus, in the chapters describing the moveable sanctuary (Exod 26:33; 40:3, 21), material commonly understood to originate in a Priestly context. This identification completes seven different references to this sacred symbol of the divine presence in Joshua 3 and 4 as it displays God's power in enabling the miraculous crossing of the boundary provided by the Jordan. Although the Ark will peregrinate in the future, it will stay west of the Jordan, only once in danger of crossing the Jordan to the other side but in the nick of time returned to Jerusalem (2 Sam 15:25–29). From there, of course, it was to disappear forever during the Babylonian exile, a reality central to the awareness of the compilers of the book of Joshua.

All is not said and done, for the memorial of stones will be at Gilgal. Gilgal is an important shrine in Joshua, although we are not certain of its exact location, and it will come to prominence again in the narratives surrounding King Saul (1 Sam 7–15). At Gilgal, the memorial of stones is again provided with a purpose. It is there so future generations will remember, the lead-in to the remembrance in both cases being "if your future children ask" (4:6, 21; cf. Exod 13:8, 14). Comparing 4:6–7 with 4:21–24 yields significant differences. The first remembrance is impersonal and terse and has a close ring construction. The meaning of the stones at the beginning and the end surrounds the cut-off waters, with the phrase regarding the Ark crossing the Jordan at the center.

Joshua 4:6–7

6 So that this will be a sign[33] in your midst:
When your children in the future ask:
What do these stones mean to you?
7 You shall say to them:
The waters of the Jordan were cut off
in front of the Ark of the Covenant of Adonai;
when it was crossing the Jordan,
the waters of the Jordan were cut off.
So these stones will be for an enduring memorial to the
Israelites.

33. As in Exod 13:16, the work of God is called a "sign."

In contrast, the recital at the end of the chapter is more expansive, moving from the third person to the second and explicitly referring to the drying up of the waters of the Sea of Reeds (4:23). Most telling are the very last lines, which spell out the objective of this remembering.

Joshua 4:21–24

21 He said to the Israelites:
When your future children ask their fathers:
What are these stones?
22 You shall inform your children as follows:
On dry land the Israelites crossed this Jordan.
23 Because Adonai your God dried up
the waters of the Jordan in front of them until they crossed,
just as Adonai your God did to the Sea of Reeds,
which God dried up in front of us until we crossed.
24 In order that all peoples of the earth will know
that the hand of Adonai is strong,
in order that you may be in awe of Adonai your God always.

The stones provide a witness and a history lesson, a testimony to the power and care of God for God's people in Israel's past. Recalling past experience is, however, not merely an intellectual exercise but is also intended to powerfully re-create a present sense of God's presence—hence the transitions from third to first person plural. "The Israelites crossed the Jordan" becomes "the Sea of Reeds . . . we crossed"; "the waters of the Jordan in front of them" becomes the waters of "the Sea of Reeds . . . in front of us." Furthermore, the stated goal of the remembrance is the acknowledgment by "all peoples of the earth" of the power of Adonai "your" God, a confession first voiced by Rahab (2:11). Many standard translations render the final line "so that you may be in awe," but the consonantal text of the Hebrew can also be read "they may be in awe," blurring the boundary between insider and outsider.

Act I, Scene 3: Circumcision and Celebration (Joshua 5:1–12)

Reports of melting Canaanites encompass the story of a stopped-up river.[34]

Joshua is at the helm not only of Israel's military life, but of its religious life as well.[35]

The Israelites have entered the land with everything ready for the first battle, but the next episode halts movement and progress toward the capture of the first city once again to focus on ritual and the first religious celebration in the land west of the Jordan. In view of the significance of the occasion, I take it as a separate scene, with its climax the Pesach celebration of the last three verses. Leading up to this last sequence, a brief narrative statement (1) precedes a new instruction from God to Joshua (2–3), followed by completion of the action (7–8) headed by a relatively long interpretive comment (4–6). The last three verses (10–12) maintain the timeline announced in 4:19 as "the first month" (i.e., Nisan), continued in 5:2 with the general notation "at that time," with the precise datum of the Pesach observance as the "fourteenth day of the month" (5:10). Registering time in this precise manner is unique in Joshua and serves to underline the importance of the event. As Lebhar Hall observes, the journey from Egypt to Canaan "has at last come to its end. This particular Passover marks the completion of the Exodus journey, and thus serves narratively to frame Israel's wilderness experience."[36]

The chapter begins with a comment from the perspective of peoples under threat from the invaders (1), reporting that Amorites and Canaanites are quaking in their boots when they hear of the miraculous crossing of the Jordan. The expressions about God's miraculous deeds that cause "the heart" to "melt" and the "spirit" to fail are in line with Rahab's report to the spies (2:10–11) and that of the spies to Joshua (2:24), and they are stereotypical of fear in the face

34. Hawk, *Joshua*, 76.

35. Lebhar Hall, *Conquering Character*, 63.

36. Lebhar Hall, *Conquering Character*, 71.

of defeat to come (see Josh 7:5; Num 22:3; Deut 1:28; 20:8; Isa 19:1).[37] The notation of reports going out to the native inhabitants and their reactions will continue in subsequent episodes (cf. 9:1, 3; 10:1; 11:1). At this point, it causes one to look for a moment at what transpires from the point of view of indigenous peoples, shifts the geographical perspective, and also anticipates in a contrastive fashion the openings of chapters 9, 10, and 11, which begin with the same phrase ("when . . . heard"), making clear that news about the actions of the invaders is going around and that it provokes reactions. In chapter 5, the important links to the language used by Joshua, Rahab, and the spies in chapter 2 are carefully preserved.

A short instruction to Joshua commands him to make flint knives and circumcise the Israelites at a place literally called Foreskin Hill (5:2–3). The explanation for the procedure (4–7) makes clear that the Israelites who had been circumcised in Egypt have perished and that their children have not been circumcised; they were "foreskins" because they were not circumcised on the journey. It may seem odd, for it would surely have been simpler to circumcise infants (see Gen 17:10–14) rather than adult males, even during the trek through the desert, but the intention of the perhaps artificial construct is clear: The crowd that enters the land is different from those who "came out of Egypt," a phrase repeated five times in verses 4–6. These lines also reiterate the totality of the group of escaped slaves ("all the people" 3× in vv. 4–5; "all the nation" in v. 6); all of them "did not listen" to the voice of God. In contrast to that generation, now perished, the ones who crossed the Jordan bind themselves anew to God, since circumcision is a sign of the covenant between God and God's people. The first Pesach in the land God has promised to them must be celebrated by those marked as God's covenant people, separated from the disobedient generation of the wilderness wanderings.

The signal is that the time for ignoring God's guidance, for not "listening to the voice of Adonai," has come to an end. The argument unfolds slowly: The males of military age who came out of Egypt (5:4–5, 4×) were circumcised (5:5), but they died, with their death

37. McConville and Williams, *Joshua*, 26.

being the first fact mentioned about them in verse 4 and repeated in verse 6. The frequency of the phrase pointing to the exodus, "came out of Egypt/coming out of Egypt," indicates the importance of the closure of that event. The closing line presents a direct statement from God to Joshua with a pun on the place name Gilgal (9). At "Gilgal" God has "rolled away" (*gallivoti*) the "disgrace of Egypt," possibly a reference to the condition of the people when they languished there under oppression. More likely it is a direct allusion to Deut 9:28 with its reference to hypothetical mocking by the Egyptians.[38]

The timeline continues in the last sequence (10–12) with a description of Pesach observance, which includes eating from the fruit of the land. Earlier in the chapter, the land is indicated with the phrase "a land flowing with milk and honey"—a unique reference in Joshua.

Joshua 5:10–12

10 The Israelites encamped at Gilgal,
and they made Pesach on the fourteenth day of the month
in the evening, in the plains of Jericho.
11 They ate from the produce of the land
on the day after the Pesach, matzot and grain on that very day.
12 And the manna stopped on the day after
they ate from the produce of the land.
And there was no longer manna for the Israelites;
they ate the yield of the land of Canaan in that year.

Both space and time receive precise markers, picking up from 4:19. The place is Gilgal, near Jericho; the month is the first, the day the fourteenth. There "they made Pesach," "they ate from the produce of the land" (2×), and "they ate the yield of the land." Specific moments

38. McConville and Willams (*Joshua*, 27) adhere to the first view, Lebhar Hall (*Conquering Character*, 70) and Polzin (*Moses and the Deuteronomist*, 111) to the second. Lebhar Hall correctly notes the "threat of international reproach . . . specifically related to Israel's ability to maintain military control of their land, or to their stability within it."

in time get repeated and receive detailed emphasis: "the fourteenth day of the month in the evening, the day after Pesach, that very day, the day after . . ." These moments extend into the final notation of "that year." In other words, this eating of the land like settled people was not a momentary condition but stretched into the future. Eating as settled people do, from the land's yield, anticipates their becoming Canaan's inhabitants. It takes place against the backdrop of the emphatic notation that the food from heaven, the "manna," stopped.

As once Pesach marked the escape from Egypt, Pesach again sets them apart on the eve of the campaigns that herald their establishing themselves in the land. Circumcision and food from what the land produces are a sign of the people's passing from wilderness existence, with its attendant rebellion and disloyalty to its leaders and to God, to settled existence with a mindset of listening and loyalty, above all exhibited by Joshua. The cessation of manna is the exclamation mark on this episode (5:12).

Act I, Scene 4: The Battle of Jericho (Joshua 5:13–6:27)

It is as if Joshua is momentarily taken out of the normal process of rational planning to see where the real heart and cause of things lie.[39]

We thought we were in the outside world and then—whoops! It all turns out to have been something else entirely.[40]

Once again bearing the sign of the covenant, having put the wilderness behind and ready to conquer and settle the land, the armies of the Israelites can begin their task of conquest. In the scene that follows, the city of Jericho indeed falls to the invaders, but the account that unfolds is unlike any battle described in the Bible. It begins with the appearance of a divine messenger to Joshua and continues with ritual processions around the city, the eventual collapse of its walls,

39. McConville and Williams, *Joshua*, 29.

40. James L. Kugel, *The God of Old: Inside the Lost World of the Bible* (New York, Toronto, London, Sydney, Singapore: The Free Press, 2003), 70.

and the enactment of the *herem* (described in one line), to conclude with a relatively detailed report of the rescue of Rahab and a curse uttered by Joshua on potential future rebuilders of Jericho.

The air of the miraculous that dominated chapter 4 picks up at the end of the fifth chapter and continues through the sixth.

JOSHUA 5:13–15

13 When Joshua was in Jericho,
he lifted his eyes and saw—and look!—
a man standing opposite him
with a drawn sword in his hand.
Joshua went up to him and said to him:
Are you for us or for our enemies?
14 He said: No! For I am the commander of the host of Adonai;
now I have come!
And Joshua fell on his face to the ground in worship and said to him:
What does my lord speak to his servant?
15 The commander of the host of Adonai said to Joshua:
Take your sandal from your foot,
for the place where you are standing is holy.
And Joshua did so.

Following the mundane activity of eating (5:12), these lines present a sudden turn to a sphere that does not quite belong to this world. In the words of James Kugel, the episode in Joshua 5:13–15 provides a "visionary journey, traveling from ordinary to extraordinary reality." Such stories, as he points out, may have a "latch" or a "trapdoor" that opens up into another reality.[41] Such stories may also be extremely puzzling. First, the Hebrew text places Joshua "in Jericho." Most translations render "near" or "by," but the Hebrew preposition attached to the name of a location ordinarily means "in." Logically, Joshua cannot be *in* Jericho before the city has been taken, but logic is not what prevails in this sequence. Placing the location of Joshua

41. Kugel, *The God of Old*, 70.

in Jericho signals that what is taking place does not belong within ordinary time or space. The encounter itself seems at first blush to be common enough, for Joshua sees a man standing across from him. The phrasing at this point is, however, of some interest. Although "he saw—and look!" may occur in ordinary circumstances, there are a number of occasions in which the phrase appears in the context of the numinous, as when Abraham lifts his eyes and "he saw—and look!—three men" are standing before him, who will eventually turn into the presence of Adonai (Gen 18:2), or when he discerns the ram that will furnish the vicarious burnt offering in the place of Isaac (Gen 22:13). When Moses encountered a bush that appeared invulnerable to fire, "he saw—and look!—the bush was burning with fire and the bush was not consumed" (Exod 3:2).[42] For the careful listener, then, the encounter has the potential to draw us into something extraordinary. "A drawn sword" can indicate a number of things: perhaps that this figure is no ordinary soldier, or that battle is about to commence, or even that there is danger present. A drawn sword is also in the hand of the angel of Adonai during the encounter with Balaam (Num 22:23), as well as in the vision of David (1 Chr. 21:16)—both representations of a threatening presence. Certainly, the figure is imposing enough that it elicits Joshua's question about whose side he is on, an appropriate enough inquiry when someone meets you with a drawn sword. Dialogue, and especially questions, on Joshua's part is not common in the book and is unique in this set of chapters—perhaps another sign of the befogged state of our protagonist on this occasion.

The first word from the warrior, preceding the self-identification, does not seem to fit the question; "no" could just as well be "yes," for neither response would shed light on the issue of what side the figure will take. How are we to understand the peculiar negative?[43] Many translations provide the word "neither," meaning that the com-

42. See also the occasion when Elisha's servant sees horses and chariots of fire around Elisha (2 Kgs 6:17).

43. Some versions, including the Septuagint and the Syriac, solve the issue by reading "he said to him," substituting the personal pronoun, which has the identical sound as the word "no/not," albeit with a different consonant.

mander is not on anyone's side. While this is a possibility, it sounds unlikely in the context of a book in which both leader and people receive repeated assurance of the presence of God in their efforts to conquer the land (Josh 1:5, 9; 3:7, 10; 4:13). The self-identification at least clarifies that this is no ordinary human person but a commander of heavenly forces. The phrase "now I have come" is found in other ancient conquest accounts at the onset of battle from a military leader on the verge of announcing success. Divine aid is also a part of the pattern of describing military campaigns outside of ancient Israel.[44] Once Joshua recognizes the fact that he is in the presence of the holy, he bows in worship and receives the command to remove his sandals, for he is standing on holy ground—wording that clearly draws on the episode of Moses facing the bush that was not consumed by fire (Exod 3:5). Unlike Moses, Joshua does not receive a charge, however. In the opinion of Daniel Hawk, the negative response as to whose side the commander is on together with the absence of a specific commission creates a "profound ambivalence. Israel has . . . expressed its fidelity to [Adonai] through circumcision and Passover but [Adonai] has not responded in kind."[45]

Besides links to the burning bush episode, the reference to an otherworldly warrior also recalls Judges 4 and 5 with their descriptions of God and the heavenly armies fighting to defeat the Canaanites (Judg 4:15; 5:20). In Judges 5, the Song of Deborah, Meroz, together with its inhabitants, is cursed because it "did not come to the help of Adonai, to the help of Adonai among the heroes" (Judg 5:23).[46] Perhaps the negative response from the commander means

44. See, for example, the speech of King Kamose (1555–1550 BCE) of ancient Egypt to a Hyksos ruler: "It is an attack./ Behold, I have come . . ." (K. Lawson Younger Jr., *Ancient Conquest Accounts: A Study in Ancient Near Eastern and Biblical History Writing*, JSOTSup 98 [Sheffield: Sheffield Academic Press, 1990], 73, 133, 180).

45. Hawk, *Joshua*, 85.

46. The place name Meroz is obscure, although it may have been in the neighborhood of the Kishon stream. It may be of some interest that in the expanded Old Latin version of this verse, it is "the angel of Adonai" who does the cursing (Susan Niditch, *Judges*, OTL [Louisville: Westminster John Knox, 2008], 75).

that Joshua is asking the wrong question. The heavenly armies, as they represent God's Holy Presence, do not belong to anyone; the question is not whose side they are on, for that decision has been made and clearly stated. The issue is rather: Will the Israelite armies come to the aid of the heavenly ones? Will they be firm and courageous and not falter in their efforts, as has been enjoined upon them from the start (Josh 1:6, 7, 9, 18)? The orders Joshua will receive to prepare for the conquest of Jericho will not be along the usual lines of armed combat, an aspect that may be hinted at in the enigmatic response from the heavenly warrior in front of Joshua.

A final question concerns the declaration of holiness issued by the commander of the heavenly armies (15). The instruction is almost identical to that of Exodus 3:5, words addressed by God to Moses. That section begins with the appearance of a messenger or angel of Adonai (Exod 3:2), who changes in verse 5 to Adonai calling to Moses from the middle of the burning bush to take his sandals off his feet because the ground he stands on is holy. There, the place is presumably holy because of the nearness of the presence of the Holy God. Does the presence of the commander make the place holy? One variation between the two passages is that in Exodus it is the "ground" (*adamah*) that is declared holy, while in Joshua 5:15 it is the "place" (*maqom*), presumably referring to Jericho. At the site of the burning bush, one assumes it is the presence of the Holy God that renders the ground holy. What makes Jericho a holy place? The presence of the commander does not morph into the presence of God, unlike the presence of the messenger/angel in Exodus 3. I believe we must seek a solution in the direction of the *herem*, which has already been placed on Jericho. Jericho will be "consecrated," that is devoted to destruction (6:17), but in this section the consecration is a fait accompli. The Jericho where Joshua stands in 5:13–15 is the city where he cannot yet be and also the city that already is no more because it is consecrated to God.

All in all, this short section does not provide a satisfactory or rounded description and exchange. It is somewhat like Moses at the burning bush, but then again it is not like Moses, who receives clear instructions in terms of his future role with the oppressed Israelites in Egypt. Medieval Jewish commentators Rashi and Kimhi identify the commander with the messenger/angel of Exodus 33:2, who was promised by God to Moses but rejected by Moses in favor of the very presence of God. The passage has an odd feel, truncated, with pieces missing, perhaps fitting the oddity of its context. It takes place in Jericho, but not really in Jericho, with two men, one of whom is not really human. A straightforward question is asked that receives a far from straightforward response. In its own way it may prepare adequately for all the strange events that are to follow.

Chapter 6 consists of a set of two sequences. The first, 6:1–15, shows a familiar pattern: instructions from Adonai to Joshua are relayed to the appropriate groups and people; action follows. The first verses (6:1–5) open with a statement about Jericho.

> JOSHUA 6:1
>
> Now Jericho was shut and shut up tight
> before the Israelites;
> no one going out, no one coming in.

Emphatic repetition marks the comment: two verbs express a closed-up town; the last line restates this fact by highlighting the resulting absence of movement, in or out. A short sentence, easily overlooked, indicates peculiar aspects of the city as a battle site. The Israelites are present, and the city has withdrawn into itself behind closed walls. Surely, either party should be getting ready for something resembling armed struggle. Those of Jericho should be exiting the city to pursue the Israelites as those of Ai will do in a future episode (Josh 7:4–5; 8:14); or in the absence of any sorties from Jericho, the Israelites would be getting ready for the siege. A curious passivity has enveloped Jericho. Following this statement, Adonai issues instructions to Joshua, first stipulating the encircling of the city with the warriors, but then, contrary to expectations, continuing with the command to go *walking* around the city for seven days, and on the seventh day seven times. All this walking will be accompanied by the sound of seven shofars carried by seven priests. These proceedings will culminate in a "great shout" from all the people, upon which the wall of the city will fall down.

The next units, in 6:6–15, present two speeches by Joshua (6–7 and 10), alternating with descriptions of actions (8–9 and 11–15). Joshua's instructions are first to the priests who will carry the Ark, already mentioned in verse 4, with seven of them in charge of carrying the shofars. Threading our way through the instructions and activities, we get the picture of priests, some of whom carry the Ark and some of whom blow the shofars, with an armed vanguard in front of them and a rear guard behind the Ark. The following section vividly paints the scene.

Joshua 6:8–9

8 When Joshua had spoken to the people,
seven priests carrying seven rams' horns
crossed before Adonai and blew the horns.
And the Ark of the Covenant of Adonai was walking behind them.
9 The vanguard was walking in front of the priests,
who were blowing the horns,
while the rear guard was walking behind the Ark,
the horns blowing all the time.

The Ark, once again the subject of a verb, "walks" behind seven priests carrying and blowing seven shofars; in front of the priests is the vanguard, while the rearguard follows the Ark. Note the emphasis on the blowing of the horns, repeated three times in the span of two verses. The priests are once again "crossing," and they are walking; the Ark is walking, and both vanguard and rear guard are walking with the horns continuously blowing. Since the Ark is the subject of the verb in the fourth line, it is not exactly clear who is carrying it, making it sound as if God personally walks in the midst of the procession. At the end of verse 11, the circumambulation has taken place one time on the first day. Before that concluding note, Joshua emphatically issues a command of silence to the people until he will tell them to "shout," not yet revealing the full duration of the walking tour (10). The silence is in stark contrast with the blasting of the shofars. The entire scene is processional but also almost comical, for what city has been conquered by the ceremonious walking of the enemy around the city walls in deep silence accompanied by the sound of shofars, which even singly are loud as well as eerie? Why don't the beleaguered citizens of Jericho take the opportunity to send out a party to attack this strange procession? Are they mesmerized by the strangeness of it all?

The final unit of the sequence, 6:12–15, narrates action, moving it along until the climactic seventh day. Twice the narrative mentions an early rising, on the part of Joshua on the second day and of the people on the seventh (12, 15). The verb used for the early start indicates haste and urgency (see p. 75) in contrast to the perambulation around the city, which cannot move at great speed with participants in the parade transporting the Ark as well as a group carrying and blowing the shofars the entire time.

The final sequence, 6:16–27, brings the walking to a halt and recounts the initial collapse of the wall before continuing with the capture and destruction of Jericho. A large amount of text is devoted to the rescue of Rahab. Except for the final unit (26–27), Rahab is present each time Joshua speaks, as well as in an action unit (22–23). Thus, the lines alternate between emphasis on the city that is being put under the *herem,* its capture and destruction, and the violation of the *herem* through the liberation of Rahab. As the priests blow the horns during the seventh circuit on the seventh day, Joshua commands the people to shout, and before the shouting can commence, he launches into a speech. Part of the speech is not surprising: As he announces the consecration of the city, meaning the annihilation of all that breathes in it, he issues a warning. Care needs to be taken that the Israelites do not take anything that is consecrated, that is to say under the *herem,* for such a consecration will infect the entire camp (6:18). To this warning he makes two exceptions: The first is Rahab; the second is vessels made of expensive metals. In other words, the consecration is not total. Joshua refers to Rahab as "the whore" and states as the reason for her survival the service she rendered to the "messengers we sent." The spies sent by Joshua alone in secret (2:1) have become "the messengers *we* sent." He refers to Rahab and her action as if it were common knowledge, something that would not be surprising except that, in the text, the spies talk about their adventures in Jericho only to Joshua (2:23–24). The rephrasing in chapter 6 could indicate an effort on Joshua's part to spread the responsibility for violating the *herem*. Two items are for Adonai: the city for destruction and the precious vessels for treasure. These two surround the reference to Rahab, who "will live." Rahab is outside the *herem*, and her survival is in direct violation of it.

Verse 20 picks up the action, congruent with Joshua's instruction. The first sentence summarizes what is repeated in detail in the next lines: "the people shouted and the horns blew" (20). The people shout, the horns sound, and the walls collapse; the troops capture the city, and all in it fall, human and beast, "to the sword" (21). Swiftly, the narrative moves to the rescue of Rahab, to which more lines are devoted than to the specifics of the city's capture.

Joshua 6:22–23

22 To the two men who had spied out the land Joshua said:
Go to the house of the woman, the whore,
and bring out from there the woman
and all who are with her, as you swore to her.
23 So the young spies went and brought out Rahab
and her father and her mother,
her brothers and all who were with her;
all her kin they brought out
and stationed them outside the Israelite camp.

The two spies appear again, receiving instructions from Joshua to go to Rahab's house and bring her and all those found in her house to safety. It is in this episode that we find out the spies were "young men" (23). Joshua refers to Rahab as "the woman, the whore," but in the next breath she appears by name. Everything that is general in verse 22 becomes specific in verse 23 ("the two men who had spied" = "the young spies"; "the woman, the whore" = "Rahab"; "all who are with her" = "her father and her mother, her brothers and all who were with her; all her kin"). The spies "bring them out," a root that is repeated three times. The verb is common enough but is notably used in this stem variation for God "bringing the people out" of Egypt (e.g., Exod 20:2; Deut 26:8). The young men's actions are thus of a liberative and salvific nature. The attention paid to the outsiders is noteworthy because they were, after all, part of the consecrated city, and they escape the wholesale slaughter in violation of Adonai's command. Joshua himself takes the lead in the saving of Rahab's family, referring to the oath the spies took: "as you swore to her" (22).

Finally, after the burning of Jericho is noted, the two exceptions, the treasure for Adonai and the saving of Rahab, once again receive mention (6:24–25). Both exceptions signal the future. The saved treasure links to the next episode, when other treasure that was not part of the exception leads to a disastrous defeat for the Israelites. The presence of Rahab signals future times when Israel will continue to live with many neighbors, because the narrator announces her continued presence: "She stayed in the midst of Israel until this day" (25). For the second and last time, her service to the Israelite men who had come to her house is mentioned. Apparently, loyalty to those of Israel and deeds of faithfulness (*hesed*), even from outsiders, trump perceived commandments to destroy. The editors make no comment and let the incongruities stand, not for the last time in the book. The chapter ends with Joshua uttering a proleptic curse, a unique occurrence in the Bible, and with mention of God's presence with Joshua (in case the incident with the commander of the heavenly armies had left any doubt?) and his fame throughout the land.

Act I in Review

Four scenes form the first act, which establishes Israel's first foothold west of the Jordan. Only one of the scenes concerns itself directly with Jericho and its capture; everything else is preparation. The chain of instruction and follow-through is clear: God speaks, Joshua listens and speaks to the people, action follows. Only in chapter 2 is divine speech lacking; there human protagonists carry the story line forward. The chapters have a stop-and-go tempo, and a great deal of narrative space is spent in preparation. Also, ceremonial matters, sometimes coinciding with the miraculous, punctuate the accounts: crossing the river with its dammed-up waters in the presence of the Ark, building stone memorials, celebrating wondrous deliverance within the covenant bond, marching around city walls, which tumble down at a shout from the people. Noise and marching, again in the presence of the Ark, mark the collapse of Jericho.

After the commissioning of Joshua in chapter 1, the presence of Rahab frames the episodes that eventually lead to the capture of Jericho. She is the one who first mentions the *herem* in the book, and she and hers are the ones who escape the *herem* at the end of the act on account of her earlier act of *hesed.* God promises presence and the gift of the land at the opening of Joshua, and the theme of divine presence runs through Joshua 1–6; it is especially made clear in the appearance of the Ark, both in the crossing of the river and the march around Jericho. Important boundaries are crossed throughout: The spies cross the boundaries of the Jordan and appropriate behavior when they visit Rahab; Rahab herself crosses the boundary of loyalty to her fellow citizens; the people cross the boundary presented by the Jordan, and God crosses this boundary with them; with God's help, the people cross the boundary presented by city walls; finally, the boundary presented by the practice of the *herem* is crossed by the rescue of Rahab and her family.

Once the river crossing has begun, miraculous incidents mark the narrative: waters stand in a heap, a commander of the heavenly armies meets Joshua in Jericho on the eve of its capture, and the walls of Jericho collapse as a result of the people's shout. Ceremony and religious ritual punctuate the forward movement of the story: Once the river is crossed, stone memorials mark the event; at a crucial moment, a newly dedicated people celebrates Pesach and begins to eat of the land's produce, which spells the cessation of the provision of the miraculous food of the wilderness. Wilderness existence has ceased, and settled existence has been inaugurated.

Jericho did not exist in the way it is described in Joshua 2 and 6 in the latter part of the thirteenth century BCE, the Late Bronze Age. While there had been a city before and one existed again long afterward, there is no evidence for a walled city between the fourth quarter of the fifteenth and the first of the thirteenth century BCE. Jericho had once been a powerfully fortified town but had fallen in 1550 BCE; it was without doubt a town of the size and fame that caused it to be widely known well past its actual existence. The name and the place were symbols for what was most powerful and well-defended in the land Israel was about to invade, and therefore it is the symbol of the first place they conquer. Everything in the last scene (5:13–6:27) has a dreamlike quality, beginning with the meeting of Joshua and the heavenly commander and continuing into chapter 6 with its ceremonial marches and the crumbling of walls upon a shout of the invading Israelites. Even the rescue of Rahab has odd features. If the walls fell down, her house, which was in the wall according to 2:15, must have come down with it, yet her rescue is reported in detail. No mention is made of the red cord which was prominent in chapter 2 (2:18, 21). The story partakes of the mythical qualities that make up the memories of a defeated people who celebrate their past, with its mixture of the miraculous and the quotidian, the ideal and the real, the total loyalty to divine instructions and the bold violation of them on behalf of those who found no place for themselves except "in the wall" and precisely from that place were able to accomplish acts of keeping faith. Like the walls of Jericho, the picture of complete loyalty and follow-through, of leading a fenced-off existence and keeping outsiders at bay, is already disintegrating.

Act II: Taking and Being Taken (Joshua 7–9)

The shadow of possible disobedience to the law and the problematic presence of unconquered people left in the land . . . has started to loom over the book of Joshua.[47]

Three chapters make up the second act, central to which is the capture of Ai in chapter 8, an affair that does not take place without a

47. Richard D. Nelson, *Joshua: A Commentary* (Louisville: Westminster John Knox, 1997), 132.

major delay (ch. 7) caused by one of the Israelites having procured for himself a part of the spoil intended as treasure for God, an act that initially causes an Israelite defeat and loss of courage. Once the contamination of the camp caused by the theft has been contained and wiped out, the capture of Ai takes place with a detailed account of strategy and military maneuver (ch. 8). The final scene, chapter 9, presents a counterpoint to hostile takeovers with the account of Canaanite inhabitants using a ruse to trick Joshua and the Israelite leaders into making a treaty with them. Each episode centers on *taking*, the first through the illicit *taking* of goods that prevents the *taking* of another town, the second through the successful *taking* of said town, the third on clever inhabitants *taking* along just the right stuff and employing the right words to manipulate the Israelites, who are thus "taken" by the Gibeonites and lose the opportunity for *taking* another part of the region. Chapters 7 and 9 form a type of frame around the defeat of Ai, both episodes portraying the inability to conquer: the first by enemy tactics and Israelite loss of courage in the face of possible defeat, the second by enemy wiles and Israelite incapacity to break faith with those they perceived as no threat.

Act II, Scene 1: The Taking of Ai (Joshua 7:1–8:29)

A different kind of story appears in connection with Ai.[48]

So far, obstacles facing the invading Israelites have been overcome with the help of God, but the next stage of conquest does not proceed smoothly. Ai, the next city on the list, is not as easily or miraculously captured as Jericho; there is "capture" of another nature. Goods have been appropriated, and the culprit, a member of the community, is caught, with resulting consequences. The first attempt to conquer the second city meets with resounding failure, and it is only after the restoration of the God-community relationship that the action against Ai succeeds. Joshua 7:1–8:29 show a departure from patterns of the first act, in which divine speech met with

48. Hawk, *Joshua*, 107.

appropriate action on the part of Joshua and the people with few exceptions; the road to the capture of Ai is a bumpy one. Broken pattern signals broken relationship. Rather than the faithful action of leader and people, we come across theft, lies, secrecy, anger, and the horrendous annihilation of an Israelite family before the sequences once again take on the familiar character of faithful response to divine initiative.

In addition, the successful second campaign against Ai is described in unusual detail. In stark contrast to the seizure of Jericho with its ceremonial and extraordinary nature, Joshua 8:1–29 specifies military maneuvers and deployment of troops not present in the earlier chapters. Once again, Adonai joins forces with the Israelites and is actively present to support Joshua in his military leadership.

Scene 1, Part 1: Breaking Faith (Joshua 7)

The ritually unclean Rahab is prudently kept outside the war camp . . . but it is Achan the pedigreed Judahite who contaminates the camp with herem.[49]

A note precedes a harrowing narrative. The effect of the first verse is that the reader has information not shared by the characters in the story; the characters' lack of this knowledge causes them to commit military blunders with disastrous consequences.

JOSHUA 7:1

And they committed infidelity, the Israelites,
infidelity with respect to the *herem*;
and Achan, descendant of Carmi,
descendant of Zafdi, descendant of Zerach,
of the tribe of Judah, took from the *herem*.
So the wrath of Adonai burned against the Israelites.

49. Richard D. Nelson, *Joshua: A Commentary* (Louisville: Westminster John Knox, 1997), 103.

The first line announces abruptly that events have taken a wrong turn. The verb, sometimes translated "transgressed" or "trespassed" is specifically related to committing an act of infidelity (cf. Lev 5:15–26 [5:15–6:7]; Num 5:6; 31:16; Deut 32:51). It is notably used in connection with the episode in Ezra that concerns intermarriage with indigenous peoples, proscribed in Deuteronomic regulation (Ezra 9:2–4; 10:6). For good measure, the sentence repeats the root in its nominal form: "They committed infidelity . . . infidelity with respect to the *herem*."[50] Following on the heels of the statement about Joshua, who is assured of divine support, whose fame is throughout the land at the end of chapter 6 (6:27), the announcement comes as a shock. The entire people is declared guilty of infidelity, and the anger of Adonai is against the community.

References to "the Israelites" frame the notation in 7:1, which moves from the larger group to the individual. One Israelite, Achan, "took"—by itself an innocuous verb, the impact of which the narrator delays by putting its object at the end of the phrase. It comes as no surprise, however, that the "taking" concerned the *herem*—that is to say, that which was consecrated to Adonai—something expressly prohibited by Joshua before the capture of Jericho when he warned the people not to "take from *herem*" lest the people and the camp "become *herem*" (i.e., consecrated) and thus become a "ruin" (Josh 6:18).

Achan receives a detailed line of descendancy, and a distinguished one at that. The names deserve some attention, because although the ancestor of Achan is identified as Judah, the father of Zerach (Gen 38:30; 46:12), another ancestor is Carmi, who is mentioned as a son of Reuben (Gen 46:9). The names of Achan's ancestors, whether going back to Judah or Reuben, have positive connotations of vineyard/fruitfulness, endowment or gift, and sunrise. Yet the Zerach ancestry is also one of inappropriate sexual conduct on the part of Judah, and Zerach, identified as the older of his mother Tamar's twins, pulls back at the moment of exiting the womb to let

50. Cf. Martin Buber and Franz Rosenzweig, *Bücher der Geschichte: Verdeutscht von Martin Buber gemeinsam mit Franz Rosenzweig* (Cologne: Jakob Hegner, 1965), 22: "Die Sohne Israels veruntreuten, Untreue am Bann."

his brother Peres come first so that Peres is the one taking pride of place in ancestor lists (Gen 38:28–29; 46:12; Ruth 4:12). Achan is a name with no known derivation, and it occurs only here in the Bible. Some view his name as a play on the word Achor (meaning "disaster" or "trouble"), the name of the valley where Achan will lie under a pile of stones (7:26).[51] One may also hear in his name the sound of woe present in the first syllable, which reminds one of the Hebrew word *ekhah*, an exclamation of sorrow (see Lam 1:1). Achan, the man with the name that evokes sorrow, son of the vineyard/gift/sunrise, descended from either Reuben or Judah, has not acted according to his status and illustrious ancestry but has taken from that which was expressly reserved for God, and surely nothing good will come of it. His act has infected the entire community and spread like a contagion.

A short episode describes the disastrous attempt to take Ai (7:2–5), a city to the west of Jericho in the central hill country, identified as being near to Bethel. Ai is, in Joshua, always cited with the definite article in Hebrew, meaning "the ruin." Its geographical placement in verse 2 is near Beth-Aven (i.e., "house of evil") east of Bethel (i.e. "house of God"), names that signal the predicament of the Israelites. Unknowingly infected by the evil that Achan has spread around, neither Joshua nor the troops act on a divine directive, a feature present in every episode that precedes chapter 7. The spies who go out to reconnoiter do not view "the ruin" as much of a threat and advise to send only a part of the troops to a place without walls and few inhabitants (3). Verse 4 recounts that "about three thousand" warriors go up against Ai, a phrase that is immediately followed by the note that "they fled from the men of Ai." This note does not cite a reason for the rout. The damage done by the theft of the consecrated goods may have seeped into the mentality of the

51. Nelson, *Joshua*, 99. Hawk (*Joshua*, 120) suggests that Achan is an anagram of the root related to the name of the land, Canaan, and argues that Achan "represents the presence of *kena'im* within Israel," a "hidden presence" which is "personified by this now Canaanized Israelite." In Chronicles, Achan is named Akhar, a name that literally translated means "trouble." See 1 Chr 2:7: "Trouble, troubler of Israel who committed infidelity with respect to the *herem*."

army so that their courage failed when faced with the enemy. Certainly, the final observation of the sequence underlines the disheartened state of the troops whose "heart melted and turned to water" (5). This is a feature that heretofore marked the Canaanites (Josh 2:11; 5:1) but is now clinging to the Israelites in an ironic reaction to the falling of "about thirty-six" victims to the pursuit of Ai, surely not a significant enough number to react in this dramatic way, as if they had suffered a great defeat. Yet the men of "the ruin" pursue the Israelites from the gate to *Shevarim*, which is to say "the collapse." Lack of courage and strength—mental predispositions strongly recommended in the initial commissioning of Joshua (Josh 1:6, 7, 9, 18) stains the camp of the Israelites.

The next sequence (7:6–15) stands out in this scene, as well as in the entire book, because of the nature of the exchange between God and Joshua. Here we find not a divine directive faithfully executed by Joshua but a Joshua who is downcast and reproachful and a Deity who is angry and impatient with his adjutant. Joshua and the leadership of the community lie in front of the Ark with signs and posture of mourning until Joshua utters his complaint. The tone and language used by Joshua remind one strongly of the rebellious episode at Kadesh in the wake of the first reconnaissance of the land recounted in Numbers 14:1–25, though here Joshua speaks the words that were there ascribed to the people. Like the community in the wilderness, Joshua questions God's actions in bringing the people into the land, apparently in order to accomplish their destruction; and like the people, he then wishes for a return to an earlier, safer existence "on the other side of the Jordan" (7). Like Moses, he calls God's reputation into question, but unlike Moses, his plea centers on the danger that now faces the Israelites rather than on God's forgiving nature (cf. Num 14:17–18).

A long response in two parts of equal length follows Joshua's lament. The first part (10–12) concentrates on the situation created by the breaking of the *herem* using the third person plural. The second part instructs the remedy for the removal of the contagion and uses the second person plural. Twice, Adonai admonishes Joshua to "arise" (10, 13) to pay attention to what has happened and what he should do about it.

Joshua 7:10–12

10 And Adonai said to Joshua:
Arise, you! Why are you falling down on your face?
11 Israel has sinned,
and also they crossed my covenant that I commanded them.
Also, they took from the *herem*,
and also they stole;
also they concealed,
and also they put it with their own stuff.
12 So the Israelites will not be able to arise before their enemies;
they will turn their back on their enemies,
for they have become *herem*.
I will no longer be with you if you do not exterminate
the *herem* from your midst.

A sharp tone and urgent admonishment infuse the entire directive, beginning with the demand to get up, using the command form and personal pronoun: literally, "Arise to yourself!" Lying down and lamenting will not accomplish the needed change. The repetitive clauses in verse 11 convey in a striking manner the severity of the offense, beginning with the general identification of it as a breach of the covenant, a breach indicated with the verb "to cross," a word of such significance in these initial stages of the entrance into and conquest of the land (cf. Deut 17:2). This general statement is followed by four verbs specifying what took place, each time preceded by "also": "Also *they took*. . . , and also *they stole*; also *they concealed*, and also *they put it with their own stuff*." Four charges: first, there is the *taking*, a serious enough offense in itself; second, the taking constituted *theft*; third, the entire business was conducted in *secret*; and finally, it was kept strictly for *personal* use. Taking, stealing, lying, and hoarding—the accusations fall down thick and fast. It is because of these actions, notably ascribed to all the people rather than to an individual, that defeat awaits them and God threatens to withdraw support.

Two commands follow the accusation: First, there is a repetition of the admonition to "arise"; second, there is a charge to engage in sanctification, as they once did in anticipation of crossing of the river (Josh 3:5). The threat that Israel will not be able to maintain itself in the face of its enemies is picked up again in verse 13: "the Israelites will not be able to arise before their enemies" (12) // "you [sg.] will not be able to arise before your enemies" (13); "they have become *herem*" (12) // "there is *herem* in your midst, Israel" (13); "I will no longer be with you [pl.] if you do not exterminate the *herem* from your midst" (12) // "until you [pl.] have cleared away the *herem* from your midst" (13). The process of finding the culprit will take place implicitly by the casting of lots, with the capture, or selection, of the guilty one gradually moving from the larger to the smaller group (14–15). The sentence of burning, unusually severe, is pronounced on the guilty one, and the transgression is once again identified, this time as an act of willful sin—wanton folly/sacrilege (*navelah*). Only burning will accomplish the necessary decontamination.

In the next sequence (7:16–26), all is accomplished almost exactly as prescribed. Once again, Joshua arises early, providing a sense of urgency (see pp. 75, 94 above), and then proceeds with the selection. The first unit (16–18) repeats the verb "to capture/select" four times, each time following the "approach"—first of the tribe, then of the clan, then of the house until Achan is "captured." After the process of selection, there follows an exchange between Joshua and Achan in which the latter confesses his misdeed in detail and reveals the place where the goods lie hidden (19–21). Joshua issues an invitation with four directives: two of them setting Achan on the path to restoring relations with God ("glorify now Adonai, the God of Israel, and give him thanks") and the next two urging him to reveal the truth ("tell me now what you did; do not hide it from me"). The encouragement opens with the address, "my son," lending the request a fatherly tone, an impression reinforced by the addition of a particle (*na*) to the imperatives, which adds an air of urgency but also a note of pleading, softening the straightforward imperative. Notably, the particle is absent in Adonai's speech to Joshua in the preceding sequence (10–15). It is, of course, of vital importance for Joshua to learn where the stolen items are hidden since they need to be destroyed together with Achan, his family, and his other possessions. The description of the exchange makes Joshua sound borderline deceptive, with an almost kind invitation that seems to imply, "Nothing bad will happen to you." Joshua will speak plainly to Achan only when his demise appears imminent (7:25). Perhaps Achan, too, heard merely kindness, for his confession sounds trusting, providing all the details both of what he took and where he put it. His opening word is "truly," signaling that he will make an honest admission of guilt (20). He specifies the items and declares that he "desired" or "coveted" them, so he took them. Nothing good ever comes in the Bible of "taking" what one "covets," the very inclination to which is proscribed in the Ten Words (Exod 20:17).

So they bring him and "all that was his" to the "Valley of Achor," where Joshua declares to Achan that he has "brought disaster," so Adonai will "bring disaster" on him" (25). The name of the valley echoes in the verbs of disaster (*akhar*). The end of the story is that Achan with "all that was his" is stoned in the valley of "disaster" (24–25), and subsequently everyone and everything is burned. Stoning is a mitigation, although it may not sound like much of one, of the dreadful fate of burning, which now takes place after death. This amounts to a modification on Joshua's part of the sentence pronounced by Adonai.[52]

A horrifying tale but also an instructive one. The final units of the previous chapter begged the question of the *herem.* If everyone and everything in Jericho faced destruction, there are nonetheless specific exceptions of persons and goods (6:17–19). The latter belong to Adonai while the former, in the person of Rahab and her family, belong to the Israelites because of her act of keeping faith (2:12; 6:17). Achan is clearly Rahab's negative counterpart. Like Rahab, he kept something hidden, but he hid out of covetousness, and what he hid was designated for God.[53] Rahab was rescued together with

52. Stoning as a punishment of individuals for violation of divine mandates is commanded in relatively few cases in the Torah (Lev 20:2, 27; 24:14, 16; Num 15:35; Deut 21:21), is mentioned as an actual event in two cases in the Torah (Lev 24:23; Num 15:36), and occurs only one other time in the historical books (1 Kgs 12:18 = 2 Chr 10:18). Burning as punishment of the individual is invoked once, to be subsequently retracted, in the Torah (Gen 38:24–26) and demanded in only two legislative cases (Lev 20:14; 21:9).

53. The verb used in Joshua 7:21 for hiding is identical to the action of

"all that was hers" (6:25); Achan is destroyed with "all that was his" (7:24). There is a lesson in the tale, horrifying as it may be. A deed of faithfulness from an "outsider" weighs heavy in the scale, and an act of *hesed* brings about exceptions to the *herem*, the condition that equals total destruction in warfare. Neither the insider status of Achan nor his tribal lineage provides him with an advantage. One can hardly overstate the radical nature of the message embedded in the comparative fates of Rahab and Achan. Not only was the former a Canaanite, she was also a whore, a position that put her, if not in a forbidden zone, certainly at the very low end of the scale in the ancient society. Achan, the insider, is held up to the high standard of conduct expected of those who lived life in covenant with Adonai—a covenant that laid on the community a special charge. His misstep is therefore identified as a "breach of the covenant" (7:11). Rahab is one of those in the Bible who as an outsider "subverts" an "assumed world of meaning" and "transforms . . . that world."[54] She is not the only one who plays this role in the Bible or in the Historical Books, but her story in this context, contrasted with that of Achan, paints a striking picture for the community of postexilic Israel, a context we identify often with a mentality intent on protecting the inside group from the outsider. The Rahab episode shares the theme of the text in Isaiah, which portrays welcome to outsiders (Isa 56:3), rather than the anxiety concerning "foreign" women of Ezra 9–10.[55] Indeed, Rahab exemplifies the "foreign born" with Israel lasting "to this day" (6:25). Achan's monument is of a pile of stones in the valley of "disaster," a testimony to the disaster that overcame the descendant of Judah lasting "to this day" (7:26).

Rahab in 2:6. In the historical books it occurs only once more (2 Kings 7:8), also in regard to the hiding of spoil.

54. Thomas Ogletree, *Hospitality to the Stranger: Dimensions of Moral Understanding* (Philadelphia: Fortress, 1985), 3.

55. Isaiah 56:3:

Let not the foreign born say,
she who has joined herself to the Holy God:
Separate, yes, separate God will keep me from his people!

I understand the verbal form of "join" to be a feminine participle in the *Nif'al* stem variation.

Scene 1, Part 2: Restoring Faith (Joshua 8:1–29)

The permission now to take booty is somewhat ironic after Achan's punishment for doing that very thing.[56]

Ai, "the ruin," still awaits the fate that will make it live up to its name. The city, for the existence of which there is no evidence in the period in which we place the invasion of Canaan by the Israelites, lies in the direction the invaders are taking in their first attempts to settle the central highlands and may serve as a symbol for the further steps to conquer and inhabit the land. The familiar pattern of divine instruction followed by Joshua's action is once again restored. The first sequence (8:1–9) reestablishes the presence of Adonai with the troops in a speech-unit (1–2) reassuring Joshua, as before the capture of Jericho, of God having given the city into his hand. Once more Joshua is told to "arise," and all will be done as it was to Jericho and its king—that is to say, all will be devoted to destruction, except that this time the plunder and the cattle may be kept as booty. A concluding instruction adds the detail to create an ambush behind the city (2). An exception is once again made to the *herem*, this time by divine initiative, more extensive in terms of the items that may be preserved than at Jericho and also to be kept for use by the people rather than reserved for divine treasure. The allowance raises the question whether it is an accommodation to the previous episode with the goal of forestalling further trespass in regard to the *herem*.

As in previous episodes, Joshua issues instruction in the next unit (3–9), preceded and concluded by a descriptive note recording anticipated movement and action, with a specific number of fighters who are to lie in the ambush (3, 9). Joshua's instructions paint a clear picture: A large ambush will lie in wait while he and the rest of the troops draw those of Ai out of the city, which will cause a pursuit as happened before (7:4–5). As they draw them away, the ones in the ambush will capture the undefended city and set it on fire. Joshua emphatically weaves the work of God into his instructions. God will give the city into their power (7) and his instructions are really

56. McConville and Williams, *Joshua*, 42.

God's instruction: "According to the word of Adonai, your God, you will do" (8).

The sequence that follows (8:10–17) depicts the most detailed account of a battle in the book, albeit with some confusion in those details. The strategy Joshua follows is, however, quite clear. He and his men are visibly present to those of Ai, who indeed leave the city in hot pursuit while the Israelites with Joshua go on the run.

The next half of the sequence switches perspective to Ai so that we view the chase after the Israelites from its point of view (14–17). The emptying of the city underscores the effectiveness of the ruse, with repeated reference to the haste with which "the king . . . the men of the city . . . and all his people . . . left" in ignorance of the ambush (14). "All the troops in the city assembled. . . . They pursued and were drawn away from the city" (16). The last lines repeat the evidence that the city is left undefended.

Joshua 8:16b–17

16b They pursued Joshua
and were drawn away from the city.
17 No man was left in Ai and Bethel who did not go after Israel.
They left the city open behind them
and pursued Israel.[57]

The inclusion of Bethel is peculiar and seems out of place, especially as those from Bethel would have run across the Israelites in ambush. This is not the first time that Bethel, a city that actually existed in the Late Bronze Age, is mentioned in connection with Ai, indicating a possible conflation of traditions that include Bethel in the conquest narratives, although it receives no further reference in chapter 8. Its presence here points again to the capture of Ai as symbolic of "a more extensive campaign."[58]

The final sequence (8:18–29) switches perspective back to Joshua and the Israelites, opening with a further instruction from

57. Following the sentence structure in Hawk, *Joshua*, 128.

58. McConville and Williams, *Joshua*, 44.

Adonai to Joshua to stretch out his spear toward Ai (cf. Exod 14:16) as a sign for the ambush to go into action. Five verbs accomplish the desired burning of the city: "they arose in hurry," "they ran," "they entered the city," "they captured it," and "they hurried and set fire to the city" (19). Reversing perspective once more, we view the city with the pursuers, who at the sight of it ablaze finally understand what is going on and lose all courage (lit. "they had no hands"), and they are set upon from behind and before (20–23). The unit concludes with the king being brought to Joshua. Details of the total decimation of Ai and all in it conclude the sequence (24–29), with the burned city turned into a "mound of lasting devastation as it still is today" (28), and the impaled king buried under a heap of stones, "where it still is today" (29), repeating phrases from the tale of unfortunate Achan. Perhaps the most disturbing part of the blood-soaked adventure is the moment when the victorious Israelites turn on the already decimated city to complete their task.

JOSHUA 8:24–26

24 When Israel was done slaying all the inhabitants of Ai
in the open wilderness where they had pursued them—
they all of them to the last fell by the edge of the sword—
all Israel returned to Ai and put it to the sword.
25 And all who fell that day were,
from man to woman, twelve thousand,
all the people of Ai.
26 And Joshua did not stop stretching out his hand with the javelin
until all the inhabitants of Ai were put under the herem.

As perturbing as the concentrated attention to the slaughter at Ai is to us, the message of Joshua 7 and 8 is clear. According to Daniel Hawk, "Achan represents the Canaanite presence within the community, while the king and people of Ai represent the Canaanite presence outside. . . . That which is Canaanite must be drawn from its hidden, secure place, and when exposed it must be completely eliminated."[59]

59. Hawk, *Joshua*, 131.

Act II, Scene 2: Writing and Reading at Ebal (Joshua 8:30–35)

To report the building of an altar is to make a land claim in another way.[60]

One scene, in one unit, at a location in the region of Shechem geographically quite removed from Gilgal, describes religious ceremony and has, in the words of Richard Nelson, "only a tenuous and approximate chronological connection" with its context.[61] The editors placed the tradition about a significant ceremony at Ebal and Gerizim here most likely to underscore the significance of the first successes in the process of conquering and settling the land and to round off episodes in which threats to the relationship between God and the community surfaced. At the altar at Ebal, the community is once again united both with each other and with God through the divine guidance via the teachings of Moses. Joshua's name is present only at the opening and conclusion of the scene, which otherwise contains five references to Moses. Joshua *builds* an altar of stones "which no iron has touched" (Exod 20:25) and *writes* "a copy of the Teaching of Moses, which he *reads* "before the entire assembly of Israel" (8:30, 32, 34, 35). Clear links to texts in Exodus and Deuteronomy are present. Moses *wrote* the words of Adonai, *built* an altar, and *read* them in the hearing of the people (Exod 24:4, 7). In the Exodus passage, as in Joshua, sacrifices are made by representatives and the people are present (8:31, 33). In addition, there are obvious connections between the Joshua text and Deuteronomy (Deut 11:29; 27:4–8, 12–13), albeit with some noteworthy differences.

The scene is constructed in such a way that the actions of building, making sacrifice, writing, and reading (30–32, 34–35) frame the list of those who are present in verse 33. It adds in careful detail how they are positioned around the Ark and facing the mountains.

60. Nelson, *Joshua*, 119.

61. Nelson, *Joshua*, 116. For a review of the difficulties regarding the nature and placement of Joshua 8:30–35, see Hawk, *Joshua*, 140.

JOSHUA 8:33

All Israel and its elders, officials, and its judges were standing
on either side of the Ark, in front of the priests, the Levites,
who were carrying the Ark of the Covenant of Adonai,
stranger as well as native;
half opposite Mount Gerizim, half opposite Mount Ebal,
as Moses, the servant of Adonai,
had commanded to bless the people of Israel at first.

The list follows the mention of "all Israel," adding specifics about the groups included, the ones with a leadership role in regard to sacred tasks and items cited last. Following the mention of priests and Levites, the record adds the "stranger" as well as the "native." The word for "native" appears in the Torah fourteen times but outside it only here, apart from one occurrence each in the Psalms (Ps 37:35) and in Ezekiel (47:22). In the Torah, we find it always in legislation that pertains also to the "stranger." It is the presence of the stranger (*ger*) that is especially striking in this episode. The *ger* is a protected category in the Torah, with more than forty regulations relevant to this class of people. In the ancient world, before the existence of the modern nation state, a *ger* was anyone from the outside, anyone who did not belong—most of the time someone not from Israelite tribal lineage. Its opposite here is the *ezrah,* the native, one from inside the community. The emphatic naming of the category, repeated in the last verse (8:35), may have crept into the text under the effect of the Deuteronomic vocabulary of the passage. Of course, we know that Rahab and those with her belong to this group, but perhaps there were others. Verse 35 also includes the women and the children together with the *ger,* so that the circle of those whose relationship to the God of Israel is affirmed through recital of the Teaching is widely rather than tightly drawn.

Although all present are once again confirmed in the covenant bond, of which the Ark is the visible representation, the actions here do not amount to a covenant making or renewal. If we compare the text with its model in Exodus 24:3–8, it becomes clear that important aspects of that ritual are absent, such as the sharing of the blood between altar and assembly as well as the affirmative response of those present. In addition, the terminology that accompanies the concluding of a covenant is missing.[62] The ceremony affirms a restored relationship of people and their God, and as such it serves to set up the expectation of confident progress of Israel's advance into the land of the promise. Progress will indeed take place, although not quite in the way one might anticipate.

Act II, Scene 3: Being Taken (Joshua 9)

The Gibeonites . . . like Rahab seem to have studied Deuteronomy.[63]

Chapter 9 takes proceedings in an unexpected direction in an animated narrative filled with lively exchanges among human characters. There is a noted absence of divine counsel (9:14), with no explicit negative comment from the narrators added. The first sequence (9:1–15) paints the scene in vivid colors and concludes with the success of Canaanite inhabitants to come to a peaceful understanding with the invaders, in contrast to others who gear up for battle. Two very different mindsets lead to opposite actions.

JOSHUA 9:1–5

1 When the kings across the Jordan heard,
in the hill country, in the Shephelah,
and along the coast of the Great Sea toward Lebanon
—Hittites, Amorites, Canaanites, Perizites, Hivites, and Jebusites—
2 they gathered together to do battle with Joshua and Israel
with one accord.

62. Contra Nelson (*Joshua*, 119) and others and in agreement with Lebhar Hall (*Conquering Character*, 148). I also agree with the latter that Joshua is not taking on royal stature here (149).

63. Frymer-Kensky, *Reading the Women of the Bible*, 42.

3 When the inhabitants of Gibeon heard
what Joshua had done to Jericho and Ai,
4 they, for their part, acted with cunning:
They made provisions ready,
they took worn-out sacks for their donkeys,
and worn-out wine skins, cracked and patched.
5 Worn-out patched sandals on their feet,
threadbare clothes on their bodies,
with their food provisions dry and crumbly.

Two groups "have heard" something. In the first case, what they have heard remains general, but one assumes that it relates to the capture of Ai or that it is simply that the Israelites are upon them. Unlike the earlier reference to Amorite and Canaanite kings whose courage fails them when they hear of the miraculous crossing of the Jordan (5:1), these kings are described with specificity in terms of location and ethnicity; and in contrast to the earlier crowd, they gear up for battle. They are chieftains of different groups, all named in verse 1, and they "gathered together . . . in one accord" (lit. "with one voice"). Unity lends them courage and determination. Once again, we look at this collective from the east, "across" the Jordan (cf. 5:1). In verse 3, we are back in Canaan and review the situation from the perspective of the Gibeonites. They too "have heard," specifically about "what Joshua had done to Jericho and Ai," and they too act upon their information, but differently than the kings of the south. The reader knows that their actions involve something clever and thus anticipates a trick. The word used here for "cunning" does not have negative connotations and can mean careful deliberation.[64] There is no mention of a king or any leadership; the story refers simply to the "inhabitants of Gibeon," unlike the references to the groups mentioned at the chapter opening. Clearly, also, they are not gearing up for battle to go by the accoutrements cited in their preparations. Old clothes, old packaging,

64. It is so used in Exod 21:14, albeit with negative consequences. It occurs in a positive sense in Prov 1:4 and is an altogether positive quality ascribed to Wisdom in Prov 8:5, 12.

and deteriorated provisions—rather than armor and weaponry—are what they take along.

In the next sentence they have reached the Israelite camp. It was not a long distance, and they open negotiations right off the bat, perhaps counting on stunning the Israelites into refraining from hostilities. They certainly do not have a threatening mien and may have given the impression of exhausted haste. They do not reveal who they are; in fact they never clearly state their identity and give no one time to ask at first. No doubt dirty and perhaps panting with exhaustion, they immediately ask for a treaty, a "covenant." Of course, as they would have counted on, a conversation ensues. They address both Joshua and the Israelites, but only the Israelites reply to their demand. It is worth noting that Israelites and Gibeonites are each presented as one person. Verse 7 literally reads: "The man of Israel said to the Hivite:/ Perhaps you live close by?/ How could I make a treaty with you?"[65] Those from Gibeon reply in turn to Joshua, declaring that they are his "servants," the usual polite phrase from inferior to superior. In his turn, Joshua answers with the habitual polite inquiry to persons unknown about their identity and place of origin.[66]

With remarkable dexterity, the Gibeonites deflect attention from their identity and the place they hail from, which they must of course do at all cost, and repeat only their first vague declaration that they have come from "a far country," this time making it "a *very* far country" ("from a very far country they have come, your servants," 9:9). They continue with references to the Name of Adonai and the great deeds about which they have "heard." The actions to which they refer have nothing to do with the capture of Jericho and Ai, which as we know had set them in motion, but rather, much like Rahab, they recite the conquest of the Amorite kings "across the

65. The second person in Hebrew has four different forms and occurs here in the 2nd per. m. sg.

66. Such questions, as Ferdinand Deist (*The Material Culture of the Bible: An Introduction* [Sheffield: Sheffield Academic, 2000], 241) points out, belong to the usual conversational questions that are put to "newcomers on a scene, aimed at ascertaining their identity, social status, affiliations, domicile, occupation, aims and intentions."

Jordan" (cf. 2:10) and the orders they received from every one back home to enter into negotiations (9:11). For good measure, they show the rotten foodstuff they have with them and their clothes worn out from the long trek (12–13). A narrative comment concludes everything to the satisfaction of Gibeon.

JOSHUA 9:14–15

14 The men took their provisions
and did not ask Adonai.
15 Joshua made peace with them,
and made a covenant to let them live.
And the community leaders swore an oath to them.

A terse and revealing comment, the second line in Hebrew literally states that they did not "ask the mouth of Adonai," an expression that occurs in only two other places in the Hebrew Bible (Gen 24:57; Isa 30:1–2).[67] The "taking" of the provisions is obviously for the purpose of examining the truth of the claim that the foodstuff is in as bad a shape as the Gibeonites claim. It is a consultation of sorts, while they refrain from consulting with the source that could have provided them with the real truth: Adonai. The comment implies a criticism of the way the Israelites go about this business with Gibeon, albeit a mild one, and they are not taken to task for their omission in any part of the story, leaving it up to the reader to decide if the result of the affair was positive or negative. In the next breath, Joshua has stepped up to the plate and makes the desired treaty with them, while the "community leaders" pledge their oath. Such an action is by Deuteronomic regulation allowed in the case of places far removed from Canaan (Deut 20:15). The phrasing in verse 15 is once again reminiscent of the episodes involving Rahab, who pled for her life with the spies (2:13) and whom "Joshua let live" (6:22).

67. For an insightful discussion, see Lebhar Hall, *Conquering Character*, 155. The Genesis text concerns the family of Rebekah consulting her wishes; the Isaiah text concerns alliances Israel makes with Egypt without consulting Adonai.

The pledging of the oath takes place also in the Rahab context (2:12, 17, 20). Here then is another group of outsiders (a large one at that!) who will be allowed to coexist peacefully.

The tale is not yet done and takes some more turns before it is finished (16–27). Of course, it does not take long for the Israelites to find out the truth that those from Gibeon "were very near and lived among them" (16), because on their way west they happen upon four of their cities. Their oath prevents them from hostile encounters, which causes dissent in the ranks. In a unit from which Joshua is notably absent (19–21), the leaders solve the issue by assigning low-status jobs to the community they have taken into covenant. Woodcutters and water bearers they shall be.[68]

Somewhat belatedly, Joshua enters into the negotiations, summoning the Gibeonites and asking them an accusatory question in a tone that renders the innocence of the questioner ambiguous.[69] Joshua has, after all, colluded in being taken in by the Gibeonites by not consulting God and by not making further inquiries about their place of origin. He ends by pronouncing them cursed to perpetual servitude (9:23). At the same time, he redefines their task as confined to the "altar of the house of my God." Lebhar Hall understands this assignment as an attempt by Joshua "to apply the *herem* prescription in the only way available to him at this point," since the *herem* means consecration as well as destruction.[70] It is indeed possible that Joshua is forced to contain the damage somewhat in this way. In any case, I agree with Hall that the action is strategic rather than naïve.

A final unit concludes with the Gibeonites, who certainly have the gift of gab, revealing why they acted deceptively. In their reply, they refer to Moses as the "servant" of God who received the command to destroy "all the land's inhabitants." Because of what "was

68. Apparently a position with low status. They are mentioned as those who appear before God to be taken into covenant in Deuteronomy 29:10[11] in a list ending as follows: "women, children, and your stranger who is in your midst,/ from your woodcutter to your water bearer."

69. Cf. 1 Sam 19:17; 28:12; Lebhar Hall, *Conquering Character*, 155.

70. Lebhar Hall, *Conquering Character*, 162.

told" to them, they feared for their lives and "acted like this"—a phrase reminiscent of Achan's confession. They have acted unlike Achan, however: not out of greed but out of knowledge of what God is able to accomplish through God's servant and out of justified fear. Fear in the face of Adonai is never a bad thing in the Bible. With their last words, they put themselves into Joshua's power (9:25). Verse 26 makes Joshua the rescuer of Gibeon: "He delivered them from the hand of the Israelites/ and they did not slay them," a comment that implies the community may not have been entirely satisfied with the solution of the leaders. The delivering role is also assigned to the spies in the Rahab story (2:13) and, as it is in the Torah, to the God of Israel in the final chapter of the book (24:10). Being in covenant and acting as a deliverer will yet have a part to play in the next episode.

The word for "servant" gets great play in the narrative. It is first employed as a term of self-deprecating politeness (almost to excess) by Gibeon (3× in vv. 9–11), but Joshua makes the identity a reality by assigning them a task of servitude, to which they reply by referring to Moses as God's "servant," both in accordance with Israelite terminology and likely as a cheeky pun. In some ways, the Gibeonites appear more like Israelites than the Israelites themselves. They have no king to lead them, which makes them closer in terms of social and political organization to Israel than to other groups in Canaan, and they act with one accord in a united way in order to save their lives, while the Israelites exhibit dissension and some division. There is a frequent mention of leaders in Joshua 9 in distinction from and sometimes in opposition to the "whole community" (cf. 9:18).

Chapter 9 presents an instructive and at the same time entertaining story, providing some light relief after the bloody episodes that precede it. Like the Rahabites, the Gibeonites live with Israel "until this day" (9:27). Just in case anyone had questions about this strange arrangement of Canaanites coexisting with the covenant community, here is the answer. Lighthearted as I believe the account to be, it shows clear connections to the account of Rahab in theme as well as terminology. Rahab, as an outsider, also managed to save herself and guaranteed her family's ongoing existence among Israel. Both narratives provide strong testimony to the impossibility of the ancient Israelites living an enclosed existence, fenced off from their neighbors, as much as this may have seemed desirable to some of the theological voices among the editors.

It is not unreasonable to assume that the tale represents an old tradition, since attempts to make a treaty with a powerful enemy are not unknown in ancient conquest accounts, and even something like the ruse of Gibeon exists in surviving Hittite documents.[71] The reasons for preserving it in the collection of Joshua texts can only be surmised. It may just have been too good a story to pass up; but at the same time, it expresses a theological theme of great importance.

Act III: The Mouth of the Sword (Joshua 10–12)

For all our hermeneutical imagination, we still have before us texts that wound.[72]

The grim account of Israelite conquests recommences in chapter 10. Initially, a coalition of five kings and peoples in the south set upon Gibeon, which appeals to Joshua for help. In what follows, God and Joshua together achieve a great victory, the Israelites receive divine aid through natural and unnatural phenomena, and the five kings are slaughtered and buried in the cave where they had initially hidden themselves. The second half of the chapter recites the defeat of six cities and a region, one city after another in a long sequence of units with strong repetitive phrases concerning the totality of the destruction of cities, their kings, and all the people in them. The entire series closes with a short section that reviews the capture of the entire region and a return of Joshua with the troops to Gilgal.

71. *Annals of Murshili* as cited in Younger, *Ancient Conquest Accounts*, 202. The sending of weaker parts of the population, in this case old women and men, by a ruler who feared the Hittite army, does not sound entirely unlike the machinations of the Gibeonites. As Younger observes: "This is a ruse of the rank of the Gibeonites" (203).

72. Walter Brueggemann, "The God of Joshua: An Ambivalent Field of Negotiation," in *Joshua and Judges*, ed. Athalya Brenner and Gale A. Yee (Minneapolis: Fortress, 2013), 14.

Chapter 11 continues the report with a new coalition under Jabin, the king of Hazor, in the north. The Israelites execute a complete defeat on these armies with their kings, with specific mention of the treatment of Hazor as the only city that was burned. After battles in which Joshua defeats the coalition and captures and burns down Hazor, the recital ends with the note that "Joshua took the entire country/ . . ./ and the land had rest from war" (11:23). While chapter 10 provides a preliminary ending, with the Israelites encamping at Gilgal, chapter 11 closes off the stage of fighting the wars of conquest by announcing the impending allotment of the land to the tribes. Both chapters depict the Deity as actively participating in the battles, so that ultimately victory is due to the fact that "Adonai, the God of Israel, fought for Israel." Finally, chapter 12 ends the act with two lists of defeated regions and their rulers, east and west of the Jordan.

Act III, Scene 1: The Longest Day (Joshua 10)

There is no reason to maintain that the account in Joshua 9–12 portrays a complete *conquest.*[73]

Once again, an episode opens with news about Israelite advances reaching the Canaanites. This time, a leader is mentioned by name as well as location: Adonizedeq, king of Jerusalem. The name, meaning something like "my lord is righteousness," combined with the place, Jerusalem, lends a particular edge to the story, which is at first told from a Canaanite perspective.[74] Name and place are heralds of a future beyond what is taking place at this particular time. Adonizedeq has heard not only about Jericho and Ai but also about the

73. Younger, *Ancient Conquest Accounts*, 243.

74. McConville: "Adonizedek's very name, 'the Lord is righteousness,' bears an irony. . . . It was from Salem (Jerusalem; cf. Ps 76:3[2]) that the mysterious priest-king Melchizedek had once blessed Abraham (Gen 14:18–20)." According to McConville, both names convey that "the *god* worshiped at Jerusalem is righteousness. . . . The name points to a goal of the story well beyond himself, while in the meantime he stands in defiant opposition to it" (McConville and Willams, *Joshua*, 51–52).

peace treaty with the Gibeonites, and it worries him greatly. From Adonizedeq's point of view, Gibeon is a "big city, like one of the royal cities, bigger than Ai" (2). Subsequently, the Jerusalem king forms a coalition of five kings with their cities to the south rather than going out on his own to fight the invaders (3), an event anticipated at the beginning of chapter 9, which announced the formation of an alliance in broad general terms. Now, it is the pact between Gibeon and the Israelites which sparks a pact between specific indigenous leaders in a region south of Gibeon. Instead of taking on Joshua and his army, the kings besiege Gibeon, which, naturally, sends word to Joshua with an appeal for aid (6). The perspective turns back to Joshua and the Israelite army on the march from Gilgal to relieve Gibeon.

This first sequence of the chapter (10:1–15) describes the engagement of the Israelite troops, the "mighty warriors" (7) of Israel led by Joshua and aided by divine interventions, with the Canaanite coalition. Rather than the detailed strategy before the capture of Ai in chapter 8, we encounter general phrases such as "they struck them a great blow" and "they pursued them as far as . . . and struck them until" (10:10). Any specificity is reserved for divine activity: "Adonai sowed confusion among them . . . cast great stones down on them . . . on the day Adonai gave the Amorites to Israel . . . Adonai fought for Israel" (10:10, 11, 12, 14). Everything gives the impression of Joshua and his "mighty warriors" achieving a quick and decisive victory to a great extent because of divine intervention. Stones hurled at the enemy from heaven are known from other ancient conquest accounts.[75] Celestial bodies participate and help decide the outcome of the battle. In Joshua 10, these bodies include the sun and the moon.

Joshua 10:13–14

13 Then the sun was still,
and the moon stood,
while a people took vengeance on its foes.

75. In the *Annals of Murshili* it is a "meteor"; regarding Sargon's campaign, "flood, cloud and (hail)stones" are mentioned (Younger, *Ancient Conquest Accounts,* 208–210).

Is it not written in the scroll of Yashar:
The sun stood midway in the sky
and did not hasten to come in for a whole day.
14 There has been no day like it
before or after
that Adonai heeded the voice of a man,
and Adonai fought for Israel.

It is clear enough that the intention of the miracle is to create a long day and that the phenomenon takes place on the word of Joshua to Adonai. K. Lawson Younger asserts that both sun and moon "were visible in the heavens at the time," and the prayer of Joshua involved the petition for God not to let "the sun and the moon . . . set till Israel had taken vengeance upon its foes."[76] Younger also points out the significance of "a single day" in this context used as hyperbole, citing a number of parallels from ancient accounts, among them one that includes the phrase "the like had never happened."[77] In other words, the picture of the hailstones and of sun and the moon together providing light to lengthen the stage for defeating the enemy is standard fare in this type of literature, shared by Israel with its neighbors, since miraculous events accompanying the proceedings appear to be a familiar trope of ancient conquest accounts. For contemporary readers, the sun and the moon together in the sky stopping their natural progress (as far as the ancients were concerned) should be no more surprising than the waters of the Jordan "standing in one heap" (3:16). The last comment of the segment lends great authority to the person of Joshua while at the same time underlining the personal engagement of the God of Israel in the battle (10:14). The verse that links the episode to what follows notes a return of the Israelite army to Gilgal while the five kings hide in a cave at Makkedah. Kings finding refuge in a cave may be viewed as a logical step in a hilly region, one taken by other groups or persons on the run in the Historical Books—notably by David when he is

76. Younger, *Ancient Conquest Accounts*, 215.
77. Younger, *Ancient Conquest Accounts*, 217.

hiding out from Saul.[78] In addition, defeated kings, according to ancient transmission codes, are often said to "flee and take refuge in some hiding place such as a cave."[79]

The next sequence at this stage of Israelite progress (10:17–27) reveals that there are still enemies to conquer, followed by a more detailed account of the execution of the five kings. Joshua commands the army to go in pursuit of the enemy, and in the end they strike them "a great blow until they were finished" (20)—that is to say, until they were wiped out. In the same breath, the narrator notes that "survivors of them escaped into the fortified cities," the very thing Joshua had tried to prevent (10:19). Evidently, the Canaanites are not quite "finished," and this campaign does not involve the conquest of cities. A complete conquest is apparently not quite complete, and not everybody is as "finished" as might be desired.

The armies return to Makkedah to seal the fate of the five kings. They are led out of their hiding place and displayed in total defeat, with the commanders' feet on their necks. Joshua thus involves others in a symbolic action that depicts dominion over the conquered kings. As others have observed, the display of the vanquished kings on trees or stakes (10:26) is attested elsewhere, as is the piling up of stones to commemorate the site.[80] Lebhar Hall views the account of the southern campaign as implicitly critical of kingship. The offensive against Israel is led by kings, whose actions and defeat receive detailed attention, while Joshua by contrast shares the victorious moment with his commanders.[81] Certainly, the narrators depict the Israelite army under Joshua's leadership in a way that diverges from that of the Canaanites, in line with the

78. Judg 6:2 and 1 Sam 13:6 of the Israelites; 1 Sam 22:1 and 24:3 of David; 1 Kgs 18:13 and 19:9 of Elijah and other prophets.

79. Younger, *Ancient Conquest Accounts*, 222.

80. Younger, *Ancient Conquest Accounts*, 223–24. Younger also views the account of the heap of stones as "non-etiological."

81. Lebhar Hall, *Conquering Character*, 178: "This anti-monarchic perspective, no doubt informed by theological preference for direct theocracy over monarchy (Judg 8:22–23; 1 Sam 8), is evident in the remainder of the chapter as well. It implicitly legitimizes Joshua's (non-royal) position in Israel."

ambiguous perspective on the virtues of kingship which will be present throughout the Historical Books. In this respect also, the conquest accounts differ from other ancient literature, which for the most part highlights the roles of individual leaders and is told from a first-person point of view.

It is clear from the previous account that the defeat of enemy groups did not include the conquest of their cities. This mopping up operation takes place in the final sequence of the chapter (10:28–43). Makkedah, Libnah, Lachish, Eglon, Hebron, and Debir, three of them part of the coalition in the south, fall to the invaders in six episodes, each unit structured according to a similar literary pattern, repeating phrases such as "Joshua and all Israel with him," "did battle with," "captured it," "struck it with the mouth of the sword," "all persons who were in it," "he left no survivors," and "he did as he had done to." In addition, the line "all persons who were in it he put under the *herem*" occurs four times. We note that Jerusalem is not among the list of cities.

Joshua 10:38–39

38 Joshua and all Israel with him turned back to Debir
and did battle with it.
39 He captured it with its king and all its cities,
and struck them with the mouth of the sword.
He put them under the *herem*
and all persons who were in it;
he left no survivors, as he had done to Hebron.
Thus he did to Debir and its king
as he had done to Libnah and its king.

The chapter ends with a unit recapping the conquest of the "entire region" (40), repeating a part of the pattern and ending with the phrase "Adonai, the God of Israel, fought for Israel (10:42). A concluding line has "Joshua and all Israel with him" returning to the camp in Gilgal. The verb "to strike down" (*nakhah*) appears fourteen times in chapter 10—more than in any other chapter.

Act III, Scene 2: The Last Battles (Joshua 11)

The phrase "all the land" must be understood as hyperbole.[82]

Attention turns to the northern cities, who gather in an effort to beat off the invaders. According to the text, they do so in great multitude, "like the sand at the sea's edge" (11:4–5). As in the previous account, Joshua receives the counsel from Adonai to have no fear, for the Canaanites will be delivered "slain" to Israel. The first sequence (11:1–7) provides an overview of the battle with a successful defeat of the Canaanite alliance. A second sequence (11:8–15) has its focus on the battle against Hazor, called "the chief of those kingdoms" (10) and one of the cities that, according to archeological records, was indeed destroyed in the Late Bronze Age. It is the only city in this region that is "burned with fire" (cf. Jericho, 6:24; and Ai, 8:19, 28), an exception stated emphatically in verse 13. Hazor is also put under the *herem,* as the cities in chapter 10 were. In other cities, the people are allowed to take plunder for themselves (14).

The concluding sequence (11:16–23) reviews all the land that falls to Joshua and the Israelites, with references to Moses and the exodus. As in Egypt with Pharaoh, Adonai "hardened the hearts" of the city chiefs (11:20; cf. Exod 14:8, 17). Of course, there are exceptions to the claim of no survivors; the Gibeonites are mentioned here, as well as the Anakim, who are annihilated in the south, although not all of them: "No Anakim were left in the land of the Israelites;/ only in Gaza, Gath, and Ashkelon did they remain." Such a sentence sums up quite well what must have been the case: The attempts to conquer and settle the land met with resistance, resulting violence, and partial or impermanent success. The account can claim that "Joshua took all the land" (16) while in the next breath it states that Joshua "did battle with those kings for many days" (18). Yet chapter 11 ends with the statement that "Joshua took the whole land . . . and the land had rest from war" (23).

82. Younger, *Ancient Conquest Accounts,* 244.

Act III, Scene 3: All the Kings (Joshua 12)

There is but one Enemy—with a capital letter—so that whether one is looking at Adoni-zedeq, Jabin, Sihon, Og, or the Anakim, they are viewed through the same unitary ideology of enmity.[83]

Joshua 12 presents two lists, one of the territory with its kings east of the Jordan, conquered under the leadership of Moses (12:1–6), and a second of subjugated regions and kings taken under Joshua (12:7–24). Such summary statements are common to the genre and, according to K. Lawson Younger, "a natural part of the narration . . . by our comparison with the ancient Near Eastern conquest accounts."[84] The list looks back to what has been accomplished and also forms a transition to the material that follows, which equally consists for a great part of lists. The first sequence (12:1–6) is set in the frame of the territory taken in the Transjordan, looking from west to east "across the Jordan" and from south to north. The land is initially taken by "the Israelites" (12:1), but the sequence closes with "Moses, the servant of Adonai," as told in Deuteronomy 1–3. In the opening verse, "the Israelites took possession"; in the closing lines it is Moses who "gave" it as a possession to the Transjordanian tribes.

Then follows the listing (12:7–24) of kings of cities seized under Joshua "across the Jordan to the west"—that is, looking from the Transjordanian side, north to south. Two verses serve to introduce the list, with the emphasis on Joshua as the one who "struck" the enemy down together with the Israelites and who "gave" it to the tribes, naming regions and peoples (7–8). The royal list (9–24) opens with Jericho and Ai (with renewed mention of Bethel) and continues first south then north. One should not look for accuracy or complete coherence with material available elsewhere in the text, and finding cities not named in Joshua 1–11 is thus not unusual. Names of kings are not preserved here, but rather the kings are named by their cities. In the end, there are "thirty-one kings," a large number for this relatively small territory and indicative of the political landscape of

83. Younger, *Ancient Conquest Accounts*, 233.
84. Younger, *Ancient Conquest Accounts*, 232.

the period, divided as it was into small city-states. One Israel was led by one successor of Moses, the servant of God, over against a multiplicity of groupings and their chieftains, all of whom are given a royal title—king of Such and Such and king of Such and Such—while Israel settles without kingship. Where now are all those kings of the past? In the end, it is a list of disappeared powers, symbolic of the ephemeral nature of human sovereignty.

Crossing and Conquest Review: Joshua 1–12

The juxtaposition of the stories [of Achan and Rahab] implies that the herem *is not absolute, and is superseded by issues of justice and mercy.*[85]

The first twelve chapters present a narrative with distinct connections between episodes in terms of literary motifs, themes and theological point of view. Joshua is appointed directly by God as successor to Moses and commissioned with admonitions to be strong and of good courage (1:6, 7, 9), an affirmation that will recur in the shape of the encouragement not to be afraid (8:1; 10:8; 11:6). The phrase that God "*has* given" or "*will* give" a city or a people into the hand of the Israelites, implying that the land is thus a *gift* from God to the people, occurs throughout the Cycle, beginning in chapter 1 (1:2, 15; 2:9, 24; 6:2, 16; 8:1; 10:8; 11:6). God is directly present with Joshua, addressing and counseling him, speaking to him in each chapter except chapters 2, 9, and 12. God is said to "fight" on behalf of Israel (10:14, 42), an expression used elsewhere only on the occasion of the miraculous crossing of the Sea of Reeds (Exod 14:25), a tradition in which the God of Israel is also called a "man of war" (Exod 15:3). In theme and terminology, the cycle exhibits strong links with the exodus: crossing the Jordan in a miraculous way as erstwhile the people had crossed the Sea of Reeds, celebrating Pesach after circumcision, punctuating events with ceremony and liturgical celebration, and marking them for historical reference. This is done in such a way that what began with the exodus—liberation from bondage—is now

85. Frymer-Kensky, *Reading the Women of the Bible*, 42.

brought to a successful end—entry into the land God promised to the ancestors. At the same time, Deuteronomic regulations receive follow-through in Joshua, especially in the portrayal of the complete decimation of indigenous peoples and the application of the *herem*. "Listening" to Torah regulations receives emphatic mention from the beginning of the cycle, and transgression is punished severely. The theological point of view presents a Deity who strongly supports the effort to conquer and settle the land to decimate the indigenous population, and who even *fights* on behalf of the invading Israelites, as long as they adhere to the regulations reflected in Deuteronomic perspective and text.

Chapters 2 and 9 stand out in the cycle because they lack divine address to Joshua and depict in rich detail two exceptions to hostile encounters with indigenous peoples ending in peaceful relations. Each fits into the fabric of the composition in a specific way. Chapter 2 closely links to the first chapter as well as the material that follows by relating an episode of "crossing" the Jordan that entails a "gift" from one of the Canaanite inhabitants to Israelite representatives, saving their lives and making possible the ensuing crossing of the river by all of the tribes. In addition, it opens up the chance for permanent coexistence of indigenous groups with the Israelites. Chapter 9, placed between the destruction of Ai and the impending capture of a series of places and people in the south and the north, opens a window of peace in the midst of the relentless march to violence on the part of the Israelites. Both chapters also offer relief with lively characterization of individuals and groups.

Every chapter in this first part of Joshua has its own purpose and place in the construction of the whole, with distinct connections to its context. Chapters 3 and 4 feature the presence of the Ark, guiding the people to safety through the river that represents the border between wilderness existence and occupation of the land. Chapter 5 presents a pause in the action with the liturgical marking of the occasion of entry, while in chapter 6 the Ark returns as God's presence at the downfall of Jericho. Movement into the land continues in chapters 7 and 8, though it is temporarily halted by disobedience and momentary defeat, and the first conquests are emphatically concluded with a ceremonial reading of the Teaching of Moses on Mount Ebal. Chapter 9 stops the action with a detailed account of the successful ploy by an indigenous group desiring peaceful relations with the Israelites. Chapters 10 and 11 portray violent conquest scenes, according to which the Israelites under Joshua secure footholds in the south and the north of the country. Rahabites, Gibeonites, and Anakim remain to exist in Canaan. Cities, though conquered, are ordinarily not razed and burned, as were Jericho, Ai, and Hazor, and they may have been only temporarily in Israelite possession.

It is clear enough that the claim that the whole country is under Israel's sway is an exaggerated one, but all the same, the tale makes for grim reading, especially in the episodes concerning Jericho, Ai, and the capture of individuals, cities, and regions in the south and north. What can believers today have to do with a God who encourages the wholesale annihilation of peoples and groups and is even said to *fight* on behalf of a marauding crowd that overruns a country? Stephen Williams, in his attempt to come to terms with the God we encounter in Joshua—the God who not only condones but encourages violence—concludes that we must seek a solution in the direction of God accommodating to the fact that evil, though detested by God according to biblical witness, is not abolished, and that Israel's God is in the thick of it with God's people.[86] In addition, as Williams also recognizes, this text narrates Israel's memories and is therefore descriptive rather than prescriptive. Glorification of past violence is part and parcel of these memories and not intended to inform present practices. We have also seen how closely patterned the texts are on related ancient Near Eastern literature. Divine aid during warfare represents a common theological theme; in its context, it was not surprising and did not set Israelite perspectives and literature apart.

Surprises are located in episodes that do not fit the pattern and in the ways they do not fit. Why are the Rahabites and the Gibeonites saved from the fate of the *herem*? Does one good deed (Rahab) outweigh the danger of mingling with the peoples of the land and thus running the risk of becoming idolaters? Is tricky cleverness

86. McConnville and Williams, *Joshua*, 108–24.

(Gibeon) enough to set aside determination to annihilate all that breathes and strike it down by the mouth of the sword? Why are "strangers" mentioned at the reading of the Teaching of Moses on Mount Ebal? Both Rahab and the Gibeonites receive a sworn oath from the Israelites. In the case of Rahab, she requests the oath as a return for her deed of loyalty by hiding the spies, and because of the oath sworn to her, Joshua saves her life and that of her family during the destruction of Jericho. The Gibeonites trick the Israelites into swearing an oath to them also, to let them live and not hurt them. The oath is in both cases sworn "by Adonai"—that is to say, it includes an invocation of God to be a witness and as such is unbreakable. With the Gibeonites, the commitment includes a covenant—a significant moment in Joshua, in which covenant, apart from 7:11 and references to the Ark, is mentioned only in the final chapters. The fact that Achan has broken the covenant, to which Adonai had obligated the Israelites, opens him to the extreme punishment he receives.

Arguably, the oath for protection and the covenant making still beg the question why this aspect trumped the obligation to annihilate all Canaanites. Joshua and the Israelites are under obligation to follow the Teaching of Moses. This Teaching included, in every legal code of the Torah, the protection demanded for the stranger (*ger*) in the community. The Torah contains more regulations for the protection of the stranger—the one who lacks the privileges and rights of the insider—than for any other social category, even in the Deuteronomic code, which demands the annihilation of the indigenous population of Canaan. Both Rahab and Gibeon may make a claim on Israelite protection because of their outsider status. Rahab makes the claim on the basis of her safeguarding the life of the spies, but Gibeon has no such case to make and argues only that they come from "far away." Rahab is an outsider to Israel because of both her social status and her Canaanite identity. Gibeon asserts an outsider category it does not in truth possess; but even so, the oath, once given, cannot be broken, and in truth they do belong to the *ger* category because they are indigenous to the land.

At Mount Ebal, it is no coincidence that the stranger is included in the list of those who listen to and may rely on the Teaching of Moses together with the kinship group that survived the trek through the wilderness. The Canaanite insider/outsider was perceived as a threat to Israel and its unity and identity, both in the days of conquest and in later days, when a small community was attempting to survive as an island in a sea of religious and political entities that had overpowered it. While it remembered the glory days of past victories and heroic deeds, it maintained at the same time the Teaching of Moses in regard to protection of the stranger. It is in this direction that we must look for instruction that still carries validity. Care for and even love of the stranger set Israel's ethical code apart from that of other peoples. It stands in direct contradiction to the violent warfare perpetrated on the peoples that inhabited Canaan, violence that is also mandated. The violence we must consign to a troubled past, when it may have been the only recourse for Israel to establish itself and survive. Violent treatment of neighbors was common ideological and literary territory. Ultimately, it was care for the outsider, unique to Israel and also mandated in the Teaching of Moses, that held and holds the winning cards.

Cycle II: Occupation (Joshua 13–21)

Although a transition in leadership is at hand, the tribes have to find their place before Joshua goes the way of all flesh.[1]

The second Cycle of Joshua can be divided in two acts, the first (chs. 13–19) containing the division of the land both east and west of the Jordan and the second (chs. 20–21) devoted to assigning cities of refuge and Levitical cities. The review that follows will be selective, reserving a close reading of the text mostly for narrative segments within the listings of regions and cities. The entire cycle is framed by a promise/fulfillment scheme, with God promising eventual possession in 13:6 and the narrator reporting that God has indeed given Israel the land in 21:43–45.

JOSHUA 21:43–45

43 Adonai gave to Israel the whole land
that he swore to give to their ancestors.
They took possession of it and lived in it.
44 Adonai gave them rest round about,
according to all he swore to their ancestors,
and no one stood against them of all their enemies;
Adonai gave all their enemies into their hand.

1. Author's translation of Piet van Midden, "Jozua," in *De Bijbel Literair*, ed. Jan Fokkelman and Wim Weren (Zoetermeer: Meinema, 2003), 141.

45 Not a word failed of all the good things Adonai spoke;
it all came to pass.

Act I: Dividing the Land (Joshua 13–19)

Because the book of Joshua is concerned with the entire nation, land distribution includes all the tribes.[2]

Seven chapters review the division of the land, beginning in chapter 13 with the region east of the Jordan already assigned to Reuben, Gad, and half of Manasseh and continuing in chapters 14–17 with the apportionment in Canaan proper, first to the tribe of Judah, then to Ephraim and the other half of Manasseh. Chapters 18 and 19 are devoted to casting lots at Shiloh after a survey is taken and dividing the land among the rest of the tribes, beginning with Benjamin and ending with Dan. From the start, it is made clear that the tribe of Levi is an exception and that it will receive towns with only minor landholdings, an exception which will unfold in Act II of the cycle.

While land assignments in the Transjordan are accredited to Moses in chapter 13 (vv. 8, 33), the division of Canaan is framed by references to the priest El'azar as well as to Joshua, who are together in charge of the casting of the lot in 14:1 and 19:51. Still, references to Moses persist also in chapter 14, harkening back to the account in Numbers 32:1–40. Announcements of land divisions and listings of regions and towns are regularly interrupted by narratives concerning individuals and their claims (14:6–15; 15:13–19; 17:3–6), which lend liveliness to the monotony of the list recitations. There are also occasions for tribal query or complaint regarding the amount of land assigned (17:14–18), as well as regular notations of specific ethnic groups which the Israelites are not able to dislodge from the land (13:1, 13; 15:63; 16:10; 17:12), adding an air of tension and uncertainty to the survey.

2. Richard D. Nelson, *Joshua: A Commentary* (Louisville: Westminster John Knox, 1997), 170.

Act I, Scene 1: Settling the East (Joshua 13)

How can boundaries be fixed when they cannot be clearly determined?[3]

Chapter 13 mainly centers on the Transjordan, with assignments of land to Reuben, Gad, and half of Manasseh, moving from south to north and opening with an address from God to Joshua (1–7). This is the only place in the cycle to feature direct speech from Adonai, whose presence hereafter will be symbolized by the casting of lots. The larger part of the speech consists of a series of announcements about the great amount of land that has *not* been taken into possession west of the Jordan (13:2–6), preceded by the comment that Joshua is "old, advanced in years"—that is to say, probably not capable of doing much more conquering. This opening would not be propitious except for the concluding statement that God will step up to the plate and accomplish everything in the end so that Joshua can make provisional land assignments.

JOSHUA 13:6C–7

6c I myself will dispossess them for the Israelites.
Only allot the land as Israel's inherited share
as I have commanded you.
7 Therefore, divide this territory as an inherited share
to the nine tribes and the half tribe of Manasseh.

Although the direct referent for "them" in the first line is a group of peoples in the north, we may take it to refer to all the peoples and districts that are mentioned in verses 2–6: Canaanites, Geshurites, Avvim, Sidonians, and Amorites, a daunting list of regions and inhabitants that have not given way before the Israelites, among them the Philistines, who will provide trouble for many years to come.

The first communities to be assigned territory are the two and a half tribes whose portion fell in the Transjordan (13:8–33), men-

3. L. Daniel Hawk, *Joshua*, Berit Olam (Collegeville, MN: Liturgical Press, 2000), 188.

tioned first in the review list of chapter 12: Reuben, Gad, and half of Manasseh. They appeared also in the first chapter of the book, when Joshua commanded them to engage with their kin in the capture of the land west of the Jordan in accordance with the Mosaic instruction in Numbers 32 (Josh 1:12–16). Manasseh's division in half is emphatically noted by including it with the nine tribes to be located in Canaan at the end of verse 7 and by opening with it at the beginning of verse 8, where it is included with Reuben and Gad. The emphasis on tribes living both east of the Jordan and in particular on the one tribe divided in half by the Jordan River signals a potential conflict.

Just as in Joshua 12, chapter 13 refers to Moses, the servant of Adonai, as the one who gave them "their inherited share" (13:8). The list of the Transjordanian rulers and territories that "Moses struck down and dispossessed" parallels the opening section of chapter 12, with some differences. Notably, there is mention of the Geshurites and Ma'acites, populations in the far north whom they were not able to dislodge, so that "Geshur and Ma'acah live among Israel until this day" (13:13), echoing the situation of the Rahabites and Gibeonites in chapters 6 and 9. In addition, the tribe of Levi gets special mention for not receiving a land allotment because their inherited share consists of "the burnt offerings of Adonai" (13:14). This observation will be repeated at the end of the chapter, with a variation in the wording. The tribe of Levi will come to the fore again in the next chapter and then once more in chapter 18, each time with some variation in the reasons cited for being singled out, perhaps a token of conflicting perspectives concerning their position among the tribes. Land assignments are made with the question "what about the Levites?" hovering over the lists. They will receive their assigned cities at the end of the cycle.[4]

Each unit in the sequence (13:8–33) begins with a reference to Moses who "gave the inherited share," first to the two and a half

4. The tasks of the Levites are described in Numbers 1, 3, 4, and 18 in specific detail, and they amount to housekeeping tasks. In Deuteronomy 18:1, they are assigned the burnt offerings intended for Adonai as their "inherited share" (*nahalah*). Moses and Aaron are, of course, Levites, but there is tension concerning tribal place and function, and there is some conflict in the traditions.

tribes as a whole, then to each in turn (13:8, 15, 24, 29), and the entire segment is enclosed by references to the agency of Moses (13:8, 33). L. Daniel Hawk points out a "gradual degeneration of the paradigm," which is especially prominent in the review of the Manassite holdings with its reference to "half of this" and "half of that"—the word "half" occurring three times in as many verses.[5] The Manasseh review also lacks the concluding statement: "This is the inherited share of . . . according to their clans, the towns and their villages" (13:23, 28). Hawk discerns a similar pattern in regard to Judah and Joseph in the next chapter and surmises that vagueness of description parallels ambiguity and uncertainty regarding actual possession versus claims on the land.[6] Such uncertainty coheres with the regular mention of peoples that continue to live in a land promised as an "inherited share" to the Israelites.

Act I, Scene 2: Allotment Interrupted (Joshua 14:1–15:19)

The stories challenge the notion that "Israel" is to be defined in exclusively masculine terms.[7]

Chapter 14 begins with a narrative note looking back while at the same time anticipating the division of land west of the Jordan as apportioned by "El'azar, the priest, and Joshua, the son of Nun, and the ancestral heads of the tribes"—dividing the task among the leadership rather than assigning it to Joshua alone (14:1–5). The explanation of what has taken place and what is still in the future strains to clarify who is in charge of which task, who will receive land, and how the tribes reach the number twelve. Moses had already assigned land to two and a half tribes, but not to the Levites, a fact that reduces the tribal number to eleven. Joseph, however, is in reality two tribes, Ephraim and Manasseh, bringing the number back to twelve. Once again, the Levites are in the spotlight for *not*

5. Hawk, *Joshua*, 190.
6. Hawk, *Joshua*, 185–90.
7. Hawk, *Joshua*, 199.

receiving a share, clarifying that they did not receive land anywhere, one supposes (although in the next breath they do get towns with pasturelands!), and making the number of tribal lands amount to twelve.[8] Finally, the Israelites did everything according to the way God directed Moses. In this opening unit, the word "inheritance" or "inherited share," together with "portion," is repeated in every verse. The concern is thus with the land that the tribes may lay claim to by order of God through Moses.

In contrast to the positions of authority announced in the opening lines, the next sequence moves to the story of an individual who takes the initiative to argue for the possession of land (14:6–15). The opening words set up the expectation that the tribe of Judah is about to receive its land but instead continues with a focus on one individual: Caleb, the son of Yefunneh, the Kenizite, a people listed in Genesis as indigenous to Canaan (Gen 15:19). Is he a member of a tribe that was originally non-Israelite but now belongs to Judah, having insider/outsider status? The ambiguity is subtle but present all the same.[9] Caleb opens with a reference to Moses, calling him "the man of God," an unusual epithet for Moses and in the Historical Books reserved mostly for prophets, especially Elijah and Elisha.[10] Before Caleb gets around to his request, he presents his bona fides, pointing out his abiding loyalty in taking a stand against his companions who had joined in the mission to reconnoiter Canaan (Num 13:1–33). "I myself," Caleb claims, "stayed loyal to Adonai, my God." The phrase employs a form of the verb meaning "to fill," here with the sense of completely answering to expectation or demand. It is also used with this meaning in the Numbers narrative referring to

8. The denial of a land allotment to Levi is stated emphatically: once in v. 3 as originating with Moses ("and to the Levites he did not give an inherited share in their midst"); and once again in v. 4 regarding allotments made by El'azar and Joshua ("and they did not give an inherited share to the Levites in the land").

9. Hawk (*Joshua*, 198) suggests that the Kenizite reference presents "a narrative frame against which to comprehend Caleb's request in the manner of other 'outsiders' in the book."

10. Moses is otherwise only once identified as "the man of God," preceding his blessing over the tribes in Deut 33:1.

Caleb and again in Deuteronomy (Num 14:24; 32:12; Deut 1:36).[11] In the next breath, Caleb comes close to making his request, referring to the promise of land Moses made to him and again emphasizing his loyalty, but he veers off in another direction. He states his great age, 85, and his nevertheless remarkable strength, which is still as it was in the old days.

JOSHUA 14:10–12

10 And now, see, Adonai kept me alive forty-five years
since God made this promise to Moses,
while Israel wandered in the wilderness;
and now, see, I am today 85 years old.
11 I am today as strong as on the day Moses sent me—
as my strength was then, so it is now—
for battle, for going out and coming in.
12 And now, please give me this hill,
of which Adonai spoke on that day,
for you yourself heard on that day that Anakim were there
and great fortified towns.
Perhaps Adonai will be with me
and I will drive them out as Adonai said.

Notably, Caleb joins the declaration of his advanced age to one about his vigor, perhaps a deliberate contrast to the initial statement about Joshua in 13:1, where the implication is that the time of Joshua's active participation in leading armed conflict is coming to a close because of his age. The urgency of the request—four times repeating "now," twice followed by "see," with an emphasis on "today" while at the same time referring back to "that day"—manifests a certain anxiety on Caleb's part. He encloses his request in references to God. Moses swore an oath which issued from a divine promise, after all. Caleb's possession of Hebron (formerly

11. In contrast, the other spies do *not* fulfill the demand and are *not* loyal. The other notable usage of the verb with this meaning refers to King Solomon (1 Kgs 11:6).

named Kiryat-Arba after one of the giants that had occupied it) is the successful outcome of the episode, although the tale is not quite finished.

The opening line of the next chapter looks once more as if the list of Judah's properties will follow, and those properties are indeed indicated in terms of regions, "from" this place "to" that place, assigning the borders of the possession (15:1–12). But the focus then returns to Caleb, providing more detail about the way he acquired both Hebron and Debir, each also indicated by alternative names (15:13–15). Next follows a vignette featuring the daughter of Caleb, Achsa, who is married off to her cousin as a prize for his conquest of Sefer.

Joshua 15:16–19

16 Then said Caleb: To the one who will strike down
Kiryat-Sefer and capture it,
I will give to him Achsa my daughter for a wife.
17 Then captured it Otniel,
the son of Kenaz, Caleb's brother,
and he gave to him Achsa his daughter for a wife.
18 When she came, she induced him
to ask her father for a field.
As she came down from her donkey,
Caleb said to her: What is the matter with you?
19 She said: Give me please a blessing.
For desert land you have given me;
now give me water basins.
So he gave her the upper and the lower basins.

The beginning features two male relatives, Caleb and his nephew Otniel, engaging in an exchange of *taking* and *giving*, ending with Caleb giving his daughter Achsa to his nephew. Caleb, named twice, in charge of speaking and giving, frames the lines. Otniel, in the center, has the action of capture and is named with his bloodline. Caleb's daughter Achsa is the gift. In verse 18, Achsa takes the lead and is the subject of all the verbs. There is an odd hiatus after the second line of the verse, with the husband absent after Achsa "induces" him, although we assume she received the field from what follows. Although Achsa is now the subject of a verb, her initial portrait is not positive in view of the verb "induced," a relatively rare word that occurs elsewhere only in negative contexts.[12] The message is that she talked her husband into the demand for property by means of some inducement that may not have met the standard of appropriate behavior. Perhaps a longer story was lost and we have only a fraction of what remains, now combined with Achsa's initiative. With Achsa's speech, a woman's voice sounds for the second time in the book.

After the reported request for a field (rather than an inheritance) through her husband, the scene shifts abruptly to the vivid picture of Achsa coming down from her donkey and her father asking her what she wants. The question addressed to a female (*mahlakh*), also quite rare, is fairly neutral. In contemporary slang, it might be, "What's up?" Her short and poetic request to her father literally asks for a "blessing," which here means an addition to her property. From her words, we find out the field is *negev*—that is to say, arid land—which is no gift at all without water.[13] The scene ends with Caleb complying with her request, perhaps in a more generous way than his daughter had asked for, as implied by the phrase "he gave her X *and* Y." The short section with Achsa in the center has her in charge of all the motion ("she came," "she came down") as well as most of the speaking ("she induced," "she said," "give me," "you have given me," "give me"), while the object of her speech is a straightforward request based on an untenable situation. Dry land without a water supply is not viable property. As Hawk observes, "The issues of property ownership by women has been broached" and "will appear again."[14]

12. See, for example, Deut 13:7[6]; 1 Sam 26:19; 2 Sam 24:1; Job 36:18; Jer 38:22; 43:3. Judg 1:14 uses the identical verb in the parallel passage.

13. The word I have translated with "basin" is a noun indicating a container for water. Most assume it in this context to refer to springs, as in Judges 1:15.

14. Hawk, *Joshua*, 202.

Act I, Scene 3: What's in a List? (Joshua 15:20–63)

The people's hope in the future is focused on the land of promise described in its most minute detail.[15]

The detour to Caleb and his family completed, the text is ready to present the long list of the towns of Judah (15:20–63). It consists of districts, each ending with a note on the number of the towns, to which is added the general indication "and their villages" (vv. 32, 36, 41, 44, 51, 54, 57, 59, 60, 62). It begins in the deep south of Judah and moves gradually to the north-eastern side, out to the far west and back east. There is an anomaly in the mention of Philistine cities (15:45–47, a section that also lacks the note marking the number of towns). Even according to biblical record, this was a region that was not under Israelite control for centuries. This is probably representative of the more idealized version of reality. The segment ends on an emphatic note.

Joshua 15:63

And the Jebusite
inhabitants of Jerusalem
the Israelites could not dispossess.
So the Jebusite lived
with those of Judah
in Jerusalem to this day.

The observation about a Canaanite part of the population living with Israel "to this day" is not new. It occurred earlier in Joshua and we will encounter it again (16:10; 17:2, 13). Nevertheless, the mention of Jerusalem and the Jebusites strikes an odd note, since Jerusalem is not one of the Judahite towns, although it is in a nearby region. The border of Judah was carefully delineated earlier in the chapter as following a line south of Jerusalem (15:8), and eventually Benjamin is to count Jerusalem as its inheritance (18:28), but in the Historical

15. Nelson, *Joshua*, 193.

Books the city is not captured until the time of King David (2 Sam 5:6–8). Its significance apparently looms large enough to mention it twice in the review of the territory of Judah and once again bring to attention the persistent presence of a population group indigenous to Canaan.

Whether lists of towns and regions as we find them here represent ancient inventories or scribal reconstructions is a debated issue, and it is certainly an arduous task to read the recital which many of us may experience as "mind-numbing."[16] Lists in the Bible are not uncommon; we may think of abundant bloodline accounts, the details of the accoutrements of the wilderness sanctuary, and the numerical listing of Israelites to name just a few. Most likely, they were part of the shared literary output of the ancient world. Among the lists, geographical inventories constitute their own genre, and among them the survey of towns in Judah in Joshua 15 is "the most detailed roster of towns in the Bible."[17] It may be a part of an accurate administrative record dating back to a period in the Kingdom of Judah, although its function for the compilers and editors of Joshua can hardly have been administrative. A reason for inserting it and others like it into the "conquest" story may have been to offer a view of the past in its faded glory, but there may have been other reasons.

One purpose of maintaining memories of place is to strengthen identity. To a great degree, the sense of self is defined by one's location in past and present—a definition important for both individuals and groups, especially in the ancient world. Extreme dislocation as experienced by the population of Judah was still felt by the community of the restoration, which likely occupied itself with the listing of Judahite towns especially to reestablish a sense of itself and its belonging. Losing the memory of what once was and where one came from involves losing track of groups and individuals as they are in the present. Towns would still be remembered, saved in the ancestral memory as someone's birthplace or residential site; and

16. So Nelson, *Joshua*, 193.

17. Yohanan Aharoni, *The Land of the Bible: A Historical Geography*, trans. A. F. Rainey (Philadelphia: Westminster, 1979), 88.

to those of Judah living under Persian reign, reciting the names of the once owned and occupied towns provided a crucial sense of communal identity. It was, after all, only in looking back that they could find a way forward.

Act I, Scene 4: Claims for Space (Joshua 16–17)

It is not military strength that determines the ownership of the land, but the justice the women asked of [Adonai].[18]

Chapters 16 and 17 concern themselves entirely with the tribe of Joseph, sometimes referred to as "those of Joseph" (*beney Yosef*, 16:1; 17:14, 16) but for the most part specifying Ephraim and Manasseh, a reflection of the complicated make-up of the tribe as one and yet two. This reality is reflected in verse 16:4: "Those of Joseph received their inherited share, Manasseh and Ephraim" (cf. 17:17).

The tangled and difficult language regarding their specific allotment testifies to the complication arising from this fact (16:5–8). In contrast to the survey of Judah's regions and towns, the indications of the regions are vague, zigzagging from east to west and back again, although it is clear that these allotments are north of Judah. Apparently, no detailed records remained of the districts that once belonged to those of Joseph. At the end of chapter 16, the Canaanites of Gezer are listed as living with Israel, in this case with Ephraim, "to this day" (16:10; cf. 6:25), adding another group to the peoples left in the land after the "conquest" and fracturing the picture of total compliance with the instruction to annihilate all of them.

The next sequence opens with a superabundance of male names, all descended from Joseph, whose firstborn was Manasseh. No less than twelve male names are mentioned in the span of two verses, ending with the phrase: "These are the *sons* of Manasseh,/ the *son* of

18. Kerstin Ulrich, "Joshua: Tradition and Justice: Women's Share in the Inheritance," in *Feminist Biblical Interpretation*, ed. Luise Schottroff and Marie-Theres Wacker (Grand Rapids: Eerdmans, 2012), 109.

Joseph,/ the *males* in their clans" (17:2), emphatically restating male presence. Then, the recital takes an unexpected turn.

Joshua 17:3–4

3 Zelofhad, son of Hefer, son of Machir,
son of Manasseh, had no sons,
only daughters.
These are the names of his daughters:
Mahlah, Noah, Hoglah, Milkah, and Tirzah.
4 And they approached El'azar, the priest,
and Joshua, the son of Nun,
and the leaders with the words:
Adonai commanded Moses
to give to us an inherited share among our male kin.
And he gave on the word of Adonai
an inherited share among the male kin of their father.

For the third time in the book, women are heard from; they are the daughters of Zelofhad, who come to remind Joshua, El'azar, and the leaders of a promise made to them to receive an "inherited share." Pointedly, they refer to a command given by Adonai, appealing directly to the Deity who had instructed Moses and to the exact nature of what they were to inherit. Without further ado, Joshua complies with the request. The story is brief in the extreme and echoes the longer episode told in Numbers 27:1–11, employing identical terminology. The five daughters, there as here each called by name, "draw near" or "approach" the authorities (cf. Num 27:1) and make a bold request for land. Moses takes the case to God, who grants the daughters an "inheritance" (*nahalah*; Num 27:7) rather than the more modest "property" (*ahuzzah*; Num 27:4) they had asked for. In Numbers, the case is a clear-cut example of the adaptability of ancient Israelite law-giving, as it is adjusted to protect both the land as family inheritance and women from abject poverty. Mahlah, Noah, Hoglah, Milkah, and Tirzah are orphans according to the understanding of Torah regulations, since their father is dead, an issue that is clearly stated in the Numbers episode (Num 27:3). The word ordinarily translated with "orphan" in the English versions of the Bible literally means "fatherless." These sisters belong, together with their widowed mother, to a protected category in the Torah. In addition, it was of course important to keep land within the property of clan and tribe; both goals are accomplished with the divine granting of their demand and the establishment of the statute in perpetuity (Num 27:11).

Their boldness in the Numbers narrative is evident, and the grant is given to them in direct quotation from the mouth of Adonai, whose first word is *ken* (Yes!), emphasizing that the women are right to make their request (Num 27:7).[19] In addition, the case sets a precedent that will function for other families (Num 27:11). Although the land grant is conditioned upon the endogamous marriage of the daughters in Numbers 36:1–12, that restriction may in reality not have made much difference, as marriage was most likely to be endogamous in any case (Num 36:5–12), although the restriction evidently intends to guard against the risk of breaking that tradition. In the Joshua episode, they exhibit the same determination they had in their appearance before Moses by referring to what *God* had "commanded Moses" rather than to what *Moses* had commanded upon God's word. For good measure, the narrative repeats that the daughters receive their inheritance in verse 6: "The daughters of Manasseh inherited a share among his sons," underlining the social equivalence of male and female offspring and embedding in the brief story a combined threefold reference to *inheritance* and *daughters.*

The territory of Manasseh takes up the next seven verses (17:7–13) ending with the note that the Manassites were not able to drive out the Canaanites, whom they put to forced labor when they were strong, but "they could not dispossess them" (17:13). Attention then shifts to "those of Joseph" and remains there until the end of the chapter (17:14–18).[20] The Josephites too have a demand, one based

19. This affirmation is difficult to render in translation. "Rightfully the daughters of Zelofhad speak" may be the best one can do.

20. As Hawk (*Joshua*) observes, the Josephites are not indicated with the word "tribe," a term which is reserved for the two that make up the entity, the tribes of Ephraim and Manasseh.

not on Mosaic or divine promises but on a complaint. Their size is too large for the land they have received. Why only one inheritance and one allotment when they are "a numerous people," in reality two tribes (17:14). Joshua's response is provided in direct speech, a feature that in this cycle occurs only here and in the next chapter, and it is bracketed by uncertainty. Joshua begins by repeating the rationale offered by the Josephites about being a large group, but posing it as a hypothetical ("if you are a numerous people") and concluding with a phrase that begins with an ambiguous conjunction, which could be translated "in case Ephraim's hill is too narrow for you."[21] In between, he offers them the forest, which they will need to clear and which is also the land of the "Perizites and the Refa'ites." The reference to the latter, legendary ancestors of the Canaanite population, sounds especially ominous and oddly out of place here.[22]

Those of Joseph offer a counterargument, returning to the subject of the hill country and expressing fear of the Canaanites, who are in possession of "iron" chariots. We will encounter the iron chariots again in Judges, and clearly they enter the text here to highlight the threat of the Canaanites mentioned in verse 13. In the next breath, the narrator elaborates that the "house of Joseph" consists of Ephraim and Manasseh, and Joshua sounds as if he accommodates Joseph, allowing that they are indeed large as well as powerful and extending to them the hill country "to its farthest extent." But when all is said and done, it is not quite clear what the Joseph tribe has accomplished, and they have still the task ahead of them of driving out the Canaanites.

In contrast to the episodes concerning Caleb and the daughters, the demand of the Josephites is not based on a divine promise. Unlike in the clear grants given to Caleb, Achsa, and the daughters of Zelofhad, the verb "give" is absent from this unit. In response to Caleb's request, Joshua *gives* him Hebron; Caleb *gives* his daughter Achsa water supplies; and Joshua *gives* the daughters of Zelofhad an

21. The Hebrew conjunction *ki* can also be read as a conditional in this case.

22. Refa'ites occur together with Kenizites in Gen 15:19–20 and are also reportedly the ancestors of Og, the king of Bashan (Deut 3:11; cf. Josh 12:4; 13:2).

inheritance. Whereas Caleb reportedly took the initiative to drive out the previous inhabitants of Hebron (15:14–15), here both the occupation of sufficient land and the displacement of the Canaanites are presented as a challenge in the face of great odds in ambiguous case language.[23] One imagines the representatives of Joseph coming away from the exchange scratching their heads, wondering what exactly they achieved with their negotiation.

Act I, Scene 5: Unclaimed Space (Joshua 18–19)

So what now of Shiloh?[24]

The first ten verses of chapter 18 open with a gathering of the Israelite community at Shiloh, where Joshua challenges the remaining seven tribes and directs a plan to lay claim to their land (18:1–10). The meeting has the character of a sacred gathering, taking place in the presence of the Tent of Meeting, and portrays the community as united ("the entire assembly," 18:1). There is no mention of outsiders, of Rahabites hovering on the outskirts of the gathering or of Gibeonites carrying water and wood for the many activities. They gather in Shiloh, the territory of Ephraim, a tribe that has just received its allotment. The appearance of the Tent of Meeting, without mention of the Ark, is surprising, since it appears only here and at the end of the Scene (19:51). The location, Shiloh, is unexpected also because so far Gilgal has been the place for decision-making and celebration (4:19, 20; 5:9, 10; 9:6). The description makes use of a rare derivation of the Hebrew verb *shakhan* ("to dwell") for setting up the Tent of Meeting. This verb carries echoes of God's presence,

23. Josh 17:18 includes five occurrences of the Hebrew *ki*, which cannot be consistently translated with the same word and which, taken together, destabilize the lines.

24. Susan Ackerman, "Who Is Sacrificing at Shiloh? The Priesthoods of Ancient Israel's Regional Sanctuaries," in *Levites and Priests in Biblical History and Tradition*, ed. Mark Leuchter and Jeremy M. Hutton (Atlanta: Society of Biblical Literature, 2011), 35. Ackerman makes a convincing case for the existence of many regional sanctuaries in preexilic Israel, of which Shiloh was one.

a God who "dwells" with God's people (e.g., Exod 24:16; 25:8; 29:45; Num 5:3). The movable sanctuary constructed in Exodus is called the "dwelling" (*mishkan*). It is in Shiloh that the assembly causes the Tent of Meeting to "dwell." A tradition of a sanctuary and sacred assembly at Shiloh may have constituted a separate record which found a place in these chapters of Joshua (see 22:12). Shiloh will be at center stage again in the last chapter of Judges and the first chapters of Samuel. In the end, its record will be a blemished one, but here at the beginning stages of the occupation of the land, it is, first of all, the place where the remaining tribes receive their land assignment by the casting of lots.

So far, Geshur, Ma'acah, Jebus, and the Canaanites have been named in this cycle as those who continue to live in the land, with the Canaanites prominently mentioned in chapter 17. Chapter 18 opens with a picture of Canaan as subdued land: "The land was subjugated before them" (18:1).[25] All this unclaimed space, and seven tribes who have not yet established themselves! Joshua's words, "How long will you be slack about going in?" sound like a reproach in line with the portrayal of a completed conquest in this unit, presenting the ideal of a united community and a land where no resistance remains. The stark reality of a mixed population that will constitute Israel and the armed struggles that lie ahead are left unspoken.[26] The land "has been given by God"; it remains only to "take possession" (18:3).

The next unit (18:4–10) presents Joshua's plan, with verses 5 and 7 devoted to an account of the four tribes who have already received land distribution: Judah, Joseph (i.e. Ephraim and Manasseh), Reuben, and Gad. These four are in reality five, and thus it must once again be clarified that Levi is *not* receiving a portion of land since the priesthood is their inheritance. Joshua's plan is a good one if the

25. The verb *kavash*, which occurs only here in Joshua, is notably in a Hebrew passive form, leaving aside action taken by the Israelites.

26. Daniel Hawk (*Joshua*, 214) identifies the meeting as one in which "the holistic description of the community . . . and the specific mention of the tent of meeting combine to present Israel as a coherent community in union with [Adonai]."

land is indeed open before them without opposition. Three men of each tribe will go around to create seven partitions and bring them back so the lot can be cast to determine who will receive each portion (18:4–6). For good measure, this instruction is repeated in verse 8 before the conclusion that everything went exactly as Joshua had instructed.

Joshua 18:8–10

8 And the men arose and walked.
And Joshua commanded those who were walking
to write down the land as follows:
Go and walk around in the land,
write it down, and come back to me.
And here I will cast the lot before Adonai in Shiloh.
9 The men walked and crossed through the land
and wrote it down by cities
in seven parts in a scroll
and came back to Joshua at the camp in Shiloh.
10 Then Joshua cast the lot in Shiloh before Adonai,
And Joshua divided there the land for the Israelites,
according to their divisions.

The lines begin in verse 8 with the men getting up and walking but then backtrack to Joshua's instruction about their task, already spelled out in verses 4–5. Most of verse 8 thus repeats the instructions of Joshua to the walkers, while verse 9 presents the resolution with a few additions. The result is a piled-up list of verbs of motion braided tightly together: they "arose," "walked," "were walking," "walk around," "come back," "walked," "crossed," "came back." The last line of verse 8 is picked up in verse 10, which brings all to a satisfactory conclusion and readies the text for the lists to follow. Walking about and crossing the land happen simultaneously with writing "it" down. Written documents were mentioned earlier in the book, particularly in reference to the Teaching of Moses (1:8; 8:31, 32, 34). In this unit, *writing* occurs five times in the span of six verses (4–9) and refers to the creation of an administrative document—a fact emphasized in verse 9, which adds to the repetition of the instruction that they "wrote it down . . . in a scroll." The action of writing contrasts sharply with the actions of movement, since the two activities cannot be combined; writing can hardly occur while walking! Yet there is a deliberate emphasis on the written nature of the land distribution, which at its core may point to a historical truth.

The waters of debate concerning literacy in ancient Israel are deep indeed, and wading into them constitutes a perilous undertaking. While the opinion that literacy in ancient Israel was more widespread than generally assumed is controversial (see pp. 30–31), there is general agreement among the scholars that scribal groups and other elites during the period of the divided kingdoms produced literary documents on a sophisticated level. The reference in Joshua 18 may thus be to such a written testimony, an administrative list dating to the ninth or eighth century. The list is clearly not complete, providing thorough descriptions only for the tribe of Benjamin in the rest of the chapter (18:11–28). As Daniel Hawk notes, "Benjamin's allotment is set off from the rest by a tight organization and attention to detail that rivals that of Judah's territory."[27] It is not unthinkable that following the various devastations experienced by the kingdoms, lists that were preserved, especially for the northern tribes, were extant in fragmentary condition.

The tribal allotment for Simeon (19:1–9) presents an interesting case, scattered as its possessions are within the allotment of Judah, with nine of its towns also assigned to the Judah territory.[28] The curious nature of Simeon's territory is signaled twice, surrounding the list of its seventeen towns as a frame.

JOSHUA 19:1, 9

1 Then came out the second lot for Simeon,
for the tribe of the Simeonites in their clans.

27. Hawk, *Joshua*, 216.

28. There are eigth towns also listed in chapter 15: Moladah (15:26), Hazar-Shual (15:27), Ezem (15:29), Eltolad (15:30), Hormah (15:30), Ziklag (15:31), Ain (15:32), and Ashan (15:42).

And their inheritance was in the midst
of the inheritance of those of Judah.

. . .

9 From the plot of those of Judah
was the inheritance of the Simeonites,
for the portion of those of Judah
was too large for them,
and the Simeonites inherited
in the midst of their inheritance.

The fact of the Simeon tribe "inheriting" in the midst of Judah is stated three times with the stated reason being that the size of the Judah allotment is too big for its tribe. In reality, Simeon does not receive a region of its own, and its dwelling places are distributed amid another's tribal apportionment. It could be that the reason was the size of Judah's territory, though this is unlikely in view of the size of the regions. Another possibility is that the listing of Simeon's territory echoes the ancient words of father Jacob when he addressed the brothers Levi and Simeon together: "Cursed be their anger for it is fierce/ and their rage for it is hard;/ I will disperse them in Jacob/ and scatter them in Israel" (Gen 49:7).

The rest of chapter 19 records the heritage of Zebulon, Issachar, Asher, Naftali, and Dan, generally moving south to north, to end with a brief note about the residence assigned to Joshua. The description of the territory of Dan (19:40–48) records instability in its concluding phrase. Instead of the refrain regarding the inheritance with towns and villages, it seems to say that the Danites have lost their territory and subsequently engaged in a battle of conquest (19:47), after which the lines are added about their inheritance.[29]

29. The initial line literally reads, "Then the territory of Dan went out from them." Many translations understand this to mean that the territory was too small, but see "was lost to them" (NRSV), "slipped from their grasp"(TNK), "entging ihnen" (Martin Buber and Franz Rosenzweig, *Bücher der Geschichte: Verdeutscht von Martin Buber gemeinsam mit Franz Rosenzweig* [Cologne: Jakob Hegner, 1965], 58), and "got away from them" (Everett Fox, *The Early Prophets: Joshua, Judges, Samuel and Kings* [New York: Schocken, 2014], 98). Cf. also "verloren hun gebied" in the new Dutch translation, De Nieuwe Bij-

The concluding verses of chapter 19 report the grant of a town to Joshua. Like Caleb, Joshua receives a town of his own; unlike Caleb, he does not need to fight for his possession and dislodge fearsome inhabitants from the site. Like Caleb, he apparently made a request, although this is not directly recorded; unlike Caleb he receives the property directly from "the Israelites" on a divine command (19:49). The final verse repeats the report at the beginning and end of the opening unit with a significant difference. Whereas 18:10 put Joshua alone in charge of the casting of lots, the conclusion mentions El'azar and the heads of the ancestral houses, as in 14:1. The closing lines communicate the location once more: Shiloh, at the Tent of Meeting, where they cast the lot before Adonai. "And they finished dividing the land" (19:51).

Unique features mark the scene about assigning unclaimed land to the seven tribes, Benjamin, Simeon, Zebulon, Issachar, Asher, Naftali, and Dan. First, there is the unified presence of the Israelite "congregation" at Shiloh, a place without previous reference, where they "cause to dwell" the Tent of Meeting. The verbs and nouns used in 18:1 cast the following procedure in the light of an event marked by divine presence. Gathering or assembling in a congregation takes place in Joshua on only two other occasions: at Mount Ebal in 8:35 and subsequently in 24:1. Word usage in connection with setting up the tent (see pp. 147–48) refers back to a structure designed for meeting Adonai. In contradiction to the material leading up to it, there is no acknowledgment of remaining hostility in the rest of Canaan, and Joshua is the only one in charge of the plan and its execution. Only the concluding verse (19:51) adds El'azar and other officials. Possibly the tradition represented in these chapters dates to a separate source preserved in the current collection to account for the presence of the other tribes in the land and because a record, albeit fragmentary, remained of regions and towns once in possession of the Israelites.

---

belvertaling (NBV Studiebijbel: De Nieuwe Bijbelvertaling met Uitleg, Achtergronden en Illustraties [Heerenveen: Jongbloed, 2010], 345). The instability of Dan's landholding will return as an issue in Judges 18.

Act II: Life in the Land (Joshua 20–21)

The lists in their current form are substantially products of a Judahite author's imagination and served to organize Israelite tribal life in a distantly remembered past.[30]

The second act considers the assignment of towns inside the existing allotments in two parts: the towns of refuge and the towns provided for the Levites. Chapter 20 concerns itself with cities affording asylum from blood vengeance and is noteworthy for the elaborate description of judicial process within its brief span. Both chapters speak to organizing life in the land once tribal assignments have been made. Chapter 21 has an especially schematic character that argues against the historicity of its listing, although a historical core may underlie its current configuration. As Jeremy Hutton argues, in both lists and narratives in which Levites feature "we occasionally catch glimpses of an apparent historical reality."[31] We will concern ourselves with the special position of the Levites in biblical literature rather than the specifics of the city listings.

Act II, Scene 1: Asylum (Joshua 20)

In the context of Joshua, the provision of cities of refuge marks an important step in the conceptualization of Israel as a nation in the land.[32]

JOSHUA 20:1–3

1 Adonai spoke to Joshua as follows:
2 Speak to the Israelites and tell them:

30. Jeremy M. Hutton, "The Levitical Diaspora (II): Modern Perspectives on the Levitical Cities Lists (A Review of Opinions)," in *Levites and Priests in Biblical History and Tradition*, ed. Mark Leuchter and Jeremy M. Hutton (Atlanta: Society of Biblical Literature, 2011), 80.

31. Hutton, "The Levitical Diaspora (II)."

32. J. Gordon McConville and Stephen N. Williams, *Joshua* (Grand Rapids: Eerdmans, 2010), 81.

Appoint for yourselves towns of refuge,
of which I spoke to you all through Moses.
3 There a murderer may flee
who killed a person by mistake, without knowing,
and they will serve you as refuge from blood vengeance.

In accordance with stipulations registered in the Torah, special towns must be designated where a perpetrator of accidental homicide may find asylum (cf. Exod 21:12–14; Num 35:9–34; Deut 4:41–43; 19:1–13). The six towns mentioned in 20:7–8 are also Levitical towns, and the three on the east side of the Jordan concur with the list in Deuteronomy. The nature of the lists may follow an artificial schema, but the notion of asylum for involuntary manslaughter is interesting, together with the process by which a perpetrator of such an act could escape blood vengeance. We note that the towns are to be appointed by "the Israelites," and the task is thus not assigned to Joshua personally, as indeed is borne out in 20:7–8 by the two plural verbs: "they sanctified" and "they appointed." The detail of the process by which a person guilty of manslaughter may receive asylum is striking. First, the text specifies that the "elders" of such a designated town must give the murderer a hearing and are obligated to take him in and provide a safe place for him to live. The perpetrator is called "the murderer" three times, emphasizing the unacceptable quality of the deed, expressly forbidden in the Ten Words (Exod 20:13; Deut 5:17). At the same time, it is made clear that there was no premeditation and that the act was done "by mistake, without knowing" (20:3), repeated in verse 5 and augmented by noting the absence of a previous conflict between the parties. The town elders are expressly forbidden from handing the one who committed the homicide over to the person who pursues for vengeance.

The term for the one who pursues the killer for vengeance is literally translated "blood redeemer." The rich biblical concept of redemption, for a full exploration of which there is insufficient space in this commentary, may in general be understood to cover the notion of responsibility. Redemption in the context of property, incurrence of debt, impoverishment, and crime involves the responsibility a person takes for another or on behalf of a group in order to achieve restoration. Blood was understood to pollute the land (Num 35:33), so if blood was shed, there were people responsible for cleansing the land by following the regulations established through legal procedures and representative bodies for appropriate punishment. In addition, there was a shared ancient tradition of blood vengeance—that is to say, of a relative of the victim designated to restore justice by killing the perpetrator. Needless to say, this practice could lead to endless acts of violence, and the custom of designating places and cities for asylum was intended to curb the tradition. Regulations for the establishment of such locations occur in all the law codes of the Torah, testifying to a significant concern for the ancient community.[33]

The account in Joshua 20 is detailed about some things, like where the perpetrator shall stand and to whom he must speak, but is confusing in other ways. It looks as if verses 4–6 cover at least two occasions: one in which the killer asks for asylum and receives it; the other in which he is tried in his hometown because, in a case like this, a trial should take place, and it could hardly happen in the town where the perpetrator had found asylum since no one would know the persons involved and no witnesses could be called. Finally, there is the matter of the high priest's death. When the high priest dies in the city of refuge, a death perhaps understood to achieve atonement, the murderer is allowed to return home.

The social disaster which the provision of places offering asylum is trying to prevent is clear enough. What sort of life the one who committed accidental homicide would lead in such a town must be left to the imagination, but it can hardly have been an existence in which he found the communal acceptance so necessary for an individual's well-being in the ancient community. Unfortunately, there are no narratives extant in the Bible that afford an illustration of an actual case of blood vengeance and its prevention through asylum in a town set aside for refuge. The list of these towns may be another case of an idealized view of the harmonious existence

33. Although we have only a fictive account of a putative blood redeemer, in the narratives concerning King David's court, what becomes clear in the story is the fact that David understood the Tekoite to come to him for a ruling in the case (2 Sam 14:1–20).

of the Israelites in the land given to them by divine fiat. Finally, it is worth noting that in the final verse, the "stranger who lives as a stranger" among the community is included in the opportunity to escape blood vengeance.

Joshua 20:9

These were the agreed-upon towns
for all the Israelites and for the stranger,
who lived as a stranger among them,
to flee there, for everyone who murders by mistake,
so he will not die by the hand of the blood avenger
until he stands before the congregation.

The inclusion of outsiders in this regulation agrees with the stipulations in Numbers; their presence in the Joshua text testifies to the fact that these chapters concern life as it was to be lived in the land, expressing concerns beyond the more narrow boundaries of territorial acquisition. Life in the land, after all, was always to include many "others" and had to be lived in the light of that reality, in the past as well as in the postexilic present.

Act II, Scene 2: What's with the Levites? (Joshua 21)

One must reckon critically with what is manifestly a utopian schema in the apportioning of the enumerated cities.[34]

If we did not know it already, our review of Joshua has made clear that the Levites took up a special position among the tribes. In Joshua, their exceptional place was made clear four times in earlier chapters (13:14, 33; 14:3–4; 18:7). The ground has thus been prepared for the opening of chapter 21.

34. Hutton, "The Levitical Diaspora (II)," 47. See the same article for an overview of the different scholarly opinions on the possible historicity of the list of Levitical cities.

Joshua 21:1–3

1 Then approached the ancestral heads of the Levites
El'azar, the priest, and Joshua, the son of Nun,
and the ancestral heads of the Israelite tribes.
2 They spoke to them in Shiloh, in the land of Canaan:
Adonai commanded through Moses
to give us towns to dwell in
and their pasturelands for our cattle.
3 So the Israelites gave to the Levites from their inherited
portions
on the word of Adonai
these towns and these pasturelands.

What follows is a list of forty-eight towns divided among the tribes. Setting apart cities and pasturelands for the Levites is a stipulation found in the Torah (Num 35:1–8), where it is mentioned without further specifications except the extent of the surrounding land.[35] Other texts in the Torah note the setting aside of specific cities for the Levites and their not receiving an "inheritance" in Israel (Num 18:20; Deut 10:9). We observe that not Joshua but the Israelites as a whole are in charge of assigning the towns, just as was the case with the towns of refuge.

While I leave open the issue of the historicity of the list of Levitical towns, it is an interesting question to consider why Levi was so singled out. Even if the list has no historical core, this is not the only place where Levites receive special mention in the Torah or the Historical Books. There appear to be two main traditions concerning them and the priesthood. In one, traceable to the Deuteronomic strand of the Torah and the editors called the Deuteronomists, priest and Levite are identical. We came across this assumption in the sections of Joshua that center on the Ark, where the text mentions "the priests, the Levites"—that is, the Levitical priests (Josh 3:3; 8:33), a term used in Deuteronomy (Deut 17:9, 18; 24:8) which also puts the

35. Some argue that the Numbers text is dependent on the list in Joshua. See Nelson, *Joshua,* 238.

Levites in charge of sacrificial duties (Deut 18:1–8). Another strand of the Torah ranks Levites, other than those who are direct descendants of Aaron, below those who offer sacrifice and enter the most holy part of the sanctuary (Num 18:1–7). In Joshua, various reasons have been cited for singling them out: The burnt offerings of Adonai (13:14), Adonai himself (13:33), and the priesthood of Adonai (18:7) are all listed as the basis for their peculiar place in the community. Clearly, ambiguous and contradictory traditions cling to their ancestry, continuing into the history of biblical Israel.

While there is no possibility of here unraveling the entwined threads of the customs surrounding the Levites, the earliest material available in the Bible connects both Levi and Simeon with violence.[36] In Genesis 49, by general consensus one of the most ancient texts in the Hebrew Bible, Jacob issues declarations to his sons about their character and future. Although often identified as blessings, the poem is more accurately characterized as prophecies. The text, in many places notoriously difficult to decipher, is not complimentary about every son, but no words are as harsh as the sayings about Simeon and Levi.

GENESIS 49:5–7

5 Simeon and Levi, brothers,
gear of violence their trade.[37]
6 In their circle does not enter my being;
their assembly my honor does not join;
for in their fury they slew a man,
and by their pleasure they hamstrung an ox.

36. For an exploration of this connection, see Joel S. Baden, "The Violent Origins of the Levites: Text and Tradition," in *Levites and Priests in Biblical History and Tradition*, ed. Mark Leuchter and Jeremy M. Hutton (Atlanta: Society of Biblical Literature, 2011), 103–133.

37. The word *mekherotehem* is very difficult because it occurs only here. It may derive from Hebew *mekherah*, meaning "plan, advice." I connect it with the verb *makhar* ("to sell") and the noun *mekher* ("purchase price," "trade"). The variant is "fishnet" (*mikhmeret*). See Isa 19:8 and Hab 1:15, but that metaphor seems ill fitting.

7 Cursed be their anger, for it is fierce,
and their rage, for it is hard;
I will disperse them in Jacob
and scatter them in Israel.

The saying directly refers to the episode of Jacob's daughter Dinah and the Shechemites in Genesis 34:1–31. Simeon and Levi were the instigators of the slaughter of the Shechemites. According to this tradition, also present in Exodus 32:26–29 and Deuteronomy 33:8–11, the Levites in particular trail violence in their wake, although in the Exodus and Deuteronomy passages this characteristic is spun in a positive direction. Ambiguous and contradictory testimony makes it difficult to precisely understand the position of the Levites in ancient Israel, especially in view of the changes that position underwent over time. One of these changes proved to be enduring and is already embedded in the Deuteronomy poem, where Levi is said to be in charge of the instruction of the "ordinances" and "teachings" of God to God's people (Deut 33:10) in addition to being charged with sacrificial responsibilities. The latter, in the end, disappeared entirely from the center of the faith community that succeeded ancient Israel so that the Levites eventually came to be considered first of all as teachers and interpreters of God's *torah*.

However schematic the list may be, perhaps representing an artificial construction, there are those who leave open the possibility of a historical core for the tradition that there were cities devoted to housing the Levites, though they perhaps did not solely consist of Levites.[38] Such a view would cohere with the understanding that, originally, the land contained sanctuaries scattered throughout (see p. 147n24).

A summation concludes the chapter and this cycle, creating, in the words of Daniel Hawk, "a sense of closure by affirming the fulfillment of the promises which have driven the plot up to this point."[39] The section blithely disregards all the ragged edges that remain of

38. For such a view, see A. Graeme Auld, "The Levitical Cities: Texts and History," *ZAW* 91 (1979): 194–206.

39. Hawk, *Joshua*, 224.

conquest without occupation, of different ethnic groups remaining in the land—whether by Israelite consent or because they were unable to overcome them—and of blurry boundaries and inconsistent enumeration of regions and cities.

JOSHUA 21:43–45

43 Adonai gave to Israel the whole land
that he swore to give to their ancestors.
They took possession of it and lived in it.
44 Adonai gave them rest round about,
according to all he swore to their ancestors,
and no one stood against them of all their enemies;
Adonai gave all their enemies into their hand.
45 Not a word failed of all the good things Adonai spoke;
it all came to pass.

These lines parallel the concluding verse of chapter 11, although here there is mention of neither Joshua nor of Moses. All the credit goes to Adonai, who is the one who "gave" land, rest, and enemies into their power. To some ears, this may sound like an ironic conclusion in view of what has gone before.[40] More likely, when all is said and done, the idealistic portrayal of land possession once again takes over. While such contrasts may make us uneasy, the ancient collectors and editors let the contradictions stand.

40. So K. Lawson Younger, *Ancient Conquest Accounts*, JSOTSup 98 (Sheffield: Sheffield Academic, 1998), 347.

Cycle III: Conflict and Unification (Joshua 22–24)

The sense of ending is thus drawn out, as if to work through issues that still await resolution.[1]

While the continued existence of outsider groups presented a reality that destabilized and threatened the existence of the Israelite people, the last chapters of Joshua turn to other dangers with the potential to undermine life as a community in the land. Each chapter forms a coherent unit, but all of them are concerned with idolatry, an inherently Deuteronomic theme that dominates these final episodes. Tribal disunity connects to this concern in the sense that splintered worship causes a possible splintering of the community. I divide the material into three acts. The first, chapter 22, concerns the division of the tribes into those who live in the newly settled land and those to whom land had already been allotted by Moses east of the Jordan, with altar construction the focus of disputation and potential hostilities. The second, chapter 23, presents a farewell address by Joshua and returns to the issue of threats inherent in the existence of the outsiders within the land. It reiterates themes of gratitude, emphasizes loyalty to the God of Israel, and dictates that the people should refrain from mingling with the peoples of the land because this will lead to adopting their gods and will cause God to bring destruction upon them. Finally, the last chapter of the book, 24, describes a covenant ceremony conducted at Shechem by Joshua, who sets "statutes and rules of justice" for the people, erecting a

1. L. Daniel Hawk, *Joshua*, Berit Olam (Collegeville, MN: Liturgical Press, 2000), 227.

stone as witness (24:1–28). Concluding notes are concerned with Joshua's death and with various burials (24:29–33).

Act I: All in the Family (Joshua 22)

This chapter previews the impending intertribal tensions that will be reported in the book of Judges.[2]

Argument and disagreement, which have been on the scene heretofore in, for example, the Achan episode in chapter 7, the accord with the Gibeonites in chapter 9, and beneath the surface during the exchange with Joseph at the end of chapter 17, stand front and center in chapter 22, with the tribes on the verge of armed conflict. The divisive issue concerns altar construction by those who settled east of the Jordan, which points to the threat of idolatry looming over these final chapters. It takes a good deal of convincing by those of Reuben, Gad, and half of Manasseh before the danger of a rupture is averted.

Act I, Scene 1: Settling the Transjordanian Tribes (Joshua 22:1–10)

Membership in the community of Israel is at stake here.[3]

A first sequence (22:1–8) begins peacefully enough with Joshua calling together the tribes that had been allocated space east of the Jordan and allowing them to return to their property, bringing to a resolution the instructions in chapter 1 to aid their kin in acquiring land on the other side of the river. The first part of Joshua's address thus amounts to a commendation of Reuben, Gad, and half of Manasseh (1–3). Kinship with the tribes west of the Jordan is emphasized in phrasing that refers to them as "your kin" twice (vv. 3, 4). Subsequently, Joshua

2. Richard D. Nelson, *Joshua: A Commentary* (Louisville: Westminster John Knox, 1997), 247.

3. Robert Polzin, *Moses and the Deuteronomist: A Literary Study of the Deuteronomistic History*, vol. 1 (New York: Seabury, 1980), 237.

exhorts the Transjordanians to continue as they have begun. What they have *kept* (i.e., the commandments of Moses), they need to go on *keeping*. "You kept, you heeded, you did not abandon" is followed by "and now turn to . . . only keep firmly to do." The tail end of this admonition contains the Deuteronomic instruction "to love Adonai your God," to "walk" in God's ways and to "keep" God's "commandments," and to "cling" to God and serve God with "all your heart and being" (5). Joshua's blessing caps the short section, and it seems that all's well that ends well. But the final description emphasizes the split in the tribe of Manasseh, which lives on both the west and the east side of the Jordan, an issue that highlights potential trouble down the road. The next lines repeat the blessing and detail the wealth of the returned warriors, with words for "great/many/much" defining their goods of cattle and clothing, besides references to precious metals (8).

The last unit of this scene establishes the return with a double mention of the specific tribes involved. Reuben, Gad, and half the tribe of Manasseh frame the description.

JOSHUA 22:9–10

9 So the Reubenites returned and went
with the Gadites and half the tribe of Manasseh,
from the Israelites from Shiloh,
that is in the land of Canaan,
to go to the land of Gilead,
to the land of their holdings which they held
by the mouth of Adonai through the hand of Moses.
10 When they came to the districts of the Jordan,
that is in the land of Canaan,
the Reubenites, Gadites, and half the tribe of Manasseh
built an altar there at the Jordan,
an altar of mighty appearance.

The first part sounds redundant. Who they are, where they came from, and where they are going have been made abundantly clear. Once again, the separate geographical location emphasizes the difference between these tribes and the rest of the people. They come "from the Israelites," the rest of the tribes who are named as one entity throughout the chapter. For good measure the narrator adds "from Shiloh," a place with connotations of sanctity on account of the presence of the Tent of Meeting. Both the Israelites and the sacred presence are noted as being "in the land of Canaan." They—that is, those of Reuben, Gad, and Manasseh—"go to the land of Gilead," to their "holdings" (*ahuzzot*) rather than their "inheritances" (*nahalot*), the acquisition of which is described in Numbers and Deuteronomy (Num 21:21–35; Deut 2:24–3:22).

So far so good—until the sequel to their settling causes a kind of stutter in the account, although in itself it may not feel as shocking. So far there has been mention of an altar at Mount Ebal (Josh 8:30–31), although not in Shiloh. That there is trouble ahead is mostly signaled by the description of the altar (lit. "big to see"). Altars may be described as adhering to instructions provided in the Torah (Exod 20:24–25; Deut 27:5–6; cf. Josh 8:31), but nothing of that sort is stated here. It's simply really big. People who build really big things should be ready to be taken down a peg or two. It draws the mind to the project of Babel and its builders. The location of the altar is described as on the border, "at the Jordan," which, although vague, could point to a structure visible from the other side.

Act I, Scene 2: A Tear in the Fabric (Joshua 22:11–34)

Who belongs to Israel? Who belongs to the whole community of Israel?[4]

The next scene takes us back to the other side of the Jordan, where the "Israelites" are reported not to have seen but to have "heard" of the altar across the river. The word "Israelites" occurs three times in verse 11, begging the question of who exactly belongs to this group. The phrasing here reminds one of the Canaanite kings in earlier episodes who got ready for hostilities when they "heard" (10:1–5; 11:1–5). Just like the indigenous opponents to the Israelites, they

4. Polzin, *Moses and the Deuteronomist*, 135.

themselves now gather for battle (22:12). It sounds out of proportion to the crime committed, if crime it was, which is by no means clear. Perhaps their disproportionate reaction causes some second thoughts on the part of the Israelites, for instead of an army they send a delegation consisting of Pinhas and ten leaders who represent the ancestral houses. That there are ten leaders means that a Manassite is present, underscoring the fact that this is a matter of kin strife, tribe member against tribe member. In addition, the presence of Pinhas is ominous because of his history with the punishment of idolatrous acts in the context of the goings on at Shittim with Baal-Peor (Num 25:7–8).

Two long speeches follow, first by the delegation (22:15–20), then by the altar builders (22:22–29). The representatives of Israel refer to the building of the altar as "disloyalty" and "rebellion," words used in connection with previous activities against God, and they refer explicitly to "the sin of Peor." The word "disloyalty" recalls also the actions of Achan, whom the Israelites mention specifically in the final lines of their speech. Such actions are prone to provoke the anger of God against everyone, implying that those of Reuben, Gad, and half of Manasseh have brought danger on the entire people by building an altar (20). The reply of the Transjordanians is a masterpiece of avoidance and prevarication, beginning with a spluttering invocation of the Holy Name, followed by a bunch of "ifs," and ending in a resounding "No!" (22–25). Divided from the other tribes by the river, they were merely worried about the future and the impending separation from their kin west of the Jordan. Not *they* but *future generations* will feel themselves cut off, and those will be able to use the altar as a model for altar building and sacrifices, which they certainly do not intend to do themselves (22:24–29). No, no, this altar is meant as a "witness" (22:27, 28). It sounds odd, because usually stones suffice as a witness, but their words are a masterpiece of renaming something that loomed as a danger into a model of innocence and faithful action.

There is little doubt that there were multiple sanctuaries and altars in the early period of ancient Israel (see pp. 147n24, 159). The anxiety about worship in "one place" is Deuteronomic (Deut 12:5, 11, 21, 26; 14:24, 25; 16:6; 17:8; 18:6; 26:2); a variety of worship opportunities would naturally make it difficult to keep idolatry in check. The obvious issue of the chapter is the existence of more than one such place, but on the other hand, the text of Joshua testifies to a number of different places where sacred activities take place. It could be that the existence of an altar on the "wrong" side of the Jordan occasions the tumult, as is implied by the statement of the delegation that this piece of land may be "unclean" (19)—a term that appears only here in Joshua and may point to a Priestly tradition in the story. What is truly going on is tribal conflict, which is exacerbated by the separation created by the Jordan River. Hawk argues that the "Israelites" of the narrative are more concerned with land, while the tribes east of the Jordan care most about kinship.[5] How, then, did these concerns play a role in the period after the exile? While both perspectives continued to be significant, surrounded by continued tension, it was in the end the tie of kinship, fragile and frayed, and their common orientation to a text that preserved the descendants of ancient Israel as a community.

Apart from other considerations, this narrative, like others in the Bible, testifies to sibling rivalry—of all human conflicts one of the most cruel and destructive. The ones on the "correct" side of the Jordan, not so well established and still fighting off the outsiders that threaten them, see their siblings departing laden with loot and able to build themselves a large structure, apparently at ease enough and rich enough to do so. How dare they! Who are they that they no longer have to fight for their land? And what kind of land is it? Is it really the land promised by God? Sure, it was given by God through Moses, but that's now some time ago, and there they are staring across the Jordan from their ostentatious altar! "And Cain said to his brother Abel. . . . And when they were in the field, Cain arose against his brother Abel and slew him" (Gen 4:8). It has not come that far yet, but it will.

5. Hawk, *Joshua*, 229: "The tribes west of the Jordan equate national identity with *the possession of land*, particularly the land west of the Jordan. . . . The eastern tribes regard *bonds of kinship* as more definitive for Israelite identity than the possession of specific territory and are concerned to preserve these bonds."

Act II: The State of the Nation (Joshua 23)

Chapter 23 modifies the totally positive outlook of 21:43–45 to conform to the reality of the rest of Israel's story in the land.[6]

The entirety of Joshua 23 consists of a speech in the Deuteronomic style and theme. It emphasizes the great deeds of God on behalf of the people and sets out to warn them about the importance of keeping strict boundaries between themselves and those who remain in the land, "the peoples that remain with you" (7). Mingling with "what is left of these peoples" (12) will lead to idolatry, which will stir up God's wrath so that they and their land will perish. In considering his own death (14), Joshua looks toward possible futures for the people, both positive and negative.

Following a summary statement about the peaceful state of the people in their land (v. 1), which reiterates 21:43–45, Joshua's farewell address opens with a declaration about his age ("I am old and advanced in years"), a theme picked up again in verse 14: "See, I am going today the way of all the earth." Other individuals who announce their old age are Isaac (Gen 27:2), Naomi (Ruth 1:12), and Samuel (1 Sam 12:2), and in all these cases the news carries a negative implication. Before he goes to his grave, Joshua points out some crucial aspects of life in the land, the overriding one of which, in contradiction to the opening verse, is the continued existence of "these peoples" (3, 7, 12, 13), "remaining nations" (4), "great and mighty peoples" (9) in the land where "all Israel" now lives. The land is "their inheritance," but it is not yet wholly theirs. Nor will it be unless they can also make the people as well as the land their inheritance, which they can only do by keeping themselves strictly apart from "these peoples who are still with you" (23:12), because mingling with them, or marrying them (God forbid!), will occasion their falling into idolatry. They must "cling" to their God, otherwise they will "perish away from this good land" Adonai has given to them.

6. Nelson, *Joshua*, 259.

The speech consists of a series of admonitions to "be strong" (6), as Joshua was once himself commissioned to "be strong" and not to veer from the written instruction of Moses (1:7–8). The terminology for refraining from idolatry and for serving God alone is Deuteronomic, as is the theme of the speech. God has done such and such for them; now they must render back, trusting that God will bring the beginning to successful completion, or else. The state of the nation is still fragile, and only the strictest loyalty will maintain them in the land. Those who entered this speech into the composition of Joshua did so, no doubt, in the awareness of their loss, and they issued the warnings in a new context so they could maintain themselves and their small holding even as servants of a foreign power.

Act III: A Covenant at Shechem (Joshua 24)

Is it possible that Israel established some sort of rapprochement with the inhabitants of the city?[7]

For the most part, this chapter presents a long speech by Joshua reviewing selected events of the past concerning the ancestors, the exodus, and the allocation of tribal territories on both sides of the Jordan. The climax of the speech is the call for those who are present to make a choice of allegiance to the God of Israel: "Choose for yourselves today whom you will serve" (15). The speech is followed by a covenant and witness ceremony, after which Joshua sends everyone home, "each man to his inheritance" (28). The chapter, together with the entire book of Joshua, is rounded off by a brief account of Joshua's death and burial and two other burial notes (29–33).

7. Hawk, *Joshua*, 266.

Act III, Scene I: Code of Conduct (Joshua 24:1–28)

Reminding people that God is holy reminds them that God is someone you can't mess with.[8]

Chapter 23 would have made a suitable ending for the book, with the official representatives of Israel gathered by Joshua, but his encouragements and warnings there do not meet with a response from the people, and thus the last line of that speech leaves an opening for further transactions. Chapter 24 provides an elaboration on God´s gifts to Israel and pursues the issue of what it means to be loyal to Adonai alone. Like chapter 23, it contains a review, but this time it is of the more distant past as the basis to posit a demand that requires a response. Demand and response are formulated three times before a concluding action can take place.[9]

An introductory verse locates the gathering of the tribes in Shechem, where the representatives of the people "stood before God," indicating Shechem as a location of a sanctuary. The Shechem region was also the place in an earlier episode where a sacred event took place in the presence of the Ark (Josh 8:30–35; see p. 111), an event many scholars associate with this final chapter. Without further ado, Joshua begins to speak in the name of God, usually a feature of prophetic speech, so that the words following for the most part present the Deity speaking in the first person. The speech, which forms the first sequence (24:2–13), contains a review of the past in three parts: God's gift of offspring to the ancestors in Canaan (2–4); God's dealings with Egypt followed by God's gift of the Transjordan (5–10); and God's gift of Canaan (11–13). In each section, the verb "give" dominates divine action. In the Egypt unit, this verb is substituted by "I did" and "I led out" (5, 6, 7). Altogether, there are twenty-one verbs with God as subject in these twelve verses.

8. John Goldingay, *Joshua, Judges and Ruth for Everyone* (Louisville: Westminster John Knox, 2011), 24.

9. For detailed analyses of the chapter see Hawk, *Joshua,* 261–81; and Nelson, *Joshua,* 262–83.

Rhetorically the speech serves to present the good gifts of God to Israel: of offspring, deliverance, and land. The review is economical and touches only on the salient points of God's largesse toward Israel. Following the brief review of the ancestors' sojourn in Canaan and the eventual emigration to Egypt, the style moves to personal address, first alternating with references to "your ancestors" but eventually moving to a complete identification of the gathering in Joshua's presence with those who escaped from Egypt and lived in the wilderness: "I led your ancestors out of Egypt/ and you came to the sea./ The Egyptians pursued your ancestors . . ./ . . ./ they cried . . ./ your eyes saw . . ./ . . ./ you dwelt in the wilderness" (24:6–7). It's all between "me" (God) and "you" (people) and leads up to God delivering the land to them.

Joshua 24:12–13

12 I sent the hornet ahead of you;
it drove out before you the two Amorite kings—
not by your sword or your bow.
13 And I gave to you a land
for which you did not labor,
and cities you did not build:
you lived in them;
vineyards and olive groves you did not plant:
you ate from them.

This powerful review, which ignores any efforts the Israelites may have made on their own behalf, ascribing everything to the hand of Adonai alone, raises a number of questions. The reference to Terah and Abraham mentions that "they served other gods" before God took Abraham and began to shower him and his descendants with gifts (2). The service of "other gods" can be found elsewhere in the Torah, mostly in Deuteronomy, and is mentioned elsewhere in the Historical Books, but it is never used in connection with the patriarchs outside of this verse, where it provides an essential link with the demand made of the people at Shechem in verse 15 to "put aside the gods your ancestors served." In addition, the recital has significant omissions: *the promise* of land made to the ancestors according to Torah tradition is missing, as is mention of the *Sinai covenant* and the entire experience there, as well as the miraculous *crossing of the Jordan*, to name the most glaring ones. *Moses* receives scant mention outside of one reference in verse 5, where he is named alongside Aaron. As observed, virtually no action is ascribed to the people, and there is no mention of past rebellion and disloyal behavior. One hears of "chiefs of Jericho," who along with other groups provided resistance—a picture that is inconsistent with the narrative in Joshua. A different tradition may be at work in this chapter, as many have argued, or it may be that only the most relevant matters are touched on, which consist of God's delivering, benevolent action on behalf of the people, who did nothing to be the recipients of such largesse but who now need to face the demands that such gracious activity on the part of the Deity puts on them. One might think that reminders of past disloyalty and idolatry would have served well in this context, especially the Sinai and golden calf episode, but these are simply missing apart from the reference to the remote ancestors who "served other gods."

A second sequence (23:14–24) turns to demand and response, signaled by the words "and now."

Joshua 24:14

And now, be in awe of Adonai
and serve him in wholeness and truth.
Put aside the gods your ancestors served,
across the Great River and in Egypt,
and serve Adonai.

Altogether, Joshua issues seven straightforward commands, culminating in the charge to "choose." In the sequence, tacking back and forth from demand to response (14–24), the root "to serve" repeats thirteen times. The first response from the people is entirely positive, strongly avowing disinclination to "abandon" their God in order to "serve other gods" and stating in creedal fashion their convictions about what God has done for them: "The people responded and said:/ Far be it from us to abandon Adonai/ and serve other gods. . . ./ Adonai drove out all the peoples,/ the Amorites who lived in the land in our presence./ We also will serve Adonai,/ for He is our God" (16, 18).

The pledge in verse 16 ("far be it from us to abandon and serve other gods") turns into the positive "we also will serve Adonai, for He is our God" at the end of 18, framing the reasons on which they base their commitment. They reiterate the great deeds of Adonai as the basis for their promise, deeds that concerned the "ancestors" but that are recited as affecting those present: "God . . . brought *us* up," etc. The people's avowal provokes a negative and threatening reiteration of the demand by Joshua, eliciting a simple repetition of the people's promise (21). Upon this second response, Joshua declares the matter a legal one, calling the people to be witnesses against themselves that they have made their choice: "You have chosen." The people give the required response that they are indeed witnesses, and still Joshua exhorts them to "put away the foreign gods in your midst" (22–24). The people have the last word with their pledge that they will serve Adonai alone and that they will "listen" to God's voice, a pledge reminiscent of the one made by the community at Sinai (cf. Exod 24:7).[10]

Finally, in a third sequence (24:25–28), the last pledge judged satisfactory, Joshua ratifies the decision and makes a covenant; literally, "He cut a covenant for the people on that day" (25). This is not a *renewal* of the Sinai covenant or of any other covenant.[11] The

10. On the importance of translating the Hebrew *shama* with "listen" rather than "obey," see Johanna W. H. van Wijk-Bos, *Making Wise the Simple: The Torah in Christian Faith and Practice* (Grand Rapids: Eerdmans, 2005), 18.

11. Assumptions that the occasion is one of *covenant renewal* are numerous. Such a celebration was first argued by Artur Weiser in his influential commentary on the Psalms (*The Psalms*, trans. Herbert Hartwell, OTL [Philadelphia: Westminster, 1962], 23–51), which appeared in the late fifties in Germany and in English in 1962, whereupon an ancient Israelite liturgical celebration of regular covenant renewal was assumed to have existed and reference to it has been repeated in many scholarly works. There is no evidence in the Hebrew Bible that there ever was a covenant renewal festival, and Weiser's arguments suffer from circular reasoning by which the texts he

covenant made by Joshua constitutes the pledge of the assembled people to devote themselves to the service of Adonai alone to the exclusion of worship of "other gods." He makes the covenant on their behalf as a permanent commitment, writing down "statute and justice" in Shechem in "the scroll of the Teaching of God" (with another conspicuous omission of a reference to Moses!), and erects a stone to mark the occasion. Once all is completed to satisfaction, Joshua can send the people each to their own location.

The opening of the chapter presents a gathering of "all the tribes," with important representatives standing "before God." Joshua's address, however, is "to all the people" (24:2). The issue obviously concerns idolatry and the choice the people must make in God's presence of total and exclusive loyalty to Adonai alone. They make this choice on the basis of God's gracious actions toward them in the more remote as well as the recent past. God is not a party to this pledge as God was at Sinai; God is not pledging anything, for God has already done everything, with the people playing the role of recipient. It is now time for them to step up to the plate and provide the proper response, which is to "put aside the gods the ancestors served," also called "other gods" and "foreign gods" (2, 14, 15, 20, 23), for those gods belong "on the other side." Still, we may wonder. Idolatry, so significant in Deuteronomy and to the editors named after that book, has so far not taken up a prominent place in Joshua and occurs in this particular phrasing for the first time in chapter 23:16 (cf. 23:7, 13). Where do these gods come from? Why do they take on such significance in these last chapters?

---

analyzed on behalf of his thesis were used both as hypothesis and proof for the theory. References to Joshua 24 as a covenant renewal may be found in, for example, Robert G. Boling and G. Ernest Wright, *Joshua: A New Translation and Commentary* (New York: Doubleday, 1982), 544; Jerome F. D. Creach, *Joshua*, Interpretation: A Bible Commentary for Teaching and Preaching (Louisville: Westminster John Knox, 2003), 82; Thomas W. Mann, *The Book of the Former Prophets* (Eugene, OR: Cascade, 2001), 43; J. Gordon McConville and Stephen N. Williams, *Joshua*, The Two Horizons Old Testament Commentary (Grand Rapids: Eerdmans, 2010), 91; J. Alberto Soggin, *Joshua: A Commentary* (Philadelphia: Westminster, 1972), 231; Marten H. Woudstra, *The Book of Joshua* (Grand Rapids: Eerdmans, 1981), 340, 356.

Intermarriage, a significant concern in Deuteronomy, is mentioned for the first time in 23:12. I suggest that for these last chapters, the reality of the "remaining peoples" in the land takes on greater force than before. This reality has been mentioned often enough but mostly as an observation without possible consequences. It is a reality that will become central in Judges, and thus it fits well here in the final sections of Joshua. In this context, the overriding importance of "putting away other/foreign gods" points to the possibility that Joshua 24 reflects the inclusion of groups originally not a part of the invading kinship units. If there are indeed connections between the covenant making at Shechem and the celebration at Mount Ebal in Joshua 8, we recall that the "stranger" was notably present among those assembled to witness the ceremonies there and to listen to the "Teaching, the blessing as well as the curse" (Josh 8:33–34).

Joshua's review of the past in chapter 24 is a history lesson that mentions only what is salient and should cause adherence to the God who gives and delivers. The consistent address in the second person plural points to the complete embrace of those who have joined the "children of Israel" in one community. Joshua is here acting as the true successor of Moses, creating the motley crowd into a community with clear commitments to adhere to the God of Israel alone and to listen to God's voice, thus in truth forming a new beginning to the adventure of becoming God's people. Biblical scholar John Goldingay argues that one of the odd features of Shechem as a location is that there is no record in Joshua of a fight there or an attack on the city and that this is an occasion where "such people" made their commitment to the God of Israel, "the whole community doing what Rahab did." I agree with Goldingay that this would "fit in with other indications that the Israelites' becoming a settled and united people in Canaan was not just a matter of Israel killing off or chasing off its previous inhabitants."[12] Clearly, it was important to include others in the Teaching of God, to which they could subscribe if they abandoned their service to other gods.

12. Goldingay, *Joshua, Judges and Ruth*, 87.

Act III, Scene 2: Grave Matters (Joshua 24:29–33)

Remembering burials and land purchases . . . are ways for a people to claim land and identity, similar in function to battle reports and topographic lists.[13]

A final scene forms a fitting conclusion to the book with the mention of the death of Joshua, who has played the role of commander, priest and administrator, and who only now is called "the servant of Adonai." His age and burial place get mention as well as an additional note on the faithfulness of the people in his time and for a period following, because "they knew the work that Adonai had done for Israel" (24:31). After that period, as we already suspect, things will not go so well. Another loose end is picked up with the burial of Joseph's bones according to a stipulation made in Exodus 13:19. Shechem is the place where Jacob had bought a field (Gen 33:19). We know of other events that took place in Shechem that are not so positive (Gen 34:1–31), and this note thus brings an accent of ambiguity back into the tale that first seemed to end peacefully. Finally, the death of the priest El'azar, who has played a significant role in the preceding episodes, gets mention, as well as his burial place, Gibeah. Where Shechem casts a shadow backward and forward (Judg 9:1–49), Gibeah has echoes that resound into the future (Judg 19–20; 1 Sam 11–26).

13. Nelson, *Joshua*, 279.

Looking Back

From the first chapter to the last, the book of Joshua has presented its story in an arc that leads from God commissioning Joshua to be faithful to Moses's Teaching to Joshua pledging the people to be faithful to the Teaching of God. Joshua's commission to be strong and courageous and to listen to the instruction delivered to him sets in motion the story of compromise and concessions to inhabitants next to armed conflict and deeds of horrific violence. Liturgical processions and celebrations punctuate the attempts to settle the land, and constant reminders of the existence of other peoples among them "to this day" bring to awareness the fact that the Israelites live there with others, at times in deliberate inclusion and at other times faced with the inability to overcome and annihilate them. There is always the "stranger" in their midst who is also listening, first perhaps on the outskirts of the camp, but before they know it inside the "gates," present in the assembly.

It's a story of group activity with, now and then, exceptional individuals poking through the fabric of communal achievement and their names taking their place among the ranks of remembered ancestors. One of them, the Canaanite prostitute Rahab, becomes a model of fidelity to a pair of invaders in a tight spot and receives "loyalty" for "loyalty" when her town falls into Israelite hands. Caleb, the one Israelite who in the wilderness had proven faithful together with Joshua, comes to claim an inheritance, and his daughter Achsa boldly demands the possibility of productive land. The daughters of Zelofhad once again step forward to demand that the leaders make good on the promise they received to inherit land as offspring of a man who had only daughters. Amid the grim business of war and slashing swords, the Gibeonites, with their moldy food, tattered clothes, and worn wineskins, neatly trick the conquering horde.

Conquest accounts give way to distribution lists and memories of anticipated, once-inhabited possessions, lost again in the end. Some lists are better organized than others; some are more complete; many are ragged at the edges. Nothing, to be sure, happened according to the vision that "Joshua took the entire country . . . and the land had rest from war" (Josh 11:23; 14:15; 18:1; 21:44; 23:1), for references to powerful and hostile groups remaining in the land point to a messy reality fraught with obstacles and an uncertain future (Josh 13:13; 15:63; 16:10; 17:12, 16). The final chapters bring to mind anxious questions regarding intertribal tensions and the possibility of exclusive adherence to the God of Israel, thereby providing a fitting opening for the next chapter in their history. Judges will unfold in full the difficulties occasioned by life in a land that is not wholly theirs—the result of the inability to live in exclusive loyalty to Adonai—as well as the friction that exists among those who believe themselves kin but whose first loyalty is more to clan and tribe than to a larger entity.

Latecomers to the story and outsiders to the memories preserved in these texts, as we are, may wonder what we can take from the accounts in terms of guidance or inspiration for our lives as communities and individuals. In many places, the biblical accounts remind one of rabbinical discussions in the Talmud, where conflicting arguments are presented side with side without arbitration to judge who is right or more accurate, more inspiring or more true to the text. Similarly, we must read and interpret biblical texts without the benefit of a final arbiter. Ancient conquest accounts depicting human violence and atrocity have been and still are chosen to sanction imperialist and racist undertakings and to privilege the conqueror. Today such cannot be the road to interpreting a text like Joshua for people of goodwill who consider it their ethical and religious mandate to create a human community of greater equality and less violence than the world currently has. The text argues with itself as to what is taking place, and we are free to make our choice, whether for violence and exclusion, to which the text witnesses, or for loyalty and kindness—the Teaching of wholeness and peace of a community that includes the stranger inside its gates.

JUDGES

Delivering the Land

Introduction

Content

When all hell breaks loose, when the militia volunteer, bless Adonai.[1]

A lengthy introduction (1:1–3:6) sets the stage for what is to follow, beginning with the efforts of the Judah tribe, joined by Simeon, to establish itself in its territory. Judah is depicted as successful (1:1–20), but its achievement is followed by a list of failures on the part of the tribes who did not accomplish the goal of driving out the resident occupants and therefore had to be content to live "among" the inhabitants (1:27–36). "The Canaanites lived among them" and "they lived among the Canaanites" (1:29, 30, 32, 33). The introductory chapters underline the distinction between the generation that benefitted from Joshua's guidance and those who came after: "And a new generation arose after them/ and did not know Adonai/ or the work he had done for Israel" (2:10). The Joshua text has prepared the ground well both for the reality of living "among the Canaanites" and for the possibility of abandoning the worship of the God of Israel and serving other gods, together with the harmful consequences (Josh 24:1–26, esp. 20).

In the main part, Judges tells the stories of individual leaders, identified as divinely appointed "saviors" or "judges," who go on military campaigns to guarantee a period of peace after the Israelites have been subjected to hostile forces, which as often as not originate from outside the land (Judg 3:7–16:31). In the opening section, these characters are introduced as "judges" (*shofetim*), a word from a root with

1. Marc Zvi Brettler, *The Book of Judges* (London: Routledge, 2002), 73.

a wide range of meanings, from administering or providing justice, to passing judgment, to ruling (2:16). Yet few of the protagonists in the narratives receive this title (although a number of them are said to "have judged" Israel). Some of these characters receive only a few lines, beginning with Otniel and Shamgar (3:7–11, 31), continuing with Tola and Ya'ir (10:2, 3), and concluding with Ibsan, Elon, and Avdon (12:8, 11, 13). Another set function as central figures in detailed stories of violent conflict—sometimes military campaigns, sometimes acts of deceit to vanquish the foe—beginning with Ehud of Benjamin (3:15–30); followed by Deborah and Barak of Naftali (chs. 4–5), who are aided by Yael, a Kenite woman; Gideon of Manasseh (6:11–8:32); Jefta of Gilead in the Transjordan (11:1–12:7), perhaps also a Manassite; and, finally, Samson of Dan (13:2–16:31). In between the actions of Gideon and Jefta, about midway through the book, Gideon's son Abimelek enforces royal rule (9:1–57), an adventure that does not end well, with Abimelek the first of the Israelite leaders to die a violent death (9:53–54). Although it is difficult to find a representative of each tribe in the combined list of "major" and "minor" leaders, their total does number twelve.

The final chapters, Judges 17–21, feature narratives with prominent roles played by individuals, most of them nameless, as well as tribes. Micah of Ephraim serves to depict a situation of cultic confusion and is a foil for an unnamed Levite (17:6) who joins a band of roving and pillaging Danites (ch. 18). Another Levite appears in chapter 19 as the protagonist in a sordid tale of rape and murder which eventually leads to intertribal warfare (chs. 20–21). The book ends with the observation "in those days there was no king in Israel," a refrain that occurs four times in the final five chapters, twice with the added notation that "everyone did what was right in their own eyes" (17:6; 18:1; 19:1; 21:25).[2]

Judges contrasts starkly with Joshua in terms of content. The forces of hostility and danger, though mentioned in Joshua, appear in full force in Judges to paint the Israelites as an embattled group, struggling to maintain itself against the odds. The genre of conquest

2. Literally, the phrase reads, "In those days there was no king in Israel;/ every man would do what was right in his eyes." Outside of Judges, the phrase "a man" doing "what is right in his eyes" occurs only in Deut 12:8. For further discussion, see pp. 187–88, 191, 277, 286 below.

account, so prevalent in certain chapters of Joshua, is thus missing; the *herem* receives only rare mention. There are very few gatherings of the people as a whole in either a cultic setting or for a secular purpose. The cultic acts referred to do not always conform to expectation; the Ark, a central unifying symbol of divine presence in Joshua, is virtually absent, mentioned only in passing in one of the final chapters (20:27). As Amit has observed, there is no sense here of a central place of worship, no reference to a scroll with the Teaching of Moses.[3] On the other hand, the presence of Adonai permeates the stories. God seems to be everywhere, accessible to everyone. Rather than the Deity communicating through one leader as in Joshua, Deity and individuals—as well as groups—interact continuously, albeit in sometimes fraught circumstances. In the confessional section of chapter 10, there is no mention of representatives approaching God, whether leaders, elders, heads of ancestral houses, or priests. At the beginning, the ones who inquire of Adonai about leadership are called "the Israelites." Those who cry out and confess their wrongdoing are also "the Israelites," and God addresses the entire people (10:10–15). Only in chapters 20 and 21 is there mention of the "congregation" or "assembly," of leaders, of a priest, and of customs of worship (20:1–2, 28; 21:10, 13, 16), but even then, as often as not, the gathering is referred to as "the Israelites" (20:18, 26–27; 21:1–5).

Historical Setting of Events

You may imagine then that this Book of Judges is not pleasant to read—much of it is quite ghastly.[4]

The children loved it.[5]

3. Yairah Amit, *The Book of Judges: The Art of Editing*, trans. Jonathan Chipman, BibInt 38 (Leiden: Brill, 1999), 367.

4. From T. Rhondda Williams, *Old Testament Stories in a Modern Light: A Bible Guide for the Young* (London: T&T Clark, 1911), 66–67; cited in David M. Gunn, *Judges* (Oxford: Blackwell, 2003), 9.

5. Bertram F. Simpson, *The Story of the Bible* (c. 1938), 281; as cited in Gunn, *Judges*, 9.

The events narrated in Judges take place following the death of Joshua and the first tentative conquest of the land before the beginning of the first millennium BCE. In terms of historical time, the period actually covers approximately 150 years up until the end of the eleventh century BCE, although the total of accumulated time in the text itself amounts to more than 400 years. The period forms a bridge between the initial entry of the Israelites into the land and the establishment of the monarchy as told in the books of Samuel. In contrast with Joshua, where Israel is the aggressor, Judges portrays the tribes as falling victim to hostility and oppression, sometimes from peoples inside their borders but predominantly from those outside Canaan. This situation is ascribed by the narrator to the people's failure to abide by their sworn loyalty to Adonai and their falling prey to idol worship (2:11–3:6). The campaigns of various hostile groups are thus the means by which God punishes the people and at the same time attempts to woo them back, to change their faithless ways. God's response to the people's cries of distress is to send a "savior/deliverer," who rises up to create resistance and defeat the enemy, upon which there follows a period of peace, marked at times by the phrase "then rested the land for . . . years" (3:11, 30; 5:31; 8:28; cf. Josh 11:23; 14:15).

The opening chapters establish the turbulence of a situation, already prepared for in Joshua, in which total conquest of all the indigenous inhabitants of Canaan by invaders from outside has proved to be unsuccessful, so that either by choice or force the fledgling nation is consigned to live among different ethnic groups in the land (see pp. 141–42, 146, 148, 174, 176–77 above). As long as there was strong leadership, represented by Joshua and those around him (the priests, leaders, heads of ancestral houses, etc.), the situation was containable or contained, but as the beginning of Judges makes clear, Joshua's death left a vacuum, and there was no one to take his place. Individuals are thus appointed by God to act for a specific military purpose at a given time. These leaders who appear in the central section of the book are depicted as active on a local rather than a national level. They put out the fires that are burning at the time, but they establish no central leadership, and the one attempt to achieve this goal falters (9:1–53). At times, the saviors sent by God are "unlikely heroes," as, for example, left-handed Ehud (3:15–30), the female Deborah (4:1–16), or the outcast Jefta (11:1). Regularly, however, they are persons of standing in the community, beginning with Otniel, whom we already met as a landowner in Joshua (Judg 1:13; 3:9); the prophet Deborah, who is depicted as dispensing justice even before she joins Barak on the battlefield (Judg 4:1–5:31); and Gideon, a son of a family of some means (6:11–8:32), himself in possession of multitudinous offspring (8:30), a signifier of wealth. Two of the minor judges listed in chapter 12 are similarly described (12:8–15).[6]

Following the exploits of Samson—who is said to have "judged Israel" for twenty years but during whose time there is no mention of peace or prosperity in the face of Philistine aggression (16:31)—the closing section of the book (chs. 17–21), although filled with violent and immoral activity on a sociopolitical and religious level, veers away from the focus on charismatic, episodic leaders to depict turmoil and intertribal conflict. Yet according to some perspectives, the situation, especially as painted in chapters 19–21, portrays more tribal cooperation and combined actions against injustice than anything that came before. Somehow, against the odds, something like a people was able to establish itself and find enough cohesion and stability to continue its existence in the land with the possibility of a future.

The period, though hard to reconstruct with historical verisimilitude, assumes for the Israelites localized leadership in the political realm and the absence of a standing army, with ad hoc military forces, at times poorly equipped and faced with enemies in possession of superior weaponry and organization. Socially, the context appears rural-agricultural, centered on clan and tribal kinship ties, accompanied by the cooperation as well as the conflict that such

6. Some commentaries classify all the judges in the mold of "unlikely hero." So, for example, J. Cheryl Exum in her essay, "The Centre Cannot Hold: Thematic and Textual Instabilities in Judges," in *Reconsidering Israel and Judah: Recent Studies on the Deuteronomistic History*, ed. Gary N. Knoppers and J. Gordon McConville (Winona Lake, IN: Eisenbrauns, 2000), 580. See also Susan Niditch (*Judges*, OTL [Louisville: Westminster John Knox, 2008], 3–4), who identifies the judges as "social bandits." Such classifications paint the different characters with too broad a brush.

ties may bring. As observed by many commentators, the tales are notable for the presence of women. In the words of Tammi Schneider, "One of the major components affecting the evaluation of the judges is the role of women in their lives."[7] Women walk through the stories in all their complexity, as leaders, schemers, and seducers, as perpetrators and victors, as family members and as victims of collective violence. The fluctuations in the depiction of women in Judges may testify to a period when their function and role in the social and economic setting had a degree of fluidity, when appreciation of deeds of valor and violence was not limited by rigid perceptions of gender boundaries.

Historical Period of Composition and Themes of the Text

In spite of her continual disobedience, she survived, and, more often than not, thrived.[8]

The world proposed in Judges is stamped by the search of the people of Israel for a successful life in the promised land.[9]

Like Joshua, Judges was not composed in the period of which it tells, the twelfth or eleventh century BCE, but was compiled and edited from older existing materials at a much later date. Its final shape and placement may date to the postexilic period, although it is possible that an early edition was created in the late eighth or early seventh century BCE in the aftermath of the destruction of the Northern Kingdom by Assyria in 722, as argued by biblical scholar Yairah Amit.[10] In either case, disintegration and cataclys-

7. Tammi Schneider, *Judges*, Berit Olam (Collegeville, MN: Liturgical Press, 2000), xiv.

8. Robert Polzin, *Moses and the Deuteronomist: A Literary Study of the Deuteronomic History*, vol. 1 (New York: Seabury, 1980), 211.

9. Susanne Gillmayr-Bucher, *Erzählte Welten im Richterbuch: Narratologische Aspekte eines Polyfonen Diskurses* (Leiden: Brill, 2013), 9; translation mine.

10. Amit, *Judges*, 364. The point is argued most cogently in a close

mic destruction provided both impetus for and influence on the shape of the book. Theoretically, the book of Samuel could have served as a continuation of Joshua, and it was not strictly necessary to devote an entire scroll to the period leading up to the beginnings of the monarchy, so there must have been compelling reasons to provide accounts of the years in which the tribes were still struggling to guarantee an existence for themselves in land on which they had only a tentative grasp. Teasing out these reasons, which gets the reader closer to the main theme or themes of the book, is no easy task; witness the multitude of varying responses in commentary and interpretation.

We may assume that the story collection in Judges served the general urge to preserve the memories of the past in order to reestablish and solidify the identity of a fragile and threatened community and to redefine its relationships vis-à-vis one another, its God, and its land in the aftermath of the traumatic experience of exile (see pp. 23–25, 28). Ancient hero accounts extant in oral and written form needed to be collected into a cohesive whole. The ancient date of the so-called Song of Deborah in chapter 5 is virtually undisputed, but also other material—such as, for example, the Samson stories, portraying one of the most gratuitously violent and amoral of the main characters—breathes the air of ancient storytelling, drawing the reader deeper and deeper into its twists and turns until its ending. There was most likely general comfort experienced by a diminished and subjected people in preserving these memories. Unexpected swashbuckling heroes, such as left-handed protagonists like Ehud, the tent-dwelling woman Yael, or the rogue judge Samson, certainly also fulfilled the desire to entertain as well as to enlighten. In addition, as reviewed in the introduction (see p. 7), remembrance of the past provides guidelines for a future filled with uncertainty and thus holds up standards to follow and contains warnings about what paths to avoid.

---

analysis of the text of Judges: "We may argue with equal plausibility that Judges reflects the literary materials that influenced the shaping of Deuteronomy and its school and that its own composition preceded the reign of Josiah."

About the actual historical existence of the characters depicted in Judges or the historical realities underlying the period, it is extremely difficult to speak with certainty. There must have been a stage between the first attempts to settle the land and the establishment of the monarchy in the tenth century. The portrait of communities out of which something like a nation under central leadership came into existence is likely not wholly inaccurate. The way Judges presents the situation—the presence of hostile groups both inside and outside the land in periods of land scarcity, the spontaneous and localized nature of military and administrative leadership to fight off hostile forces, the ad hoc nature of raising a fighting force, agricultural customs, a social context in which women lived less circumscribed lives and could step outside of the roles defined by the patriarchal family, the absence of any kind of centralized worship, the fragmented nature of kinship ties among the tribes—all these sound as if they could have been possibilities in the less settled world of the days before the monarchy, "when there was no king in Israel and everyone did what was right in their own eyes." It is not a "chronicle of ancient history" but history written as mythos peopled by characters larger than life.[11]

It is possible that none of the characters, women or men, actually lived in this ancient period, but it is equally possible that people *like* them were at some point significant for the period. It is difficult to imagine that a woman like Deborah, a female leader in an administrative as well as military sense, would have been invented out of whole cloth at a later date, especially in the community of the restoration.[12] I understand the main characters in Judges to be

11. Susan Ackerman's (*Warrior, Dancer, Seductress, Queen: Women in Judges and Biblical Israel* [New York: Doubleday, 1998], 14) observations in this regard—maintaining that Judges is best not analyzed as a "chronicle of ancient history"; that, to her view, "no historical reality . . . underlies the narratives"; and that "none of the women actors of these stories actually lived"—miss the point of ancient history writing and the importance of the category of mythos. See pp. 2–3, 11n23 above.

12. Ackerman's (*Warrior, Dancer*, 14) question in regard to Deborah ("Can we really imagine warrior women thriving within the context of Israel's highly androcentric culture?") is thus illogical, since Israelite society certainly

folk heroes indeed, much like the sea heroes from the seventeenth century remembered in my country of origin: historical figures augmented by legends and folktales until they are larger than life.

Opinions on the central theme or "editorial guideline" of Judges differ widely.[13] While the book concerns itself clearly with leadership, it presents different examples of governance. Some of the judges are deceitful (Ehud and Yael), some hesitant (Barak and Gideon), some overweening (Abimelek), some overstep the boundaries of acceptable behavior (Jefta and Samson), and the whole thing ends with an example of revolting torture and murder followed by violent conflict among the tribes. The entire period is marked by abandonment of central commitments to Adonai, with the people engaging in the worship of "other" gods—a result of miscegenation with the peoples of the land—or at best a blurring of the boundaries that constitute the worship of Adonai alone. Although often characterized as a book of repentance, punishment, and deliverance, there is very little actual repentance in Judges. The people are said "to cry out" when things go ill for them, upon which cry God sends a savior (Judg 3:9, 15; 4:3; 6:6, 7; 10:12), but the one time they make a confession that they have "sinned" (Judg 10:10, 15) and implore God to help them, there is a sarcastic response (Judg 10:14) from the Deity. The evaluative comments from the narrator in the final chapters that there was "no king in Israel" twice accompanied by the phrase "everyone did what was right in their own eyes" (17:6; 18:1; 19:1; 21:25), one of which concludes the entire book, could lead in the direction of an argument on behalf of kingship as the one element lacking in restoring the community to its true task of living as God's people. The course that lies ahead will of course include kingship, but that fact does not entirely clarify the intention of the statement.

---

did not become less androcentric as time went on. If no historical reality underlies such a figure, how does one explain its invention in such a culture?

13. For the concept and analysis of the "editorial guideline" of Judges, see Amit, *The Book of Judges*, 9. Amit proposes the double guideline of "sign" and "leadership" for the book. She understands the "sign" guideline to consist of a "five-stage model—sin, punishment, crying out, deliverance, peace" (36).

Many scholars are of the opinion that the disintegration evident in the final chapters combined with this narrative comment leads directly to the approval of kingship, specifically Davidic kingship. Others view the final scenes as a victory of order and appropriate behavior, albeit including punitive methods of tribal organization.[14] Thus biblical scholar Susan Niditch declares, "The section ends with a victory, the cessation of hostility. . . . At the end, harmony prevails, at least in the view of the androcentric author. . . . A renewal of order has taken place."[15] German scholar Susanne Gillmayr-Bucher seeks the theme of Judges in the very polyphonic character of the text and its narrative sections that present not only a variety of situations but also different interpretations of the events.[16] To my view, the latter perspective yields the most satisfactory results for interpreting and understanding the material and does the least violence to texts that most likely originate from different sources and perspectives and therefore do not lend themselves to being viewed through one lens only.

Establishing a place in the land, living there under threat of hostile oppression from outside and inside, living together among other peoples without worshiping "other" gods, maintaining right

14. Thus, Marc Brettler (*The Book of Judges* [London: Routledge, 2002], 113) argues that Judges "is a highly political work, which echoes the following sentiment, found elsewhere in the Bible (1 Kgs 1:31): 'May my lord King David live forever!' " Others view the issue as presented in an ambiguous way rather than in terms of a specific monarchy. See, for example, Polzin, *Moses and the Deuteronomist*. In Amit's (*The Book of Judges*, 96, 342) opinion, the narrator creates a balanced position (i.e., kingship is a pragmatic solution), while chs. 17 and 18 argue specifically in a pro-Davidic, anti-Saul direction. Schneider (*Judges*, 287) takes a similar position. Gregory T. K. Wong (*Compositional Strategy of the Book of Judges*, VTSup 111 [Leiden: Brill, 2006], 252), on the other hand, does not view the issue of advocacy for kingship as central, but rather the relationship to Adonai: "Israel's problem is . . . a spiritual one, the centre of which lies in Israel's relationship with [Adonai]."

15. Niditch, *Judges*, 208.

16. Susanne Gillmayr-Bucher, *Erzählte Welten im Richterbuch*, 9. She identifies the collection as a "polyphonic dialogue" and suggests that all efforts to discern one theme or perspective suffer defeat on account of this characteristic.

relationship with Adonai, a search for proper leadership—these are all concerns that weave themselves through the fabric of Judges. All of these remained perpetual concerns of ancient Israel, taking on new shape in different periods, including in the postexilic period. We may look in vain for the one overriding theme that holds it all together, and what feels to us to be fragmentary may rather testify to a multiplicity of valid concerns that do not easily reduce themselves to the orderly and organized unity we desire. The voices do not always sing in harmony; disharmony did not disturb the final collectors and editors. Uncertainty and a degree of chaos marked the days of the judges, when "hair hung unbraided in Israel," as it will do when, in Brettler's words, "all hell breaks loose" (Judg 5:2).[17] We will mark the various voices, those of the old tales, what Niditch calls the "epic-bardic" voice, and the one that evaluates and comments especially on the relationship of the people to their God.[18] As often as not, readers are left to judge on their own whether this event or that was for good or for ill.

In terms of theological understandings of the book, I agree with Robert Polzin that Judges argues against a mechanistic understanding of theology that equates obedience with blessing and disobedience with punishment and that the book is not so much about repentance and deliverance as it is about deliverance in spite of constant backsliding.[19] Concerns concentrate themselves on the issue of God's mercy in the face of the communal abandonment of God, a refusal to listen to the voice of Adonai, and neglect of the moral compass provided for the community. The violation of the divine-human relationship extends from the religious into the social realm so that the people not only engage in idolatry (10:10) but also violate codes of decency and moral behavior to an increasing degree instead of loving kin and stranger in their midst as they are obligated

17. Brettler, *The Book of Judges*, 73.

18. Niditch, *Judges*, 8–13. Niditch discerns three layers or voices in Judges: the epic-bardic, the theological, and the humanistic, with the first being the oldest, the second not necessarily Deuteronomic, and the third the non-critical voice in particular present in the first and the final chapters (1; 17–21).

19. Polzin, *Moses and the Deuteronomist*, 155.

to do. The deliverers God raises up, barring a few, are hardly models of leadership, but perhaps they were the best Israel could have had at the time. The people did, after all, survive in spite of chaos and destruction.

Style

To be so deluded about such complex affairs means that one ceases to read, no matter how many pages we continue to turn.[20]

Judges presents a far greater variety of genres than Joshua. It's a heroic narrative that blurs the boundaries between prose and poetry: Battle hymn, riddle, parable, and proverb all make their appearance. In contrast to Joshua, the tales in Judges give evidence of daily life: food, drink, household items, agricultural customs and devices, and implements used for singular violent acts and for battle come into view. As already observed, there is regular consultation with the Deity, at times initiated by a divine emissary or introduced by the phrase "X inquired of Adonai." A good deal of speech and human interaction marks the episodes. Phrases that identify the situation as unstable because of Israelite backsliding and Adonai's wrath in the face of such behavior receive frequent notation: "The Israelites did what was wrong in the eyes of Adonai" (2:11; 3:7; 3:12; 6:1), alternating with the phrase, "they continued to do what was wrong in the eyes of Adonai" (3:12; 4:1; 10:6; 13:1). The declaration in the final chapters that "everyone did what was right in their own eyes" represents the other side of the same theme. Repeated mention of idolatry occurs in such typical expressions as "they abandoned Adonai" (2:12, 13; 10:6), "went whoring" after other gods (2:17; 8:27; 8:33), and "served the Baal" (2:11, 13; 3:7; 6:25, 30, 31, 32; 8:33; 10:6).

In response to these misdeeds on the part of the Israelites, the "wrath of Adonai flared up" (2:14, 20; 3:8; 10:7), and Adonai is said to "sell" or "give" them into "the hand of X" (2:14; 3:8; 4:2; 6:1; 10:7;

20. Polzin, *Moses and the Deuteronomist*, 162.

13:1). Then the Israelites "cry out" in their distress (3:9, 15; 6:6, 7; 10:10), and Adonai sends a "judge" or "deliverer" (2:16; 3:9, 15). Some of them are said to act because the spirit of Adonai "was upon," "stirred," or "overpowered" them (3:10; 11:29; 13:25; 14:6, 19; 15:14). A form of the root "to judge/rule" occurs more than a dozen times (3:10; 4:4; 10:2; 11:27; 12:7, 8, 9, 11, 13, 14; 15:20; 16:31). In the early part of the narrative sections, the land is said to "have rest" for certain periods of time (3:11, 30; 5:31; 8:28), a phrase that we find also in Joshua 11:23 and 14:15. We note that following the reign of Abimelek, no more references are made to intervals of peace or rest.

Whereas the book of Joshua has a clear sequential arc, from the appointment of Joshua to be the leader of the campaign to occupy the land to his final speech and death, following the model of his teacher Moses in Deuteronomy, Judges is far more episodic in nature. In view of the localized nature of the activities of different leaders, a number of them were most likely active at the same time. The framing chapters (1:1–3:6 and 17:1–21:25), unlike the central sections of the book, contain no temporal markers except for the notation of the death of Joshua in 2:8–9; the marker "in those days" of the final chapters serves merely as a vague reference to the period before the monarchy. In what follows, I have divided the material into three cycles, each with their own acts and smaller subdivisions: Judges 1:1–3:6 ("Setting the Stage"), Judges 3:7–16:31 ("Oppressors and Saviors"), and Judges 17:1–21:25 ("To Do What Is Right").

Cycle I: Setting the Stage (Judges 1:1–3:6)

The book of Judges goes a step further than Joshua by tackling the question not of how much of the land Israel would occupy but why *they had not been able to drive out the inhabitants of the land.*[1]

Two acts in this first cycle prepare the ground for the rest of the book, continuing the theme of conquest begun in Joshua and introducing the topic of the people's continuous disloyalty to Adonai through falling into idolatry—warned against in Joshua 24.

Act I: Success and Failure (Judges 1)

Chapter 1 serves as the first link in a model of a causal chain.[2]

Act I surveys, in descriptive narrative, the partial success of Judah and the failure of the other tribes in establishing themselves as the sole occupiers of the land. It lays the groundwork for confrontations to come, since surely there is trouble ahead with Jebusites, Canaanites, and Amorites living among the Israelites. The second act (2:1–3:6), beginning with a short illustrative narrative (2:1–5), provides the rationale for the struggles that lie ahead, reaching back to the death of Joshua and emphasizing the separation between the generations.

1. Robert Polzin, *Moses and the Deuteronomist: A Literary Study of the Deuteronomic History*, vol. 1 (New York: Seabury, 1980), 148.

2. Yairah Amit, *History and Ideology: An Introduction to Historiography in the Hebrew Bible* (Sheffield: Sheffield Academic Press, 1999), 144.

Act I, Scene 1: Judah First (Judges 1:1–20)

We have seen between the lines of Joshua . . . that in reality it was more complicated.[3]

The first chapter divides easily into halves, with one that centers on the tribe of Judah and its successful settling in the land (1:1–20) and the other presenting a list of seven tribes and their mostly failed attempts to drive out the local inhabitants (1:21–36). As Joshua does, Judges begins with the notation of a death marking a transition point, but then it goes in an entirely different direction. After the death of Joshua, instead of God commissioning and instructing a new leader, the Israelites as a group inquire of God, who "shall go up for us first against the Canaanites to fight for us?" (1). The terse opening of this unit (1–3) reveals first of all that there is at this time no leader to take Joshua's place. No "assistant of Joshua" (cf. Josh 1:1) is available to lead the Israelites under the present circumstances. Before Moses died, Joshua had already been appointed to guide the entry into the land. There has been, however, no initiative either on God's part or Joshua's to seek someone to succeed him, a serious matter in view of the "reality" indicated by John Goldingay in the quote above.

The reality is that there are still Canaanites in the land and there is still fighting to be done, so who will take the lead in the battles that lie ahead? Adonai answers the question, but perhaps not in the way expected—that is to say, not with the name of a leader but with that of a tribe. The tribe of Judah is appointed to "go up"; God declares the land to be given into Judah's hand (cf. Josh 1:2–4). Judah then invites Simeon, the tribe that lives among the Judahites, to join in the enterprise—not to drive the Canaanites out of the entire land, but rather to get rid of them in their joint land allotment (1:3). In four units (4–6, 8–11, 17–18, 19–20), victories take place in the region of Judah. Judah does not drive the Canaanites out of the *land* but out of the region around Jerusalem, out of Jerusalem itself, and

3. John Goldingay, *Joshua, Judges and Ruth for Everyone* (Louisville: Westminster John Knox, 2011), 90.

subsequently out of the area south to Hebron and west and northwest to Hormah, Gaza, and other Philistine cities in a rough square encompassing the land allotments to Judah and Simeon. The section is proleptic, making the anachronistic leap forward to future conquests: Jerusalem will not become Israelite until the reign of David (2 Sam 5:6–9), and there is still mention of the Philistines as a hostile power to be conquered in the time of King Hezekiah (2 Kgs 18:8). In Judges, the *herem*, so frequent in Joshua, occurs only here (1:17) and once again in the final chapter (21:11). The question of who shall go up first also links to the final chapters and the tragic context of intertribal war, when Judah will be first to go up against Benjamin (20:18). If the notion of putting Judah in a central leadership position is that not one person but an entire tribe will perform the task of vanquishing the foe and guiding the people, that idea proves to be illusory. Judah is not entirely successful in its endeavors in this first chapter, and in the final chapters it turns out to be a major instigator of intertribal warfare.

The recital of Judah's endeavors is interrupted three times. First, there is the appearance of the defeated king of Jerusalem, Adoni-Bezek (7), who opines that he has received his just deserts from Adonai in being a prisoner ("picking up scraps under the table") with toes and thumbs cut off—a comment that paints the Israelite Deity from an outsider point of view as one who requires an eye for an eye.[4] The second interruption (11–15) repeats the story of Caleb, Achsa, and Otniel as it is found in Joshua 15:15–19. Finally, there is mention of the Kenites settling with the Judahites in the Negev (16). All three interruptions anticipate subsequent developments. Jerusalem, captured by Judah, is cited as *not* captured by Benjamin (21), thus depicting a contrast that will return with emphasis in the last two chapters of the book. Otniel will become the first "deliverer" when the Israelites cry out under oppression (3:9–11), and the Kenites will return in chapter 4 (4:11–21; 5:24–27). The most striking feature of the interrupting

4. In Joshua 10, we met Adonizedeq, a king of Jerusalem with a similar name. The reference could be to the same king originating in another tradition or to another king of the same city.

episodes is the repetition of Achsa's appearance and her request from her father for water wells. Not only Otniel but also Achsa reaches into future episodes in the sense that, already in the first chapter of Judges, a woman appears where the text could reasonably have continued without her. Achsa is the prize presented to her cousin on a promise by her father to "give" his daughter to the man who will capture the town of Sefer, but also he commits to "giving" her the blessing of water upon her request. She talks her husband into requesting land, and it is clear that she considers the land hers from her appeal to her father.

JUDGES 1:13–15[5]

13 Then captured it Otniel,
the son of Kenaz, Caleb's younger brother.
And he gave him Achsa his daughter for a wife.

14 When she came, she induced him
to ask her father for a field.
As she came down from her donkey,
Caleb asked: What is the matter?
15 She said to him: Give me please a blessing,
for desert land you have given me;
now, give me water basins.
And Caleb gave her both upper and lower basins.

Women as deliverers and at the side of Israel's appointed strong men will play important roles in the main part of the book. Achsa, coming on the scene as someone "given as a wife," takes initiative, induces her husband, rides to her father, and "is given" the blessing of water for her land.[6] In this way, she models the great variety of

5. With some slight variations, these verses are a verbatim repetition of the report in Joshua 15:17–19 (see p. 139).

6. It is worth noting that two narratives focused on women are repeated in the traditions and that both concern women and the possession of land (Num 27:1–11 and Josh 17:3–6; Josh 15:17–19 and Judg 1:13–15).

female presence the narratives in Judges will display. Women will appear in later episodes as recipients of male dominance, wrong-headed commitments, and violence (5:28–30; 11:30–40; 19:22–30; 21:1–25). They will also take initiative and fight on the battlefield (4:1–16, 17–21), become a blessing instead of receiving one (5:24), and communicate with the Deity (13:2–23). They will, in addition, play the role of the inveigler, inducing the deliverer into giving up his secrets to his undoing (16:4–20).[7]

Act I, Scene 2: The Others (Judges 1:21–36)

It is not a question of one Israel, but of separate tribes who each act on their own behalf and cooperate with one another only to a very limited degree.[8]

In the second scene, Benjamin heads the list of tribes who did not "drive out" native peoples, which continues with Manasseh, Ephraim, Zebulon, Asher, Naftali, and Dan (1:21–36). The list of failures is interrupted by the ostensible success of Joseph in the capture of Bethel (23–26). Subsequently, however, Ephraim and Manasseh, who make up the tribe of Joseph, are not able to drive out those of Beth Shan, Tanakh, Dor, and a number of other cities (27–29). The record of Joseph's victory may serve the purpose of drawing attention to Bethel. Deborah will dispense "justice" in that region (4:5), and above all it will be the place where the Israelites will consult Adonai in the presence of the Ark in the final chapters (20:26).[9] In their accessing the city with the

7. To identify Achsa as "sex toy," "sex-kitten-prize," or "supplicant daughter" risks a tendency to read contemporary western gender stereotypes into the ancient text. See Lillian R. Klein, "Achsah: What Price This Prize?" in *Judges: A Feminist Companion to the Bible*, ed. Athalya Brenner (Sheffield: Sheffield Academic, 1999), 26.

8. Author's translation of Susanne Gillmayr-Bucher, *Erzählte Welten im Richterbuch*, 43: "Es gibt nicht ein Israel, sondern einzelne Stämme die jeder für sich agieren und nur sehr eingeschränkt miteinander kooperieren."

9. Bethel has a complex history in biblical tradition (see Gen 28:10–22;

help of a local resident (24), there are echoes of the Rahab story in Joshua 2:1–24, especially in the pledge of the spies at Bethel to "deal kindly" with the man; but unlike Rahab, the one from Bethel does not continue residence with the Israelites, and the next verses show the victory of Joseph to be a very partial one. Unlike the period of the entry in Joshua, there are no examples of alliances made with local inhabitants in Judges, and the one example provided here may include implicit critique. References to continuous presence of local occupants of towns abound: "The Canaanites resolved to live in that region" (27); "they put the Canaanites to heavy labor,/ but did not in fact drive them out" (28); "the Canaanites lived among them in Gezer" (29); "the Canaanites lived among them" (30); "those of Asher lived among the Canaanites" (32); "Naftali . . . lived among the Canaanites" (33); "the Amorites continued to live in Har Heres" (34).

The positive light shed on Judah as compared to its neighbor tribes is easy to discern. Amit suggests that the extensive portrayal of Judah and its success in the opening chapter is there to make up for its virtual disappearance in the rest of the book until the final chapters.[10] With the exception of Otniel, the deliverers appointed by Adonai in the subsequent episodes will hail from tribes of the center and the north. The contrast painted between Judah and the rest of the tribes is indeed stark. We note also that, unlike Judah, the other tribes do not act in cooperation but engage individually, one tribe at times acting to the disadvantage of the others (34–36). In this context, the absence of a reason for the failure of the other tribes is worth observing, whereas for Judah, the inhabitants' possession of iron chariots is provided as the cause of their inability to get rid of those who live on the plain (19).

35:6, 15; Josh 16:2; 1 Sam 7:16; 1 Kgs 12:29–33; 2 Kgs 23:15; Hos 10:15; Amos 3:14).

10. Amit, *The Book of Judges*, 147: "Judah enjoys an extensive presentation and positive characterization in the exposition as compensation for its limited appearance throughout the book."

Act II: A Pattern Is Set (Judges 2:1–3:6)

Judges views Israel's history though a theological lens; it makes faith claims.[11]

The second act (2:1–3:6), beginning with a short illustrative narrative (2:1–5), performs the function of providing the rationale for the struggles that lie ahead, reaching back to the death of Joshua and emphasizing the separation between the generations. The pattern sets up the schema of wrongdoing, punishment, crying out, and deliverance that will frame subsequent episodes. It forms the background for the first concrete example of hostile invasion and deliverance by means of a judge in the following scene.

Act II, Scene 1: Interlude (Judges 2:1–5)

A careful reader will note the admixture of historical explanations, i.e. those dealing chiefly with human actions and motivations, and theological rationales.[12]

The first five verses of chapter 2 present an interlude that ostensibly offers an explanation of the place name Bochim. Within the structure of the initial acts, the unit serves as a bridge, moving from brief descriptions of conquest to commentary on the way Adonai views the situation. There is no known place called Bochim, although some identify it with Bethel. More important than the location is the naming of the place as "weepers," a reaction to an indictment voiced by God's messenger.[13] The indictment begins with a reminder of God´s saving action in bringing the people out of Egypt. The

11. Mark E. Biddle, *Reading Judges: A Literary and Theological Commentary* (Macon, GA: Smyth and Helwys, 2012), 31.

12. Biddle, *Reading Judges,* 35.

13. Because of the freight in contemporary culture attached to the word "angel," I opt throughout for the word "messenger," a literal translation of the Hebrew word. There is no doubt that this figure is an emissary of Adonai and at moments turns into the Deity itself.

people, throughout addressed with the second person plural, are identified in the last lines as "all the Israelites" (4). In addition, the message announces that God made them a promise not to "break" the covenant—God's religious and political bond with the people—at any time (1). The demand put upon the people is for them not to make a covenant with the peoples of the land in view of God's devotion to them: "I will not break my covenant" (1) and "you will not make a covenant" (2). On the heels of this statement follows the accusation: "You have not listened to my voice./ What have you done?" (2). Not listening to the voice of Adonai points to the core of covenant disloyalty and leads to a question revealing a serious breach in "proper relations between parties, human and divine or human."[14] God asks the question "What have you done?" of Eve in the garden (Gen 3:13) and of Cain after he has killed his brother (Gen 4:10). The people raise this question to Moses when they discover that Pharaoh's army is pursuing them after their escape from Egypt (Exod 14:11). In the face of the people's disloyalty, God makes a new promise: not to "drive out" these inhabitants of the land so that they will become a trap and lead the people into idolatry (3). From this perspective, the inability of the northern tribes to dispossess the local people is God's doing and is a consequence of their disloyalty.

By referring to the people not listening to God's voice, the implication is that they have made covenants with "the people of the land" and not destroyed their altars, which constitutes an abandonment of their covenant bond with Adonai. The unit thus reaches back to the first chapter and the reality that they live among the Canaanites and the Canaanites live among them. The danger presented by this state of affairs, as observed in Joshua 23:13, echoes in the words of the messenger: While the indigenous population will remain hostile to the Israelites, their gods will be a "lure" for them. At the same time, the unit anticipates what is to come, with the people's repeated disloyalty and their "crying" out to God upon suffering under the oppression of their foes. "The people lifted their voices and wept" (4) reminds one of the episode in Numbers after the people have received word about the land from the spies (cf. Num 14:1). Weep-

14. Susan Niditch, *Judges* (Louisville: Westminster John Knox, 2008), 47.

ing is not always the same as repentance and can as easily precede dissonance between community and the leaders, as well as between the community and God. The last line, referring to sacrifice, calms at least temporarily any intimations of that sort.

Act II, Scene 2: A New Generation (Judges 2:6–19)

Like subsequent judges, Joshua is treated as one who inspires Israel's faithfulness.[15]

The initial scene (2:1–5) having emphatically invoked the presence of Joshua and his warnings, the opening lines of the next scene (2:6–19) occupy themselves with the generation of his lifetime, depicting that era in an idealized manner and noting his death and burial (6–10). This sequence ends with the announcement that after that generation has passed, a new generation comes about who "did not know Adonai or what God had done for Israel" (10). Then comes a description of the entire schema on which the narratives to follow are constructed:

Judges 2:11–16

11 The Israelites did what was wrong in the eyes of Adonai,
and they served the Baals.
12 They abandoned Adonai,
the God of their ancestors,
who led them out of the land of Egypt;
they went after other gods,
from the gods of the peoples that were round about,
and bowed down to them
and vexed Adonai.
13 They abandoned Adonai
and served the Baal,
and bowed down to him.

15. Niditch, *Judges*, 49.

14 Then the wrath of Adonai burned against Israel,
and he gave them into the hand of their ravagers,
who plundered them.
He sold them into the hand of their enemies round about,
and they could not stand against their foes.
15 Every time they went out,
the hand of Adonai was against them for evil,
as Adonai had promised and sworn to them;
and they were in sore distress.

16 Then Adonai raised up judges,
Who delivered them from the hand of their plunderers.

The first unit (11–13) of this sequence resounds with expressions of the people's wrongdoing: "They did what was wrong" (2×, vv. 11, 13), "they abandoned," "they vexed." The recipient of all these actions is Adonai, called "the God of their ancestors" who brought them out of Egypt. An observation missing here is that God brought them to the land of promise and gave it to them. The stress thus falls on the delivering action of God. The content of the people's wrongful actions is further spelled out as "serving the Baals," following "other gods," and "bowing down to them." The very thing that Joshua at Shechem pledged the people to avoid has come to pass. The charge against the people is framed with the phrase "they abandoned Adonai" (2:12, 13) in such a way that the plural "Baals" of verse 11 becomes the singular "Baal" of verse 13 and "bowed down to them" becomes "bowed down to him" (12, 13), sharpening the accusation by pitting the one Israelite God, Adonai, against the Baal of Canaan.

These actions of the people provoke a counteraction on the part of God, who is in charge in the corresponding unit (14–16). Adonai's wrath is kindled: "Then the wrath of Adonai burned against Israel" (14), the first of four times that this expression is used in the book, with two others in the opening chapters (2:20; 3:8) and the other following the rule of Abimelek and three of the "minor" judges (10:7). The introductory section of the book thus makes repeated use of a phrase that is relatively rare outside of these chapters. The result of God's anger is that Adonai "gave them into the hand" or "sold them into the hand" of those who oppose the Israelites: "ravagers," "their enemies round about," their "foes." The repetitious style hammers home the seriousness of both the people's misdeeds and God's reaction, of which the result is that the people are "in sore distress" (2:15). It is because of this distress that God raises up "judges" for them. The final action is thus benevolent, in spite of the people's wrongdoing. The judges/deliverers are presented in the plural to indicate this happened not only once but repeatedly. Amit notes that up until this point, the "stage of crying out to God" is missing, which "contributes to the severe tone of the description." It also leaves the impression that the deliverance provided by the Deity is provided without the people's request for assistance.[16]

A subsequent unit (17–19) points out that at times even the presence of the God-appointed leaders did not stop the people from "whoring" after other gods (17). They heed neither the voice of their leaders nor the voice of their God. The pattern is set: The Israelites continue to do what is wrong, going after the gods of the people around them. And the oppression by hostile forces is due to God's initiative; it is the means by which God faces the people with the consequences of their actions. At other times, they return to their "practices and stubborn ways" after the death of the judge (19). These lines announce general patterns that lie ahead in the narratives about the judges/deliverers that Adonai will send to save the people from complete disaster and to bring them back to the covenant loyalty their ancestors swore.

Act II, Scene 3: The Test (Judges 2:20–3:6)

The multi-voiced discourses in the narratives do not lend themselves to a reduction into one perspective or one statement of its intention.[17]

Three times in this scene, God is said to "test" Israel (2:22; 3:1; 3:4), a Hebrew verb that appears only eight times in the Hebrew

16. Amit, *The Book of Judges*, 155.

17. Gillmayr-Bucher, *Erzählte Welten*, 7.

Bible with Adonai as subject.[18] Each time, the people are the target of God's testing. The first and third time, the test has the same objective: loyalty to the God of Israel, by "walking in God's way" (2:22) or "heeding Adonai's commandments" (3:4). This phrase is strongly reminiscent of usage in Exodus and Deuteronomy. God tested the people to see whether they would *walk in God's* torah/ *instruction* (Exod 16:4) and to find out whether they would *keep his commandments* (Deut 8:2). God gave the people good instructions, but they chose to not walk in God's way but to walk after "other" gods. Still, it is of some interest that in both places, the remaining presence of indigenous inhabitants in the promised land is ascribed to the Deity rather than to the inability of the people to displace them as depicted in the first chapter (1:21–36). The statement goes to a central conviction in Judges that it is ultimately Adonai who is in charge. Human leaders come and go, but both weal and woe are due to the guiding hand of the Most High. Yet much is made of the responsibility laid on the people to abide by the ways laid out for them in the commandments they received "through Moses" (3:4). They are given a choice, and they choose wrong consistently. Their very wrongdoing then becomes an opportunity for Adonai to show them kindness. In regard to the purpose of the test, the observations in 2:22 and 3:4 are consistent.

There is, however, a third explanation which goes in another direction.

Judges 3:1–2

1 These are the peoples Adonai left
to test by them Israel,
all who had not known all the battles with Canaan.
2 Only for the knowledge of generations of Israelites
to teach them warfare;
only the ones who had not known it before.

18. The usage of the *Pi'el* of *nasa'* elsewhere (roughly 25×) frequently occurs with Adonai as the target of the "testing."

The peoples are left by God as a test. So far so good—except that this time, the test is not directly related to walking in God's ways but is rather for the practical purpose of teaching the Israelites to fight! The assumption is that the generation following the one that entered the land was unacquainted with the art of battle. This distinct "take" on the significance of the abiding presence of indigenous peoples in Canaan raises a question as to which response is the one intended by the editor/writer of Judges. The goal in each case can be said to be educational, but the lessons to be learned are different: listening to and heeding God's instructions or learning to fight. One might perhaps argue that the fight was, after all, intended to abolish those who would lead the people into idolatry, and in that sense the two goals coalesce. Yet the voice sounds different in 3:4 than in 3:1, where, in Amit's words, the "nations were allowed to remain in order to serve as a kind of 'punching bag,' by means of which the Israelites may train and practice the art of war."[19] Apparently, the editor/writer thought it important to maintain a multi-vocal approach to this issue, and in 3:1 we may hear a note of ancient enthusiasm about engagement in warfare, one that we will see reflected also in the Song of Deborah in Judges 5. Niditch calls this the voice that "captures well the bardic ideology of war."[20] Two or perhaps even three different voices propose a purpose for the continued presence of indigenous peoples in the land, voices left in the text without an attempt to harmonize them.[21]

To begin with, the list of peoples includes Philistines, Canaanites, Sidonians, and Hivites (3:3), which are familiar from other pop-

19. Amit, *The Book of Judges,* 156.

20. Niditch, *Judges,* 55.

21. Amit (*The Book of Judges,* 156–57) sees distinctions between 2:22 and 3:4 and describes 2:20–3:4 as an "addition of an anthological or aggregational nature, the result of an editing that sought answers to the questions as to why Joshua did not drive out all the Canaanites and why the other nations remained in the country." She suggests a smooth transition between 2:19 and 3:5–6. While this solution is possible and may even be likely in terms of the original coherence of the text, it does not solve the intriguing question of the desire of the final editor to retain the verses that Amit views as dissonant and a later addition.

ulation lists (cf. Josh 13:4), although neither Sidonians nor Hivites will be among the groups from which the Israelites will need deliverance in subsequent episodes. The second list, in 3:5, is identical to Exodus 3:17 and 33:2, and the same listing with a slightly different order appears in Deuteronomy 20:17. Of the people on this inventory, only Canaanites and Amorites will present a problem in what follows. These catalogs are largely symbolic of the inimical presence in Canaan. What happens because of their existence is what counts: The Israelites' living among them and intermarrying with them cause them to "serve their gods" (3:6).

Cycle II: Oppressors and Saviors (Judges 3:7–16:31)

It is the nature of the story to interest and to excite its reader; . . . its penetrative and persuasive powers are often greater than those of other kinds of biblical literature.[1]

The deliverer narratives that make up the main part of the book are here presented in six acts. Acts I, II, III, and VI open with the statement that the Israelites did what was wrong or continued to do what was wrong in the eyes of Adonai, and Act V includes it (10:6). Reference to doing the wrong is missing only in Act IV, which stands out for other reasons. Brief notes on a named deliverer, rather than a detailed narrative, follow Acts I, IV, and V, each indicating the predecessor with the word "after him" (3:31; 10:3; 12:8, 11, 13), except that in Act IV the predecessor is named ("after Abimelek," 10:1). Abimelek is the only example of a leader grasping for monarchial power. Following Deborah, the episodes show a gradual decline in the actions of the delivering judges, and violent deaths of Israelite groups and individuals begin to mark the stories.

Act I: Enemies Round About—Otniel and Ehud (Judges 3:7–31)

The first two heroes to come to the rescue of the beleaguered Israelites are Otniel and Ehud. Otniel's activities take place outside of Canaan and, outside of the notation that Adonai "raised him

1. Yairah Amit, *The Book of Judges: The Art of Editing,* trans. Jonathan Chipman (Leiden: Brill, 1999), 11.

up" as "a deliverer," the narrative provides no detail of any strategy or armed combat (3:7–11). Ehud, on the other hand, arises as an unlikely hero whose assassination of the enemy lord is described in fine detail (12–30). A third judge, Shamgar, is mentioned in what constitutes an abbreviated note, perhaps a snippet left from a lost story (31).

Act I, Scene 1: Double-Trouble from Two-Stream Land (Judges 3:7–11)

The impression is created that only a judge from Judah would set out to do battle in a remote region.[2]

While I connect the Otniel story with the opening of the second cycle, it could also serve as a fitting conclusion to the first. As Judah was the first to successfully occupy its territory, a deliverer from Judah is the first to defend the people from an enemy outside the borders of Canaan. The short narrative provides an appropriate illustration of the foundational description in chapter 2 and the beginning of chapter 3. What was general in the description becomes specific in the Otniel story: "The Israelites did what was wrong . . ./ served the Baals and Astartes/ . . . God sold them into the hand of . . . the king of . . ." (7–8).

Rather than an appearance by one of the hostile groups already listed, who present to the Israelites the test of faithfulness and skill in battle, an outside force comes to the fore. The introduction paints the Israelites as faithless and in *service* to the gods of Canaan, as a consequence of which they are made to *serve* a foreign lord—in Hebrew, Cushan Rishatayim from Aram Naharaim, translated something like Cushan Double-Trouble from Two-Stream Land, a reference to Mesopotamia. The name and place resound through the short story, mentioned no less than four times (8, 10). While most likely no trouble came from that direction to fledgling Israel in the days before the monarchy, it

2. Amit, *The Book of Judges*, 165.

was to loom large in the subsequent history of ancient Israel, and here we may well have a creative imagining of a period when little Judah in the person of Judahite Otniel had the upper hand over this oppressive power.

Verse 9 introduces the cry of the Israelites to Adonai.

Judges 3:9

Then the Israelites cried to Adonai,
and Adonai raised up a deliverer
for the Israelites who delivered them:
Otniel, son of Kenaz, younger brother of Caleb.

Otniel is a proven war hero and a good candidate to embody the military nature of the task at hand. He is the only one of the major protagonists whose story is told entirely in the descriptive voice. He is said to have "judged Israel" and gone "out to battle," without further details about him or the enemy, as, for example, an invasion by King Cushan Rishatayim. Amit notes that verses 7–11 contain a total of fifteen "formulaic phrases," of which the lines quoted above are an example, so that we may term the entire passage a "reservoir of formulae" that will in part occur in subsequent episodes. Likely, the function of the story is to serve as a template for the characteristic features of all the hero stories that follow.[3] Amit also points out that the character sets out to do battle in a remote region and "displays concerns for national needs" rather than just for his own tribe. As such, he is a "kind of precursor of David," the future conqueror from Judah of areas outside of the country.[4] In this context, it should be noted also that Otniel did battle with "the spirit of Adonai upon him" (3:10), a power that later will overcome other judges but notably also the first kings of Israel, Saul and David.[5]

3. Amit, *The Book of Judges,* 162. Amit lists all of the phrases in 3:7–11 that will recur elsewhere in the book.

4. Amit, *The Book of Judges,* 165.

5. In Judges, the spirit also overcomes Jefta (11:29) and Samson (13:25; 14:6, 19; 15:14); in 1 Samuel, Saul (1 Sam 10:6, 10; 11:6) and David (1 Sam 16:13).

Act I, Scene 2: A Knife in the Belly (Judges 3:12–30)

Like his sword, Ehud's words are double-edged.[6]

The story of Ehud and the fat king of Moab, Eglon, plays itself out in three units. An introduction recites the state of affairs with Israel and sets Ehud on the stage (3:12–15). This part is followed by the central action in which Ehud, as a leader of the party, brings tribute to the Moabite stronghold and manages to assassinate the king inside a private room of the residence (16–23). A final unit recounts Ehud's escape during the delay provided by the king's entourage (24–26) and ends with a victorious battle against the Moabites (27–30).

At the opening of the scene, a majority of translations render the verse as if there was a pause in the wrongdoing of Israel, which picks up again after the forty-year rest following the judgeship of Otniel; a more accurate translation leaves open to doubt that they ever stopped doing wrong. Again, an enemy arises from outside; and again, it is the Holy God who is behind the enemy's actions.

JUDGES 3:12–14

12 And the Israelites continued to do
what was wrong in the eyes of Adonai,
and Adonai strengthened Eglon, king of Moab,
over Israel, because they did
what was wrong in the eyes of Adonai.
13 He gathered to himself Ammonites and Amalekites
and went and struck down Israel,
and they took possession of the City of Palms.
14 The Israelites served Eglon,
king of Moab, for eighteen years.

God's "strengthening" of the enemy in verse 12 is bracketed by the repeated assertion of the wrongdoing of the Israelites, an

6. Author's translation of Susanne Gillmayr-Bucher, *Erzählte Welten im Richterbuch: Narratologische Aspekte eines Polyfonen Diskurses* (Leiden: Brill, 2013), 75.

emphatic general reference which we may certainly apply to the specifics of idolatry and abandonment of Adonai recorded in chapter 2. Moab, Ammon, and Amalek go to battle with Israel, which in the end becomes subservient to Moab. As in the Otniel report, the Israelites cry to Adonai, who sends a deliverer. This time, the deliverer is from Benjamin, one Ehud, a left-handed man. The next units (16–23, 24–30) may be recapped briefly as follows: Ehud casts a double-edged sword or dagger, hiding it under his clothes on the right side—an advantage when meeting unsuspecting adversaries. He is the one commissioned to bring tribute to Eglon, an indication that he was a man of some standing in the community, and he does so. After sending his party on their way, he turns back at a place with "carved images at Gilgal" and, securing a private audience with the king, kills Eglon, skewering him through the belly. Then he makes his escape while the attendants of the king are dithering at the entrance to the private chamber, which was probably a type of bathroom. Finally, Ehud rounds up Israelite forces, which pursue the Moabites and defeat them at the Jordan fords. Then "the land had rest for eighty years" (30).

As the narrative unfolds, it presents an entertaining and comical episode with a number of prominent references to body parts, physical size, and bodily functions, creating, in Yairah Amit's words, "a ribald atmosphere that gives pleasure to the reader and increases his interest in what is being told, all without harming the primary message."[7] The Moabite king is called a "well-fed" or "very fat" man (17), with his armed forces notably "robust," or also "fat" (29). His name is reminiscent of the Hebrew word for "bull" or "bull-calf," an animal used for sacrifice (Lev 9:2, 3, 8), but also for the idolatrous images made at the foot of Mt. Sinai in the wilderness (Exod 32:4, 8, 19, 20, 24, 35). In the Historical Books, the same word is used for the images set up by Jeroboam at Bethel and Dan in the Northern

7. Amit, *The Book of Judges*, 197. Amit presents a detailed analysis of the entire story (174–99). We note the frequent references to "hand" (5×), "thigh" (2×; the word for "thigh" also means loins), the "belly," and "feet" (used euphemistically for genitals). Niditch (*Judges*, 58) and others observe a "play between eroticism and death."

Kingdom (1 Kgs 12:28, 29), the sinful act by which all the kings of the north would subsequently be measured. Eglon is the one to be sacrificed, and he is also a symbol of all idol worship, the "wrong" committed by Israel in the eyes of Adonai.

The story, told with great economy of words, slows the action at certain points to provide significant detail: Ehud's weapon, where it is hidden, the method of the killing, and the scene of the bewildered attendants outside the king's chamber. The crucial aspects hold our attention while at the same time leaving gaps that raise a number of questions. Even if the dagger was hidden on the "wrong" side of the body, would guards at a king's palace not conduct a careful search on members of a subjected people bringing tribute? The story skips blithely to the moment following the delivery of the tribute, when Ehud presumably leaves with the party that carried whatever they carried, sending them home while "he returned from the carved images at Gilgal." The information about Ehud hiding the weapon early in the story raises expectations of an act of violence, but nothing has happened so far, and it looks as if the right moment passed while they were in the presence of the king. Did Ehud have second thoughts when faced with the over-sized king Eglon? Did he have second thoughts again at the sight of the "carved images"? What were these images precisely? Their location, Gilgal, we recognize as the place where Joshua put up stones as a testimony to the miraculous and saving deeds of God toward Israel after the crossing of the Jordan (Josh 4:20–24).

The Hebrew word for the images where Ehud makes his turn is *pesilim*, a term used in the Bible exclusively for the carved images that led Israel to idolatry.[8] Is this another hint that the Israelites have continued their wrongdoing even under Moabite oppression? Or are the images a testimony to Moabite worship at the very place in-

8. The word *pesilim* occurs 23 times, always in the plural (Deut 7:5, 25; 12:3; Judg 3:19, 26; 2 Kgs 17:41; 2 Chr 33:19, 22; 34:3, 4, 7; Ps 78:58; Isa 10:10; 21:9; 30:22; 42:8; Jer 8:19; 50:38; 51:47, 52; Hos 11:2; Mic 1:7; 5:12[13]). It is connected with the root *psl* ("to hew, cut") and also to the noun *pesel* ("a hewn image"), which occurs in Judges 17 and 18, with most of its 20 occurrences also in a negative context.

tended for a witness to the faithful deeds of the Israelite Deity? What causes Ehud to return just at this spot? Is the referent by implication one that recalls the monument erected by Joshua, and does it serve as a reminder to our hero that his task is not complete?[9] Whatever the case may be, the word *pesilim* functions to recall the misdeeds not only of outsiders but of the Israelites who have "continued to do what was wrong in the eyes of Adonai" (3:12). Allusions to worship and idols together serve to highlight the area in which the Israelites have lost their way. This, then, is precisely the place where Ehud finds his way back, from the *pesilim* to the king's residence. Close attention to the phrasing of Ehud's return ("He himself returned from the carved images at Gilgal," 3:19) may hint that Ehud is turning his back on the idols in more than only a literal way.[10]

Once he is back in the palace, how is it exactly that Ehud manages to get a private audience with the king? He announces that he has something "secret," a word used elsewhere for political as well as sexual intimacy. Apparently, the statement is important enough that the Moabite king sends his servants away, allowing him the one word of direct speech in the Sequence—"hush" or "still"—one word from the king who, at the end of the exchange with Ehud, will be "fallen to the ground dead" (3:25). The presence of servants was probably common enough at the time, even in a room that contained a royal lavatory. But why is the king so easily convinced? Is it because the secret thing or word hints at an oracle received at the place of worship where Ehud turned around? Why is Eglon so unsuspecting? The story has a number of elements in common with the assassination of Sisera by Yael, but in that tale, we are told why

9. The significance of Ehud turning around at just this spot was brought to my attention in the first instance by my student Timothy McNinch, who wrote in an exegesis paper on Judges 3:15–25 (Spring 2015) that the detail in the narrative "appears to intensify 'Ehud's motivation to carry out his assassination attempt. Such motivation could have come from seeing the Israelite ebenezer at Gilgal (stirring up his sense of divine right to the land), or he may have witnessed Moabite idols in the area (stirring up his wrath at the profaning of Israel's worship)."

10. The Hebrew verb *shuv* is, especially in prophetic literature, indicative of a return to a commitment to Israel's God.

Sisera suspected no harm. It is clear why Ehud leaves the dagger in the king's belly—so that he may escape "bloodless"—but it is not precisely clear how he gets out of what must have been a closely guarded place. The reader tends to become entangled in obscure words and the difficulty of reconstructing the events. What becomes evident is that the picture of the hesitant servants mumbling and shuffling their feet outside the locked door of their dead master creates the necessary delay for Ehud to get out of the place and to continue his actions of "deliverer."

The victorious battle takes place in three verses (27–29), beginning with Ehud blowing the shofar after he once again passes the *pesilim* and makes his escape, eventually to the hill country of Ephraim. The shofar can be used in the context of religious ceremony or to gather troops in a battle setting. In Judges, it is used outside of this chapter only in the story of Gideon, where the shofar is blown with some frequency. The verb for blowing the instrument, which makes a loud and eerie sound, is the same one used for the death blow Ehud deals to Eglon (cf. vv. 21 and 27). The question here is why the death blow to Eglon meant such an easy defeat of the Moabites.

JUDGES 3:28–29

28 He said to them: Go in pursuit,
for Adonai has given your enemy Moab into your hand.
They went down after him
and took the fords of the Jordan to Moab;
they let no one cross.
29 They struck down Moab at that time,
ten thousand men, all robust warriors;
no one escaped.

It is possible that the death of Eglon took the fighting spirit from the Moabites while at the same time invigorating the Israelites. Yet the story gives credit for the victory to the Deity before the fighting even begins (28). Unlike Otniel, Ehud is not said to have received the "spirit of Adonai" (3:10). Adonai is mentioned explicitly at the beginning and end of the story, while Adonai's further guidance of

Ehud goes unrecorded. In his initial approach to Eglon, Ehud mentions a "secret" (19), which he specifies in a follow-up as "a word [or thing] from God" (20), using the general word for Deity. It may be that the guiding hand of the God of Israel is supposed to be read into all the fortuitous coincidences that eventuate in Ehud's and finally Israel's success, answering all the questions raised by the story. It was seemingly Ehud and his cleverness that accomplished the death of the Moabite king and the victory over the enemy, but in truth, the unseen hand of Israel's God made it all happen just as it did.[11] Or perhaps the episode furnishes an example of the divine-human cooperation often on display in biblical narrative. The human beings called into God's service are the ones God has to work with to accomplish a desired goal. At times, it goes well and the end is achieved; at other times, events may come to a bad and even disastrous end. They are, after all, *human beings*, warts and all, who are engaged in this enterprise. The Holy God of Israel is not just a remote, immutable Deity pulling the strings of the play that is enacted on earth but is shown as One who leaves humanity its freedom, even its freedom to make a mess of things. In the course of the twists and turns of the history of Israel, God too may have need to adjust to new realities as they develop.

Act I, Scene 3: A Footnote (Judges 3:31)

God is not bound to ethnocentrism.[12]

JUDGES 3:31

After him was Shamgar, the son of Anat,
and he struck down six hundred Philistines with a cattle prod.
He also delivered Israel.

11. Such is Amit's reading throughout her analysis of Judges 3:12–30 (*The Book of Judges*, 174–99).

12. John Goldingay, *Joshua, Judges and Ruth for Everyone* (Louisville: Westminster John Knox, 2011), 97.

Stuck in between Ehud, whose death is not reported until the next episode (4:1), and Deborah, the protagonist of the next chapters, appears one Shamgar. The brevity of the report is not what sets this reference to another deliverer apart, for we find this feature also with other judges (10:1–5; 12:8–15). The other short accounts, however, all report on "judges" hailing from tribes or regions in Israel and list the duration of their activity. There is no mention of judgeship in the case of Shamgar, his name includes reference to a Canaanite deity, Anat, and his activity consists of one single deed of prowess in battle. Goldingay observes that "it is not too adventurous to infer that Shamgar was a Canaanite" who was also under pressure from the Philistines, and that any victory over the Philistines was a relief for Israel.[13] It may be that there was a full story about Shamgar and this is simply the snippet that was left, added here because he comes back into the story in Judges 5:6. Niditch suggests that "some of the traditions assigned to [Yael] in Judges 4–5 may have been assigned to Shamgar in other tellings" and compares this dual-tradition to the mention of Goliath's killing by one Elhanan in 2 Sam 21:19, a story told in detail in 1 Samuel 17 with David as the hero.[14]

Act II: Without Restraint—Deborah, Barak, and Yael (Judges 4–5)

Women in their tents are not always victims.[15]

In the next act, the first person to appear is the only female judge in the book, Deborah—probably an Ephraimite, who, accompanied by general Barak from Naftali, defeats a Canaanite army in possession of the latest in military equipment. Yael turns up at the end of chapter 4 and shares certain characteristics with Ehud. Ehud's physical difference and Yael's belonging to a different ethnic group than the Israelites mark

13. Goldingay, *Joshua, Judges and Ruth*, 98.

14. Niditch, *Judges*, 59.

15. Tikva Frymer-Kensky, *Reading the Women of the Bible*, (New York: Schocken, 2002), 56.

them as somehow set apart. Their methods also share common traits, and the texts about them braid together violence and hints at intimacy. Ehud, Deborah, and Yael are all outsiders of a sort in a time when the outsider perhaps had a better chance of taking on a pivotal role, when there was no central administration or standing army, and when the people constantly did "what was wrong in the eyes of Adonai."

Chapters 4 and 5 present the same events—one in narration, the other in song.[16] The song, a composition judged by many scholars to be one of the most ancient texts in the Hebrew Bible, has produced volumes of writing.[17] Rather than taking the material in order, I present the two chapters as interlaced, reviewing the Deborah/Barak/Yael episodes from the perspective of both battle hymn and story and dividing the chapters into two scenes: one with Deborah and Barak as protagonists (4:1–16; 5:1–22) and a second with its focus on Yael and Sisera (4:17–22; 5:23–31). Deborah is the lone woman among the judges and is also the one who composed the song, which makes her character unique even in a book noted for the presence of women.

Act II, Scene 1: A Prophet under the Palm (Judges 4:1–16; 5:1–22)

Deborah functions as the alter ego of Adonai.[18]

Deborah is fiercely protective of her own—she is not a member of some international club of mothers.[19]

The setting for both story and song is the period following the death of Ehud, when the Israelites are under the boot of the Canaanites.

16. The distinction between "prose" and "poetry" is to my view not accurate, because Hebrew biblical narration has many stylistic qualities that are poetic in nature.

17. For a bibliography, see Charles L. Echols, *Tell Me, O Muse: The Song of Deborah (Judges 5) in the Light of Hebrew Poetry*, Library of Old Testament Studies 487 (New York; London: T&T Clark, 2008), 8–9.

18. Wilda C. Gafney, *Daughters of Miriam: Women Prophets in Ancient Israel* (Minneapolis: Fortress, 2008), 91.

19. Frymer-Kensky, *Reading the Women of the Bible*, 50.

Action and consequence follow one another: "The Israelites continued to do what was wrong in the eyes of Adonai," who "sold them into the hand of Jabin"; "the Israelites cried to Adonai"; "he oppressed the Israelites cruelly" (4:1–3). The subject of "oppressed" is Jabin or his commander, Sisera, and we note that *oppression*, rather than the arrival of a deliverer, follows the cry to Adonai. At the same time, Deborah, a judge, is dispensing justice under a palm tree in Ephraim. The author of the song, Deborah opens with a reference to the absence of rule or restraint in a time when the army depends on volunteerism (5:2).

Judges 5:1–3

1 Then sang Deborah with Barak,
son of Abinoam, on that day:

2 When restraint gave way in Israel,[20]
when troops volunteered—

20. The opening lines are variously translated, often with a reference to unbound hair; so NRSV: "When locks are long in Israel." Others see a reference to leadership; thus NAS: "That the leaders led in Israel." Isaac Leeser renders, "When depravity had broken out in Israel." The difficulty lies in the Hebrew verb *para'*, here used emphatically without a direct object. Where the verb elsewhere indicates loosened hair, the word for head (*rosh*) is present (Lev 10:6; 13:45; 21:10; Num 5:18; 6:5; Deut 32:42). In other contexts, the verb, which occurs only 18 times in the Bible, indicates setting aside norms of sociopolitical or cosmic-religious order (Exod 5:4; 32:25; 2 Chr 28:19; Prov 1:24–25; 4:14–15; 8:32–36; 13:18–19; 15:32). In his careful review of the expression, Gerald Janzen ("The Root pr' in Judges V 2 and Deuteronomy XXXII 42," *VT* 39 [1989]: 405) proposes that in Judg 5:2, the words mean that Israel cast off the restraint of oppression and engaged in rebellion against the Canaanites. He translates, "When the rebels cast off restraint in Israel/ when the people offered themselves freely/ bless [Adonai]." I am largely in agreement with Janzen, and my translation comes close to that of Robert G. Boling (*Judges*, AB 6a [New York: Doubleday, 1975], 107), which was earlier argued by Theodor Gaster (*Myth, Legend, and Custom in the Old Testament* [New York: Harper, 1969], 529). The parallel line referring to volunteers is echoed in v. 9, where the parallel word in the *a* line is not entirely clear either, though most translations read "commanders" or "leaders."

Bless Adonai!
3 Hear, O kings; give ear, O rulers;
I to Adonai, I myself will sing,
make melody to Adonai,
the God of Israel.

The song abounds with references to Adonai: three times in the opening stanza alone and repeated three times more in the next verses (4–5), twice coupled with the epithet "the God of Israel." God's name and Israel's are closely interwoven in the first eighteen verses, with "Adonai" occurring nine times and "Israel" seven. The multiple references bring home the point that Adonai is the God of Israel and that they are God's people.[21] Eventually, the song breaks the unity of the people down to the various tribes, some of which volunteer in dangerous times (5:14–15, 18) while others may hesitate (5:16–17).

JUDGES 4:4–5

4 Deborah, a woman, a prophet—
a woman of fire she[22]—
was judging Israel at that time.
5 She was sitting under Deborah's palm tree
between Ramah and Bethel,
in Ephraim's hill country;
and the Israelites would come up to her for justice.

In the narrative, Deborah appears with emphatic female naming. Literally translated, the Hebrew text of 4:4 reads, "Deborah, a *woman*, a *female* prophet, a *woman* of Lappidot, *she*, she was judging," a quadruple identification in which the second reference "a

21. Martin Buber (*The Prophetic Faith* [New York: Harper & Row, 1960], 10) calls this connection between Adonai and people the "motive force of the Song and the meaning of the victory of which it sings: the connection of the deity '[Adonai]' with the people 'Israel.' "

22. So Niditch, *Judges*, 60, 62.

woman" coupled with the personal pronoun "she" before the verb is redundant in Hebrew; in addition, the Hebrew grammar does not need the personal pronoun "she." Traditionally, her social status has been understood to be the "wife of Lappidot." The Hebrew word *lappid* means "torch" or "lightning," and the word *lappidot* does not occur as a proper name elsewhere in the Bible. Today, a number of scholars name Deborah as "a fiery woman" or "torch lady."[23] In either case, as a wife or a single woman, her presence is associated with fire.[24] The name Deborah means "bee" or "wasp."[25] The participles that follow her introduction indicate that her activity was customary: She *used* to sit and dispense judgment. In the song, she identifies herself as a "mother in Israel" in tumultuous times (5:6–8). She is a honeybee who is a mother to her people, a prophet who speaks for the Deity, a judge who dispenses justice, and a force of nature delivering a sting—a compounding string of epithets that point to the complex nature of this woman judge. Unlike male judges, Deborah receives no antecedents; she is no one's daughter, she may be no one's wife, she is no mother except of her people. In Wil Gafney's words, "As a mother, Deborah provided military and political security for all of her children."[26] Gafney identifies her as a "wordsmith," whose voice raises itself in triumph, in praise of Adonai, rousing herself and her companion, the general Barak, whose name also means "lightning," to action (5:12).[27] Marked by strong rhythms, short lines, repeated exclamations, and rhyme, the song in its first lines drums like the hoof beats it cites in verse 22. In the narrative, she calls Barak to muster troops of Naftali and Zebulon on Adonai's command (4:6–7). In the song, she urges him to "arise to capture his captives" (5:12).

23. Frymer-Kensky, *Reading the Women of the Bible*, 45–46; for an extensive discussion, see Tammi Schneider, *Judges*, Berit Olam (Collegeville, MN: Liturgical Press, 2000), 64–69.

24. Gillmayr-Bucher, *Erzählte Welten*, 91: "On the associative level Deborah is the woman of torches, a woman who sets things on fire."

25. Gafney (*Daughters of Miriam*, 90) prefers to derive the name from the root for speaking, *dbr*, and understands it as *dibberah* ("she spoke").

26. Gafney, *Daughters of Miriam*, 92.

27. Gafney, *Daughters of Miriam*, 92.

Following its opening lines, the song continues with an epiphanic celebration of the God of Israel, who marches out, and in whose presence nature is in tumultuous upheaval (5:4–5)—references that recall God's appearance at Sinai.[28] That Adonai actively participates in the battle is clear from the statements made by Deborah to Barak in the story (4:9, 14). While Barak comes down with his fighters, it is God who throws Sisera and his army "into confusion" (4:15), giving the impression that all Barak has to do is the mopping up. In the song, heavenly and earthly powers join in the battle, with the stars fighting from heaven and the waters of the Kishon sweeping the enemy away: "Wadi Kishon swept them away,/ the ancient wadi,/ Wadi Kishon" (5:19–21).

Deborah's general Barak will go only if she accompanies him (4:8), a request oftentimes interpreted as a lack of self-confidence, even cowardice; but the presence of Deborah at his side, a woman of standing in the community who is known by many and bears the title prophet, may also be seen as a logical and justifiable request. Deborah, at least, does not reprimand him but accepts without hesitation.

Judges 4:8–9

8 Barak said to her:
If you go with me, I will go;
and if you will not go with me, I will not go.

28. The verses read
4 Adonai, when you went out from Seir,
when you marched from Edom's fields,
the land shook;
also the heavens poured,
even dark clouds poured water.
5 The mountains dripped down rain
before Adonai—
this Sinai—
before Adonai the God of Israel.
A similar exclamatory recital may be found in Psalm 68:9[8], with an identical reference to Sinai, the only other place this occurs in the Bible.

9 She said: I will certainly go with you;
only there will be no glory for you[29]
on the road where you are going,
for Adonai will sell Sisera
into the hand of a woman.
Then Deborah arose and went with Barak to Kedesh.

Barak needs Deborah at his side, but as his prophet/counselor or as a fellow fighter? Frymer-Kensky assumes the people who came to Deborah for judgment (4:5) to be the ones to issue the call both to her and Barak to rouse themselves, as rendered in the song (5:12), eager as they are for someone to deliver them from their oppression. She also judges Deborah not to have taken part in the battle, since her "role is to inspire, predict and celebrate."[30] The narrative leaves the issue of her participation in the fighting ambiguous; it is certainly possible that this woman with the sting of the wasp and the fire of a torch was also a warrior woman who fought alongside her general, who was himself lightning.[31] The song puts her at the side of the tribes that support Barak (5:15). Deborah is, after all, not limited by gender stereotypes, not a typical "mother" who stays "home protecting her children, and awaiting the return of her husband or other male relatives."[32] If we take the subject of 4:7 to be Deborah, then she makes Barak the promise to deliver Sisera and his troops into his hand.[33] Human cooperation with the work of Adonai is both mandated and necessary for accomplishing the task.

29. The conjunction *efes ki* occurs in only four other places, each time providing a condition on what has already been stated (cf. Num 13:28; Deut 15:4; 2 Sam 12:14; Amos 9:8).

30. Frymer-Kensky, *Reading the Women of the Bible*, 49.

31. So Gafney (*Daughters of Miriam*, 91), who ascribes to Deborah the roles of both "military strategist and warrior."

32. Frymer-Kensky, *Reading the Women of the Bible*, 50.

33. Wilda Gafney (*Daughters of Miriam*, 91), assigns the promise of victory to Deborah in a "predictive oracle of military victory" with Deborah functioning as "YHWH's emissary with her own authoritative autonomy."

Act II, Scene 2: A Peg in the Head (Judges 4:17–22; 5:23–31)

All peace-loving folk will find the violence of her actions disturbing.[34]

Preparation for the appearance of Yael in 4:17 occurs in the narrative as well as in the song. In the narrative, a reference to the Kenites is wedged between Barak and Sisera mustering their troops in 4:11, with the notation that a group of Kenites had separated themselves from their kin and moved to the far north.[35] In the song, a desolate landscape in Israel is situated "in the days of Shamgar, the son of Anat,/ in the days of Yael" (5:6). In the story, Deborah announces to Barak that she will go to war with him and warns him that there "will be no glory for you on the road where you are going" because "Adonai will sell Sisera into the hand of a woman" (4:9). While her statement may put down a false trail by raising the expectation that she, Deborah, will be that woman, the text in short order places another woman on the scene, Yael, to whose tent Sisera flees after the defeat (4:17). Yael belongs to the Kenite clan, with the textual notation in verse 17 that there were peaceful relations between the Kenites and the Canaanites, making Yael's tent a plausible place for Sisera to flee toward.[36]

The song presents Yael with the word "blessed," in counterpoint to the curse pronounced on Meroz in the preceding verse (5:23): "Cursed be Meroz . . . cursed, yes cursed its inhabitants/ because they did not come to the help of Adonai/ to the help of Adonai among the heroes." In contrast to the triple curse on those who refuse to aid Adonai in delivering Israel, Yael is twice blessed.

34. Alice Ogden Bellis, *Helpmates, Harlots, and Heroes: Women's Stories in the Hebrew Bible* (Louisville: Westminster John Knox, 1994), 123.

35. Reference to the Kenites and their movements go back to 1:16, where their location is mentioned between notations about Caleb/Achsa and Judah.

36. I take the notation about *shalom* between Jabin and the Kenites to mean that the latter took a neutral position toward both parties, which would be logical for a tribe skilled as metal workers and smiths.

Judges 5:24–25

24 Blessed above women Yael,
wife of Heber the Kenite,
above women in the tent be she blessed![37]
25 Water he asked, milk she gave.
In a precious bowl, she brought cream.

In the narrative, Yael goes out to meet Sisera, inviting him into her tent and telling him to "have no fear." The tale is filled with innuendo and a mix of eroticism and violence. Sisera asked for water and she gave him milk, in the song augmented by the word cream and adding the vessel in which she offers it to him. Yael is a woman, and conceivably a wife, who acts in a possibly seductive and certainly a deceptive manner[38]; she closes the tent flap and covers the milk container, all the while covering what she is about to do.[39] Sisera orders her around as if she were one of his soldiers once she has complied with his wish for liquid refreshment.[40] She picks up the tent peg and hammer, her tools for setting

37. This translation of v. 24 follows Robert Alter, *Ancient Israel: The Former Prophets: Joshua, Judges, Samuel, and Kings* (New York: Norton, 2013), 136.

38. In the story, her introduction can also be read to mean that she was "a woman of the Kenite clan."

39. I read the act of covering in both v. 18 and v. 19 as closing the tent and later the vessel from which she gives him to drink. Covering Sisera seems illogical, and she need not cover him if her tent flap is closed. The covering and uncovering are of course also hinting at illicit or erotic action. See Johanna W. H. van Wijk-Bos, "Out of the Shadows: Genesis 38; Judges 4:17–22; Ruth 3," in *Reasoning with the Foxes: Female Wit in a World of Male Power*, ed. J. Cheryl Exum and Johanna W. H. van Wijk-Bos, Semeia 42 (Atlanta: Society of Biblical Literature, 1988), 51.

40. Judg 4:20: "He said to her:/ Stand at the tent opening." The form of the verb "to stand" is the masculine singular imperative. In a thought-provoking article, Deryn Guest ("From Gender Reversal to Genderfuck: Reading Jael through a Lesbian Lens," in *Bible Trouble: Queer Reading at the Boundaries of Biblical Scholarship*, ed. Teresa J. Hornsby and Ken Stone [Atlanta: SBL, 2011], 26) proposes that this verb form is one of the signals that testify to the fact that Yael is "a figure who unsettles and destabilizes, whose performativity provides one of those unintelligible genders that give the lie to ideas of sex as abiding substance." Robyn Fleming ("Jael's Gender: A Story of Appropriation"

up her tent, and hits him in the back of the neck, severing his spinal cord. He falls over and dies. The song renders its violent subject with eloquent short lines whose cadence mimics the hammer in Yael's hand.

Judges 5:26–27

26 Her hand to the peg she stretched,
her right hand to the worker's hammer;
she hammered Sisera,
she crushed his head,
she smashed and split his skull.
27 Between her legs he sank,
he fell, lay still;
between her legs he sank and fell;
where he sank, he fell,
ruined.

In the narrative, Yael tells Sisera not to be afraid (4:18), an ironic encouragement from a woman who lives on her own to a soldier who, even on the run, must have loomed formidably and most likely had not shed all of his weapons. The expression "have no fear" in the biblical text usually comes from the mouth of a superior, many times from Adonai; in this episode it is a hint at the turning of the tables that is soon to happen between Yael and Sisera. In addition, the narrative version in chapter 4 does not end with fallen Sisera but adds the sequel of Barak in hot pursuit, invited into Yael's tent, and "look! Sisera fallen, dead, the peg still in his head" (4:22). Sisera had instructed Yael not to tell anyone passing by that there was a man in her tent, an instruction that anticipates his death, for the man in her tent is in reality a dead man and therefore not a man at all.[41] In the song, he lies dead, "ruined," a Hebrew root that indicates total destruction.[42]

[Dec. 1, 2005], http://revena.livejournal.com/140803.html), in her essay on Jael, also argues that the condemnation of Jael on the part of biblical scholars is based on her challenging notions of gender construction.

41. Van Wijk-Bos, "Out of the Shadows," 54.

42. The root *shadad* occurs especially in the Prophetic literature of places

In the song, the attention turns from the murdered general to his kinfolk, the women who are waiting at home, anticipating a delay on account of their victorious son and lord dividing the loot, including the violation of women: "a womb, two wombs for each hero" (5:30).[43] The turn to the anxiously waiting mother is a natural one, for although erotic hints are present in both story and song, the associations with mothering actions are more obvious. In both versions, Yael provides milk, and in the song, Sisera falls down "between her legs" in a mimicry of childbirth. In this context, Yael's soothing words in the narrative for Sisera to "have no fear" make sense also, for she speaks as a mother to a child. In the words of Tikva Frymer-Kensky, "Sisera doesn't find sexual release and the *petit mort* ("little death") of orgasm; he finds total death. Rather than being delivered to life, he is delivered to death." As Frymer-Kensky puts it, "Yael is Sisera's last 'mother,' and as he lies there, defeated, the scene shifts to Sisera's birth mother."[44] His waiting kinswomen have no illusions about a quick

---

and cities destined for devastation. See especially Jer 4:13, 20, 30; 5:6; 6:26; 9:18[19]; 10:20; 12:12; 47:4; 48:1, 8, 15.

43. The *Hebrew and Aramaic Lexicon of the Old Testament* lists the Hebrew words used here, *raham rahamatayim*, as a "euphemism for vaginas" (*HALOT*, 3:1218, s.v. *raham*).

44. Frymer-Kensky, *Reading the Women of the Bible*, 52. Rabbinical tradition tends more toward finding in Yael a seductive presence and emphasizes the erotic suggestiveness of both story and song, as do many modern commentators. The Israeli scholar Gili Zivan (as cited by Rabbi David Ariel Joel in a written communication with author, October 16, 2016) suggests keeping both options open. Cheryl J. Exum ("Judges: Encoded Messages to Women," in *Feminist Biblical Interpretation*, ed. Luise Schottroff and Marie-Theres Wacker [Grand Rapids: Eerdmans, 2012], 116) suggests an interweaving of the erotic and the maternal. An entirely different interpretation for the place and function of Yael is provided by Ora Brison ("Jael, *'eshet heber* the Kenite: A Diviner?" in *Joshua and Judges*, ed. Athalya Brenner and Gale A. Yee [Minneapolis: Fortress, 2013], 141), who understands her to be associated with magic and divination as a "cultic intermediary/diviner." Susan Ackerman (*Warrior, Dancer, Seductress, Queen: Women in Biblical Israel* [New York: Doubleday, 1998], 93) also views Yael as a "cultic functionary," mostly because of her tribal association. While both understandings offer intriguing alternatives to more common interpretations, the explanations do not exactly arise naturally from the text.

return, although they are of course wrong about the nature of the delay. Some interpreters read the perspective on the women who wait at home for Sisera in 5:28–30 as mocking or lacking sympathy for them, or as implying they deserve violation themselves.[45] Whether with the author's approval or simply inserted as a logical explanation for their son and lord's delay, the women in these episodes—in story and song, on the Israelite as well as the Canaanite side—are a part of the war culture of the time and reflect the violence of war.[46] According to the introduction of this episode, the Israelites had suffered defeat at the hand of the Canaanites for 20 years. Mockery of the oppressor is a habitual trope of war literature, continuing until the present day and something I remember well from the period in Europe after the Second World War. Others see here a sympathetic portrait and the "composer's capacity to identify with the enemy," a device through which the "author leads us to sympathize with them, even while rejoicing in the defeat of Israel's enemies, as in v. 31."[47]

The reports of Yael's actions are more detailed and therefore grislier than those of Deborah, reminiscent of the assassination of Eglon by Ehud. There too, a weapon seemingly comes out of nowhere toward an unsuspecting enemy. The verb used for Yael's death

45. See Cheryl J. Exum, "Feminist Criticism: Whose Interests Are Being Served?" in *Judges and Method: New Approaches in Biblical Studies*, ed. Gale A. Yee (Minneapolis: Fortress, 1995), 73; Danna Nolan Fewell, "Judges," in *Women's Bible Commentary*, ed. Carol A. Newsom and Sharon H. Ringe, expanded ed. (Louisville: Westminster John Knox), 76. Jenni Williams (*God Remembered Rachel: Women's Stories in the Old Testament and Why They Matter* [London: SPCK, 2014], 88) takes this line, reading the words ascribed to Sisera's mother as if she were comforting herself with the thought of the violation of Israelite women while her own son lies violated. In Williams's words, the language "marks Deborah as a construct of patriarchy."

46. That women, then as now, would be in agreement with violent activity, even activity that affects them, is not unusual either. Witness the many women who continued to support Donald Trump as a presidential candidate in October 2016, even in light of revelations not only of boorish behavior and language but also of sexually predatorial behavior toward women.

47. Niditch, *Judges*, 82. Niditch also points out the contrast in this section between "the mighty and the weak, the urban and the rural, Canaanite and Israelite, a theme that recurs in the book of Judges."

blow (*taqa'*, 4:21) is used in Judges in a context of violence only here and in the Ehud episode (3:21). In that episode, as with the Canaanite women, a group of attendants comes up with a likely but erroneous excuse for their lord's absence. Both Ehud and Yael are unlikely characters—Yael more so than Ehud as a woman and a non-Israelite. It is possible that Shamgar (3:31) was also an outsider; his name, "son of Anat," may hint at this possibility, and he receives no patronymic or tribal identification. His tool of destruction, the ox-goad or cattle prod, is more outlandish even than that of Yael. By sliding from the Yael episode into one where Sisera's kin explicitly mention the action of rape, it is not too farfetched to read the same perspective into Yael's view of the general. Even if she did not defend herself against rape, she had the courage to invite a known rapist into her tent and to dispatch him in a manner that mirrored his own violation of women.[48]

A Look Back

We are clearly meant to identify with the protagonist and to enjoy the sheer virtuosity of his performance. It is a classic example of the underdog coming out on top, a scenario with universal comic appeal.[49]

When it comes to gender, western culture expects one to be either wholly male or wholly female.[50]

48. See Johanna W. H. van Wijk-Bos, *Reformed and Feminist: A Challenge to the Church* (Louisville: Westminster John Knox, 1991), 70–77; "Out of the Shadows," 37–67. Ryan Bonfiglio ("Choosing Sides in Judges 4–5: Rethinking Representations of Jael," in *Joshua and Judges*, ed. Athalya Brenner and Gale A. Yee [Minneapolis: Fortress, 2013], 168) offers a similar argument: "In situating Jael's murder of Sisera as resistance to rape, Judges 5 represents Jael more as a heroine *among women* than as a heroine for Israel."

49. Barry G. Webb, *The Book of Judges: An Integrated Reading*, JSOTSup 46 (Sheffield: Sheffield Academic, 1987), 131.

50. Sandra L. Gravett, Karla Bohmbach, F. V. Greifenhagen, and Donald C. Polaski, *An Introduction to the Hebrew Bible: A Thematic Approach* (Louisville: Westminster John Knox, 2008), 131.

There are very few positive things to be said about war. I have personally suffered from the fear and deprivation, the misery and murder of war. My early recollections are filled with blackened skeletons of ruined buildings. I carry with me the kinds of traumatic memories that mar one's outlook on humanity for a lifetime. This is the reality of one who lost no one close to her and whose entire family survived the war, whose losses are only those of others implanted on the psyche of a young child. In my memory book, there is nothing good to be said about war.

Yet when I watched the 1977 film *A Bridge Too Far* for the first time—a film based on events that had taken place scant miles from my home, events of which the results plunged people north of the rivers, where we lived, and in the western part of the country into six more months of German occupation, accompanied by a devastating famine—when I watched the airlift setting out from England to our shore, the largest airlift of troops ever assembled, my spirits were thrilled by the spectacle, even knowing its disastrous end and all the lives that would be lost. There is nothing good about this kind of exaltation, but it exists. I believe that something of this spirit imbues the "Song of Deborah," which brings home more than many other texts—through pounding rhythms and sound play—the exhilaration that may overtake those who prepare for and engage in battle.

The first of the deliverer heroes in Judges present us with individual as well as communal violence, and our reaction to this may be one of revulsion. Here we find a man whose left hand was the one that brandished the weapon to kill the enemy in his bathroom; another man whose story was largely forgotten, barring the farmer's tool he used for the destruction of a large number of foes, and who only seems worth remembering for that one act of horrific force; a woman who was a prophet and who went to war together with her general, aided by a divine hand guiding the forces of nature to the enemy's destruction; and a female outsider who used a household tool to destroy the man who presented a major threat to herself and her kind. When the stories were told, there could not be a thought of emulating these characters in either their militant or their moral behavior. They most likely provided laughter and entertainment, and the quotation from Webb at the beginning of this section about the comic appeal of "underdogs" goes for all of the protagonists who are in such a position—a position shared by the community after the exile, even if at that time they had not "come out on top." In addition, the stories may cause a sense of awe that, under these circumstances, anything at all had survived—even the small population of Judah after the Assyrian conquest or of Jerusalem following the Babylonian exile. Surely, somewhere in all that turmoil—the clattering of swords, the devastation of military combat, the thundering of horses' hooves, the being taken into captivity—the mercy of God must have been at work.

It is clear that both Deborah and Yael cross into territory that violates rigid gender boundaries—certainly the boundaries set up by Western culture and its influence on traditional biblical interpretation (see pp. 21–22, 32, 185, 222, 224). Deborah is traditionally assigned to be the "wife of Lappidot," and her participation in the story according to such readings did not extend to armed combat; even her judgeship is not always taken seriously. Yael's deed is considered an abhorrent violation of the ethics of "desert hospitality," an ethic that clearly does not extend to hammering and crushing a guest's head. Yael is also cunning and deceptive, traits assuredly ascribed to women and used to undermine female autonomy and authority in Christian theological tradition.[51] Today in Western culture, the gender binary is still powerful and easy to read into the pages of Scripture. Existing gender stereotypes may inhibit a clear-eyed view of the portrayal of two women who played a vital role in the early years of ancient Israel's existence.[52] To be sure, Deborah

51. In this respect, Tertullian, with his condemnation of women's vanity, stupidity and cunning, is only too typical. See Marie Turcan, "Être Femme selon Tertullien," *Vita Latina* 119 (1990): 15–21, http://www.tertullian.org/articles/turcan_etre_femme.htm.

52. For a more thorough investigation of the blurring of gender boundaries, see Fleming, "Jael's Gender: A Story of Appropriation": "The problem is not that she breaks with laws of hospitality, or even that she is a rapist quite. The problem is that by doing those things, and in order to do those things, she destabilizes both her own gender construction and the gendered identities of others. . . . The phallocentric reader sees . . . the disturbing imagery of his own methods turned against him."

is the only woman judge—a fact that is underlined by her emphatic female naming. She is also prominent in two chapters as a prophet and judge, a military strategist, possibly a fighter in chapter 4, and the author of the powerful song in chapter 5. Composing songs and giving voice to them in the Bible is not the domain of women only and not to be associated with "femininity." Next to Miriam, Moses is recorded to have composed songs; David is known as the "sweet singer of Israel." The one who writes the interpretation of events is accorded great authority, no less in song than in narrative.[53] On Deborah's word, Yael takes her place in the annals as a celebrated character who, as an outsider, a Kenite woman, achieved what the Israelite general Barak could not: the death of the adversary who had ravaged the country and its women for years.

Act III: Who Will Be Master?—Gideon (Judges 6–8)

Gideon is a guy maybe more like most of us.[54]

The next candidate to bring deliverance from oppression is Gideon, a Manassite who lives west of the Jordan. The lead-up to his story (6:1–10) paints a dire situation in the land, with the country and its people overrun by a Genghis Khan–like conquering horde of Midianites. A short review in 6:2–6 offers, in fine detail, a picture of agricultural pursuits in disarray—sowing, harvesting, and animal husbandry made impossible by the ravaging marauders who have come up from the southeast; the Israelites made homeless, driven off their land to hide in hills and caves. In response to the cry of the people, Adonai first sends a prophet rather than a deliverer. In starkly reproachful words, the prophet rebukes the people, chiding

53. Thus Gravett et al. (*An Introduction to the Hebrew Bible: A Thematic Approach*, 149) in their otherwise measured approach to the subject of gender in the Bible assign "femininity" to Deborah's singing a victory song. Instead, authoring text, be it poetry or prose, was and is a sign of authority and power in the ancient world, as it still is today.

54. Goldingay, *Joshua, Judges and Ruth*, 108.

them that they have not "listened" to the voice of Adonai (6:10), in counterpoint to the opening line of the unit that "the Israelites cried out to Adonai" (6:7). The Israelites cry out in the expectation that God will listen without extending God the same courtesy.

In the narrative that follows, Gideon is appointed by God (6:11–7:14) and Midian is defeated (7:15–8:21). Chapter 8 revisits the Midianite defeat, depicting a different Gideon than the one encountered in earlier events, with details of intertribal quarreling (8:1–3, 16–17) followed by Gideon's harsh treatment of tribal kin and the slaughter of two Midianite kings. A final unit (8:22–35) raises the question of kingship (rejected by Gideon), the danger of divided loyalties, and the aftermath of his leadership. The unresolved question that hangs over the tale concerns the ruler of Israel. Will it be Adonai, a human leader, or another master altogether? If Adonai is the ultimate leader of the people, then what qualities should the human representative of the divine ruler display?

There is much in the Gideon story that is new: Through the direct exchanges between the divine and the human realm that mark the first chapters, the hearer/reader gets a direct view of the specifics of such an appointment. The protagonist, Gideon, appears first resentful and then mistrustful and afraid until shortly before the decisive encounter with Midian (7:15), almost exactly halfway through the entire narrative. Gideon, whose name means something like "hacker," receives also the name Jerubbaal from his father (6:32), a name pointing to the struggle with or on the part of Baal, the Canaanite deity.[55] While he is in his state of uncertainty and fear, Gideon acts mostly at night. His last nocturnal exploit takes place during the march on the Midianite camp. After that moment, his character becomes more resolute, but he engages in harsh actions against his own people at moments when his leadership is called into question or support is slow in coming. Although he rejects the idea of "rule," his deeds exhibit a character that remains

55. Robert Polzin, *Moses and the Deuteronomist: A Literary Study of the Deuteronomic History*, vol. 1 (New York: Seabury, 1980), 169: "Somehow or other, the story means to emphasize through its hero's names a basic tension concerning his loyalty to [Adonai]."

divided on the question of where the loyalty of the people should be directed. While possibly different sources form the basis for the current account, I believe we should resist attempts at harmonizing the whole and agree with Elie Assis when he concludes that "Gideon oscillates between a positive and a negative approach to his leadership."[56] Editors of the book apparently intended to present Gideon in just this way.

Act III, Scene 1: A Messenger under the Oak Tree (Judges 6:1–7:14)

He needed numerous signs like a person addicted to tranquilizers.[57]

Almost all of Gideon's first activities take place around his household, and all of them are conducted in secret. In daylight, he acts out of sight of everyone because he is afraid of the enemy, and at night in the same way because he is afraid of his neighbors. A messenger of Adonai appears to him (lit. "is seen by him"), although it is far from clear how much Gideon actually sees at first. What the hearer/reader knows, that indeed he is in the presence of the Holy God, only gradually dawns on Gideon himself. Once he is on to the fact that he has been in the presence of more than an ordinary visitor, he gets his first task: not to go on the warpath but rather to overthrow a Baal altar, which he does at night "because he was too afraid of his family and the people of the town to do it by day" (6:27). From one thing and another, it is quite clear that the entire place is involved in worship of the wrong master and that building altars to Adonai is an extraordinary and dangerous thing.

Ofra, the name of Gideon's town, has associations with the word for dust, which may also connote the grave or underworld. Precisely at this place, the membrane between the natural and the supernatural world has become thin, and the messenger of Adonai

56. Elie Assis, *Self-Interest or Communal Interest: An Ideology of Leadership in the Gideon, Abimelech and Jephthah Narratives (Judg 6–12)*, trans. Stephanie Nakache, VTSup 106 (Leiden: Brill, 2005), 109.

57. Amit, *The Book of Judges*, 238.

enters the story. A divine messenger has appeared twice before in Judges (2:1, 4; 5:23), both times with a negative message. The being is seated under the oak or terebinth, a tree with cultic significance and identified with Gideon's father, Joash, who will turn out to own an altar to Baal. The messenger has not come to reproach Gideon, and all its words are encouraging, even flattering, calling him "a valiant hero" and the one who "will deliver Israel from the hand of Midian." It ultimately promises divine presence (6:12, 14, 16). When the food put on the rock goes up in flames (6:21), this action turns the rock into an altar and the food into a sacrifice.[58] An altar to Adonai, erected by Gideon and called Adonai Shalom ("Adonai is healing/wholeness," 6:24), points to the life-giving presence of the Holy God of Israel in contrast to Ofra, the dry dusty place where the Canaanite Baal (i.e., "the master") is worshiped.

Gideon is slow to catch on, but at the same time he is an extremely busy man. While the divine messenger sits and speaks, Gideon works. First, he is busy with the wheat; then he prepares a substantial meal; he builds one altar and pulls another one down, and events are far from complete. Gideon is in constant motion. Not until the very end of the story does he get to sit down in his own house (8:29). He disavows having any worth, his clan the poorest in Manasseh and he the least in his family (6:15), but clearly his family is one of substance—possessing wheat even in these times of deprivation along with animals fit for food preparation (6:19), ten servants available to help with a nocturnal task, and cattle used in the destruction of the Baal altar and the sacrifice to Adonai (6:25–26). He is fearful, but he has reasons to be afraid: He has been in the presence of the living God, he has pulled down the altar of a deity his neighbors revere and thus roused their anger, and he knows he has to go on the warpath against the Midianites. Gideon is involved in a struggle against his family, his townspeople, and his own inner fears.

Gideon's father, Joash, once he is made aware of his son's actions by the riled-up town, which clamors for Gideon's death, wards off

58. Elie Assis, *Self-Interest or Communal Interest*, 37. Assis points out that the words used in 6:18–24, "offering" (*minhah*), an "ephah of flour," and "presented" (*wayyiggash*) speak to a "ritual context."

the threat by throwing the entire matter to the gods. If Baal is indeed a mighty god, he will take care of it. The short interchange is filled with wordplay on the word "quarrel," "dispute" (*riv*), often used in a legal context and maintained in the new name for Gideon: Jerubbaal.

JUDGES 6:31–32

31 Joash said to all who stood against him:
Will you fight for Baal
and come to his rescue?
The one who fights for him may die come morning!
If he is a god, he will fight for himself
now that someone tore down his altar.
32 They called him on that day Jerubbaal, saying:
Let Baal fight with him
because he tore down his altar.

"If he is a god . . ." It's a clever answer, throwing the matter to the gods—an answer that does not commit Gideon's father, for it leaves the outcome of the struggle up in the air while at the same time underscoring the significance of what is at stake. The fight is not truly of one god with Gideon but of two gods with one another. With Elie Assis and Robert Polzin, I read Joash's statement as one from a person who still needs to be convinced about the issue of which god is more powerful and therefore deserves allegiance. Time will tell which one will win the day. The two names assigned to Gideon, "Hacker" and "Let Baal Contend," also testify to the unresolved nature of the matter and highlight "the basic tension concerning loyalty" to the God of Israel.[59] That Gideon takes part in the ambivalent attitude of kin and neighbor becomes clear from the sequel to the altar incident.[60]

59. Assis, *Self-Interest or Communal Interest*, 49–50; Polzin, *Moses and the Deuteronomist*, 169. Others hold a different view. Barry G. Webb (*The Book of Judges* [Grand Rapids: Eerdmans, 2012], 236), for example, declares that Joash has morphed "into a proto-Elijah," having switched sides overnight apparently.

60. Polzin (*Moses and the Deuteronomist*, 170) also draws attention to the

First, it looks as if all will be resolved quickly, for while the Midianites go on the warpath accompanied by allies, Gideon, under the power of Adonai's spirit, summons his own troops in a gathering that includes Asher, Zebulon and Naftali, besides his own clan of Manasseh. The text has it that these tribes "were called out behind him" (6:34 2×), with a variation of the verb used for the Israelites' "crying" to God from their distress (6:5, 7). The call to God for help thus finds an echo in Gideon's call to the neighboring tribes.[61] Then everything halts once more because Gideon requests another sign. He requests the sign from "God" rather than from "Adonai," perhaps a signal from the narrator that Gideon is not sure who will be the winner in the contest. In any case, he wants a sign that God really means for him to deliver Israel.

Judges 6:36–38

36 Gideon said to God:
If you have gotten yourself a deliverer through my hand
as you said,
37 see, I am putting a fleece of wool on the threshing floor;
if there is dew on the fleece alone,
while the rest of the land is dry,
I will know that you will deliver Israel by my hand,
as you said.

---

shifts in naming the Deity throughout the story, which, although not a feature peculiar to the Gideon story, "serves a more obvious ideological purpose here than perhaps in any other story in Judges." On this point, see also Assis, *Self-Interest or Communal Interest*, 54.

61.The unit makes use of abundant *a-u* sounds in repetitive cadence, evoking the march of troops and the blowing of a shofar.

We'ruah [Adonai] lavesha et gid'on
Wayyitqa' bashofar
Wayyizza'eq abi'ezer aharav
Umal'akhim shalah bekhol menasseh
Wayyizza'eq gam hu aharav
Umal'akhim shalah be'asher uvizvulun uvenaftali
Wayya'alu liqra'tam. (6:34–35)

38 So it was when he rose early the next day,
he squeezed the fleece,
and wrung dew from the fleece
to fill a bowl with water.

Not satisfied with the one sign, he asks for another—the opposite one: for the ground to be wet and the fleece to be dry. The second time, Gideon asks to "*do the test* with the fleece again" (6:39), using a term otherwise employed in Judges only of the Deity testing Israel (2:22; 3:1, 4). Lack of confidence and trust still marks the relationship between Adonai and his deliverer. Gideon is torn between doubt and confidence, allegiance to the familiar gods and to this new disturbing reality; he is still contending with Baal. The fractured nature of the relationship between Adonai and Israel is evident also in Gideon.[62]

God complies, and our hero can get underway with the enterprise of defeating the Midianites, for in the next breath, "Jerubbaal, that is Gideon, arose early" (7:1), a verb that in the narratives points to energetic activity (see pp. 89, 109, 119). The armies camp at a place called Harod's Spring, meaning literally the spring of fearing, anticipating the state of mind of a good number of the fighters (7:3). In a humorous twist, the Deity takes a turn requesting a sign, assuring that the credit will indeed go to the God of Israel and not to the people's own might and power (7:2). In the words of Assis, "Gideon delayed the commencement of the battle when he asked for the signs; God delayed the commencement of the battle subsequently when He reduced the number of soldiers."[63]

First, the frightened are sent home, then the ones who take too much trouble with quenching their thirst from the spring of fear (7:3, 5). Two ways of culling the troops leave three hundred men with Gideon to fight an army "as numerous as locusts" with "camels as sand on the seashore" (7:12). When faced with a choice "that night" to

62. Assis (*Self-Interest or Communal Interest*, 56) points out the use of day and night in this scene: "Belief in God prevails at night" (as when Gideon breaks down the Baal altar), and God acts to confirm the requested signs, while doubts prevail in the daytime.

63. Assis, *Self-Interest or Communal Interest*, 67.

attack right away or to go and investigate the Midianite camp, Gideon chooses the road of fear once again and sneaks up to the enemy. He overhears a dream together with its interpretation. While this may seem to us an unlikely means to strengthen the courage of the faint-hearted, dreams and their interpretation had great power in the ancient world and were understood as divine messages. When a Midianite interprets his companion's dream to predict the defeat of his own people, prophesying that "God has given Midian and all its host into his [i.e., Israel's] hand" (7:14), it suffices to convince Gideon, who arranges a surprise attack on the Midianite camp that same night.

Act III, Scene 2: Defeat of Midian (Judges 7:15–8:21)

Gideon has developed a new self-assertive destructiveness.[64]

It is not easy to kill, even in a war setting.[65]

In an event reminiscent of the capture of Jericho, a frightful amount of noise—in this case at night, creating confusion with the wavering light of many torches and giving the impression of a far larger unit about to attack than is actually the case—is enough to send the Midianites running (7:19–21), and through Adonai's intervention they turn their weapons on each other. Niditch compares the tactics to those of "bandit warriors" in the *Iliad,* for whom "trickery, luck and divine favor sometimes figure more prominently than skill and weaponry."[66] The Midianite camp flees with Israelite tribes in pursuit. All seems well.

There is, however, a good deal still to be taken care of to make sure Midian is put down for good. Three units relate events during the pursuit of the Midianites to accomplish this end; all three involve

64. J. Cheryl Exum, "The Centre Cannot Hold: Thematic and Textual Instabilities in Judges," in *Reconsidering Israel and Judah: Recent Studies on the Deuteronomistic History,* ed. Gary N. Knoppers and J. Gordon McConville (Winona Lake, IN: Eisenbrauns, 2000), 587.

65. Susan Niditch, *War in the Hebrew Bible: A Study in the Ethics of Violence* (Oxford: Oxford University Press, 1993), 100.

66. Niditch, *Judges,* 98.

intertribal quarrels. These quarrels stand at the center of the events rather than the chase itself. First, Ephraim, called upon to hold the Jordan against the fleeing Midianites, captures two chiefs, Oref and Ze'ev ("Raven" and "Wolf") and sends their heads to Gideon from across the Jordan (7:24–25). As a follow-up, perhaps with success gone to their head, the Ephraimites berate Gideon for not having called on them sooner. In his response, Gideon exhibits a model of diplomacy, successfully calming down the indignant Ephraimites by rating his own performance far below theirs in comparison (8:1–3).

There will not be such propitious outcomes in the next exchanges. Gideon marches on, crosses the Jordan with his band of three hundred, all notably fatigued, and requests refreshment from the inhabitants of Succoth and Penuel. Both times, his request is refused mockingly, and Gideon threatens to punish them on his return (8:4–9). The narrator's voice provides no additional reason, so we can only surmise that there was as yet little trust on the part of Israelites in the ability of Gideon to put down the enemy for good. Gideon, however, completes his mission successfully, captures two kings, Zevach and Tsalmuna (8:10–12), and follows through on his earlier threat against the two Israelite cities to the extent that he kills those of Penuel (8:13–17). Remarkably, more attention is paid in the text to the hostile exchanges with Succoth and Penuel and their subsequent punishment than to the battle with the Midianite camp. The result is a different portrait of Gideon than the earlier one. Gone is the diffident, hesitant man who needed constant convincing; in his stead, a powerful and vindictive leader has arisen. Is the same man at work—one who is still hesitant and mistrustful of both his own worth and the power of his God and thus overreaching in his quest to establish himself? Or is this a man who, constantly needing to reassure himself of his self-worth, has turned into a bully now that he has the upper hand?

The two captured kings still need to be dispatched. Before killing them, Gideon asks them a question.

Judges 8:18–19

18 He said to Zevach and Tsalmuna:
Where are the men whom you slew in Tabor?

They said: Like you, so were they,
each the form of the sons of a king.
19 He said: They were my brothers,
the sons of my mother.
As Adonai lives,
had you let them live,
I would not slay you.

As it turns out, Gideon has a personal stake in the demise of the kings, which in some respects resembles the execution of the five kings in Joshua 10:22–27 (see p. 123). His question to the two captives ("where are . . . ?") makes little sense, because he knows the men are dead and also knows where they died. It is reminiscent of God's query to Cain after he killed Abel: "Where [is] Abel, your brother?" (Gen 4:9). Like God in the Genesis story, Gideon hides an accusation in his inquiry; like Cain, the Midianite kings give an answer that is not straightforward but is a revealing one all the same. The kings declare that the men they dispatched had a royal mien, just like Gideon: the "form" of royal offspring. There was thus honor in killing Gideon's brothers because of their stature. Gideon reveals that they were his brothers, not sons of a king, but sons of his mother. It is going to be a life for a life. The kings' death has to be humiliating, so Gideon hands the task to his son who is "only a lad" (8:20). But this lad is afraid, just as Gideon was once afraid and as Saul's weapon bearer will be afraid (1 Sam 31:4); thus, the kings get their wish and are executed by Gideon himself, by a man with royal mien in full strength.

Niditch maintains that the interaction between Gideon and the two kings "richly evokes a heroic ethos of war in which respect is expressed between combatants and in which it is considered proper for men of equal skill and training to confront one another."[67] She compares the admiring phrases of the kings with those of warriors in the *Song of Roland*. When Gideon's son withdraws from the job, the captives invite Gideon to do the deed: "You yourself arise and strike us,/ for like the man is his strength" (8:21). Such a phrase too, according to Niditch, testifies to the mutual respect with which "no-

67. Niditch, *Judges*, 105.

ble enemies" negotiate "their own execution."[68] Such observations are on the mark, and yet a question remains. What does it mean to have royal form? Did Gideon's brothers exude authority? Did they appear formidable and strong? Were they tall? Or are the two kings simply flattering the person who is about to execute them "in the bardic tradition"? The most striking fact is that the word "king" has been uttered for the first time in Judges in relation to an Israelite deliverer. It will resound with frequency again in chapter 9 in relation to Gideon's offspring, Abimelek. The presence or absence of an Israelite king has been raised as a subject.

Act III, Scene 3: A Refusal to Rule (Judges 8:22–35)

The main problem in the Gideon account is Gideon's self-contradiction.[69]

The trap closes fast upon the Israelites.[70]

JUDGES 8:22–23

22 Then said the men of Israel to Gideon:
Rule over us, you and your son
and the son of your son,
for you delivered us from the hand of Midian.
23 Then said to them Gideon:
I will not rule over you myself,
and my son will not rule over you;
Adonai will rule over you.

Not surprisingly, the people invite Gideon, the man of royal bearing, the one with royal habits, "to rule" over them, seeking to institute a hereditary monarchy no less. He refuses, properly observing that Adonai is the ruler of Israel. And yet, overtly refusing

68. Niditch, *Judges*, 105; see also Niditch, *War*, 90–105.
69. Assis, *Self-Interest or Communal Interest*, 105.
70. Polzin, *Moses and the Deuteronomist*, 173.

the notion may not mean that a part of Gideon does not embrace it at the same time. As Assis points out, there are motifs here that point to royal aspects of Gideon's behavior, including taking the crescents from the necks of the Midianite camels, which were most likely "royal ornaments" (8:26).[71] In addition, upon refusing the role of ruler, Gideon requests part of the booty taken by the troops. What follows is eerily reminiscent of the incident of the golden calves at Mt. Sinai (Exod 32:2–4). The people give their gold willingly in both cases, and the leader makes an image (8:24–27). In Gideon's case, it is an "ephod," a word that sometimes points to a garment in the biblical texts but here is clearly some sort of image. Though it was perhaps not initially made for a nefarious purpose, the narrator declares about the ephod that "all Israel prostituted itself before it there/ and it became for Gideon and his house a snare" (8:27), language used elsewhere in Judges and the Torah for idolatry.[72]

Notwithstanding the coda on the humbling of the Midianites and a forty-year peace in the land "in the days of Gideon" (8:28), alarming sounds of discord are present also at the end of the Gideon story. In a final unit (8:30–35), his multitudinous offspring is noted: seventy sons and many wives. Many wives and a great number of offspring mark those who conduct themselves in the manner of kings in the ancient world; this specific behavior is expressly forbidden in the case of kingship in Israel in Deuteronomy 17:17. Gideon names one of his sons "Abimelek" ("my father [is] king").[73] Assis observes that Gideon is buried "in the tomb of his father Joash," a notation used mostly in reference to kings.[74] The concluding observation

71. Assis, *Self-Interest or Communal Interest*, 102.

72. Cf. Exod 23:33; 34:12, 14, 16; Lev 17:7; Num 25:2; Deut 7:16; 31:16; Josh 23:13; Judg 2:3. Assis (*Self-Interest or Communal Interest*, 107) suggests that the false worship could also be directed at Gideon himself, with an intentional ambiguity in the text.

73. The fact that Abimelek is the son of Gideon's "concubine in Shechem" (8:31) may also point to royal habits, as the term "concubine" (*pilegesh*) occurs especially in the context of royal polygyny. See Mark E. Biddle, *Reading Judges: A Literary and Theological Commentary* (Macon, GA: Smyth and Helwys, 2012), 100.

74. Assis, *Self-Interest or Communal Interest*, 114.

that the Israelites once again prostituted themselves in idolatry after Gideon's death is almost superfluous, although the epitaph on Gideon is a positive one. While Gideon is not a failed leader, his story is shot through with ambiguity. First resentful, mistrustful, and afraid, then overweening and punitive to his own people, and in the end at least enabling backsliding on the part of his people, he is perhaps ruler in all but name.[75] Both the approving and the disapproving voice remain in the story and, when all is said and done, the jury is still out on who will be master in Israel.

Act IV: The Man Who Would Be King—Abimelek (Judges 9)

The Abimelech account . . . is not a deliverance account.[76]

The two adventurers who set out to become kings in a remote part of Afghanistan in Kipling's story do not come to a good end, and neither does the man who makes a similar effort in the sequel to Gideon's story. Unlike the Gideon narrative, which takes a long time to get off the ground, chapter 9 plunges immediately into the intrigue and bloodshed, ending in the crowning of a king, Abimelek, Gideon's son mentioned in the previous chapter (8:31). Abimelek presents a portrait in contrast to his father. He is far from hesitant or fearful, enters the story speaking, grasps for kingship, and buys himself a position at the cost of murdering all of Gideon's other sons. As happens in some folk tales, one of the potential victims, the youngest of the massacred brothers, survives and proclaims a prophetic parable announcing a bad end for the new ruler and those who have elected him (9:7–21). A final series of episodes describes intertribal conflict and protracted hostilities, concluding with the violent demise of Abimelek (9:22–54).

75. Assis (*Self-Interest or Communal Interest,* 109) judges Gideon to oscillate between a positive and negative approach to leadership, refusing kingship while carrying on as a king. I agree with Assis to the extent that Gideon, in Goldingay's words "a guy . . . like most of us" (*Joshua, Judges and Ruth,* 108), shows inconsistency in his conduct.

76. Assis, *Self-Interest or Communal Interest,* 131.

Unlike in previous contexts, there is no enemy oppressing the Israelites, and all the violence comes from within. The verb *harag* ("to slay, murder") is in Judges concentrated in the Gideon and Abimelek chapters, occurring seven times in each. In addition, the narrative stands out for the abundance of verbal exchanges, including the extended parable told by the surviving member of Abimelek's family. The leadership of Abimelek is called into question in the chapter, as well as the behavior of the leaders of Shechem, both of which are judged negatively by the narrator. Hints of inappropriate leadership that were present already in the Gideon narrative here become full-blown problems that, in the end, undo all the participants. Rather than an experience of threat from outsiders, Judges 9 depicts peril that comes from within the community.

Act IV, Scene 1: A King in Shechem (Judges 9:1–6)

Mother's kin/father's kin—does it make a difference?[77]

JUDGES 9:1–2

1 Abimelek, the son of Jerubbaal,
went to Shechem, to his mother's brothers,
and spoke to them and the entire clan of his mother's
household:
2 Say now in the hearing of all the masters of Shechem:
What is better for you?
That seventy men, all the sons of Jerubbaal, rule over you
or that one man rule over you?
And remember that I am your flesh and blood!

With the Abimelek episode, the theater of operations has shrunk to two towns and two households. Gideon´s town of origin

77. Naomi Steinberg, "Social Scientific Criticism: Judges 9 and Issues of Kinship," in *Judges and Method: New Approaches in Biblical Studies*, ed. Gale A. Yee (Minneapolis: Fortress, 2007), 54.

and his domicile, Ofra, now stands in opposition to Shechem, the site of Abimelek´s mother´s clan. In the first five verses, Abimelek is the subject of five verbs: he went, he spoke, he paid, he entered, he killed. The direction of his movements is first to Shechem to put a proposition before his uncles, members of his mother's household. His final action is to return to Ofra, the household of his father, to massacre Gideon's entire male offspring, his own kin on his father's side. His words to his uncles are in the form of a rhetorical question ending in a reminder of kinship obligations: "Remember that I am your flesh and blood!" (9:2).[78] Abimelek's question assumes that Gideon's offspring has inherited a leadership role, something Gideon himself disavowed (8:23), and it ignores the rule of Adonai, which Gideon emphasized. The question of rule is reduced to who will be the human master.

Abimelek's uncles understand very well what he is actually asking, and they convince the "masters" (*baalim*) of Shechem to provide the funds so Abimelek can wipe out potential rivals. With the money, he hires a group of mercenaries—worthless and reckless men, the riffraff of Shechem—and goes back to Ofra to accomplish what he has in mind, sacrificing his paternal kin to his ambitions (9:4–5). The episode ends with the "masters of Shechem" crowning Abimelek as king at the "terebinth of the pillar of Shechem," a place with sacred connotations, which indicates ambiguous allegiances.

Shechem was an ancient Canaanite town. We came across this place as a location with sacred significance, symbolized by the Ark of the Covenant, in Joshua 8:30–35, and in Joshua 24 it was the place where Joshua pledged the people by a solemn covenant to be loyal to Adonai alone. This aura of holiness also clings to Shechem in Judges 9. Yet, in contrast to the role it serves in the Joshua text, here it stands out as a place of sacrilege and idolatrous worship. The term *baal* is present in some form in every verse of the episode. Gideon is named Jerubbaal throughout (1, 2, 5). The leaders of Shechem are called the *baalim* of Shechem, the owners or masters (2, 3, 6)—a noun used only one other time in Judges (also with a negative connotation) apart from the fifteen times in this chapter (20:5). Almost

78. The phrase in Hebrew reads literally, "your bone and flesh."

exactly in the center of the scene (4), there is reference to the "covenant Baal" mentioned at the end of the Gideon narrative (8:33). The phrase encountered previously, that the "Israelites continued to do the wrong in the eyes of Adonai," is lacking in the tale of Abimelek, for it would be superfluous. There are three households in the story: the household of Abimelek's mother, the doomed household of his father, and, in between these two, the "house of the covenant Baal." Abimelek does not stand in any relationship to the God of Israel, never mentions Adonai, and acts throughout on his own initiative and for his own benefit. The money he pays his band of worthless, murderous followers comes from the worship of the covenant Baal. He ends up as king in a house where the Baal instead of Adonai is master.

Act IV, Scene 2: King Bramble (Judges 9:7–21)

Appointment of a king out of self-interest is liable to lead ultimately to a conflict of interest that will result in disaster.[79]

While Shechem represents the site of exclusive loyalty to Adonai in Joshua and emphasizes service of a different master in Judges 9, the site of Ebal and Gerizim is identified with the holy ritual by which Joshua ratifies the Teaching of Moses for the people by sacrifice and inscription (Josh 8:30–35). Although the words ascribed to Yotam in Judges 9 may have no original connection to these locations, surely the collectors and editors were aware of their significance. Yotam, the one escapee of the massacre of his brothers, of which his half brother was the ringleader, sets himself on Mount Gerizim and speaks to the Shechemites through parable and warning. His name in Hebrew contains an abbreviation (*y)* of the name of the Deity together with a word connoting uprightness, absence of blame, wholeness, and perfection. The one man whose name contains the sole reference to Adonai in the narrative speaks as a prophet on a site that elsewhere has a strong connection to the sacred Teaching of Moses.

79. Assis, *Self-Interest or Communal Interest*, 153.

Even though the title prophet is not explicit in the chapter, Yotam, in the manner of a prophet, calls on the "masters of Shechem" to listen to his words because it will earn them God's attention (7). Like a prophet, he speaks in sayings with ethical implications (8–15).[80] Like a prophet, he presents a warning to the Shechemites and thus confronts them with the consequence of their choices (16–20).

I agree with Assis that story (8–15) and warning (16–20) in Yotam's parable should be viewed in correspondence, intending "to present a set of different and complementary arguments."[81] In the story or parable of the trees who go out to "anoint themselves a king," they are reduced to asking the lowliest of them, the bramble, to take on the task.[82] In response to the invitation, the bramble issues a conditional promise and a threat. If the trees are serious, then the thorn bush invites them to "take shelter" in its shade. The phrase "take shelter" (*hasah*) occurs for the most part in poetic language in reference to finding refuge in Adonai.[83] The threat spells out the consequences of their not following through on their intention and promises a devouring fire (15). The specific type of bush or tree mentioned in the parable (*atad*) is not entirely clear since it occurs elsewhere only in two other places, but it is common enough in other Semitic languages to identify it as some type of thorny bush. Taking shelter in its shade is not a viable option, and coming too close to it might even cause serious harm. An ironic promise combined with a threat spells a far from promising future for the relationship between the king and his subjects, a relationship which, in the context of the real world, was already marked by violence and greed rather than mutual trust.

In the moral or warning that follows, Yotam appeals to the Shechemites' obligation to his father, Gideon/Jerubbaal, who

80. Niditch (*Judges*, 116) identifies Yotam's story as a *mashal*, "a form of oblique and artful communication (a saying, an icon, a narrative, a symbolic action, or another form) that sets up an analogy between the communication and the real-life settings of the listeners."

81. Assis, *Self-Interest or Communal Interest*, 152.

82. With the emphatic opening in v. 8, one might even say that the trees go out of their way to accomplish their goal: "Going out, they went, the trees . . ."

83. For example, see Deut 32:37; 2 Sam 22:3, 31; Pss 2:12; 5:12[11]; 7:2[1]; 16:1; 17:7.

"fought for them, risked his life" on their behalf, and "delivered" them, framing his challenge by calling into question the good faith of their actions (16, 19). While the analogies between story and "real" events are not literal, the story concerns the worthiness as well as the threat of someone like Abimelek with the warning addressed to the loyalty of the Shechemites. At the end of chapter 8, the narrator charges the Israelites with not "keeping loyalty" (*hesed*) with "the house of Jerubbaal." Yotam sharpens the charge by casting it in ironic rhetorical questions ("if . . . you acted"), adding "truth and integrity" to the qualities desirable in those who benefitted from Gideon's leadership. Once again, the focus is on the "house" of one over against the other. References to Jerubbaal and his house abound in the warning. Yet in the end, all are kin. Abimelek is a son of the same house as Yotam, and so the house in truth is divided against itself. There is no question that only disaster will be the result of such a situation.

Yotam's words have clear implications for the context of Abimelek's kingship. While the story contains an ironic reversal, presenting a community in search of a king rather than a king in search of a crown, the core truth is that Abimelek is a worthless specimen who should have been the last choice of any community for leadership. The townsmen have clearly not acted in good faith, in truth and integrity toward Gideon and his house, and Yotam's warning about a devouring fire that will consume them all (20) serves as a prophetic announcement of disaster. Less clear are the implications of Yotam's speech for kingship in general, and scholars have different opinions. Assis holds that story and warning both underline the importance of motivation: on the one hand for those who make the appointment to kingship and on the other for the one who takes on the monarchial role. In his view, the parable is neither pro- nor anti-monarchic. It is, rather, "a censure of Abimelech's egocentric personality, his unsuitability for the office of king, and the egotistical motives of the citizens of Shechem in making him king."[84]

84. Assis, *Self-Interest or Communal Interest*, 153. Cf. Amit (*The Book of Judges*, 111), who argues that "Jotham's parable brings out the problematic of the absence of monarchy."

Act IV, Scene 3: A Devouring Fire (Judges 9:22–57)

Does the promise of a full stop encourage the telling of a story, does narrative need boundaries?[85]

Judges 9:22–24

22 And Abimelek ruled over Israel three years.
23 Then God sent an evil spirit
between Abimelek and the masters of Shechem.
And the masters of Shechem broke faith with Abimelek
24 so that should come home the violence
of the seventy sons of Jerubbaal
and their blood settle on Abimelek, their brother,
who slew them,
and on the masters of Shechem,
who strengthened his hands
in slaying his brothers.

The opening lines provide a capsule of what is to come and, together with the closing verses of the chapter (55–57), establish the framework in which alliances appear to be founded on shifting sands and hostilities between the parties are the order of the day. The unit reveals ahead of time that nothing good will come of Abimelek's rule—that the violence perpetrated by him and the Shechemites will come home to roost—and so prevents tension from building up in the following narrative. Between the "masters" (*baalim*) of Shechem, mentioned three times, and Abimelek, also mentioned three times, the relationship will founder on the treachery of the Shechemites. The narrator assigns the cause of the breach to an "evil spirit" sent by God. Only one other time in the Bible is the sending of an evil spirit ascribed to the Deity, which makes the declaration highly unusual, but it announces conclusively that what follows will be a descending spiral of betrayal and violence.[86] The purpose of the sending

85. Francesca Kay, *The Long Room* (Portland: Tin House Books, 2014), 62.

86. Cf. 1 Sam 16:14, where Saul is the recipient of an "evil spirit" sent from Adonai.

will be for the violence done by Shechem and Abimelek to rebound on their heads, as observed again in the closing lines (56–57): The "wrong" that Abimelek had perpetrated by killing his brothers and the "wrong" of the Shechemites acted like a boomerang.

While the story set inside the brackets of verses 23–25 and 55–57 lacks tension because the hearer/listener knows where it will lead, it is filled with interesting and confusing detail about action and dialogue among characters. One Gaal wins the trust of the "masters of Shechem" and gets them to denounce Abimelek during cultic festivities (26–27). Before he enters the story, the narrator recounts that the "masters" of Shechem have created a situation of highway robbery to the disadvantage of Abimelek. In the words of Robert Boling, the picture "depicts a wide-open city, ripe for the plucking by another."[87] The town's commander, Zevul, is on the side of Abimelek, and in the end Gaal and his cohorts are defeated. Different groups are lying in "ambush" (25, 32, 34, 35, 43), and there is gratuitous use of force and cruelty (47–49). Fire indeed breaks out against Shechem when Abimelek is not satisfied to only demolish and raze the town (45) but also sets fire to a great number of people who have fled into a tower: "one thousand, male and female" (49)—that is to say, not warriors. Finally, Abimelek lays siege to Tebes and is killed by a woman dropping a millstone on his skull. Before he expires from the blow, he begs his weapon bearer to kill him because he does not want to go down in history as the victim of a woman's attack: "Lest they say of me:/ A woman slew him" (9:54). No reasons are provided for Abimelek's reason to go to war with Tebes, but clearly his comeuppance with a stone provides a satisfactory end for those who know that he killed his brothers "on one stone" (5).

Our Abimelek is no deliverer but rather a fire that devours everyone who comes in his path until he finds his own violent end, an ignominious death that will become proverbial in Israel.

Judges 9:55–57

55 When they saw, the people of Israel,
that Abimelek was dead,

87. Boling, *Judges*, 176.

each went to his place.
56 So returned God the wrong of Abimelek
that he did to his father
by killing his seventy brothers.
57 And all the wrong of the people of Shechem,
returned God on their heads.
And so came on them the curse of Yotam,
the son of Jerubbaal.

All that happened after Abimelek became king was due to God, who sent an evil spirit to divide the loyalties of the Shechemites (23). It is God who stirred them up and God who brought down on all their heads the wrong they did. There is no outside oppressive force and no deliverer in this tale. The spirit God sends is not one to strengthen and embolden the hero but rather one that sows discord and contention. The hero who was victorious in battle throughout the story falls in the end, like Sisera, by the hand of a woman. Once he is dead, the people do not get a deserved respite from their troubles but simply return home, "each to his place" (55). As Robert Polzin observes, "Abimelech is portrayed as a true villain."[88]

Act V: Who Is the Man? (Judges 10–12)

Do the brief notices suggest that some of the traditions about judges were less well preserved than others?[89]

Chapter 10 acts as an interlude, leading into the next story with a major protagonist, Jefta. First there is a summary list of two "judges" preceding Jefta (10:1–5), presenting an image of smooth transitions and absence of conflict. Then follows a period of tremendous violence as a result of pervasive apostasy, in the wake of which the Israelites not only "cry out" but also, for the first and last time in Judges, confess their misdeeds and change their practices (10:6–18).

88. Polzin, *Moses and the Deuteronomist*, 175.
89. Niditch, *Judges*, 121.

In contrast to previous circumstances, Adonai does not raise up a deliverer but stands aside, which forces the people to go in search of a leader (10:18).

Gilead in the Transjordan is especially in need, and it is thus Jefta, the Gileadite, who is invited to come to the rescue of the beleaguered people. In the Jefta account (11:1–12:7), Jefta is successful in his assault on the Ammonites, but by his own doing the victory costs him the life of his only child. There are echoes of the Gideon and Abimelek narratives in the Jefta chapters. During Jefta's leadership, another quarrel with Ephraim erupts, reminiscent of altercations during the leadership of Gideon. Unlike Gideon, Jefta chooses to quash the rebellion by military might. Like Abimelek, Jefta is chosen by the people, but unlike Abimelek, Jefta himself does not go looking for the position. His people elect him, and at this point kingship is apparently not a viable option. Another summary recital regarding three "judges" closes the Jefta stories (12:8–15), creating, together with the opening unit, a frame that provides both continuity and contrast.

Act V, Scene 1: From Tola to Avdon (Judges 10:1–5; 12:8–15)

The major contribution of the list of minor judges to the book of Judges in its final form is to "frame" the Jephthah story as a critical juncture in the overarching story.[90]

Tola, Ya'ir, Ibsan, Elon, and Avdon are each said to have "judged" Israel, with the terrain expanding beyond the narrow context of one town or region to include all Israel, although this most likely presents an idealized picture (10:2, 3; 12:8, 11, 13). The language of the short sections presents a repetitive pattern with the verb in first and the subject in last place of the sentence. Each "judge" is located in a specific region, with Tola at the beginning and Avdon at the end both buried in the hill country of Ephraim (10:2; 12:15). Only the first of the five, Tola, comes on the stage "to deliver Israel" (10:1). Since no introductory statement is provided regarding oppression of the Israelites by a hos-

90. Biddle, *Reading Judges*, 116.

tile force, one assumes that the death of Abimelek has brought no rest to the land. For each of the five, their death and a place of burial are cited (10:2, 5; 12:10, 12, 15). Three of them, Ya'ir, Ibsan, and Avdon have numerous offspring, a sign of wealth and high status—even pointing to kingship, since large harems could usually only be maintained at a court. The temporal and regional notations provide sequential and tribal/geographical specifics, with references to the tribes of Issachar, Zebulon, and Ephraim. The frame around Jefta possibly represents fragments of originally longer stories of leaders present in different localities at the same time. In our text, they are portrayed as active during sequential time periods with leadership over the entire people.

Connections and contrasts between the frame and the main story of Jefta are not hard to find. The region of Gilead, home of Ya'ir, is at the center of Judges 11–12:7, and Jefta is, like Ya'ir, a Gileadite. The threefold mention of large families in the case of Ya'ir, Ibsan, and Abdon, with a mention of the third generation for the latter (12:14), presents a stark contrast with Jefta, who has only one child and deprives himself of his only offspring. Although Tola is said to "deliver" Israel, the descriptions are on the whole free of the tumult and chaos of conflict and exude a more tranquil atmosphere, thus respectively setting the stage for the events surrounding Jefta and concluding the continued apostasy of Israel reported in 10:6–18. The purpose of the editors in placing these short references exactly here may have been to highlight contrast or to provide a narrative pause in between stories filled with tension and reports of leadership that fails in one way or another.

Act V, Scene 2: Belated Repentance (Judges 10:6–18)

Adonai's failure, in a sense, to keep his word points to a profound insight into the character of the biblical God. . . . While not capricious or wavering in character, the God of Israel adapts in response to altered behavior.[91]

First, there appears to be nothing new under the sun, as Israel continues to do what is "wrong in the eyes of Adonai," and once again God

91. Biddle, *Reading Judges*, 117.

punishes it by delivering the people into the hand of hostile forces. This time, however, the people not only cry out to God but engage in confession and repentance, a unique occurrence in Judges. Twice in the short section, the people proclaim that they have sinned, the second time adding actions consistent with their proclamation.

JUDGES 10:10, 15–16

10 And cried out the Israelites to Adonai saying:
We have sinned against you,
because we have abandoned our God
and served the Baals.
. . .
15 And said the Israelites to Adonai:
We have sinned!
Do to us as is good in your eyes.
Only deliver us today!

16 They removed the alien gods from their midst
and served Adonai,
and his soul was vexed by the trouble of Israel.

Unlike the incident at Bochim (2:2–5) or the announcement by the prophet in view of the people's transgressions preceding the Gideon story (6:7–9), no intermediary is present, and the exchange takes place directly between God and Israel. After the first confession, Adonai refuses to come to their aid, instead reminding the people of previous rescue missions that were met with faithless behavior and sarcastically counseling them to appeal to the gods they have chosen to serve instead of Adonai, declaring, "I will not continue to deliver you" (10:13). The people continue to confess their sins and add deed to word, setting aside the Baals and serving Adonai. The people's words and actions elicit no speech or action in return; instead, the narrator reports on the mood of God with an ambiguous phrase indicating that God is in low spirits on account of the trouble Israel faces (16).[92]

92. The verb *qatsar* connected to *ruah* or *nefesh* indicates low spirits,

The chapter ends with the Ammonites and the Israelites readying themselves for battle and the Gileadites deliberating as to who will take the initiative to face the enemy (18).

How should we understand God's refusal to intervene in the face of what appears to be genuine repentance and return to loyalty? A standard refrain in the Hebrew Bible refers to God as "gracious and compassionate, slow to anger and abounding in steadfast love."[93] Is it not always a part of the character of the biblical God to respond with grace and forgiveness to sincere human contrition and determination to change course? Even murderous outsiders may encounter God's long-suffering patience with human waywardness (see Jonah 3:10). Surely God's covenant people deserve the mercy that so often trumps God's anger! God's reaction to the community's repentance in this chapter is, however, not anger but dejection of the spirit—impatience aroused by fruitless effort (16). There is a sense of giving up on God's part, possibly with the method that so far has not rendered either adequate leadership or continued loyalty on the part of the people. Assis is of the opinion that God's refusal to send a deliverer even in the face of genuine repentance highlights the problem with the leadership model presented in Judges.[94] Jefta is thus explicitly not sent by Adonai to deliver the people but sought out by the Gileadites as one who "will *begin* to do battle against the Ammonites" (18). Similarly, Samson "will *begin* to deliver Israel from the hand of the Philistines" (13:5).

---

loss of patience, perhaps annoyance. This construction is used in reference to the people in Exod 6:9 as they labor in Egypt and during the trek through the wilderness in Num 21:4. Job uses it speaking of himself (Job 21:4), and both Miçah and Zechariah employ the expression with reference to God, referring to God's *ruah* and God's *nefesh* respectively (Mic 2:7; Zech 11:8). "At this state in all the other accounts, God sends a deliverer to save Israel from their enemies, but here only God's 'feelings' are related!" (Assis, *Self Interest or Communal Interest*, 184).

93. Cf. Exod 34:6; Num 14:18; Pss 86:15; 103:8; 145:8; Jonah 4:2; Neh 9:17; Joel 2:13.

94. Assis, *Self-Interest or Communal Interest*, 189. It should be noted that Assis, with this analysis, does not propose reading Judges as a defense of the monarchy but rather as "a discussion of the advantages and disadvantages" of different leadership models, including the monarchy (239–248).

Act V, Scene 3: Jefta the Gileadite (Judges 11:1–12:7)

In the story of Jephthah and his daughter, somewhere nobility turns into a nightmare, devotion turns into death.[95]

The story of Jefta unfolds in four stages. First, the outsider Jefta, cast out on account of his being the son of a prostitute, is courted by the elders of Gilead to fight the Ammonites on their behalf and bargains with them to become their leader (11:1–11). In the second stage, Jefta attempts in vain to come to a peaceful agreement with the Ammonites through diplomatic efforts (11:12–28). The third stage recounts the victory over Ammon and the results of a vow undertaken by Jefta on the eve of the battle (11:29–40), with a disproportionate amount of space devoted to the articulation of the vow and its fatal aftermath. A final stage consists of an account of intertribal mayhem and murder and ends with the death of Jefta (12:1–7).

These episodes, especially the section in which the vow is prominent, have received a torrent of detailed and insightful attention from a great number of scholars in the last decades. In what follows, I address especially important questions left by gaps in the story and by the pictures drawn of the various characters.

Jefta's name, in Hebrew *Yiftach* ("he will open"), can be seen as a hope-filled name that points to a promise embedded in this person vis-à-vis the closed-off possibilities for the Israelites, specifically the Gileadites, in their present dire circumstances without a deliverer to rescue them. Chapter 10 ends with the question, "Who is the man who will begin to do battle against the Ammonites?" (10:18). In the next breath, the name "he will open" could be heard as a positive response (11:1). In addition, he receives the appellation "valiant hero," a title also given to Gideon by the heavenly messenger (6:12), an indication of *Yiftach*'s military capabilities. A question arises, however, as to who is the subject of the action of opening.[96] Has Adonai re-

95. Renita J. Weems, *Just A Sister Away: Understanding the Timeless Connection Between Women of Today and Women in the Bible* (New York; Boston: Warner Books, 2005), 58.

96. Boling (*Judges*, 197) suggests that the name is short for the place name

lented to now open up an escape hatch for the beleaguered people? Is Jefta the one sent by God as a new deliverer to save them, and is he the one opening new opportunities for survival? Jefta indeed opens up a new chapter, but it will be one with negative as well as positive sides. Also, hopes located in name and epithet are quickly destabilized because Jefta is the offspring of a prostitute (*zonah*), and his brothers, sons of his father's wife, cast him out as soon as they are able for fear of having to share the inheritance. Is there a valid reason for this fear, or is this once again a sign of a family where discord and kin strife take prominent place, a foreshadowing on the family stage of the larger kin strife to follow in chapter 12 and the final chapters of the book?

The first steps taken by our "valiant hero" are in any case not promising, for he flees his domicile to settle in a region called Tov, a name that means "good," together with a band of "worthless men," giving the impression that he is living the life of a bandit. The other protagonist in Judges who surrounded himself with characters of that sort was Abimelek before he and his followers went to kill his brothers (9:4–5).[97] Again, a name that seems to hold promise is undercut, this time by characterizing the company Jefta keeps as worthless. When the elders of Gilead come to recruit him for battle against the Ammonites, Jefta, not one to be at a loss for words, castigates the elders for his exile and prods them into accepting him as "head" on the condition that victory over Ammon is achieved. In verse 11, before the battle can be joined, he is appointed "head" and commander and Jefta speaks "all his words before Adonai at Mizpah." A premature appointment causes the reader to wonder about the degree of trust the Gileadites put in Jefta and his readiness to follow through on his commitment. Their new head and commander, for his part, speaks "his words," but we are left to wonder what they

Yiftach El ("God will open [the womb?]") in Joshua 19:14, 27. See also J. Cheryl Exum, *Tragedy and Biblical Narrative: Arrows of the Almighty* (Cambridge: Cambridge University Press, 1992), 48.

97. The term *reqam* is derived from a root meaning "to empty out," and as adjective applied to a group of men it occurs only here (11:3), in Judg 9:4, and in 2 Chr 13:7 in reference to a band of useless men surrounding Rehoboam, Solomon's son. Their "emptiness" refers to a lack of principle and worth.

were. Is this a type of oath-taking on Jefta's part that he will follow through on his promise to take on the Ammonites? The phrase puts him in contact with Adonai, and his subsequent action represents the first opening move of a battle phase in the guise of an attempt at diplomacy (11:12–28).

Through a delegation, Jefta weaves a complex argument that puts Ammon clearly in the wrong. Although it does not convince Ammon to cease hostilities, this may not have been Jefta's intention anyway. He may instead be looking for an "opening" to engage in battle. The report is that the king of Ammon did not listen to Jefta's words (11:28), most likely evident from continuing raids and forays to the west side of the Jordan. No sooner are the negotiations done than Jefta comes under the influence of the spirit of Adonai, an event that sets him in motion to begin crossing through the region.

JUDGES 11:29–31

29 Then was upon Jefta
the spirit of Adonai,
and he crossed Gilead and Manasseh,
and he crossed to Mizpah of Gilead;
and from Mizpah of Gilead
he crossed to the Ammonites.

30 And vowed Jefta a vow to Adonai,
and he said:
If you will indeed give
the Ammonites into my hand,
31 then what comes out from the doors of my house[98]
to meet me on my return in peace
from the Ammonites,
it will be for Adonai,
and I will send it up as a burnt offering.

98. Niditch, *Judges*, 127: "the emerging thing that emerges/ from the doors of my house."

Jefta makes his request and his vow as he crosses the land toward the Ammonites, apparently under the motivating force of the spirit of Adonai. Although sometimes assumed to be the power that propels *all* the judges into action, the influence of the spirit of Adonai is mentioned only in connection with Otniel, Jefta, and Samson. The spirit is for all three protagonists the motivating force to set them on the move, in Jefta's case emphasized by the threefold mention of the verb "to cross," a verb that will occur once again at the onset of the battle with the Ammonites. In his bargaining with Ammon, Jefta has referred three times to the efforts of the Israelites to "cross" peacefully through Edomite and Amorite land on its way to Canaan. His own crossing through the regions does not depend on anyone's permission, and there is little doubt as to its purpose. We note that on no occasion does Jefta muster troops, and Israelite participation in the battle is only mentioned at the end of the short report on the victory over the Ammonites (11:33), the effect of which is to put Jefta in the center of all the action.

The verb "to cross" is central to verse 29, where it is mentioned three times in one sentence, immediately followed in verse 30 by the verb "to vow": "He crossed . . . he crossed . . . he crossed. . . . And he vowed." To cross (*avar*) means literally to pass through or cross over, but it is also used for transgression and occurs at least twice in the Bible in connection with human sacrifice. Its emphatic use at this point may at least hint at a serious overstepping of boundaries.[99] Only in this text in Judges does a character make a pledge to Adonai called a "vow." It is a pledge predicated on the condition that God will indeed cause victory for Jefta and defeat to the Ammonites.[100] Is his request for victory a sign of a lack of trust in God's power and presence, or is it nothing more than an ordinary prewar battle ritual

99. For *avar* with the connotation of transgression, see, for example, Josh 7:11–15; 23:16; 2 Chr 24:20. For the connection with sacrifice, see Exod 13:12, where the dedication of human firstborns demands a substitute, and 2 Kgs 16:3, where the sacrifice of a son is cited as an example of the misdeeds of king Ahaz.

100. A conditional pledge under similar circumstances is recorded in Numbers 21 on the verge of Israel's forays into the Transjordan and is also reminiscent of the promise of Hannah in 1 Samuel on the condition of God granting her pregnancy.

in ancient Israel? While the particular vow he makes is reminiscent of the one cited in Numbers 21:2 with the Israelites about to cross through peoples and regions on their way to the Jordan, no other war leader in Judges makes a promise of this kind. Moreover, Jefta makes an agreement which entails a great deal of uncertainty, for who knows what or who will come forth first from the doors of his house? An excessive promise demanding an excessive sacrifice shows Jefta, adept at deliberate and lengthy negotiations, also capable of rash and thoughtless behavior. As Mark Biddle observes, "Either he intentionally vowed to make a human sacrifice in exchange for victory over the Ammonites, or he spoke so carelessly that his statement included the possibility."[101] The question arises why he felt it necessary to make the request and utter a vow of such a radical nature. The one who "will open" has now opened his mouth with at best a thoughtless and at worst a murderous promise. He is said to be under the power of the spirit, the *ruah*, of Adonai. Are we to assume that it is the spirit who drives him to this excess as it drove him across the territories?

The short report of Jefta's victory makes no mention of the tactics or the details of the battle, only echoing Jefta's request that Adonai would give the Ammonites into his hand (11:32) and recording a "very great slaughter" (11:33). When, on his return, he finds that his daughter, in fact his only child, is the first one to exit his house in celebration of his victory, his reaction is one of mourning and complaint verging on accusation.

JUDGES 11:35

It was when he saw her,
he rent his clothes,
and he said:

101. Biddle, *Reading Judges*, 127. Together with others, Biddle also points out that the "most likely scenario for greeting a hero returning from victory on the battlefield would have been a human welcoming party" and that "indeed, in ancient Israel, such homecomings were typically occasions for the women to celebrate the hero's exploits."

Alas, my daughter,
you have rendered, oh rendered me low,
have become one who brings me disaster.[102]
As for me, I have opened my mouth to Adonai,
and I cannot take it back.

The sound of tearing echoes through the lines in the repeated consonants of the verbs, resonances difficult to convey in the translation.[103] It is a heart-rending complaint, but also one that turns the tables of responsibility. Where one might expect a cry of "what have I done?" Jefta instead declares his daughter to be the cause of his misfortune. In addition, he asserts that nothing can be done to take back the oath he spoke when he "opened" his mouth (11:35), driving the question located in his name in a disastrous direction. Are his declaration and the absence of a word of comfort for his daughter signs of a character flaw, of not being able to take responsibility? Or is this simply, as Frymer-Kensky would have it, the way a parent speaks?[104] Jefta appears to exist in isolation. There is no one around him to speak up for the daughter; notably there are no cultic personnel, no priest to consult or to counsel him that he could perhaps take back the literal nature of the vow and look for a substitute. Earlier he spoke "words before Adonai" in Mizpah without mention of any of the usual items present at a place of worship: no altar, no sanctuary, no personnel. While he is now set to bring a burnt offering, why is there no one present to inform him regarding appropriate substitutes for the dedication of a human being as stipulated in biblical law, cohering with prohibitions against child sacrifice? (cf. Exod 13:11–15; 34:19–20; Lev 18:21; 20:1–5; Deut 12:31; 18:10). In failing to look for a way out of his

102. Cf. 1 Sam 14:29, the words of Jonathan about his father Saul.

103. Verbs with the *k-r* sound occur four times.

104. Frymer-Kensky, *Reading the Women of the Bible*, 109. Phyllis Trible (*Texts of Terror: Literary-Feminist Readings of Biblical Narratives* [Philadelphia: Fortress, 1984], 102), for example, emphasizes the way Jefta's words overwhelmingly "blame the victim." Exum (*Tragedy and Biblical Narrative*, 52) agrees in part but also views Jefta's cry of horror as giving voice to an "experience of being trapped in an intolerable situation" that one did not intend but is still somehow responsible for.

predicament by emphasizing that there is no turning back on what he promised, he cements his own fate and that of his daughter, who, as the text notes emphatically, was his only child (11:34). He will go to his grave a childless man, and his daughter will pay for her father's opening his mouth.

Following the daughter's return from the mountains, the narrator concludes the actions of Jefta in this episode with the words "he did to her his vow that he vowed" (11:39). As many have observed, this phrase leaves some uncertainty as to the daughter´s fate, which has given rise to a tradition that Jefta did not really go through with the sacrifice.[105] Or does the narrator opt for a euphemism to avoid the phrase that "he offered his daughter up as a burnt offering"? The ritual for a burnt offering, including the slaughter and dismembering of the sacrifice, can be found in detail in Leviticus 1.

Before Jefta goes to his grave, additional trouble brews and breaks out, once again from the direction of Ephraim. Gideon was able to contain the discontent of the Ephraimites who considered themselves left out of a fight ending in victory (8:1–3), but Jefta has only words of blame in return. Two conflicting versions of the facts cause a conflagration with the result of massive intertribal slaughter (12:6). All is thus not well that ends well. There is no mention of a period of peace following the defeat of Ammon and Jefta's death, but, in contrast to Jefta's childless house, a recital of judges with prodigious progeny follows before the story moves to the last of the deliverers: Samson (see p. 253 above).

Jefta is a man of many words, issuing one of the longest continuous speeches in the book (11:15–27). He also comes across as a pious man who makes bargains and only engages in battle when all else fails. As is perhaps logical for someone in his circumstances, he is not one who trusts easily or totally, either in his tribal kin or in God. He is also stubborn or steadfast, depending on one's point of view; he stands by what he has said in the cases of both his daughter and the Ephraimites. In the case of his daughter, it is a word that has come from his mouth he cannot take back that determines her fate. In the case of the Ephraimites, he claims to have spoken a word

105. See Biddle, *Reading Judges*, 129.

to which they did not respond (12:2–3) and it is, ironically, the pronunciation of a word that will determine the fate of the Ephraimite victims (12:5–6).

The Women in the Story

Not all the woman fared well.[106]

Women are present in many of the Judges narratives, but after chapter 5 the only one to be given a name is the Philistine Delilah. Jefta's narrative is bracketed by his unnamed mother and his daughter. His mother is called a *zonah,* a prostitute, like Rahab, and she seems to serve in the story merely as a reason for her son's exile. She is one, however, in a line of women in Judges whose positions on the margin have an influence on the turn of events, all without names in contrast to the central roles and explicit names of the heroic women in the first five chapters of the book. A *zonah,* although not a forbidden profession, had a lower status than a concubine (*pilegesh*), the word used for the mother of Abimelek (8:31). Jefta's kin, who cast him out, call Jefta's mother "another woman" (*ishah aheret,* 11:2). In the Torah and the Historical Books, the word "other" is most frequently used in connection with Israel's idolatrous worship of the gods of "other" people.[107] There is at least a hint here that associates the mother with illegitimate associations in the religious sphere.

Once Jefta is driven away, where does his mother go? Does she share in his exile and subsequently in the rise of his fortunes once he is able to establish his own house as a leader in Gilead? Since women were often those to welcome the victorious warrior home in the Bible, did Jefta expect his mother to come out and meet him with timbrels and dance? When faced with his daughter, he laments

106. Frymer-Kensky, *Reading the Women of the Bible,* xviii.

107. Of the forty-six times that false gods are indicated with the term *elohim aherim* in the Bible, more than a third occur in Deuteronomy. See, for example, Deut 5:7; 6:14; 7:4; 8:19; 11:16, 28; 13:3[2], 7[6], 14[13]; 17:3; 18:20; 28:14, 36, 64; 29:25[26]; 31:18, 20.

that she has become as one who brings him "woe" (11:35). Earlier, it had been on account of his mother that he was exiled by his kin. She too brought him woe, although the story does not make this explicit. Is there just a hint that the loss of a *zonah* who had caused much woe in his life would be no great loss? It is doubly hard to bear that he will now be the one to "bring woe" on his only child—far worse than his mother once brought on him.

Also, where is Jefta's wife—presumably the mother of his daughter? She is his only child and, one may thus assume, also the only child of a mother. Is the name "he will open," insofar as it may refer to God opening the womb, ironic in relation to this woman with only one child, and a daughter at that? Clearly, the narrator does not intend to show the spotlight on these women who exist on the sidelines of the narrative, but their shadows move across the story and make us aware that more than one person suffered the loss of Jefta's daughter. Like her mother and grandmother, the girl goes unnamed. She is, however given voice in the narrative, which brings her more into the center than the other women in the story. When she speaks, she underlines the irreversible nature of the vow by repeating her father's phrase.

JUDGES 11:36–37

36 And said she to him: My father,
you opened your mouth to Adonai.
Do to me as what came out of your mouth,
because Adonai did for you an act of vengeance
on your enemies, the Ammonites.
37 And she said to her father:
Let this thing be done to me:
Leave me be for two months,
so I may go and ascend to the mountains,
and weep over my virginity,
I and my companions.

Jefta's daughter utters a dignified assent without complaint. Her elegant reply emphatically uses the verb "to do" three times:

"*do* to me," "because Adonai *did* for you," "let this thing/word be *done* to me." In her asking for a respite, a time of separation in the mountains, she creates for herself a small space of self-determination. She breaks, moreover, through her isolation in asking to spend time not with her family but with her female companions, making a contrasting picture to the isolation of her father. This companionship in the story continues after her death, for when her father has completed his vow, "she became a statute in Israel:/ that year upon year the daughters of Israel/ go out to chant the daughter of Jefta/ the Gileadite/ four days in the year" (11:38).[108] Her retreat is for the purpose of lamenting her "virginity." The mourning concerns thus not only her death but her lack of a husband and family. The notation that "she had not known a man" (11:39) makes clear that the entire house dies without issue, a fate that also redounds on Jefta.

God

The feature that plays the most important role in interpreting the account . . . involves the silence with regard to YHWH's view of the events, a silence that hangs over the entire story.[109]

The rabbis, who hold Jefta in low regard, have no trouble assigning the role of the daughter as victim to the hand of God. They judge Jefta's request for victory to have been "unfitting" and see God thus responding in the same manner.[110] Cheryl Exum considers divine silence in the story of Jefta to be the tragic element.[111] It is clear that neither here nor elsewhere in the Bible is the presence of the spirit of Adonai, the *ruah*, entirely benevolent.

108. I take the translation "to chant"—a verb also occurring in Judg 5:11—from Tikva Frymer-Kensky's translation in *Reading the Women of the Bible*, 113.

109. Biddle, *Reading Judges*, 128.

110. *Midrash Rabbah Genesis*, trans. Rabbi Dr. H. Freedman (London: Soncino, 1951), 527.

111. Exum, *Tragedy and Biblical Narrative*, 59.

It is, rather, a disturbing, powerful force setting a hero in motion. Susan Niditch calls the spirit "empowering, dangerous and difficult to control."[112] According to Richard Bowman, "When human freedom to act in destructive ways is exercised, God does not intervene and compromise the exercise of this freedom. Instead, the deity allows divine power to be constrained." Bowman thus argues that the presence of God with a human leader "does not guarantee success."[113]

Biblical narrators are known for not chewing a story, belaboring the obvious, which makes for interesting spaces for the reader/hearer to step into. In this case, they left the horror of a human sacrifice to speak for itself, perhaps considering the house of Jefta dying without issue sufficiently clear punishment that it obviates stating it explicitly. The rabbis were not hesitant, however, to add gruesome detail to Jefta's death. Because the text has him buried in the "towns" of Gilead rather than in one specific place, they determine that he died with his limbs dropping off in different places, each limb buried in a particular locale.[114]

This narrative, more perhaps than any other in the Bible, has a deeply disquieting effect. Whether we view Jefta's vow as acceptable within the culture and religion or see it as unwise and against God's will, the daughter's sacrifice as an inevitable result of patriarchal structures where women's lives in the end are expendable, or as only one in a string of "foundation myths" extant also in other cultures where daughters are sacrificed for the greater good of (male) conquest and glory, it cannot help but cause profound unease and grief as a story in sacred Scripture. Biblical scholar Renita Weems writes, "There is a sorrow known only to women, a sorrow so profound and so bottomless it can be shared only by a woman."[115] Finally, Phyllis Trible:

112. Niditch, *Judges*, 133.

113. Richard G. Bowman, "Narrative Criticism: Human Purpose in Conflict with Divine Presence," in *Judges and Method: New Approaches in Biblical Studies*, ed. Gale A. Yee (Minneapolis: Fortress, 2007), 41.

114. *Midrash Rabbah Genesis*, 528.

115. Weems, *Just a Sister Away*, 62.

The daughter of Jephthah lies slain upon thy high places.
I weep for you little sister.
Very poignant is your story to me;
your courage to me is wonderful,
surpassing the courage of men.[116]

Are we to assume that the effect of the story was any less disquieting in ancient Israel's past? Does the violence perpetrated in it, one of an altogether different sort than that of the hero in battle, not flag that the entire period was on a trajectory spiraling downward within the recital of the stories of the judges, and that yet more gruesome violence, including the dismemberment of a woman, is to follow? Is the name *Yiftach*, "he will open," not also the emblem of one who opens up yet more horrifying possibilities in the life of the people? Is not his title of "valiant hero" in the end also judged by narrator and ancient reader/hearer as the ultimate irony?

Act VI: The Riddle of Samson (Judges 13–16)

Throughout the cycle, the compilers have woven a rich tapestry of interconnected themes and motifs: knowing and not knowing, telling and keeping secrets.[117]

There is no one like Samson in Judges—indeed, not in the entire Bible. He strides through the text, wreaking havoc in the lives of animals and humans; he is wanton and promiscuous, flamboyantly destructive and self-destructive. Yet so well-known is Samson in a Christian context, and even in the wider culture, that one who has grown up in this tradition feels like meeting an old friend when coming upon his story. The main elements, the miraculous birth, the encounters with women that prove his eventual undoing, and

116. Phyllis Trible, *Texts of Terror*, 109.

117. Royce M. Victor, "Delilah—A Forgotten Hero (Judges 16:4–21): A Cross-Cultural Reading." Pages 235–55 in *Joshua and Judges*, ed. Athalya Brenner and Gale A. Yee (Minneapolis: Fortress, 2013), 237.

his final destructive act in the temple of Dagon, are familiar to many. One recognizes characters, especially Samson's parents and Delilah, as well as the folkloristic features, the riddles, deceptions, and feats of superhuman strength perpetrated by our trickster hero. This story, with its depiction of a larger-than-life, brawling, libidinous protagonist was for certain meant to entertain and amuse the ancient community. Once Samson appears, the tale unfolds in a series of fast-moving episodes, each of which ends in the devastation of the Philistine enemy, slowing down when he is tricked into giving up the secret of his superhuman strength, and even then coming to a conclusion of devastating destruction for the oppressor.

Four scenes spin the tale: First, there is the visit by a divine messenger and the announcement of Samson's birth to an infertile woman and her husband (13:1–23). This part contains much detail, conversation between the parents-to-be, and quite a bit of befuddlement on the part of the human recipients of a divine promise. The second scene paints adventures of Samson ensuing from his entanglement with a Philistine woman, an affair that prefigures his later liaison with Delilah and exhibits features similar to it (14:1–15:8). The third, a scene that constitutes a key interlude, details Samson's capture and handing over to the Philistines by his own people, albeit by those of a different tribe (15:9–20). Although the treacherous dealings of his countrymen are not effective, the episode anticipates the eventual undoing of Samson by an intimate and his being bound by the Philistines in bronze shackles (16:21) in the final scene (16:1–31).[118] Yet in the end, the loser ends up destroying a great number of his Philistine captors, so that "the dead he made die in his death/ were more than the dead he made die in his life" (16:30).

The scenes are marked by the divine presence, first in the form of the messenger who visits Samson's parents and subsequently through the spirit of Adonai, which engages with Samson more than with any other judge (13:25; 14:6, 19; 15:14). Adonai blesses Samson (13:24), moves events in a deliberate direction to provoke the Philistines (14:4), is negatively involved in turning away from Samson

118. The root *asar* ("to bind") occurs in Judges only in the Samson narratives, 5× in ch. 15 and 12× in ch. 16.

(16:20), and twice responds to Samson's prayer (15:18; 16:28–30). Whether this presence of God with the rogue judge benefits the peace and well-being of the Israelite tribes is not obvious, and the placement of the Samson narrative at precisely this point in the chain of accounts could be interpreted as part of the downward spiral; much, after all, depends on the human instruments at God's disposal. Besides showing brute strength, Samson is uncommonly wanton in his behavior, and throughout the story his task as deliverer of Israel remains ambiguous, for apart from his killing groups of Philistines, the larger issue of their control over the tribes remains unresolved. It should also be noted that, throughout the story, Samson acts on his own without mustering or leading troops, unlike any of the other leaders we encounter in Judges.

On the other hand, as pointed out above (see p. 268), each episode with Samson in the center ends with destructive action against the Philistines so that, in some way, Samson indeed *begins* the project of deliverance (13:5). It can be said that even when Samson loses, as in the cases of the riddle and the machinations of Delilah, he wins. In a murky way, then, the beginning of the end of the Philistine threat takes place here.

Act VI, Scene 1: You Are My Sunshine[119] *(Judges 13)*

Alas, you can be the best parents in the world but that doesn't guarantee how your son will turn out.[120]

More than any of the other judges, Samson is surrounded by women. While only one of the four women who play a role in his life receives a name, the result of their lack of names is an abundant presence in these chapters of the Hebrew word *ishah*, "woman."

119. Many commentators note the connection between the name Samson (Hebrew *Shimshon*) and the Hebrew word for "sun," *shemesh.* John Goldingay (*Joshua, Judges and Ruth for Everyone*, 133) writes that his name "would make people think of sunshine."

120. Goldingay, *Joshua, Judges and Ruth*, 134.

At the same time that the absence of a name points to a lack of significance, the frequency of the gender designation highlights female presence. Almost half of the word's roughly sixty occurrences in the book are in Judges 13–16. Three of the women have voices in the different episodes; only the prostitute in Gaza is not heard from (16:1–3). After the setting of the initial context, which establishes the continuing wrongdoing of the Israelites and their oppression under the Philistines, a man, Manoah, is introduced by clan and region, but immediately the account veers off in the direction of the woman. The man's name is related to the word for "rest," but rest will be far off in the adventures that follow. Even the initial episode is marked by constant movement, with characters moving to and fro, sometimes running. Manoah's wife, in Hebrew "his woman," is introduced by her childless state with a double notation: "She was barren/ and had not given birth" (13:2). But this negative note is juxtaposed by the appearance of a messenger of Adonai who comes with the good news of pregnancy, although once again the absence of childbirth is doubly noted, echoing the earlier phrase.

Judges 13:3

And became visible a messenger of Adonai to the woman.
And he said to her:
Behold now, you are barren
and have not given birth,
and you are pregnant
and will give birth to a son.

When she tells her husband of the visit and part of what the messenger told her, Manoah prays for another visitation, and once again the messenger comes to the woman, who then summons her husband. She may not be fully aware of the identity of her visitor but she is not quite as befogged as her husband, calling him initially "a man of God" and "a messenger of God" (13:6–7). Not until the angel disappears in the flame of the burnt offering are both husband and wife aware of the truth. Yet, while the man reacts in fear to this reality, the woman reasons logically and theologically that if God wanted them to die, the offering would not have been accepted, and above all there would not have been any need for all the promises about their future (13:23). The theme of the infertile woman is a recurring one in biblical narrative, each story displaying its own characteristics.[121] The repeated reference to Manoah's wife's infertility is most like the one describing Sarai, introduced in Genesis 11:30 as Abram's wife who is "barren, she had no child." In addition, the word barren (*aqarah*) juxtaposed to a reference to giving birth (*yalad*) occurs elsewhere a few times but is especially telling in Isaiah 54:1, where it is a metaphor for restoration.[122] The fertility of the infertile woman is thus also a metaphor for God keeping faith with God's people.

If the episode has much in common with related tales of divine visitations and birth announcements to a woman heretofore childless, there are also close connections with the visitation of God's messenger to Gideon in chapter 6, including the disappearance of the visitor, which causes a lifting of the fog of confusion and reveals his identity (cf. 6:21–22). While many features connect closely to other biblical tales, there is also much here that is unique, especially in the gaps left by the narrator, which raise a number of questions.

The messenger of Adonai announces, among other things, that their son will be a deliverer, but like Jefta before him he will only make a *beginning* of the process of deliverance (13:5; cf. 10:18). The report, at first provided by Manoah's wife, opens with a description

121. For a classification of the six infertile woman stories, see Saskia Ketelaar, "De Onvruchtbare Moeders in de Hebreeuwse Bijbel," in *Amsterdamse Cahiers voor Exegese en Bijbelse Theologie 12*, ed. Karel A. Deurloo et al. (Kampen: Kok, 1993), 7–19. The texts are Gen 16:1–6 + 18:1–15 + 21; 25:21–26; 29:31–30:24; Judg 13:2–24; 1 Sam 1:1–20; 2 Kgs 4:8–37.

122. Isa 54:1:
Rejoice, barren one who did not give birth;
break forth in joy and jubilation,
you who had no labor pains;
for more are the children of the desolate
than the children of the betrothed, says Adonai.

of the messenger who appeared to her, presumably to impress her husband with the possibility that the announcement would come true. A man of God/messenger of God, very fearful and without name or place of origin, told her of her pregnancy and the impending birth of a son. Naturally, she wants to get the most important thing out, the fact that they will have a son. She does add instructions she received about her own conduct, but about the child says only that he will be a *nazir* without mentioning any of the obligations that accompany such a person and adds that he will be so dedicated until his death, thus announcing the ending of his life even before it has begun. Are the commitments about the Nazirite status—refraining from alcohol, haircuts, and contact with dead bodies—clear enough that they need no repeating? Does the role of deliverer from the Philistine power frighten her so that she omits it? Or is it not impressive enough (since it is only a "beginning") for her to pass it on? The phrase about deliverance from the Philistines will not be repeated in the episode, and the verb "to deliver" will not receive further mention in either the Samson story or the rest of the book of Judges.

Manoah appears pious enough; he prays, possesses an altar, and eventually is clear on having been in God's presence, but he is not exactly trusting. Like Gideon, he needs repeated reassurance. It also takes him a long time to catch on to what is happening, even after the messenger makes clear that food will not be consumed by him but will serve as an offering to Adonai. In return, the divine messenger acts and speaks in mysterious ways. Much here comes across as enigmatic, leaving issues unresolved, anticipating the role of the riddle in Samson's larger story.

Samson is born, and his mother names him *Shimshon* in Hebrew, a name that evokes the word for sun (*shemesh*). Following the comment that the boy grew up and Adonai blessed him, the narrator remarks that the "spirit of Adonai began to trouble him" with a rare verb that elsewhere occurs in relation to Pharaoh after his dream (Gen 41:8) and King Nebuchadnezzar, also in reaction to a dream (Dan 2:1, 3). As elsewhere in Judges, the not entirely benevolent presence of the spirit (see pp. 265–66 above) serves as the force to set the character in motion.

Act VI, Scene 2: Samson the Riddler (Judges 14:1–15:8)

Often in folklore, solving a riddle leads to winning, not losing, the bride.[123]

Tell me who is the ruler,
the ruler without land?
Tell me where I find water,
yes, water without sand?[124]

What have I got in my pocket? he said aloud. . . . Gollum thought it was a riddle, and he was frightfully upset.[125]

The first movement made by Samson is to "go down" to Timnah, a Philistine town, where he sees a woman who pleases him. The verb "to go down" is indicative of the emphasis on movement in this first Samson adventure; verbs of motion ("going down" and "going up") occur six times in the first eleven verses of chapter 14, with an emphatic placement of the verbs at the beginning of the sentence. It all ends in Samson's "going down" to Ashkelon, where he inflicts his first damage on the Philistines (14:19).

Although his father and mother both protest the alliance, arguing that surely there is a woman of their own people, rather than one of the Philistine "foreskins," who would make a fine wife for him, they eventually go along with it, and they all "go down" together. Tellingly, Samson counters his parents by saying to his father that the woman is "right in my eyes" (14:3; repeated in 14:7). The narrator inserts here that really it was God's plan to have this close association between Samson and the Philistines (14:4), one assumes because the relationship would provide an occasion for creating havoc and destruction among the Philistines, as indeed it

123. Everett Fox, *The Early Prophets* (New York: Schocken, 2014), 214.

124. From an old Dutch rhyming ballad (author's translation) in which a girl in love with a soldier must save his life by solving the riddles put to her by the military commander. "Zeg my waar is een koning/ een koning zonder land./ Zeg mij waar is het water/ het water zonder zand?"

125. J. R. R. Tolkien, *The Hobbit*, rev. ed. (New York: Ballantine, 1970), 85.

will. In the course of the trip, Samson, apparently off on his own, kills a marauding lion while the spirit of Adonai is upon him. The encounter between Samson and lion (14:5–9) is the hinge between the main episodes of finding his potential bride and the wedding feast. Upon a return journey, he and his parents eat honey from the carcass, although he hides the origin of the sustenance from his father and mother—the first secret occurring in Samson's adventures, which are all filled with hiding and revealing. Mystery intensifies at the wedding feast when Samson poses a riddle to the wedding guests.

JUDGES 14:12–14

12 Said Samson to them:
Let me riddle you, pray, a riddle.
If you tell, yes, tell it to me
within the seven days of the feast
and find it out,
I will give you thirty linen tunics
and thirty party clothes.
13 And if you cannot tell me,
you will give me thirty linen tunics
and thirty party clothes.
And they said to him:
Riddle your riddle and let us listen.

14 And he said to them:
From the eater went out eats,
and from the strong went out sweets.

The riddle and its potential answers, its cultural and folkloristic aspects, have fascinated scholars and produced varied approaches. One question concerns the nature of the riddle and whether it can be called a "neck" riddle—that is to say, one to which the riddler alone knows the solution and the unanswerable nature of which has the power to save the neck of the one who does the asking. Bilbo's "riddle" to Gollum, quoted above, is this sort of riddle. In terms of the surface structure of the Samson story, the riddle may be called a neck riddle because its solution is located in a "recent experience of the hero."[126] In another sense, there is no danger here to Samson, or not an apparent one, unless one takes into account that the period was one in which the Israelites were ruled by the Philistines (14:4; 15:11). The apparent reason for the riddle is that Samson is trying to find a way to acquire free appropriate attire for his wedding feast companions (14:11).

What transpires is that Samson's Timnite bride, forced by her people under threat to lure Samson into telling her the answer to the riddle, wheedles the solution out of him, and the Philistines provide the answer. When they do, Samson, in a rage and once again empowered by God's spirit, provides the required price by murdering thirty Philistines.[127] Nor is that the end of the story: Samson's anger is so great that he goes home to his parents and so loses his bride to another man (14:20). When he returns once again to "his woman," considering her still to be his, and her father reveals to him that he "gave" her to another man, his fury boils over once again, and this time he sets fire to Philistine crops in a particularly cruel manner (15:4–5).[128] Fire begets fire, and the Philistines take vengeance on Samson's former bride and her father by burning them both as they had previously threatened, since they hold the father indirectly accountable. Samson goes on a rampage of killing, a "great smiting," and then goes into hiding (15:8).

126. Thomas A. Green, ed., *Folklore: An Encyclopedia of Beliefs, Customs, Tales, Music, and Art*, vol. 1 (Santa Barbara: ABC-CLIO, 1998), 587.

127. The solution provided by the Philistines ("What is sweeter than honey,/ and what is stronger than a lion?" 14:18) is in itself intriguing and sounds more like a riddle than the original one asked by Samson. Samson's reply ("If you had not ploughed with my heifer/ you would not have found my riddle," 14:18) reveals that he at least understood the Philistines' solution to be the correct one. However, it is here not my intention to plumb the depths of the riddle but rather to explore the function of the riddle in the larger story.

128. Even recognizing the folkloristic and humorous nature of the tale, one's heart goes out to the poor foxes who ran through the fields with their tails on fire. We note that the spirit of Adonai is absent during this action.

Act VI, Scene 3: Samson the Lightning Rod (Judges 15:9–20)

An avenging wildman is a difficult sort of hero to deal with, even for the community he champions.[129]

In the third scene the story takes an interesting turn. The neighboring tribe of Judah is quite eager to hand Samson over to the Philistines, who have now gone on the warpath (15:11–13). Samson consents to be bound before being delivered and, while the Philistines shout with excitement at the sight of his being delivered to them, the spirit of God makes another appearance, and his bonds melt away "like flax that was burning with fire" (15:14). This time, a great carnage results, with Samson killing one thousand Philistines with the "jawbone of an ass" (15:15), a feat with some resemblance to Shamgar's, the judge who killed six hundred Philistines with a cattle prod (3:31). The entire episode ends with Adonai delivering a miraculous provision of water for a thirsty warrior (15:19) and a final note that Samson "judged Israel in the days of the Philistines for twenty years," pointing to the fact that "the days of the Philistines" are not over yet (15:20).

The Ties That Bind

Samson . . . is not a judge who is merely taken possession of by the spirit of Adonai but a man in whom it pounds, like the clapper of a bell, a man driven by inward energy in a series of pulsating motions, like the movements of violence, like sexuality itself.[130]

The announcement to Samson's mother was that her son would "begin to deliver Israel from the hand of the Philistines" who are said to "rule" over Israel (13:5; 14:4). At the end of the first adventures in

129. Niditch, *Judges*, 159.

130. Robert Alter, "Samson Without Folklore," in *The Land of Israel in Bible, History, and Theology: Studies in Honour of Ed Noort*, VTSup 124 (Leiden: Brill, 2009), 47.

Samson's life, he has indeed done them substantial damage, but the account raises a number of questions, including one about the extent to which Samson is indeed a force of deliverance. The first comment about him is that "he went down to Timnah" (14:1), apparently a town in Philistine territory. If he is the one to commence delivering Israel, some campaign of warlike action might be expected, but instead the report is that he "saw a woman ... from the daughters of the Philistines." In the next breath, he asks his parents to "take her" for him "as a woman"—that is, he wants her to become his wife. When his parents remonstrate with him that surely there are suitable young women to be found among their own kin and that one does not have to go to the foreskins to find a bride, Samson replies that it is her he wants: "Her take for me/ for she is right in my eyes" (14:3). The phrase, to be "right" in someone's eyes, calls forth echoes of its opposite. The Israelites have consistently done "the wrong in the eyes of Adonai" (2:11; 3:7, 12; 4:1; 6:1; 10:6), including at the beginning of the Samson story (13:1). At the same time, to be "right" in someone's eyes anticipates the repeated comment in the last five chapters of Judges that "everyone did what was right in their own eyes" (17:6; 21:25), a phrase that concludes the entire book. One encounters the phrase about the Timnite being "right" in Samson's eyes twice in this chapter, one time in Samson's reported speech to his parents (14:3) and once again in a narrative comment (14:7). The phrase raises questions about the rightness of Samson's actions, undercutting the narrator's assurance that the Israelite-Philistine entanglement is part of a divine plan (14:4). God may plan, but Samson executes.

What was Samson doing in Timnah? The sentence at the end of chapter 13, leading up to 14:1, informs us that the spirit of Adonai began to "stir" him up. Presumably, then, he heads toward the Philistines to do some damage, but instead of the war path he chooses the marriage path. In his bride-to-be he has met not only a woman from outside his kin but one who is kin to the Philistine oppressor, a worshiper of a god other than the One of Israel. Still, all might have proceeded in line with divine intentions had Samson not stirred discontent with his riddle and subsequent violent action. Was there an easy exchange between the two cultures at the time? Riddling may be a token of shared knowledge, and unlike the case of some other oppressive groups in Judges, these two peoples lived cheek by jowl.[131] Is it not somewhat peculiar that Samson has such easy access to this community supposedly hostile to his own, certainly considered "other" by his parents, who call the Philistines by the derogatory epithet "foreskins"? Everyone, Samson as well as his parents, goes back and forth without exchanges of a hostile nature; in fact, the first danger on the road does not come from a Philistine but from a wild animal.

Inherent contradictions are also apparent in Samson's character. While he is the ungovernable strong man, and one may judge him crude, the story assigns him clever words. His riddle is poetic, and subsequently he will speak twice in eloquent lines, once when he reproaches the Philistines for prying the solution to the conundrum loose from his bride and once when he has killed a thousand of them with the jawbone of an ass.[132] It is true that members of his own people are ready to hand him over to the Philistines (15:9–13), but they were from a different tribe than his own, a witness to the kinship tie being strongest within the clan and the tribe. Samson does not appear to be a safe person to have around, and the Philistines have gone on the warpath because of him. Was Samson aware of potential discontent among his own people resulting from his behavior? Why else does he hide in "the cleft of the rock at Etam" (15:8) after his

131. The riddling exchange between Bilbo and Gollum in the caves of the Misty Mountains in *The Hobbit* testifies to a possible shared ancestry between Gollum and Bilbo. Claudia V. Camp and Carole F. Fontaine ("The Words of the Wise and Their Riddles" in *Text and Tradition: The Hebrew Bible and Folklore*, ed. Susan Niditch [Atlanta: Scholars Press, 1990], 127–149) pose that the riddling context in Judges is rather one of competition and social disparity. In this exploration of the riddle context, they quote W. J. Pepicello and Thomas A. Green, *The Language of Riddles* (Columbus, OH: State University Press, 1984), 125: "Riddles seek to generate tension as consciously as proverbs try to ameliorate it."

132. Judg 14:18; 15:16. The latter verse is especially clever with its pun on the word donkey. In English, the translation ("with the jawbone of an ass/ a heap, a double heap;/ with the jawbone of an ass/ I slew a thousand men") does not communicate the pun in the first lines using the word *hamor* for both "ass" and "heap."

vengeful act on the Philistines? As Niditch points out, "Samson is a complex character, beloved by a deity, capable of grand and clever acts of deception, artful in his use of language, and able to perform superhuman feats. He is susceptible to women's attractions and to the delusion that his great power is self-generated."[133]

Samson's riddle in chapter 14 refers to the "eater," in the corresponding line called "the strong," who produces sweet nourishment. The surface answer refers to the lion whose carcass produced honey, and so the Philistines respond correctly with their answer: "What is sweeter than honey?/ And what is stronger than a lion?" (14:18). That answer, however, sounds more like a riddle than the one Samson posed. For is love not sweeter than honey, and is Samson not stronger than a lion?[134] The words "strong" and "strength" (*oz* and *koah*) are, in Judges, virtually exclusive to the Samson story, with especially the latter coming into prominence in chapter 16.[135] Strikingly, Samson the strong, the one-man army, is also the only man in the tales of the Judges who is said to "love" a woman (16:4), with the verb "love" in reference to human relationships appearing three times in chapters 14–16, the only times in Judges. Although love is not used directly for Samson's dealings with the woman of Timnah, she reproaches him for not "loving her" when pressing him to reveal the solution to the riddle, inferring that love was assumed to exist between them (14:16).[136]

Finally, the occasion on which troops from Judah deliver Samson to the Philistines in 15:10–15, though perhaps understandable from an Israelite perspective, raises the question of intertribal solidarity. Apparently, Judah alone feels under assault, and rather than asking Samson to raise an army for the impending battle with the Philistines, or at the very least asking him to fight on their behalf,

133. Niditch, *Judges*, 168.

134. See Edgar Slotkin, "Response to Professors Fontaine and Camp," in *Text and Tradition: The Hebrew Bible and Folklore*, ed. Susan Niditch (Atlanta: Scholars Press, 1990), 154–59. Slotkin states that what we have here is "a riddle posed as a statement" answered by "a solution posed as a riddle" (157).

135. *Koah* is used outside the Samson story only for Gideon in 6:14.

136. The Samson-Timnite episode is of course the template for the Samson-Delilah story that follows in chapter 16.

they accede to the Philistine demand to deliver a bound Samson to them. This entire sequel to Samson wreaking destruction on the Philistines in the aftermath of their retaliation on his former wife for his rampage in their fields calls into question whether one can speak of an "Israel" at this junction, or even of a loosely organized league of tribal and kin-groups. To be sure, Samson, once again under the influence of the spirit of Adonai, sheds his bonds and is able to do significant damage to the adversary, but the foundation for the statement that he "judged Israel for twenty years" is lost in a mist of uncertainty (15:20). In the book of Judges, we find the verb "to bind" only in the Samson story, occurring seventeen times in chapters 15 and 16. Samson's bonds give way every time until the moment when he is bound in shackles as a prisoner of his enemies. Are Samson's bonds also a metaphor for the bonds that tie the tribes into a people, and are those bonds as frail as those that tie Samson?

Act VI, Scene 4: Samson the Lover (Judges 16)

The glint of the dagger in the velvet hand of love is what has excited him from Timnah onward.[137]

The story of Samson and Delilah is, above all, a story about power—who has it, who uses it, and how it is used.[138]

The prelude to the main episode serves to highlight once again Samson's easy and at times unorthodox association with women, in particular Philistine women, and his extraordinary strength (16:1–3). The location this time is Gaza, a Philistine city, where Samson "sees" another woman (16:1; cf. 14:1). The woman is introduced as a prostitute (*zonah*; cf. Josh 2:1), and Samson has a sexual encounter with her. The Philistines try to trap him in an ambush at the city gate, but

137. Alter, "Samson Without Folklore," 53.

138. Carol Smith, "Delilah: A Suitable Case For (Feminist) Treatment?" in *Text and Tradition: The Hebrew Bible and Folklore*, ed. Susan Niditch (Atlanta: Scholars Press, 1990), 114.

Samson tears out the gate by its posts and walks off, carrying the doors of the gate on his shoulders all the way to Hebron.

The moment has arrived for Samson to enter into a liaison that explicitly includes *love* on his part.

JUDGES 16:4–7

4 It happened after this
he loved a woman in the Shoreq Valley,
and her name was Delilah.

5 And went up to her the Philistine leaders
and said to her:
Seduce him and see
in what is his great strength
and with what we can overcome him
so we can tie him up to abuse him.
And we, we will give to you each
eleven hundred pieces of silver.

6 And Delilah said to Samson:
Tell me, please, wherein lies your great strength
and with what may you be bound
to abuse you?
7 Samson said to her:
If they tie me with seven new bowstrings
that have not been dried,
I will become weak and be like any human being.

Samson is reported to be in the Shoreq Valley—a region if not in then close to Philistine territory—consorting with a woman who may or may not be Philistine, but who is certainly open to receiving the vast sum of money offered by the Philistine chiefs.[139] These

139. The name Delilah may be Hebrew. It is variously interpreted as someone with dangling loose hair, one of small stature, someone who is flirtatious, or one representing night (Hebrew *Laylah*) in contrast to Samson's

leaders, for their part, have learned some lessons, and this time they issue promises instead of threats. Their initial goal is to find out what will make Samson like a normal man without abnormal strength, and they instruct Delilah to trick Samson in order to find out his secret. The word "seduce" in verse 5 does not primarily carry a sexual connotation but is especially used of enticing through talk.[140] Their ultimate goal is not to kill Samson but to "tie him up in order to abuse him"; in other words, they want to torture him rather than ending his life, perhaps to hold him up as an example to those who would dare stand up against Philistine power, or perhaps simply for sadistic purposes of their own. Startling is the crass way in which Delilah announces her purpose of Samson's divulging his secret with a use of the identical verb, in Hebrew *anah*, a word used in connection with physical violation, even rape.[141] Ostensibly, Samson consents to the abuse he will face from Philistine hands, or he certainly plays with the possibility. Alter notes that "an odd intimation of sadistic fantasy hovers over the story."[142] Mark Biddle also describes the way Samson seems to "toy with Delilah," moving "ever

"sun." While there is no agreement on the meaning of her name, her identity is equally in question. Thus Biddle (*Reading Judges*, 162): "Although she collaborates with the Philistines, her name is apparently Hebrew. . . . Since the Valley of Sorek demarcated the apparently porous boundary between Israelite and Philistine territories, . . . Delilah's residence there manifests the ambiguities." Biddle also discusses the ambiguity in relation to Delilah's status. Was she a prostitute out for as much as she could get, or was she Samson's wife? Either case raises a number of interesting points (163).

140. So Prov 20:19; 25:15; Ps 78:36; Hos 2:16[14]; Jer 20:7, 10. See Frymer-Kensky, *Reading the Women of the Bible*, 79. In Judges, this root (*patah*) occurs only in the Samson story, first with his Timnite bride (14:15) and then here.

141. Lori Rowlett, "Violent Femmes and S/M: Queering Samson and Delilah," in *Queer Commentary and the Hebrew Bible*, ed. Ken Stone [Sheffield: Sheffield Academic, 2001], 106) maintains that the story of Samson and Delilah shows a classic S-M scenario. "Delilah is the female dominatrix, teasing and tormenting Samson, who has all the characteristics of a 'butch bottom.' . . . The constant give and take between the two lovers resembles S-M role-play, complete with ritual questions, hair fetishism and other power games."

142. Alter, "Samson Without Folklore," 52.

closer to the ultimate revelation of the truth" with his responses to her repeated pleas.[143]

Three times Samson deceives Delilah; three times she calls the Philistines upon him in vain (16:9, 12, 14), so that she finally reproaches him, as did the Timnite before her, with not loving her and relentlessly presses him until he is ready to die.

JUDGES 16:16–17

16 And when she pressed him
with her words day in and day out,
and importuned him,
his soul was vexed unto death.
17 And he told her all his heart.
And he said to her:
A razor has not come on my head,
for a Nazir of God I have been
from the womb of my mother.
If I am shaved, my strength will turn away from me,
and I will become weak
and be like any human being.

Samson's soul is "vexed unto death," an expression that occurs in Judges only in 10:16 of the *nefesh* of God (see p. 255) and on this occasion of Samson. The verb literally means "to be short"; in both chapter 10 and here it refers to a state of mind, in Samson's case strengthened by the word "death." Although one would think that Delilah's calling the Philistines upon him three times would alert him to the danger he is in, instead he tells her "all his heart" and Delilah recognizes that "this time" he has told the truth (18). She calls the Philistines, gets the money first, has Samson sleep on her knees, and shaves his head herself.[144] And, as the text has it, she

143. Biddle, *Reading Judges*, 164.

144. The Hebrew text has a feminine verb form. Although a number of translations read "she had him shave off," referring to the man she called, the verb is a Piel and not a causative. Both Alter and Niditch translate "she shaved

"began to abuse him" (19), calling the Philistines upon him for the last time. Samson, apparently asleep through all these proceedings, wakes up and is unable to escape, so his enemies blind him, shackle him, and take him away to become a prisoner—perhaps for sexual abuse and mockery.[145]

It remains an odd story, leaving many questions unanswered. It has something in common with the story of Sisera, vanquished at the hands of a woman, but in many ways it is more reminiscent of myths popular elsewhere in the ancient world, tales in which a woman gets the better of a strong man—perhaps pointing to the close contact at this point in time between Israelites and Philistines, a people that hailed from the Aegean.[146] There is always a satisfactory element in this type of "battle of the sexes" tale in which the (weaker) female overcomes the (stronger) male, and the Samson and Delilah story has proven to be no exception, familiar as it is even to those who know little of the Bible. In chapters 14–16, Samson "sees" a woman in Timnah, a dead lion with bees inside, and a prostitute in Gaza, but he does not "see" the truth of Delilah's capacity to betray him in spite of all the evidence. Nor perhaps does he "see" the true source of his strength, which, though outwardly residing in his long hair, in reality comes from the Deity, who abandons him when he betrays his dedication as *nazir*. His mental blindness turns into real blindness when the Philistines deprive him of his sight and, rather than killing him, use him as a prisoner to grind grain and eventually to amuse them with some kind of antics, perhaps of a sexual nature in the temple of Dagon (16:21–25). At this point, in his final hour, in spite of the erratic and unsatisfactory fulfillment of his being any kind of deliverer of his people, Samson manages to die in a manner that

off" (Niditch, *Judges*, 163; Alter, *The Former Prophets*, 191). Alter points out that she "calls the man to bring her a razor. . . . Her performance of the act herself is thematically and psychologically apt: the seductress cuts away the source of Samson's potency."

145. See Biddle, *Reading Judges*, 167.

146. Frymer-Kensky (*Reading the Women of the Bible*, 82–83) points to the many similarities between the Samson and Delilah episode and Greek mythology, including similarities between Samson and Herakles.

tricks the Philistine enemy and shows Adonai to have renewed his strength.

Judges 16:28–30

28 Then called Samson upon Adonai
and said: Adonai God,
remember me now,
and strengthen me now,
just this once, O God,
and I will take, yes, take a single vengeance
for my two eyes on the Philistines.

29 Samson took hold of the two pillars
in the center, on which the house was set,
and leaned on them;
one on his right and one on his left.
30 Then said Samson:
Will die my soul with the Philistines.
And he stretched out with his strength,
and the house fell on the chiefs
and on all the people in it.
And the dead he made die in his death
were more than the dead he made die in his life.

We observe that mention of Adonai's spirit is lacking on this occasion; yet Samson destroys the Philistine temple and all in attendance to witness his humiliation, thus becoming one of the first suicide attackers in history.

Cycle III: To Do What Is Right (Judges 17–21)

One encounters a ragtag bunch of questionable virtue.[1]

Together with the opening (1:1–3:6), the final chapters form a framework around the tales of the individual judges. Whereas the opening portrays individual tribes acting on their own to conquer hostile territory (with mixed results) and a people who persist in doing what "is wrong in the eyes of Adonai" (2:11), the end presents a fractured community in which "everyone did what was right in their own eyes." Here, there is no list of peoples from whom Israel needs deliverance; rather there are Israelites who undermine their potential cohesion and unity with their evil behavior, the textual groundwork for which has been prepared especially by the Gideon, Abimelek, Jefta, and Samson narratives but which is only now revealed in its full scope. The phrase "in those days there was no king in Israel; everyone did what was right in their own eyes" brackets the units connecting the beginning of the disintegration and its end (17:6; 21:25). Although the observation concerning human behavior is lacking in 18:1 and 19:1, which repeat the comment on the lack of a king, we may consider it implied in both places. These are the things that happen in days without leadership, when all do as they please. The phrase "the right in their own eyes" is the inverse of the frequent comment declaring that the Israelites are doing "the wrong in the eyes of

1. Gale A. Yee, "Ideological Criticism: Judges 17-21 and the Dismembered Body," in *Judges & Method: New Approaches in Biblical Studies*, ed. Gale A. Yee (Minneapolis: Fortress, 1995), 146–70, 157.

Adonai" in the days of the judges.[2] Not surprising, then, are the many words connected to wrongdoing in chapter 20.[3] There is thus no doubt that the period receives a negative judgment in the eyes of the collectors and editors. Whether the presence of a king will restore the well-being of the community and its relationship to God remains an open question.

Ironically, considering that these episodes teem with aggressively violent encounters, rape, murder, and intertribal warfare, no other narratives in Judges are as filled with references to religious practices. Accoutrements of worship, religious personnel, and gatherings of the community in a religious setting are present in this last section to an exceptional degree; the word "priest," absent in the rest of Judges, appears fifteen times in chapters 17 and 18. In chapter 20, "all the Israelites," identified as "the assembly," appear before Adonai, while further on in the episode one encounters "the Ark of the Covenant of God" (Judg 20:27)—a singular mention in Judges of this representation of the God of Israel, so prominent in Joshua. In addition, the assembly makes repeated inquiries to Adonai about a way forward with their predicament, requests eventually accompanied by sacrifice and the involvement of a member of the priesthood (20:26–28). The first responses of the Deity to the inquirers fill the gathered community with false confidence so that they initially engage in battle against their kin to their defeat (20:18–21, 23–25), casting doubt either on the trustworthiness of God's guidance or on the appropriateness of the requests. The multiple references to matters related to worship add to the aura of chaos and confusion rather than diminishing it. Everyone doing "what is right in their own eyes" evidently does not create a climate of peace and stability for the community.[4]

2. See 2:11; 3:7, 12; 4:1; 6:1; 10:6; 13:1.

3. See 20:3, 12, 13, 34, 41.

4. This reading is in disagreement with the perspective of Susan Niditch (*Judges*, OTL [Louisville: Westminster John Knox, 2008], 211), who views these chapters as representing reconciliation and the establishment of order: "Judges does not end with chaos; it ends with wholeness, reconciliation, rehabilitation, and peace, made possible in men's eyes through the taking of women." See also Susan Niditch, "Judges, Kingship, and Political Ethics: A

In what follows, the final chapters are divided into two acts. Each act begins with an introductory Scene that provides context and motivation for subsequent events. Chapter 17 furnishes background and rationale for the migration of Dan and the founding of its landholding, the focus of Act I (chs. 17–18). Events in chapter 19 afford the provocation that results in the breach of the tribal communities and the looming decimation of the tribe of Benjamin in Act II (chs. 19–21). Each act opens with episodes of family life within the confines of a house, while subsequent events show the spread of conflict and mayhem to the larger venue of the tribal settings.

Act I: The Foundation of Dan (Judges 17–18)

However much they strive, these characters and their narrator sometimes succeed, sometimes not.[5]

The subject of Judges 17–18 is the migration of the Danite tribe northward, resulting in the establishment of a sanctuary with appropriate officials but dubious worship items.[6] For this movement, the first scene (ch. 17) functions as prologue, introducing the locations (Ephraim and Bethlehem) and the protagonists: a central character, Micah, who gives way to an unnamed Levite priest, a continuing presence in the second scene. In addition, there is an elaborately described worship apparatus. Scene 2 (ch. 18) concentrates on the movements of the Danites, who are in need of land, and explains in detail the machinations by which they acquire both the worship items and the Levite priest on their way to their new homestead in the north, where they found a city called Dan (for-

---

Challenge to the Conventional Wisdom," in *Thus Says the Lord: Essays on the Former and Latter Prophets in Honor of Robert R. Wilson*, ed. John J. Ahn and Stephen L. Cook (London: T&T Clark, 2009), 59–70.

5. Polzin, *Moses and the Deuteronomist*, 199.

6. Difficulties with the landholding assigned to Dan were already mentioned in Joshua and again in the introductory chapter of Judges (Josh 19:40–48; Judg 1:34).

merly Laish) with a worship center after slaughtering the peaceful and unsuspecting Laishians.

Act I, Scene 1: A Man and a Priest[7] *(Judges 17)*

Homemade idols of stolen silver, private shrines, personal priests, self-made sacerdotal gear; these are hardly the proper trappings of one whose name means "Who is like [Adonai]?"[8]

In the first unit (17:1–5), after a standard introduction of a character (a man named by region and tribal affiliation), untoward and improper behavior comes to the fore almost immediately, as the man Micah, or sometimes Micaiah ("who is like Adonai?"), begins a discourse with his mother to confess that he stole money from her. A long, convoluted sentence, filled with words and phrases that begin going in one direction only to veer off into another, ends in a doubled confession: "See, I have the money; it was I who took it" (2). The mother subsequently blesses the son and with part of the finances (which she had previously cursed) she commissions religious imagery for her son's sanctuary, and he installs his own son there as a priest.

Judges 17:4–6

4 When he returned the silver to his mother,
his mother took two hundred pieces of silver
and gave it to the metalworker,
who made a hewn icon and a cast image;
and it was in the house of Micaiah.

7. The entire scene is framed by the words "man" and "priest" (17:1, 13). For the important inclusios in the chapter, see Robert Polzin, *Moses and the Deuteronomist: A Literary Study of the Deuteronomic History*, vol. 1 (New York: Seabury, 1980), 195–96.

8. Gale A. Yee, "Ideological Criticism: Judges 17–21 and the Dismembered Body," in *Judges and Method: New Approaches in Biblical Studies*, ed. Gale A. Yee (Minneapolis: Fortress, 2007), 149.

5 The man Micah had a sanctuary,
and made an ephod and household gods.
And he installed one of his sons,
who became his priest.

6 In those days, there was no king in Israel;
everyone did what was right in their own eyes.

Verse 4 repeats in part the previous sentence, in which the mother declares her intention, so that the words "hewn icon" (*pesel*) and "cast image" (*massekhah*) are emphatically present. The first term, with eight references in chapters 17 and 18 (17:3, 4; 18:14, 17, 18, 20, 30, 31) but not found elsewhere in Judges, is prohibited in three law codes of the Torah (Exod 20:4; Lev 26:1; Deut 4:16, 23, 25; 5:8; 27:15). The second term, used for the image of the golden calf in the wilderness (Exod 32:4, 8) and prohibited in Exodus 34:17 as well as in the other law codes (Lev 19:4; Num 33:52; Deut 9:12, 16),[9] occurs in these two chapters five times (17:3, 4; 18:14, 17, 18) and nowhere else in Judges.[10] In addition, verse 5 lists an ephod and *terafim*—some kind of household deities, perhaps with a protective function, found throughout ancient cultures, including ancient Israel. Of the fifteen times *terafim* are mentioned in the Hebrew Bible, they are not explicitly forbidden, but they are mentioned in negative contexts (1 Sam 15:23; 2 Kgs 23:24; Ezek 21:26[21]; Zech 10:2). The word occurs here five times, again unique in Judges (17:5; 18:14, 17, 18, 20). The only other reference to

9. Cf. 1 Kgs 12:28 with Exod 32:4. The *egel massekhah* ("molten calf") of Exodus becomes the *egel zahav* ("golden calf") of Jeroboam, over which he declares virtually the identical phrase used in Exodus: "See your god(s), Israel, who brought you up from the land of Egypt."

10. The carved images where Ehud turns around in Judg 3:19 represent the plural form of a related noun based on the identical Hebrew root *pasal* ("to carve, hew"). Niditch declares that these objects "are not idols but iconic representations" typical for the "early times, before the monarchy, when religious expression had not yet become uniform or orthodox." In my opinion, the narrator inserts a note of ambiguity here if not of outright condemnation. See Polzin (*Moses and the Deuteronomist*, 199), who identifies the object as an "idolatrous making."

an ephod in this book was in the Gideon story, where it had explicitly negative connotations (Judg 8:27; see p. 242 above).

Taken together, such objects hardly call for positive reactions on the part of ancient readers. They appear intended to portray a context in which worship does not follow communally agreed upon customs but, left to the imagination of the individual, piles one forbidden or negatively colored practice on top of another. To make matters more outrageous, the man Micah/Micaiah installs his son as a priest in his household sanctuary. This last notation elicits the comment of verse 6 that everyone "did what was right in their own eyes," the counterpart to the frequently repeated observation that the Israelites do "what is wrong in the eyes of Adonai" (see pp. 191, 202, 207–8, 277, 286–87 above), usually a reference to idolatrous worship.[11]

The second unit (17:6–13) introduces a wandering Levite (7–8). He finds a home with Micah, who invites him to stay and offers a stipend if he will function as his priest.[12] All seems to end well, as a legitimate person finally serves in Micah's sanctuary. Witness Micah's declaration about his good fortune and promising future on account of having a Levite as a priest (13). The Levite hails from Bethlehem in Judah, casting a shadow forward to subsequent events related to this town, a place that echoes with special significance as the eventual birth place of King David. The relationships in the unit are cast in terms of kinship ties. Micah asks the Levite to be "my father and priest" (10) and the Levite becomes "as one of his sons" (11), a member of the family (cf. v. 12). Everything so far is taking place within the confines of one household, foreshadowing that much of what follows will involve kinship relations, albeit in the larger context of clan and tribe.

We find the verb "to sojourn" (*gur*) tied to the residency of the Levite three times within the span of three verses (7–9). This verb

11. But see Niditch (*Judges*, 182) for a different opinion on the narrative statement, as she views it as a neutral observation about olden times and part of the foundation myth: "The saying in Judg 17:6 is thus not a condemnation . . . but an indication that in the old days things were different."

12. For a more extensive discussion of Levites and their position in the ancient Israelite community, see pp. 156–59.

literally means "to live as a stranger," an outsider having temporary residence without being fully a member of the community; only here and in chapter 19 is this verb used for a Levite (19:1, 16), lending an air of instability and fragility to what will turn out to be an ephemeral presence in the house of Micah. The verb, together with subsequent actions of the Levite in the next chapter, underscores the somewhat ambiguous legacy of the descendants of Levi (see pp. 156–59 above).[13]

Act I, Scene 2: "There Was No Deliverer" (Judges 18)

The Danites, on their way to steal a city, have decided to steal a sanctuary and its priest, too.[14]

A long chapter reviews in detail the perceived need of the Danites to find new territory and what comes of their explorations, beginning with a trail that leads directly back to Micah's house (18:1–6). It will veer from there but will eventually return, so that the fate of Micah's house becomes closely intertwined with that of the town of Laish in the north, to be conquered by the Danites. Both stand to lose by the movements of the tribe of Dan.[15] The unit opens with a statement about the context in view of both the absence of a king and the desire of Dan to find room for its tribe "in those days." In Joshua, an allotment had been assigned to Dan (Josh 19:40, 47–48; 21:5, 23), but here it is portrayed as not having "a heritage to live in" (18:1). In one long sentence (2), the Danites send out five spies to investigate what land might be available for them, with the spies arriving at the house of Micah in the hill country of Ephraim. The sending of spies, who in the next breath arrive somewhere, can signal trouble down the

13. Tikva Frymer-Kensky, *Reading the Women of the Bible* (New York: Schocken, 2002), 119: "In the days of our story, the Levite was a figure of both power and danger, centrality and marginality."

14. Mark E. Biddle, *Reading Judges: A Literary and Theological Commentary* (Macon, GA: Smyth and Helwys, 2012), 179.

15. For possible reconstructions of the historical movements of this tribe, see Biddle, *Reading Judges*, 175–77.

road (cf. Josh 2:1), although what sort of trouble will arrive at Micah's doorstep still lies in the future. Yet already there are signs that the Levite at Micah's is drawing a surprising amount of attention.

Judges 18:3

They were with the house of Micah,
and they considered the voice of the lad, the Levite,
and turned aside there
and said to him:
Who made you come here?
And what are you doing in this place,
and what is your business here?

First, the scouting delegation pays close attention to his "voice," perhaps the "sound" of his speech, which may have been recognizably different than that of his neighbors. So "they turned aside," a common enough verb, but also one that may herald significant events around the corner. We can think of Moses, Sisera, or Samson—all of them "turning aside" at the onset of a radical turn of events (Exod 3:3–4; Judg 4:18; Judg 14:8). In addition, the Levite is the recipient of three interesting questions, of which the upshot is that someone must have persuaded him to live there, that he must have important business, and there must be something in it for him. The colo-metric division of the lines renders emphatic statements related to place: "The house of Micah" becomes "there," then "here" and "this place" to end with another "here." Both the indications "here" have a question mark attached, hinting at instability clinging to this house. Once the Levite has satisfied them that he is working in a professional capacity, the spies feel free to draw on his professional skills and ask him to forecast the success of their explorations. The priest complies, but provides an ambiguous response, since, in the phrase "*before* Adonai is your way" (6), the preposition can mean both "opposite" and "in front of," either announcing that the spies are on a mission opposite to Adonai's intention or that their wish coheres with the divine will.

The next unit (18:7–14) introduces Laish in the north, underlining the disposition of its people by noting they are "trusting" (2×), living "after the custom of the Sidonians," and "at rest." Moreover, they live without an oppressive hierarchy, as I understand the description of their social situation in verse 7, which concludes ominously with the statement that they live "far from Sidon" and "have no dealings with anyone." On top of the description of their trusting, perhaps naïve, disposition, the double statement of their isolation portrays the Laishians as ready prey. The reaction of the spies to this situation becomes clear from the admonition to their kinsmen to get on with the job and conquer a place that looks like a veritable Eden (9–10).[16] This is indeed "a place that lacks nothing"—except, perhaps, a marauding band of Danites! Five times, the two verses repeat the word "land," calling it "wide-handed," indicating generosity and spaciousness, hinting also at a term used for the land God promised the Israelites (Exod 3:8). The encouragement is enough to make Dan set out with a fairly small military force of 600 warriors who, like the spies earlier, arrive at Micah's house, where the spies once again offer encouragement, this time to consider taking action in view of the treasures available there (14).

In the next unit (18:15–25), off go the Danites, in another instance of "turning aside," to the "house of Micah," which frames the episode—a place open to robbery at the beginning and emptied of its treasures at the end. The report on the theft itself is not always straightforward, but the result of the double account of the robbery is a resounding tripled reference to the listing of the iconic items across four verses (17–20). The priest is quickly persuaded, perhaps on account of better prospects with the tribe of Dan, or perhaps because 600 armed soldiers may have that effect on a person. In any case, he carries the images and the ephod off, as the text has it, "gladly" (20). Priest and images will reappear once more at the end of the episode. Micah and his neighbors make a futile attempt to protest and recoup their loss (22–25) but return home empty-handed after the Danites silence him rudely and threaten all of them with murder.[17]

16. According to Niditch (*Judges*, 179), the declaration of the land they have seen as "very good" deliberately evokes the recurring refrain in Genesis in regard to the creation as "good" and, in the end, "very good."

17. Verse 24 renders Micah's protest eloquently with the thrice-repeated

The last unit (18:27–31) paints the sad picture of the Danites slaughtering those of Laish, once again characterized as a "quiet and trusting people," burning down the town and rebuilding it as Dan. The narrative (without details of the battle—possibly because Laish put up no resistance) emphasizes for the second time the features that typified them. The word "at rest" (*shoqet*) is used in Joshua of the Israelites having rest after their aggressive military engagements and in Judges of the land resting after oppressive hostilities because of a God-sent deliverer (Josh 11:23; 14:15; Judg 3:11, 30; 5:31; 8:28).[18] "Trusting" (*boteah*) occurs in Deuteronomy in reference to the Israelites living at peace and carefree in the land through God's help and in Judges of false trust on the part of the enemy in superior power or of the citizenry in troublemakers (Deut 12:10; 33:28; Judg 8:11; 9:26).[19] In Kings, the Israelites are said to live "trusting"—that is, without care—under the reign of Solomon (1 Kgs 5:5 [4:25]). In regard to a population, both words refer predominantly, though not exclusively, to Israel. The expression "there was no deliverer" in verse 28 is thus especially poignant. A picture is painted not of an aggressive oppressor from which Israel needs "deliverance" but of a people like Israel coveting peace and freedom from war who are overrun by a tribe of thieving and murdering Israelites.

The tail of the entire episode (30–31) traces the lineage of the Levite priest to Moses, or via scribal notation to King Manasseh, a name associated with a Judean king held up for special denunciation in terms of his idolatry (2 Kgs 21:1–16), perhaps to underline the condemnation of the worship practices of the Northern Kingdom.[20] The items are set up for worship "until the day of the exile of the land," a term that could point to a composition date for Judges either after the Assyrian conquest of the Northern Kingdom or after

"what." Literally translated, he says, "What have I left,/ and what is this you say to me:/ What is wrong with you?" (18:24), as if he stutters out "what . . . what . . . what?"

18. Cf. also 2 Kgs 11:20; 1 Chr 22:9.

19. Especially noteworthy is the "trusting" attitude on the part of the Shechemites in Gen 34:24 who are on the verge of being slaughtered by the brothers of Dina, Simeon and Levi.

20. For a detailed discussion, see Niditch, *Judges*, 184.

the Babylonian exile. A final observation that the sculptured image (made by Micah!) served as a center of worship for Dan "all the days that the house of God was in Shiloh" is a proleptic reference to the presence of the Ark in Shiloh as it will surface in 1 Samuel 3:3. At the same time, it refers back to the importance of this location in Joshua as a center for the gathering of the Israelite assembly and the activity of casting the lots to divide the land (Josh 18:1, 10; 19:51).

Act II: A Breach in the Tribes (Judges 19–21)

Episodes in this comedy of horrors unfold in a grotesque downward arc.[21]

The last act of the book progresses in three scenes. The first, chapter 19, presents the elaborate setup for the mayhem that follows. In it, a detailed description of a family and its journeys ends in horrific violence. The rape and murder within the confines of family and town of that episode in turn spread to acts of intertribal vengeance (ch. 20), which spin off into the mass abduction of hundreds of young women (ch. 21). In the last two chapters, the breach among the Israelite tribes, a threat on the horizon in Joshua (Josh 22:11–33), present in Judges as of chapter 8 (1–17; 9:22–54; 12:1–7; 15:9–20), becomes a reality and serves as a portent for the postexilic community of the eventual tearing of the fabric of the Israelites as a people.

Act II, Scene 1: A Man and His Family (Judges 19)

Somehow, without access to decades of clinical research, this text recognizes the power of constructing a traumatic narrative.[22]

Once again, a story beginning with the stock phrase "in those days there was no king in Israel" (cf. 17:6; 18:1) introduces a character

21. Biddle, *Reading Judges*, 181.

22. Janelle Stanley, "Judges 19: Text of Trauma," in *Joshua and Judges*, ed. Athalya Brenner and Gale A. Yee (Minneapolis: Fortress, 2013), 275–89.

(once again a Levite) identified by location (like Micah, in the hill country of Ephraim—although this time the expression "the reaches of Ephraim" may indicate more remote country). Certainly, this Levite, who, like the previous one, "sojourned," not having a fixed abode, proves to be unused to urban life, naïve, and perhaps fearful in what follows. Like the Levite in Micah's house, this one trails violence in his wake. The action in the scene takes place in precisely defined locations: the hill country of Ephraim, Bethlehem, Gibeah, and in between. The Levite has a *pilegesh*—a concubine, or secondary wife (see pp. 242n73, 263 above). In the Historical Books, these women are often part of the royal household, but they also receive names and status in the ancestry of Israel (cf. Gen 22:24; 25:6). While the position of such a woman in the household is not well understood, we may assume that her rights were not equal to that of a wife.

The first unit (19:1–9) implies, however, close family relations characterized by the frequent naming of persons to indicate such ties ("father," "father-in-law," and "son-in-law" appear twelve times in nine verses). At first, family disharmony occurs as the concubine leaves the Levite to go back to her father in Bethlehem, Judah (2). The Hebrew text reads that she "played the whore against him," understood by some to mean her very act of leaving constituted unfaithfulness.[23] I suggest that the expression is used deliberately to emphasize the fragility of her position and at the same time to continue the connection between "those days" and the perpetual unfaithfulness on the part of Israel in terms of its worship of other gods than Adonai, acts which are compared to prostitution elsewhere in the Bible, especially in prophetic literature, but also in Judges (Judg 2:17; 8:27, 33; Exod 34:15, 16; Deut 31:16; Isa 1:21; Jer 2:20; 3:6; 5:7; Hos 4:10, 12; 5:3; 9:1; Mic 1:7). There is no sign that the Levite tries to stop her, so there must have been some freedom of movement on

23. Frymer-Kensky, *Reading the Women of the Bible*, 119: "His concubine was faithless to him." Mark Biddle (*Reading Judges*, 184) suggests that the term *zanah* ("play the harlot") "may function hyperbolically . . . characterizing the woman's departure itself as a kind of infidelity." Niditch (*Judges*, 189) cites Greek and Latin variants that "provide a different nuance to her behavior." Gale Yee ("Ideological Criticism," 153) also understands the "harlotry" of the concubine this way.

her part. When he makes the decision to bring her back, he does so with the intention "to speak to her heart" (3), and there is initially no evidence of further conflict as the woman brings her husband to her paternal home, where he is received with joy and signs of hospitality. The word "heart," as the locus of strength or joy, permeates the entire first episode; even on the fifth day, the "father-in-law, the father of the lass" attempts to offer another night of hospitality in order to make the "heart" of his son-in-law "glad."

The description of the protracted family visit exhibits telling repetitive features in narrative comment and reported speech. The relationship of the host to both members of the couple is stated repeatedly, first as "her father," "the father of the lass" (3); then as "his father-in-law" and again as "the father of the lass" (4); and finally with the two combined in verse 9. There could hardly be a stronger statement to highlight family ties. We note that the "concubine" has in this section become "the lass" (*na'arah*), underlining her youth and her subordinate position in the household—in other words her dependence and vulnerability.[24] There are constant repetitions of the verb *lin* ("to spend the night"), which we encounter five times in the unit, twice in verse 9. "Spending the night" will take on accelerated significance in the next unit, with multiple references (10, 11, 13, 15) before the alarm-bell of the sixth and final reference in verse 20. Added to the prominence of night is the listing of "days": "three days" (4), "the fourth day" (5), "the fifth day" (8), and the triple reference to the ending of the day in verses 8 and 9 ("the day was done," "the day is drawing toward evening," and "the day is done"). "Night," observes Weston Fields, "was the time to remain within the bounds of the safe haven of the private home."[25] Just at the time that day

24. According to some commentators, the references to "the lass" serve to remind of the absence of the concubine in these episodes as an active presence. See Janelle Stanley, "Judges 19," 280; Jacqueline Lapsley, *Whispering the Word: Hearing Women's Stories in the Old Testament* (Louisville: Westminster John Knox, 2005), 40–41.

25. Weston W. Fields, "The Motif 'Night as Danger' Associated with Three Biblical Destruction Narratives," in *Sha'arei Talmon: Studies in the Bible, Qumran, and the Ancient Near East Presented to Shemaryahu Talmon*, ed. Michael Fishbane and Emmanuel Tov (Winona Lake, IN: Eisenbrauns, 1992),

is disappearing, the Levite decides to leave the safety of the family house. The phrases to indicate the threatening aspect of this feature come thick and fast, especially at the end of the unit.

JUDGES 19:9

And the man arose to go,
he and his concubine and his lad;
then said to him his father-in-law,
the father of the lass:
Look, the day is drawing toward evening.
Spend the night here, please—
the day is done;
spend the night here,
and your heart will be glad.
Then you can rise early tomorrow morning
and be on your way to your tent.

Words for household relations ("the man," "his concubine and his lad," "his father-in-law, the father of the lass") and the positive "rising early in the morning" enclose emphatic declarations about the impending night—twice a reference to day's end—and a repeated plea to spend the night.

The significance of the disappearance of day arises immediately in the next unit (19:10–21) when the servant observes that "the

22. Fields compares the narratives of Gen 19, Josh 2, and Judg 19 as carrying a significant "danger-at-night" motif combined with such other themes as "reproachable sexuality": "For the ancient reader the evening/night setting would almost certainly have imbued each narrative from the outset with an aura of foreboding and sinister premonition, of trepidation and anxiety, for night and violence, danger and darkness were inseparably joined." Susanne Gillmayr-Bucher (*Erzählte Welten im Richterbuch: Narratologische Aspekte eines Polyfonen Diskurses* [Leiden: Brill, 2013], 212; author's translation) highlights the different tempos in the narrative and how "the emphatic slow arrival of evening creates tension and leaves the impression that the impending night has a threatening aspect." Many scholars note the obvious similarities between Gen 19 and the Judg 19 narrative apart from this motif.

day is mostly done" (11). We understand that the Levite has left too late to make it home, already signaled in the speech of the concubine's father when he remarks that evening is falling (9). The first unwise decision on the part of the Levite may thus be this tardy leave-taking. He and his retinue—the donkeys, the concubine, and his servant—set out, but wandering in the countryside at nighttime "in those days" is not a sensible option, so they need to look for a town for lodging.

It happens that they are near to Jebus/Jerusalem, which the Levite declares to be a "foreign" town not belonging to Israel, so he decides to spend the night in Gibeah or Ramah.[26] This was probably his second poor decision. If, as mentioned in Judges 1:21, the Jebusites lived in Jerusalem together with Israelites, the more mixed population there may have made them less obvious as outsiders. Violence against travelers was probably not unusual, which is one reason for the frequency of protective legislation for the "stranger" in the Torah. As Tikva Frymer-Kensky points out, however, protective codes depend "on a common sense of trust" or on a safeguard from a protective authority, and such authorities are absent "in those days."[27] In verses 11–15 the verb "turn aside" (see p. 293 above) appears in every sentence except the one that announces that the "sun was setting," which in the context sounds foreboding.

Judges 19:14–16

14 They crossed and went,
and the sun was setting on them,
near Gibeah that is in Benjamin.
15 And they turned aside there
to go in and spend the night in Gibeah.

26. Conflicting traditions regarding Jerusalem are present in Joshua and Judges (cf. Josh 15:63; 18:28; Judg 1:7, 8, 21). The use of space in the narration is telling. The house stands for safety, while open space betokens danger. Likewise, a "foreign" town like Jerusalem is not considered safe, while one that "belongs to Israel" is expected to afford shelter.

27. Frymer-Kensky, *Reading the Women of the Bible*, 122.

And he arrived and stayed in the town square,
and there was no one who took them in
to their house to spend the night.
16 And, look, an old man came in
from his work from the field in the evening,
and the man was from the hill country of Ephraim,
and he was sojourning in Gibeah,
and the men of the place were Benjaminites.

The place is identified as belonging to Benjamin, an identification repeated at the end of the notation. The repeated references emphasize that the ones from Ephraim are outsiders, and Gibeah in Benjamin begins to look doubtful as a safe haven. In between the two mentions of location, there is the stark observation of the lack of hospitality. "There was no one who took them in" would have sufficed to make the situation clear; yet the narrator adds the words "to their house to spend the night."[28] "Spending the night" inside has now become an urgent matter. Next, the tension is lifted somewhat by the appearance of a man who is from the same place as the Levite, the hill country of Ephraim. What luck! Of course, there is the note that he is "sojourning," living as an outsider in Gibeah, and it remains to be seen how safe his house will be.

Hopes rise when the Ephraimite offers lodging and food to the "wanderer" in the square, perhaps because they come from the same place or perhaps because he abides by codes of hospitality. His invitation comes with a warning: "Only do not in the square spend the night!" This is the last reference to "spending the night," here raising doubts about the social conditions existing in the town. At first, all appears to have turned out well, and indeed the evening begins with

28. Oded Borowski (*Daily Life in Biblical Times* [Atlanta: Society of Biblical Literature, 2003], 21) concludes from this episode that "out-of-towners would sit in the street or town square . . . and wait for an invitation by one of the locals." There is no doubt that hospitality extended to the stranger is an obligation emphasized in biblical narrative and teaching. In Judges, it comes to light especially when characters are visited by a divine messenger who appears to them as a guest (Judg 6:19; 13:15).

their having a good time. Again, and for the last time, we hear the idiom "making the heart glad" (22).

After the momentary "gladness," events go downhill with alarming speed in the final unit of the chapter (19:22–30).[29] The decision of outsiders to lodge with another outsider turns out to be a poor one also. For even as they sit enjoying themselves, a band of ruffians, "worthless men" (*beney beliya'al*), surround the house and demand that the master of the house surrender his guest so they may "know him" (22)—that is to say, have sexual intercourse with him, an act of extreme hostility and aggression.[30] That the characters in the story so understand it is clear from the response of the host, who offers the women in the house—his virgin daughter (!) and the Levite's concubine—for the townsmen to "abuse" (24), to which he adds the telling phrase "do to them as is good in your eyes." In the context of these chapters, this phrase now takes on an even more ominous tone. Twice, the host admonishes the men he calls "his brothers" to not "do this wanton folly" (24). This term, "wanton folly" (*navelah*), is elsewhere used in the context of *herem* violation (Josh 7:15) and in connection with rape (2 Sam 13:12). It connotes an act of sacrilege more than merely something inappropriate (see p. 105 above). The term "brothers," reminiscent of the words for family connections used earlier in the story, is here clearly ironic. Family connections have broken down—between the host and his daughter and between host, guest, and the townsfolk who threaten them.

For the Levite, too, the bond with his family is broken, as becomes clear when he makes his next and fatal decision, shoving his concubine out of the door. "Girls are the coin of the realm, the bounty that men exchange as they jockey for power and survival, and sometimes the bloody fields on which men contest for power. The Levite

29. Many observe the similarities between this episode and the Sodom and Gomorra episode in Genesis 19. See, for example, Niditch, *Judges*, 192–193; Biddle, *Reading Judges*, 181–183; Frymer-Kensky, *Reading the Women of the Bible*, 124–125.

30. Frymer-Kensky: "Whether or not the 'knowledge' will be carnal, the purpose of it is to emasculate the traveler, strip him of his pride and his honor, and render him submissive and nonthreatening." Frymer-Kensky, *Reading the Women of the Bible*, 124.

has taken a long and arduous journey to retrieve the girl, but when he sees that he has to give her up to save his own life, he does not hesitate."[31] At this point we let the biblical text speak for itself:

JUDGES 19:25–28

25 And the men did not want to listen to him,
and the man seized his concubine
and brought her outside to them;
and they knew her,
and they abused her all night until morning
and sent her away at the rise of dawn.
26 The woman came at the turning of the morning
and fell at the entrance of the house of the man
where her lord was until daylight.
27 Her lord arose in the morning
and opened the doors of the house
and went out to go on his way—
behold the woman, his concubine,
fallen at the entrance of the house,
with her hands on the threshold.

28 He said to her: Get up
and we will go!
And there was no one who answered.
He put her on his donkey,
and the man arose and went to his place.

All the references to "spending the night" culminate in the phrase "they abused her *all night until morning*." The woman who was in charge of the action in the beginning ("she played the whore," "she went," "she was there," "she brought him," vv. 2–3) at the end becomes the helpless object of terror: they "seized" her, "brought her," "knew her," "abused her," "sent her away." Her presence outside the house causes her torture and violation for an entire night and,

31. Frymer-Kensky, *Reading the Women of the Bible*, 125.

unlike the beginning of the story, the man, twice here called "her lord," does not come out to "speak to her heart." For the first time, the concubine is called "the woman" in the story, and for the last time she is the subject of action. Tragically, her activity ("she came") concludes downward ("she fell"). The turning of the morning brings her no hope. At the end, she has no heart for "her lord" to speak to and no tongue to wield, for there is no one who answers his command. There are only her hands touching the threshold of the house, inside which he has safely stayed "*all night until morning*."

All is not done, for, once home, the Levite cuts up the body and sends the pieces around in Israel; whether she is dead or still alive before her husband begins to butcher her body the narrator does not say, leaving the matter for the reader to speculate about. The final verse of the scene voices the reaction of those who receive the gruesome body parts—a desecrated body further violated. What can one say beyond "nothing like this has ever happened" since the day the Israelites left Egypt? Verb forms throughout have been reversed imperfects, including in this last part: he "put," "arose," "went," "arrived," "seized," "cut," "sent" (28–29). This steady cadence changes in verse 30 to reversed perfects in the Hebrew, which can indicate repeated action (see Judg 2:19; 6:3) or future events (see Judg 4:20; 7:4; 9:33; 11:31; 21:22), in this case drawing attention to the reaction not only of the community at the time but also of the future hearer/reader:

Judges 19:30

Everyone who sees it will say:
Not has happened and not has been seen
such in the days since the Israelites came up
from the land of Egypt until today.
Pay attention, devise a plan, and speak!

Everyone who sees (i.e., reads) this, take note of something unique in the experience of Israel from the time of its beginning as a people! In other words, do not ignore what has happened. Moreover, make plans to prevent anything like this from ever taking place again. Not speaking in the face of the appalling scenes before us would amount to collusion with the crimes committed.

Janelle Stanley reads the story of chapter 19 as a trauma narrative, exhibiting traumatic features in its remembrance through omission, repetition, and fragmentation. She considers the very act of telling the story a part of the healing of trauma that needs to take place. She observes that the last words of the chapter "instruct us to speak out, to fight against our own innate instincts to silence the trauma, and, instead, give it voice."[32] Many question the absence of condemnation on the part of the narrator. With Jan Fokkelman, I understand the detailed description of the gruesome details together with the final admonition to be a more effective critique than explicit statements of censure.[33] This is a story of a broken female body signifying broken commitments, broken ethics, broken family relations—a reality that will play itself out further in the final chapters of the book.

Act II, Scene 2: "The Bad Thing" (Judges 20)

In the ideology of male prestige, it is infinitely preferable to be attacked by lords than by the local louts.[34]

The irony of the last two scenes is that the Israelites are more united than anywhere else in the book. They "gather" in the "assembly"; they arise "as one man united" (20:1–2). Words for Israel and Israelites, combined with references to "tribe," are clustered in chapters 20 and 21, amounting to more than half their occurrences in

32. Stanley, "Judges 19," 275–89, 289.

33. Jan Fokkelman, "Structural Remarks on Judges 9 and 19," in *Sha'arei Talmon: Studies in the Bible, Qumran, and the Ancient Near East Presented to Shemaryahu Talmon*, ed. Michael Fishbane and Emmanuel Tov (Winona Lake: Eisenbrauns, 1992), 40. Fokkelman observes that "quasi-objective narration and the precise description of horrors is a much more effective critique of violence than snorting out moral indignation" and that "the narrator is morally in order by the very creation and handing down of this story."

34. Gale A. Yee, "Ideological Criticism," 155.

Judges.[35] These emphatic references take place in the face of broken trust and, finally, all-out war among them.

A first unit (20:1–17) concentrates on the reaction of the people to the grisly dispatch they have received. The Levite has sent pieces of his butchered concubine to the entire territory of Israel (19:29), and "all the Israelites" gather "as one man" in response "unto Adonai" at Mizpah, in Judges the location for gathering troops against the Ammonites and eventually the residence of Jefta (Judg 10:17; 11:11, 29).[36] Every verse in the introductory note (1–3) mentions the Israelites in some way, twice in the last lines (3). In between these references is the following observation: "And the Benjaminites heard that the Israelites went to Mizpah" (3). From this one sentence, it becomes clear that Benjamin, presumably included in the communication from the Levite, is not included as a member of the party at Mizpah. Already, the Benjaminites have separated themselves from their own people, and "all the Israelites" are not, in fact, *all* the people, in spite of the threefold repetition of the word in the opening verses.

When the Israelites ask how this "bad thing" happened, the Levite tells the tale in his way from his perspective:

JUDGES 20:4–7

4 Then answered the Levite man,
the husband of the woman who was murdered:
To Gibeah in Benjamin I came,
I and my concubine, to spend the night.
5 Then rose up against me
the masters of Gibeah
and surrounded against me the house in the night;
me they thought to slay,
and my concubine they abused,
and she died.

35. *Shevet* ("tribe") occurs outside of this cycle only in Judges 5:14.

36. Samuel will call the Israelites together at Mizpah to fight the Philistines (1 Sam 7:5), and Saul will be crowned king there by the people (1 Sam 10:17).

6 And I took hold of my concubine,
and cut her up and sent her
in all the field of the heritage of Israel
because they committed depravity and wanton folly in Israel.
7 Behold, all of you, Israelites,
provide yourselves with word and counsel here.

Literally in Hebrew, the opening line repeats the word "man" once too often ("the Levite man, the man of the woman who was murdered"), underlining the juxtaposition of man and woman. This *man* delivers a masterpiece of truth-telling that hides important truths about himself and the *woman* he delivered into the hands of her abusers. He puts himself in the center. The "worthless men" of Gibeah have become the "masters" who were after *him* ("me they thought to slay") with the grammatical object in first place. He exaggerates the threat against his life and skips over his act of delivering his concubine to the mob so he could save his own skin. His action of butchering her body takes place after the verb "she died," implying that there is no doubt that he cut up a dead body, not a living one. In his own eyes, he did the right thing in the face of the ones who committed this evil. He uses the word for a deed considered shameful to describe what they did, together with the aforementioned "wanton folly." He sent her body to everyone ("all the field ... of Israel"); now it is time for everyone ("all of you, Israelites") to devise a plan of action.

The reaction of "all the Israelites" is to make logistical preparations for battle, uniting "as one man" (8, 11), and, after Benjamin refuses to deliver the wrongdoers, mustering the troops. First, they give Benjamin a chance to let only the culprits bear the consequences of the evil act, but Benjamin stands with its town, evildoers and all—the tie of tribe apparently outweighing their connection to the rest of Israel, to whom the narrator refers as "their brothers, the Israelites" (13). The consequence of the "wrong" that has been done, the "bad thing," is that another bad thing comes about: tribes mustering troops against each other. The stain of wrongdoing will not stay limited to the "worthless men" or even to one town but will spread throughout Israel. Details of preparations include the almost ridiculously mismatched numbers, with Israel outnumbering Benjamin ten to one. The last word of the unit is "war."

A second unit (20:18–28) presents repeated inquiries (18, 23) on the part of the Israelites to Adonai, to which the response is of a kind that encourages Israel to engage Benjamin in battle, during which Israel twice suffers a defeat.[37] Finally, they pull out all the stops with weeping and fasting and sacrifices, explicitly involving the priesthood and the Ark of the Covenant. And, finally, they not only receive encouragement to continue fighting but a promise that God will deliver Benjamin into their hand (28). The Israelites consistently refer to Benjamin as "our brother." As many point out, Israel follows protocol in their proceedings, and in the end it pays off, but only after much bloodshed and through a sea of tears. The drawn-out recitation of the process of inquiry, the references to Benjamin as a "brother," and the unforeseen defeats perhaps hint at the fact that Israel does not have its heart in this fight. The first question posed to Adonai does not address the issue of the justness of their cause directly but asks who will be in the lead in the altercation (18). The "war/battle," a term repeated twelve times in the chapter, is after all not against a foreign oppressor but against their "brother." Perhaps they only begin to take it seriously after God makes them a promise of personal involvement (28).

The battle itself (Judg 20:29–48) is recounted in extraordinary detail and reminiscent of the strategy followed against Ai in Joshua 8:4–22. The Israelite troops devise an ambush tactic, drawing the Benjaminites away from the city, and when the Benjaminites become overconfident, attacking from the front, another contingent strikes down Gibeah, setting fire to the town. A column of smoke is the signal of victory for one side and of defeat for the other. Twice, the account refers to the impending rout of Benjamin with the word

37. As many observe, the first question asked of the Deity is who should go up first, to which the response is identical to Judg 1:2: "Judah first." What is lacking in Adonai's response in chapter 20, however, is the assurance that there will be victory. This time there is no "I will give . . . into his hand." That promise does not arrive until the third request, when the Israelites contemplate stopping the effort and engage a priest in the negotiations (20:28).

for wrong or evil (*ra'ah*). First, the narrator notes that during the initial attack on Benjamin, "they did not know the evil that was coming near to them" (34); and in the end "they saw that evil had come near to them" (41). The evil/wrong has been near for a long time, evident from the murderous actions in Gibeah, but they recognize it only in their defeat. The sorry tale ends with the destruction of almost the entire tribe of Benjamin by their "brothers," leaving only six hundred male survivors and leading to the conclusion that "the second aftermath of the concubine's rape and murder has been the rape and murder of all the women of the tribe of Benjamin."[38] In fact, the textual note to that effect is in Judges 21:16. From one bad thing has come another and then another, and there is yet more to come.

Act II, Scene 3: "Those Were the Days, My Friend" (Judges 21)

The violence turns inward against the very heart of Israel.[39]

The chapter consists mainly of two sections. The first fourteen verses introduce the problem faced by Israel, together with its solution. Three introductory verses set the scene (21:1–2, 4), interrupted by a question (3). The section concludes with three narrative verses that introduce a new problem (12–14). The final eleven verses of the chapter follow a similar pattern, with one narrative introductory verse and three concluding notes, each with their own subject. In between these short narrative segments, seven verses report speech. While much action of an appalling nature takes place, the amount of text devoted to speech lends a curiously static character to the chapter.

In a first unit (21:1–7), the Israelites come together to deliberate what can be done for Benjamin. The unit is structured in a circular manner with triple references: to oath-taking (1, 5, 7), expressions of regret (2, 4, 6), and questioning (3, 5, 7). Three questions, "why did this happen," "who did not participate," and "what shall we do" circle

38. Frymer-Kensky, *Reading the Women of the Bible*, 132–133.
39. Frymer-Kensky, *Reading the Women of the Bible*, 136.

back to the question "who did not participate," so that the result of the deliberation is to point an accusing finger at another town in Israel, Jabesh Gilead, which sent no delegation (lit. "no man") to take part in the earlier meeting at Mizpah and the following action against Benjamin. The Israelites once again refer to Benjamin as kin, "their brother," of whom the six hundred remaining men have no possibility to procreate since the "men" of Israel had sworn not to give any of "their women" to Benjamin. The entire unit is bracketed in a reference to the swearing of an oath to this effect. The other oath mentioned relates the threat of death against those who absented themselves from the gathering at Mizpah, an oath that ultimately provides the solution for the problem, for it justifies renewed war on one of their own, the town of Jabesh Gilead.

A second unit (21:9–14) announces the total war on Jabesh Gilead, using the practice of *herem* for only the second time in Judges (11; cf. 1:17), with the exception of women who are virgins. The language underlines the importance of the matter by repeating the crucial condition: "women virgins/ who had not known a man/ by bedding a male" (11–12).[40] In contrast with the details listed in the war with Benjamin, the matter of the war on Jabesh Gilead is described in intention only so that the tempo of events speeds up until they "brought" the surviving women from Jabesh Gilead to Shiloh and "gave" them to the six hundred survivors of Benjamin. The report concludes, however, that "they did not find the right number for them" (14).

Because they have failed in solving the problem completely, another effort at procuring women is necessary. As in verse 6, the people "were sorry" for Benjamin, this time putting the blame on their God: "because Adonai had caused a breach in the tribes of Israel." Once again, they ask what they should do in view of the fact that one tribe should not go missing from the total. The oath referred to earlier in regard to the tribal decision to not themselves provide women

40. The phrasing in Hebrew is virtually identical to that of an incident in Numbers following a battle against Midian (Num 31:17, 18, 35), demonstrating that in this episode, Israelites treat Israelites as they once conducted themselves against an enemy.

for Benjamin is here articulated as a curse (18). In view of this curse, it is impossible to *give* women from the other tribes to Benjamin. But wait—perhaps there is another opportunity! If there is no question that any women can be *given*, there is always a possibility of *stealing*. That is exactly what happens when the Benjaminites, acting on the information provided to them, including precise directions, steal the daughters of Shiloh.

Judges 21:23–25

23 Then did so the Benjaminites
and carried women for their numbers
from the whirling women whom they stole.
And they went and returned to their inheritance
and built their towns
and lived in them.
24 Then went from there the Israelites
at that time each to their tribes
and their clans.
And each went from there to his inheritance.
25 In those days there was no king in Israel;
everyone did what was right in their own eyes.

Susan Ackerman and others have pointed out the parallels between chapters 19 and 21. In Ackerman's words, "A story that begins by condemning Benjamin's assault of an Ephraimite's woman concludes by condoning the Benjaminites' ravaging of the Ephraimites' women."[41] With this sad epilogue, the curtain drops on a stage that displayed the life of a society without central leadership, without much that united them, led from time to time by inspired warriors

41. Susan Ackerman, *Warrior, Dancer, Seductress, Queen: Women in Judges and Biblical Israel* (New York: Doubleday, 1999), 255. Ackerman also explores the connections of the annual festival in Shiloh, here referred to with its dancing and ritual music, to the opening chapters of 1 Samuel. See also Biddle (*Reading Judges*, 203): "The eerie symmetry evident in the account highlights the perversity of the whole affair."

to ward off the foe. The period has not played out in a romantic fog with dreams of past glory; the flaws of the heroes were many times on full display. Yet there could hardly have been a sadder coda to the era than this cowardly theft which had to take place because Israel had sworn an oath not to *give*. "Then did so the Benjaminites/ and carried women for their numbers/ from the whirling women whom they stole" (21:23). *Doing* constitutes *carrying*, which constitutes *stealing*. The rather uncommon root of the last word in the sentence (*gazal*) is related to "cutting" and "tearing" and indicates violent robbery, elsewhere in the Bible a forbidden and condemned act.[42] They lie in "ambush," a military ploy used in Judges in contexts of treachery and violent encounter.[43] But, having accomplished their goal, the Benjaminites go home to "their inheritance" as do the tribes. The word "inheritance" (*nahalah*) occurs in Judges only in the framing chapters (Judg 2:6, 9; 18:1; 20:6; 21:23, 24). The perpetual, rightful "inheritance," considered to be a gift from God to the tribes, is here the home at the end of a trail of blood and violence of kin against kin. After all, that is what it was like in "those days" when "there was no king in Israel." They go to live with their stolen wives, many of whom have witnessed the murder of their brothers, sisters, parents, and friends in Jabesh Gilead, and others who thought they were safe in their hometown but were torn from their families, who, if they even thought to protest, were told to "have compassion" (21:22)—compassion on everyone except the women that is.

42. See, for example, Lev 5:21, 23 [6:2, 4]; 19:13; Deut 28:29, 31; Isa 10:2; Mic 3:2.

43. Judg 9:25; 16:2, 9, 12; 20:29, 33, 36, 37, 38.

Taking Stock

What are we to make of Judges, and especially of its last five chapters? Differences of opinion abound as to the significance of its violent, misogynist ending, and indeed about the intended lesson to be learned from the entire book. It is clear that events have been spiraling downward from the period of Abimelek on and that the last "judge," Samson, presents more a picture of wayward and ungoverned behavior than a disciplined warrior fighting with his troops to "deliver Israel." The repeated phrase regarding the absence of a king and everyone doing "what was right" in their eyes in the last chapters echoes the earlier refrain that the Israelites continued to do "the wrong thing." Yet in the final chapters, the "wrong thing" does not constitute worship of the wrong gods, the case in the rest of the book; rather, it is behavior in violation of ethical codes belonging to the social and religious world of ancient Israel. Theft of a person's household goods and war against an innocent and unsuspecting people is followed by rape and murder, escalating into tribal war and more rape. That the narrator intends for the reader to understand the participants in these actions as aware of such codes is clear from the excuses they make for themselves when they argue that no one has violated battle ethics by stealing the young women from Shiloh (21:23).[1] Is the argument here that the presence of a king will bring resolution to the whirlpool of misdeeds that have engulfed the people at the end?[2] That is at least one voice that may

1. See, for example, the regulations for the treatment of women in times of war in Deut 21:10–14.

2. Tammi Schneider (*Judges*, Berit Olam [Collegeville, MN: Liturgical

be heard. Is the idea that women are after all dispensable and that their dishonor does not count? Just something that happened in the old days, in an old tale with folkloristic motifs, and order has after all been restored?[3]

The most clearly articulated critical note in the last chapters is that such things happened in days when there was no central leadership, no *king* in Israel. But to which leadership or king does the narrator refer? Will a king lead the people in the right path of worship and the practice of justice? Will a king guarantee for them the possession of the land of the promise? Is it not in the end the relationship of the people to their God that will steer them in the right path and allow them to continue their existence as God's covenant people, with or without the land? Do the references to the monarchy, an establishment which is just around the corner, also contain hints that none of the kings in the end will be of help when it comes to maintaining life in the land?[4] The most important guarantee for their existence, for the community to be able to do the "right thing," will not be life with a king, be that king ever so righteous (and most of the kings will not prove to be such), nor will it be life in a land they will always hold in a tenuous grasp. Rather, it will be an ear attuned

---

Press, 2000], 139): "The narrative in Judges recounts a period in Israel to which the only response could be monarchy." Yairah Amit (*The Book of Judges: The Art of Editing*, trans. Jonathan Chipman [Leiden: Brill, 1999], 342) argues for a specific anti-Benjaminite, anti-Saul, pro-Davidic agenda: "Placing this section before the book of Samuel serves the rhetorical tendency of creating a prejudice and willingness to criticize Saul and his house." See also Marc Zvi Brettler, *The Book of Judges* (London: Routledge, 2002), 113.

3. See Susan Niditch, *Judges*, OTL (Louisville: Westminster John Knox, 2008), 211; "Judges, Kingship, and Political Ethics: A Challenge to the Conventional Wisdom," in *Thus Says the Lord: Essays on the Former and Latter Prophets in Honor of Robert R. Wilson*, ed. John J. Ahn and Stephen L. Cook (London: T&T Clark, 2009), 68.

4. Mark E. Biddle, *Reading Judges: A Literary and Theological Commentary* (Macon, GA: Smyth and Helwys, 2012), 205: "Both the institutional office of king and the charismatic function of judge failed to address Israel's tendencies toward apostasy, incivility, and immorality. . . . Israel's shortcomings did not result from its form of leadership but from the constitution of the human heart."

to a God who promises them presence through words of instruction. The tales of the Judges, in counterpoint to Joshua, do not contain references to *torah* or "the Torah of Moses." When leadership was absent in the land, there was no recognition of the need for *torah*. There will need to be voices raised that speak with authority in addressing the people at the point of their covenant obligations; such a life may safeguard for them their continuation as a people in their land with a distinct heritage. From which direction these voices will come is an open question at the end of Judges.

Though we are latecomers and outsiders to the story, although we live in a world far removed in time and place from that of early Israel, some of the issues facing us may not be so different from those encountered by this ancient culture. Solving land disputes and power differences by violent measures is certainly not alien to our world. Establishing identity by warding off people who are from different places and ethnic origins than the ruling majority is all too familiar. Divided communities, citizens fostering deep hostilities toward one another, leadership that has gone rogue, countless violations of ethical principles, violations of the personhood of women and their victimization, including rape—with all of it we are sadly acquainted.[5] Can we say that central leadership in our society today helps our communities in the direction of a moral code that considers such actions sacrilege—*navelah*?

"The impulses that guide story-telling and the uses to which stories are put are infinitely complex—some of them not at all benign," observes Dorothy Allison. "Story," she says, "is more about mystery and people than about explanations and justifications" and "more

5. The latest statistics on violent deaths for women indicate that 55 percent of these "were intimate partner violence-related" for a ten-year period from 2003 to 2014 (Olga Khazan, "Nearly Half of All Murdered Women Are Killed by Romantic Partners," *The Atlantic*, July 2017, https://www.theatlantic.com/health/archive/2017/07/homicides-women/534306/). These are reported cases only. The Rape, Abuse and Incest National Network (RAINN), which gets its statistics from the annual National Crime Victimization Survey (NCVS) out of the Justice Department, cites more than 300,000 victims of rape and sexual assault each year in the US (http://www.rainn.org/statistics/scope-problem).

can be learned from a good story than from a structured essay or a monumental piece of theory."[6] The editors of the Historical Books in the Bible collected old stories and edited them to write about their past in order to teach and challenge the postexilic community of Judah. These same stories can teach and challenge today, for they face us with important questions about what it means to lack an ethical code of guidance for communal and individual life. The stories are indeed complex, and the many voices to be heard in them should probably not be considered to speak in harmony to one issue only.

Apart from the important questions and ethical conundrums with which the stories confront also contemporary readers/listeners, they make a call on our engagement with plots and characters. Which one of us does not love the outsider hero who, perhaps in the ordinary course of events mocked for having a physical difference, uses it to his advantage to get the better of a powerful and oppressive enemy? Who does not sympathize with the woman who overcomes the rapist—even by extreme means? Who is not sympathetic to the divided soul who has such a hard time finding the path forward in a confusing world where the cacophony of voices overwhelms the clarion call of God's messengers? Which one of us does not weep with the daughter sacrificed for the father's stubborn ambition, for the woman abandoned to abuse with no safe shelter, for the girls forced into unwanted marriages? In the meantime, the story of ancient Israel's existence in the land is not yet at an end, although those who read the tale both in ancient days and at present are aware that there will come an end. We are, after all, only at the end of the beginning. There is more to tell, for there are yet adventures in the future, starting with the early days of Israel's experience with kingship.

6. Dorothy Allison, "Mean Stories and Stubborn Girls" and "What It Means to Be Free," in *The Tanner Lectures on Human Values* (Stanford: Stanford University, 2001), 313, 319–320.

Appendix: Hebrew Words in This Volume

Throughout this book, Hebrew words are transliterated in italics. When reading these words, observe the following:

a is always as in father, not as in dad.

e generally as in met, sometimes a light sound as in about, rendered by '.

i generally as in fleet, sometimes as i in kiss.

o is always as in bone, not as in got.

u is always as in ruler, not as in run.

ey as in pray.

g is always hard as in gold.

Hebrew has no syllables that contain two vowels. If an *a* word is spelled with two consecutive vowels, it is pronounced with two syllables: Baal = bah-al.

Each word below is followed by a phonetic pronunciation to provide further help articulating the Hebrew words. Stressed syllables are underlined. They occur generally at the end of the word, but not always. Pronunciation of */ch/* or */kh/* is always as in Bach; Hebrew has no */ch/* as in cheese.

Abbreviations

adj. = adjective

adv. = adverb

conj. = conjunction

interj. = interjection

n. = noun

pr. = pronoun

v. = verb

adamah (ah-dah-mah) n.—ground, 91
Adonai (ah-doh-nai) n.—name of God, throughout
aher/aheret (ah-cher/ah-cheh-ret) adj.—other, 263
ahuzzah (ah-chu-zah) n.—holding/possession, 144
ahuzzot (ah-chu-zoht) pl. n.—holdings, 164
anah (ah-nah) v.—abuse, rape, 282
anahnu (ah-nach-nu) pr.—we, 7
aqarah (ah-kah-rah) adj.—barren, 271
asar (ah-sar) v.—bind, 268
atad (ah-tad) n.—thornbush; bramble, 247
avadim (a-vah-deem) n.—servants/slaves, 8
avar (ah-var) v.—cross, 259, 259n99

Baal (bah-al) name—Baal, 165, 191, 201–2, 232–35, 237, 237n62, 245
baal (bah-al) n.—master, 245
baalim (bah-ah-leem) n.—masters, 245, 249
beney (b'-nay) n.—sons, children, descendants, people
  beney belia'al (b'-nay b'-li-ah-al) n.—scoundrels, worthless men, 302
  beney Yisrael (b'-nay Yis-rah-ayl) n.—Israelites, lit. children of Israel, 18
  beney Yosef (b'-nay yoh-sayf) n.—Josephites, those of Joseph, lit. children of Joseph, 143
bo (boh) v.—come, 60n9
boteah (boh-tay-ach) v.—trusting, 295

dibberah (dib-b'-rah) v.—she spoke, 220n25

efes ki (e-fes ki) conj.—only, 222n29
egel (eh-gel) n.—calf
  egel massekhah (eh-gel mah-say-khah) n. + adj.—molten calf, 290n9
  egel zahav (eh-gel zah-hav) n. + adj.—golden calf, 290n9
ekhah (ay-khah) interj.—How! Alas! 102
emah (ay-mah) n.—terror, 66n14
emet (eh-met) n.—truth, 67n16
eshet (ay-shet) n.—woman of, 226n44
ezrah (ez-rach) n.—native, 112

gallivoti (gal-li-vo-ti) v.—I have rolled away, 86
gazal (gah-zal) v.—tear off, pull off, rob, 312
ger (gayr) n.—stranger, 112, 130

hakohanim (hah-koh-ha-neem) n.—the priests, 75n29
haleviyyim (ha-l'-vee-yeem) n.—the Levites, 75n29
hamor (cha-mohr) n.—ass, heap, 278n132
harag (hah-rag) v.—slay, murder, 244

pesel (peh-sel) n.—carved image, 290
pesilim (p'-see-leem) n.—images, 212–14
patah (pah-tach) v.—be open to deception, 282n140
pilegesh (pee-leh-gesh) n.—concubine, 242n73, 263, 297

qatsar (kah-tsar) v.—vex, 254n92
qedeshah (k'-day-shah) n.—prostitute, 62

ra'ah (rah-ah) adj.—evil, wrong, 309
raham rahamatayim (rah-cham rah-chah-mah-ta-yeem) n.—a womb, two wombs, i.e. one or two women as spoils of war, 226
rahav (rah-chav) adj.—wide, broad, 61
reqam (ray-kahm) adj.—empty, unprincipled, 257n97
riv (reev) v.—dispute, contend/fight, 235
rosh (rohsh) n.—head, 218n20
ruah (roo-ach) n.—spirit, 254n92, 260, 265

shadad (shah-dad) v.—devastate, 225n42
shakhan (shah-khan) v.—dwell, 147
shalom (shah-lohm) n.—peace, wholeness, 223n36
shama (shah-mah) v.—listen, 172n10
shaqat (shah-kat) v.—have peace/quiet, 295
shoqet (shoh-kayt) v.—being at rest, 295
shemesh (sheh-mesh) n.—sun, 269n119
shevet (sheh-vet) n.—tribe, 306n35
shofet/shofetim (shoh-fayt/shoh-f'-teem) n.—judge/judges, 180
shuv (shoov) v.—turn around, return, 213n10

taqa' (tah-kah) v.—strike, blow (weapon or instrument), 228
terafim (t'-rah-feem) n.—household gods, 290
torah (toh-rah) n.—Teaching, 155–59, 164, 170–71, 204, 242, 263, 290, 300
tov (tohv) adj.—good, beautiful, 13

wayyiggash (va-yig-gash) v.—he presented, 234n58

yalad (yah-lad) v.—give birth, 271
yarash (yah-rash) v.—take possession, 58–59
yiftach (yif-takh) v.—he will open; Jefta, 256, 257, 267

zanah (zah-nah) v.—play the harlot, 61n10, 297n23
zonah (zoh-nah) n.—whore, harlot, 61, 257, 263, 264, 280

Bibliography

Books

Ackerman, Susan. *Warrior, Dancer, Seductress, Queen: Women in Judges and Biblical Israel.* New York: Doubleday, 1998.

Aharoni, Yohanan. *The Land of the Bible: A Historical Geography.* Translated by A. F. Rainey. Philadelphia: Westminster, 1979.

Ahn, John J., and Stephen L. Cook, eds. *Thus Says the Lord: Essays on the Former and Latter Prophets in Honor of Robert R. Wilson.* New York; London: T&T Clark, 2009.

Albertz, Rainer. *A History of Israelite Religion in the Old Testament Period.* Vol. 1, *From the Beginnings to the End of the Monarchy.* Translated by John Bowden. Louisville: Westmister John Knox, 1994. Translation of *Religionsgeschichte Israels in alttestamentlicher Zeit.* Göttingen: Vandenhoeck & Ruprecht, 1992.

Alter, Robert. *Ancient Israel: The Former Prophets: Joshua, Judges, Samuel, and Kings.* New York: W. W. Norton, 2013.

———. *The Art of Biblical Narrative.* New York: Basic Books, 1981.

———. *The Art of Biblical Poetry.* New York: Basic Books, 1985.

——— and Frank Kermode, eds. *The Literary Guide to the Bible.* Cambridge, MA: Harvard University Press, 1987.

Amit, Yairah. *The Book of Judges: The Art of Editing.* Translated by Jonathan Chipman. BibInt 38. Leiden: Brill, 1999.

———. *Hidden Polemics in Biblical Narrative.* BibInt 25. Leiden: Brill, 2000.

———. *History and Ideology: An Introduction to Historiography in the Hebrew Bible.* Sheffield: Sheffield Academic Press, 1999.

———. *Reading Biblical Narratives: Literary Criticism and the Hebrew Bible.* Translated by Yael Lotan. Minneapolis: Fortress, 2001.

Andersson, Greger. *The Book and Its Narratives: A Critical Examination of Some Synchronic Studies of the Book of Judges.* Orebro Studies in Literary History and Criticism 1. Orebro: Universitetsbiblioteket, 2001.

Assis, Elie. *Self-Interest or Communal Interest: An Ideology of Leadership in the Gideon, Abimelech, and Jephthah Narratives (Judg 6–12).* Translated by Stephanie Nakache. VTSup 106. Leiden: Brill, 2005.

Bach, Alice, ed. *Women in the Hebrew Bible.* London: Routledge, 1999.

Bar-Efrat, Shimon. *Narrative Art in the Bible.* Sheffield: Almond, 1989.

Bellis, Alice Ogden. *Helpmates, Harlots and Heroes: Women's Stories in the Hebrew Bible.* Rev. ed. Westminster John Knox, 2007.

Berquist, Jon, and Claudia V. Camp, eds. *Construction of Space II: The Biblical City and Other Imagined Spaces.* New York; London: T&T Clark, 2008.

Bible and Culture Collective. *The Postmodern Bible.* New Haven; London: Yale University Press, 1995.

Biddle, Mark E. *Reading Judges: A Literary and Theological Commentary.* Macon, GA: Smyth and Helwys, 2012.

Boer, P. A. H. de. *Gedenken und Gedächtnis in der Welt des Alten Testaments.* Franz-Delitzsch Vorlesungen. Stuttgart: Kohlhammer, 1960.

Boling, Robert G. *Judges.* AB 6A. New York: Doubleday, 1975.

Borowski, Obed. *Daily Life in Biblical Times.* Atlanta: Society of Biblical Literature, 2003.

Botterweck, G. Johannes, and Helmer Ringgren, eds. *Theological Dictionary of the Old Testament.* 16 vols. Grand Rapids: Eerdmans, 2001–2018.

Brenner, Athalya, ed. *Judges: A Feminist Companion to the Bible.* Sheffield: Sheffield Academic Press, 1999.

——— and Gale A. Yee, eds. *Joshua and Judges.* Minneapolis: Fortress, 2013.

Brettler, Marc Zvi. *The Book of Judges.* London: Routledge, 2002.

Bronner, Leila Leah. *From Eve to Esther: Rabbinic Reconstructions of Biblical Women.* Louisville: Westminster John Knox, 1994.

Brueggemann, Walter. *The Land: Place as Gift, Promise, and Challenge in Biblical Faith.* Minneapolis: Fortress, 2002.

Buber, Martin, and Franz Rosenzweig. *Bücher der Geschichte: Verdeutscht von Martin Buber gemeinsam mit Franz Rosenzweig.* Cologne: Jakob Hegner, 1965.

———. *Scripture and Translation.* Translated by Lawrence Rosenwald with Everett Fox. Bloomington: Indiana University Press, 1994.

Buck, Christopher. *God and Apple Pie: Religious Myths and Visions of America.* Kingston, NY: Educator's International, 2015.

Carr, E. H. *What Is History?* 40th ann. ed. Balsingstoke, UK: Palgrave, 2001.

Clines, David A. *Interested Parties: The Ideology of Writers and Readers of the Hebrew Bible.* Sheffield: Sheffield Phoenix, 2009.

Collins, John, ed. *Worship, Women and War: Essays in Honor of Susan Niditch.* Providence: Brown University Press, 2015.

Conrad, Cherry, ed. *God's New Israel: Religious Interpretations of American*

Destiny. Revised edition. Chapel Hill, NC: University of North Carolina Press, 1998.

Coogan, Michael, ed. *The Oxford History of the Biblical World.* New York: Oxford University Press, 1998.

Cowles, C. S., Eugene H. Merril, Daniel L. Gard, and Tremper Longman III. *Show Them No Mercy: Four Views on God and Canaanite Genocide.* Grand Rapids: Zondervan, 2003.

Craigie, Peter C. *The Problem of War in the Old Testament.* Grand Rapids: Eerdmans, 1978.

Day, Peggy L,. ed. *Gender and Difference in Ancient Israel.* Minneapolis: Fortress, 1989.

Deist, Ferdinand E. *The Material Culture of the Bible: An Introduction.* Sheffield: Sheffield Academic Press, 2000.

Dijk-Hemmes, Fokkelien van. *The Double Voice of Her Desire: Texts by Fokkelien van Dijk-Hemmes.* Edited by J. Bekkenkamp and F. Dröes. Translated by David Orton. Leiden: Deo Publishing, 2004.

Exum, J. Cheryl. *Fragmented Women.* Sheffield: Almond, 1993.

———. *Tragedy and Biblical Narrative: Arrows of the Almighty*. Cambridge: Cambridge University Press, 1992.

Faraone, Christopher A., and Laura K. McClure, eds. *Prostitutes and Courtesans in the Ancient World.* Madison, WI: University of Wisconsin Press, 2006.

Fokkelman, Jan, and Wim Weren, eds. *De Bijbel Literair: Opbouw en Gedachtegang van de Bijbelse Geschriften en hun Onderlinge Relaties.* Zoetermeer; Meinema; Kapellen: Pelckmans, 2003.

Foner, Philip S., and Robert James Branham, eds. *Lift Every Voice: African-American Oratory, 1787–1900.* Tuscaloosa, AL: University of Alabama Press, 1998.

Fox, Everett. *The Early Prophets.* New York: Schocken, 2014.

———. *The Five Books of Moses: A New Translation with Introductions, Commentary, and Notes.* New York: Schocken, 1995.

Frymer-Kensky, Tikva. *In the Wake of the Goddesses: Women, Culture, and the Biblical Transformation of Pagan Myth.* New York, Toronto: Macmillan, 1992.

———. *Reading the Women of the Bible.* New York: Schocken, 2002.

Gafney, Wilda C. *Daughters of Miriam: Women Prophets in Ancient Israel.* Minneapolis: Fortress, 2008.

———. *Womanist Midrash: A Reintroduction to the Women of the Torah and the Throne.* Louisville: Westminster John Knox, 2017.

Gillmayr-Bucher, Susanne. *Erzählte Welten im Richterbuch: Narratologische Aspekte eines Polyfonen Diskurses.* Leiden, Boston: Brill, 2013.

Goldingay, John. *Joshua, Judges and Ruth for Everyone*. Louisville: Westminster John Knox, 2011.

Good, Edwin M. *Irony in the Old Testament.* Philadelphia: Westminster, 1965. Repr., Sheffield: Almond, 1981.

Gravett, Sandra L., Karla Bohmbach, F. V. Greifenhagen, and Donald C. Polaski. *An Introduction to the Hebrew Bible: A Thematic Approach*. Louisville: Westminster John Knox, 2008.

Green, Thomas A., ed. *Folklore: An Encyclopedia of Beliefs, Customs, Tales, Music, and Art*, vol. 1. Santa Barbara: ABC-CLIO, 1998.

Gunn, David M. *Judges.* Oxford: Blackwell, 2005.

——— and Danna Nolan Fewell. *Narrative in the Hebrew Bible.* Oxford; New York: Oxford University Press, 1993.

Habel, Norman C. *The Land Is Mine: Six Biblical Land Ideologies.* Minneapolis: Augsburg, 1995.

Havea, Jione, David J. Neville, and Elaine M. Wainwright, eds. *Bible, Border, Belonging(s).* Atlanta: Society of Biblical Literature, 2004.

Hawk, L. Daniel. *Joshua*. Berit Olam. Collegeville, MN: The Liturgical Press, 2000.

Hornsby, Teresa J., and Ken Stone, eds. *Bible Trouble: Queer Reading at the Boundaries of Biblical Scholarship.* Atlanta: Society of Biblical Literature, 2011.

Hughes, Richard T. *Myths America Lives By.* Chicago: University of Illinois Press, 2003.

Isserlin, B. S. J. *The Israelites.* Minneapolis: Fortress, 2001.

Kim, Wonil, ed. *Reading the Hebrew Bible for a New Millennium: Form, Concept, and Theological Perspective.* Harrisburg: Trinity, 2000.

Klein, Lillian. *From Deborah to Esther: Sexual Politics in the Hebrew Bible.* Minneapolis: Fortress, 2000.

———. *The Triumph of Irony in the Book of Judges.* JSOTSup 68. Sheffield: Sheffield Academic Press, 1988.

Knoppers, Gary N., and J. Gordon McConville, eds. *Reconsidering Israel and Judah: Recent Studies on the Deuteronomistic History.* Winona Lake, IN: Eisenbrauns, 2000.

Kugel, James L. *The God of Old: Inside the Lost World of the Bible.* New York: The Free Press, 2003.

———. *How to Read the Bible: A Guide to Scripture, Then and Now.* New York; London; Toronto; Sydney: The Free Press, 2007.

———. *The Idea of Biblical Poetry: Parallelism and Its History.* New Haven: Yale University Press, 1981.

Lapsley, Jacqueline E. *Whispering the Word: Hearing Women's Stories in the Old Testament.* Louisville: Westminster John Knox, 2005.

Lebhar Hall, Sarah. *Conquering Character: The Characterization of Joshua in Joshua 1–11.* New York; London: T&T Clark, 2010.

Leuchter, Mark, and Jeremy M. Hutton, eds. *Levites and Priests in Biblical History and Tradition.* Atlanta: Scoiety of Biblical Literature, 2011.

Mann, Thomas W. *The Book of the Former Prophets.* Eugene, OR: Wipf and Stock, 2011.

March, W. Eugene. *Israel and the Politics of Land.* Louisville: Westminster John Knox, 1994.

McConville, J. Gordon, and Stephen N. Williams. *Joshua.* Grand Rapids: Eerdmans, 2010.

McKenzie, Stephen L., and Stephen R. Haynes, eds. *To Each Its Own Meaning.* Louisville: Westminster John Knox, 1999.

Meyers, Carol. *Discovering Eve: Ancient Israelite Women in Context.* New York; Oxford: Oxford University Press, 1988.

———. *Rediscovering Eve: Ancient Israelite Women in Context.* Oxford: Oxford University Press, 2011.

Miller, J. Maxwell, and John H. Hayes. *A History of Israel and Judah.* 2nd ed. Louisville: Westminster John Knox, 2006.

Moore, Megan Bishop, and Brad E. Kelle. *Biblical History and Israel's Past: The Changing Study of the Bible and History.* Grand Rapids: Eerdmans, 2011.

Nelson, Richard D. *Joshua.* OTL. Louisville: Westminster John Knox, 1997.

Newsom, Carol A., and Sharon H. Ringe, eds. *Women's Bible Commentary.* Expanded edition. Louisville: Westminster John Knox, 1992.

Niditch, Susan. *Judges.* Louisville: Westminster John Knox, 2008.

———, ed. *Text and Tradition: The Hebrew Bible and Folklore.* Atlanta: Scholars Press, 1990.

———. *War in the Hebrew Bible: A Study in the Ethics of Violence.* Oxford: Oxford University Press, 1993.

Polzin, Robert. *Moses and the Deuteronomist: A Literary Study of the Deuteronomic History.* Volume 1. New York: Seabury, 1980.

Rollston, Christopher. *Writing and Literacy in the World of Ancient Israel: Epigraphic Evidence from the Iron Age.* Atlanta: Society of Biblical Literature, 2010.

Rosenblatt, Jason P., and Joseph C. Sitterson Jr., eds. *Not in Heaven: Coherence and Complexity in Biblical Narrative.* Bloomington, IN; Indianapolis: Indiana University Press, 1991.

Rowlett, Lori L. *Joshua and the Rhetoric of Violence: A New Historicist Analysis.* Sheffield: Sheffield Academic Press, 1996.

Schipper, Jeremy. *Parables and Conflict in the Hebrew Bible.* Cambridge: Cambridge University Press, 2009.

Schlimm, Matthew Richard. *This Strange and Sacred Scripture: Wrestling with the Old Testament and Its Oddities.* Louisville: Westminster John Knox, 2015.

Schneider, Tammi J. *Judges*. Berit Olam. Collegeville, MN: The Liturgical Press, 2000.

Schniedewind, William M. *A Social History of Hebrew: Its Origins Through the Rabbinic Period.* New Haven: Yale University Press, 2013.

Scholz, Susanne. *Sacred Witness: Rape in the Hebrew Bible.* Minneapolis: Fortress, 2010.

Schottroff, Luise, and Marie-Theres Wacher, eds. *Feminist Biblical Interpretation: A Compendium of Critical Commentary on the Books of the Bible and Related Literature.* Translated by Lisa E. Dahill. Grand Rapids: Eerdmans, 2012. Translation of *Kompendium Feministische Bibelauslegung.* Gütersloh: Gütersloher Verlagungshaus, 1999.

Schroeder, Joy A. *Deborah's Daughters: Gender Politics and Biblical Interpretation.* Oxford: Oxford University Press, 2014.

Schulz, Kathryn. *Being Wrong: Adventures in the Margin of Error.* New York: Harper Collins, 2010.

Schwartz, Regina M. *The Curse of Cain: The Violent Legacy of Monotheism.* Chicago: University of Chicago Press, 1997.

Soggin, J. A. *Joshua: A Commentary.* Translated by R. A. Wilson. 2nd ed. London: SCM, 1972.

Stone, Ken, ed. *Queer Commentary and the Hebrew Bible.* Sheffield: Sheffield Academic, 2001.

Terrien, Samuel. *The Elusive Presence: Toward a New Biblical Theology.* New York: Harper & Row, 1978.

Trible, Phyllis. *God and the Rhetoric of Sexuality.* Philadelphia: Fortress, 1978.

———. *Texts of Terror: Literary-Feminist Readings of Biblical Narratives.* Philadelphia: Fortress, 1984.

Volkmar, Fritz. *The Emergence of Israel in the Twelfth and Eleventh Centuries B.C.E.* Atlanta: Society of Biblical Literature, 2011.

Walsh, Jerome T. *The Book of Judges.* Grand Rapids: Eerdmans, 2012.

Webb, Barry. *The Book of Judges: An Integrated Reading.* Sheffield: Sheffield Academic, 1987.

Weems, Renita J. *Just A Sister Away: Understanding the Timeless Connection between Women of Today and Women in the Bible.* New York: Warner, 2005.

Weinfeld, M. *The Promise of the Land. The Inheritance of the Land of Canaan by the Israelites.* Berkeley, CA: University of California Press, 1993.

Wijk-Bos, Johanna W. H. van. *Making Wise the Simple: The Torah in Christian Faith and Practice.* Grand Rapids: Eerdmans, 2005.

———. *Reformed and Feminist: A Challenge to the Church.* Westminster John Knox, 1991.

Williams, Jenni. *God Remembered Rachel: Women's Stories in the Old Testament and Why They Matter.* London: SPCK, 2014.

Wong, Gregory T. K. *Compositional Strategy of the Book of Judges: An Inductive, Rhetorical Study.* VTSup 8. Leiden: Brill, 2006.

Yee, Gale A. ed. *Judges and Method: New Approaches in Biblical Studies.* Minneapolis: Fortress, 2007.

Yehoshua, A. B. *Kijken in de Spiegel: Over verzoening, identiteit en de toekomst van Israel.* Translated by Floor Borsboom. Amsterdam: Wereldbibliotheek, 2006. Translation of *Israel: un examen moral.* Paris: Calman-Levy, 2004.

Younger, K. Lawson. *Ancient Conquest Accounts: A Study in Ancient Near Eastern and Biblical History Writing.* JSOTSup 98. Sheffield: Sheffield Academic, 1998.

Articles and Chapters

Ackerman, Susan. "Who Is Sacrificing at Shiloh? The Priesthoods of Ancient Israel's Regional Sanctuaries." Pages 25–43 in *Levites and Priests in Biblical History and Tradition.* Edited by Mark Leuchter and Jeremy M. Hutton. Atlanta: Society of Biblical Literature, 2011.

Albertz, Rainer. "Monotheism and Violence: How to Handle a Dangerous Biblical Tradition." Pages 373–88 in *The Land of Israel in Bible, History, and Theology: Studies in Honour of Ed Noort.* Edited by Jacques van Ruiten and J. Cornelis de Vos. VTSup 124. Leiden: Brill, 2009.

Allison, Dorothy. "Mean Stories and Stubborn Girls" and "What It Means to Be Free." Pages 310–20 in *The Tanner Lectures on Human Values.* Stanford: Stanford University Press, 2001.

Alter, Robert. "Samson Without Folklore." Pages 47–56 in *The Land of Israel in Bible, History, and Theology: Studies in Honour of Ed Noort.* Edited by Jacques van Ruiten and J. Cornelis de Vos. VTSup 124. Leiden: Brill, 2009.

Amit, Yairah. "The Book of Judges: Dating and Meaning." Pages 297–322 in *Homeland and Exile: Biblical and Ancient Near Eastern Studies in Honour of Bustenay Oded.* Edited by Gershon Gall, Mark Geller, and Alan Millard. VTSup 130. Leiden: Brill, 2009.

———. "The Story of Ehud (Judges 3: 12–30): The Form and the Message." Pages 97–123 in *Signs and Wonders. Biblical Texts in Literary Focus.* Edited by J. Cheryl Exum. SemeiaSt. Atlanta: Society for Biblical Literature, 1989.

Auld, A. Graeme. "The Levitical Cities: Texts and History." *ZAW* 91 (1979): 194–206.

Baden, Joel S. "The Violent Origins of the Levites: Text and Tradition." Pages 102–33 in *Levites and Priests in Biblical History and Tradition*. Edited by Mark Leuchter and Jeremy M. Hutton. Atlanta: Society of Biblical Literature, 2011.

Bird, Phyllis A. "The Harlot as Heroine: Narrative Art and Social Presupposition in Three Old Testament Texts." Pages 99–119 in *Women in the Hebrew Bible*. Edited by Alice Bach. New York; London: Routledge, 1999.

———. "Prostitution in the Social World and Religious Rhetoric of Ancient Israel." Pages 40–58 in *Prostitutes and Courtesans in the Ancient World*. Edited by Christopher A. Faraone and Laura K. McClure. Madison, WI: University of Wisconsin Press, 2006.

Bonfiglio, Ryan. "Choosing Sides in Judges 4–5: Rethinking Representations of Jael." Pages 161–73 in *Joshua and Judges*. Edited by Athalya Brenner and Gale A. Yee. Minneapolis: Fortress, 2013.

Bowman, Richard G. "Narrative Criticism: Human Purpose in Conflict with Divine Presence." Pages 19–45 in *Judges and Method: New Approaches in Biblical Studies*. Edited by Gale A. Yee. Minneapolis: Fortress, 2007.

Brenner, Athalya. "Women Frame the Book of Judges—How and Why?" Pages 125–38 in *Joshua and Judges*. Edited by Athalya Brenner and Gale A. Yee. Minneapolis: Fortress, 2013.

Brison, Ora. "Jael, *'eshet heber* the Kenite: A Diviner?" Pages 139–60 in *Joshua and Judges*. Edited by Athalya Brenner and Gale A. Yee. Minneapolis: Fortress, 2013.

Brueggemann, Walter. "The God of Joshua: An Ambivalent Field of Negotiation." Pages 13-25 in *Joshua and Judges*. Edited by Athalya Brenner and Gale A. Yee. Minneapolis: Fortress, 2013.

Buber, Martin. "The Man of Today and the Jewish Bible." Pages 1–21 in *On the Bible: Eighteen Studies by Martin Buber*. Edited by Nahum N. Glatzer. Syracuse: Syracuse University Press, 1982.

Camp, Claudia V., and Carole F. Fontaine. "The Words of the Wise and Their Riddles." Pages 127–49 in *Text and Tradition: The Hebrew Bible and Folklore*. Edited by Susan Niditch. Atlanta: Scholars Press, 1990.

Coogan, Michael D. "Archeology and Biblical Studies: The Book of Joshua." Pages 19–32 in *The Hebrew Bible and Its Interpreters*. Edited by William H. Propp, Baruch Halpern, and David Noel Freedman. Winona Lake, IN: Eisenbrauns, 1990.

Coote, Robert. "The Book of Joshua." Pages 553–719 in *The New Interpreters Bible*. Volume 2. Nashville: Abingdon, 1998.

Davis, Ellen F. "Losing a Friend: The Loss of the Old Testament to the Church." Pages 83–94 in *Jews, Christians, and the Theology of the Hebrew Scrip-*

tures. Edited by Alice Ogden Bellis and Joel Kaminsky. Atlanta: Scholars Press, 2000.

Douglass, Frederick. "Speech on American Anti-Slavery Society." Pages 246–68 in *Lift Every Voice: African-American Oratory, 1787–1900.* Edited by Philip S. Foner and Robert James Branham. Tuscaloosa, AL: University of Alabama Press, 1998.

Dijk-Hemmes, Fokkelien van. "Blessed Among Women: A Mother in Israel and a Virgin in the Church." Pages 89–109 in *The Double Voice of Her Desire: Texts by Fokkelien van Dijk-Hemmes.* Edited by J. Bekkenkamp and F. Dröes. Translation by David E. Orton. Leiden: Deo, 2004.

Exum, J. Cheryl. "The Centre Cannot Hold: Thematic and Textual Instabilities in Judges." Pages 578–600 in *Reconsidering Israel and Judah: Recent Studies on the Deuteronomistic History.* Edited by Gary N. Knoppers and J. Gordon McConville. Winona Lake, IN: Eisenbrauns, 2000.

———. "Feminist Criticism: Whose Interests Are Being Served?" Pages 65–89 in *Judges and Method: New Approaches in Biblical Studies.* Edited by Gale A. Yee. 2nd ed. Minneapolis: Fortress, 2007.

Faigenbaum-Golovin, Shira, et al. "Algorithm Handwriting Analysis of Judah's Military Correspondence Sheds Light on Composition of Biblical Texts." *Proceedings of the National Academy of Sciences of the United States of America* 113 (2016): 4664–69.

Fewell, Danna Nolan. "Feminist Criticism." Pages 268–82 in *To Each Its Own Meaning.* Edited by Steven L. McKenzie and Stephen R. Haynes. Louisville: Westminster John Knox, 1999.

———. "Judges." Pages 73–83 in *Women's Bible Commentary.* Edited by Carol A. Newsom and Sharon H. Ringe. Expanded edition. Louisville: Westminster John Knox.

Fields, Weston W. "The Motif 'Night as Danger' Associated with Three Biblical Destruction Narratives." Pages 17–32 in *Sha'arei Talmon: Studies in the Bible, Qumran, and the Ancient Near East Presented to Shemaryahu Talmon.* Edited by Michael Fishbane and Emmanuel Tov. Winona Lake, IN: Eisenbrauns, 1992.

Fleming, Robyn C. "Jael's Gender: A Story of Appropriation." Essay published online, November 2005. http://revena.livejournal.com/140803.html.

Fokkelman, J. P. "Algemene Inleiding: Oog in Oog Met De Tekst Zelf." Pages 7–32 in *De Bijbel Literair: Opbouw en Gedachtegang van de Bijbelse Geschriften en hun Onderlinge Relaties.* Edited by J. P. Fokkelman and W. Weren. Zoetermeer; Meinema; Kapellen: Felckmans, 2003.

———. "Structural Remarks on Judges 9 and 19." Pages 33–46 in *Sha'arei Talmon: Studies in the Bible, Qumran, and the Ancient Near East Presented to Shemaryahu Talmon.* Edited by Michael Fishbane and Emmanuel Tov. Winona Lake, IN: Eisenbrauns, 1992.

Frymer-Kensky, Tikva: "Reading Rahab." Pages 57–67 in *Tehillah le-Moshe: Biblical and Judaic Studies in Honor of Moshe Greenberg*. Edited by Mordechai Cogan, Barry Eichler, and Jeffrey Tigay. Winona Lake, IN: Eisenbrauns, 1997.

Goldman, Talia. "Prostitution in Classical and Jewish Antiquity." Hashta UMD: Jewish Voices on a Secular Campus. https://sites.google.com/site/hastaumd/contents-1/prost.

Guest, Deryn. "From Gender Reversal to Genderfuck: Reading Jael Through a Lesbian Lens." Pages 9–44 in *Bible Trouble: Queer Reading at the Boundaries of Biblical Scholarship*. Edited by Teresa J. Hornsby and Ken Stone. Atlanta: Society of Biblical Literature, 2011.

Gunn, David M. "Joshua and Judges." Pages 102–121 in *The Literary Guide to the Bible*. Edited by Robert Alter and Frank Kermode. Cambridge: Harvard University Press, 1987.

———. "Narrative Criticism." Pages 201–229 in *To Each Its Own Meaning*. Edited by Steven L. McKenzie and Stephen R. Haynes. Louisville: Westminster John Knox, 1999.

Hackett, Jo Ann. " 'There was no king in Israel': The Era of the Judges." Pages 177–218 in *The Oxford History of the Biblical World*. Edited by Michael D. Coogan. New York: Oxford University Press, 1998.

Halpern, Baruch. "The State of Israelite History." Pages 540–65 in *Reconsidering Israel and Judah: Recent Studies on the Deuteronomistic History*. Edited by Gary N. Knoppers and J. Gordon McConville. Winona Lake, IN: Eisenbrauns, 2000.

Hawk, L. Daniel. "Indigenous Helpers and Invader Homelands." Pages 109–22 in *Joshua and Judges*. Edited by Athalya Brenner and Gale A. Yee. Minneapolis: Fortress, 2013.

Hutton, Jeremy M. "The Levitical Diaspora (11): Modern Perspectives on the Levitical Cities Lists (A Review of Opinions)." Pages 45–82 in *Levites and Priests in Biblical History and Tradition*. Edited by Mark Leuchter and Jeremy M. Hutton. Atlanta: Society of Biblical Literature, 2011.

Janzen, J. Gerald. "The Root *prʿ* in Judges V 2 and Deuteronomy XXXII 42." *VT* 39 (1989): 393–406.

Junger, Sebastian. "How PTSD Became a Problem Far Beyond the Battlefield." *Vanity Fair* (June 2015): https://www.vanityfair.com/news/2015/05/ptsd-war-home-sebastian-junger.

Kellermann, Natan P. F. "The Long-Term Psychological Effects and Treatment of Holocaust Trauma." *Journal of Loss and Trauma* 6 (2001): 197–218.

———. "Transmission of Holocaust Trauma: An Integrative Review." *Psychiatry* 64 (2001): 256–67.

Ketelaar, Saskia. "De Onvruchtbare Moeders in de Hebreeuwse Bijbel." Pages

7–19 in *Amsterdamse Cahiers Voor Exegese en Bijbelse Theologie* 12. Edited by Karel A. Deurloo et al. Kampen: Kok, 1993.

Klein, Lillian R. "Achsah: What Price This Prize?" Pages 18-26 in *Judges: A Feminist Companion to the Bible (Second Series).* Edited by Athalya Brenner. Sheffield: Sheffield Academic, 1999.

Lemos, Tracy M. "Were Israelite Women Chattel? Shedding Light on an Old Question." Pages 227–43 in *Worship, Women and War: Essays in Honor of Susan Niditch.* Edited by John J. Collins, T. M. Lemos, and Saul M. Olyan. BJS. Providence, RI: Brown University Press, 2015.

Midden, Piet van. "Jozua en Richteren." Pages 133–57 in *De Bijbel Literair: Opbouw en gedachtegang van de bijbelse geschriften en hun onderlinge relaties.* Edited by Jan Fokkelman and Wim Weren. Zoetermeer; Meinema; Kapellen: Pekelmans, 2003.

Morgenstern, Mira. "Samson and the Politics of Riddling." *Hebraic Political Studies* 1 (Spring 2006): 253–85.

Müllner, Ilse. "Lethal Differences: Sexual Violence as Violence Against Others in Judges 19." Pages 126–42 in *Judges: A Feminist Companion to the Bible (Second Series).* Edited by Athalya Brenner. Sheffield: Sheffield Academic Press, 1999.

Na'aman, Nadav. "David's Sojourn in Keilah in Light of the Amarna Letters." *VT* 60 (2010): 87–97.

Niditch, Susan. "Judges, Kingship, and Political Ethics: A Challenge to the Conventional Wisdom." Pages 59–70 in *Thus Says the Lord: Essays on the Former and Latter Prophets in Honor of Robert R. Wilson.* Edited by John J. Ahn and Stephen L. Cook. London: T&T Clark, 2009.

O'Connor, Michael Patrick. "The Biblical Notion of the City." Pages 18–39 in *Construction of Space II: The Biblical City and Other Imagined Spaces.* Edited by Jon Berquist and Claudia V. Camp. London: T&T Clark, 2008.

Rowlett, Lori. "Violent Femmes and S/M: Queering Samson and Delilah." Pages 106–15 in *Queer Commentary and the Hebrew Bible.* Edited by Ken Stone. Sheffield: Sheffield Academic, 2001.

Runions, Erin. "From Disgust to Humor." Pages 45–74 in *Bible Trouble: Queer Reading at the Boundaries of Biblical Scholarship.* Edited by Teresa J. Hornsby and Ken Stone. Atlanta: Society of Biblical Literature, 2011.

Shalom-Guy, Hava. "Three-Way Intertextuality: Some Reflections of Abimelech's Death at Thebez in Biblical Narrative." *JSOT* 34 (2010): 419–32.

Slotkin, Edgar. "Response to Professors Fontaine and Camp." Pages 154–59 in *Text and Tradition: The Hebrew Bible and Folklore.* Edited by Susan Niditch. Atlanta: Scholars Press, 1990.

Smith, Carol. "Delilah: A Suitable Case For (Feminist) Treatment?" Pages 93–116 in *Judges: A Feminist Companion to the Bible (Second Series).* Edited by Athalya Brenner. Sheffield: Sheffield Academic Press, 1999.

Stanley, Janelle. "Judges 19: Text of Trauma." Pages 275–89 in *Joshua and Judges*. Edited by Athalya Brenner and Gale A. Yee. Minneapolis: Fortress, 2013.

Stanley, Sara. "What, to the Toiling Millions There, Is This Boasted Liberty?" Pages 246–68 in *Lift Every Voice: African-American Oratory, 1787–1900*. Edited by Philip S. Foner and Robert James Branham. Tuscaloosa, AL: University of Alabama Press, 1998.

Steinberg, Naomi. "Social Scientific Criticism: Judges 9 and Issues of Kinship." Pages 46–64 in *Judges and Method: New Approaches in Biblical Studies*. Edited by Gale A. Yee. Minneapolis: Fortress, 2007.

Trible, Phyllis. "Exegesis for Storytellers and Other Strangers." *JBL* 114 (1995): 3–19.

Turcan, Marie. "Être Femme selon Tertullien." *Vita Latina* 119 (1990): 15–21. http://www.tertullian.org/articles/turcan_etre_femme.htm.

Ulrich, Kerstin. "Joshua: Tradition and Justice: Women's Share in the Inheritance." Pages 100–11 in *Feminist Biblical Interpretation*. Edited by Luise Schottroff and Marie-Theres Wacker. Grand Rapids: Eerdmans, 2012.

Vaka'uta, Nasili. "Border Crossing/Body Whoring: Rereading Rahab of Jericho with Native Women." Pages 143–55 in *Bible, Borders, Belonging(s): Engaging Readers from Oceania*. Edited by Jione Havea, David J. Neville, and Elaine M. Wainwright. Atlanta: Society of Biblical Literature, 2004.

Vanderhooft, David. "Dwelling Beneath the Sacred Place: A Proposal for Reading 2 Samuel 7:10. *JBL* 118 (1999): 625–33.

Vanderkam, James C. "Davidic Complicity in the Deaths of Abner and Eshbaal: A Historical and Redactional Study." *JBL* 99 (1980): 521–39.

Victor, Royce M. "Delilah—A Forgotten Hero (Judges 16:4-21): A Cross-Cultural Reading." Pages 235–55 in *Joshua and Judges*. Edited by Athalya Brenner and Gale A. Yee. Minneapolis: Fortress, 2013.

[Wijk-]Bos, Johanna W. H. [van]. "Out of the Shadows: Genesis 38; Judges 4:17–22 and Ruth 3." Pages 37–67 in *Reasoning with the Foxes: Female Wit in a World of Male Power*. Edited by Johanna W. H. [van Wijk-]Bos and J. Cheryl Exum. Semeia 42. Atlanta: Society of Biblical Literature, 1988.

Wijk-Bos, Johanna W. H. van. "Writing on the Water: The Ineffable Name of God." Pages 45–59 in *Jews, Christians, and the Theology of the Hebrew Scriptures*. Edited by Alice Ogden Bellis and Joel Kaminsky. Atlanta: Society of Biblical Literature, 2000.

Yee, Gale A. "Ideological Criticism: Judges 17–21 and the Dismembered Body." Pages 138–60 in *Judges and Method: New Approaches in Biblical Studies*. Edited by Gale A. Yee. Minneapolis: Fortress, 2007.

Author Index

Subject Index

Scripture Index

Judges